CHILDREN OF THE GHETTO

For Carol Emelda Foster, a mother of the future

KEVIN LE GENDRE

CHILDREN OF THE GHETTO

BLACK MUSIC IN BRITAIN VOLUME 2

PEEPAL TREE

First published in Great Britain in 2024
Peepal Tree Press Ltd
17 King's Avenue
Leeds LS6 1QS
England

© 2024 Kevin Le Gendre

ISBN13:9781845235642

All rights reserved
No part of this publication may be
reproduced or transmitted in any form
without permission

Supported using public funding by
ARTS COUNCIL ENGLAND

CONTENTS

Introduction   7

1. Sure It Was American   15
2. The Property of the Negro Race   31
3. All Men Are Created Equal   46
4. Only the Black Man Understand It   60
5. Whole Lotta Consciousness   73
6. Black Woman and Child   86
7. Funkin' for Jamaica… Guyana… St. Vincent… Africa   100
8. The Elephant Is Not in the Room   115
9. The Other Dubliner   129
10. The Spook Who Sang On the Floor   142
11. Open to Persuasion   155
12. The Revolution Will Not Be Capitalised   173
13. Children of the Ghetto   189
14. Blood 'n' Fire   204
15. Why Can't We Liv Togevver?   221
16. Level Vibes   238
17. Green Is the Colour   256
18. Young Americans Who Are Black… and British   273
19. The World Hears the Ghetto   289

Outroduction   307

Discography
Index

INTRODUCTION

FROM THE CONCRETE JUNGLE

Don't Stop the Carnival, the first volume of Black Music in Britain, was titled after a historic song. It is one of the great entries in the canon of calypso, an important form of West Indian folk expression that made a sizeable impact on the UK, and indeed on the world, in the post-war period, summing up the cultural significance of what is now known as the Windrush generation. The migrants brought a strong work ethic to their new home. The musicians, writers and artists among them displayed great creativity as well as determination.

Nothing makes this clearer than the monochrome Pathé newsreel that shows Lord Kitchener singing 'London Is the Place for Me', surrounded by several of the 498 Jamaicans and Trinidadians who disembarked at Tilbury Docks in Essex on 1948. The verses that wafted through the air against softly strummed guitar chords were so bathed in optimism that one would have thought the arrivals had won the grandest of all sweepstakes, because the prospect of life in Britain was about much more than employment opportunities, the chance to enjoy 'the big life' and live the dream as it had been sold to them back home, in the colonies. They were in the *mother country*.

The often reluctant parent gave a stark wake-up call to the children of empire. While there was an embrace of artists from the Caribbean and Africa in the 1950s and 1960s, notably innovative jazz and hi-life musicians, from Joe Harriott and Dizzy Reece to Ginger Johnson and Ambrose Campbell, there was also a creeping tide of bigotry that swept London and Nottingham in the form of race-related civil disturbances and the consignment of the bulk of black settlers to the slum areas of major urban centres. For every known white city there was the unprepossessing 'brown town', the side of Britain synonymous with sub-standard housing and inadequate educational facilities. Excluded from white British social life, Black people made their own entertainment, exemplified by the vibrant shebeens and house parties, that drew the contempt of the tabloid press that dubbed such areas 'the jungle.'

Despite the hostility, the 'coloured colonials' decided to lay down roots. New generations, who were either born in Britain, or in some cases, arrived here as boys or girls, would make their voices heard by way of inspirational music. *Children of the Ghetto* was thus an obvious title for this second volume of Black Music in Britain.

The song with that title was written and performed by the soul band The Real Thing in the mid-1970s and stands as one of the definitive chronicles of black youth, born on Merseyside to African and Caribbean parents, who were consigned to second-class citizenship and a lack of professional prospects, a bad hand in the game of life chances.

The lyrics of the song are freighted with meaning that extends back before the historical context in which they were written. Liverpool, home of The Real Thing, was one of the major ports through which Africans were shipped during the transatlantic slave trade of the 18th and early 19th centuries that took them to the sugar and cotton plantations of the America and the West Indies, from which would flow the gargantuan fortunes of many individuals as well as institutions, including the Anglican and Catholic churches. The industrial revolution that powered Britain into modernity was built on the basis of this inhumane bondage.

Even after slavery was abolished, the Victorian age was marked by events, including several major exhibitions, that showed a blindness to the shocking oppression of Africans and others who lived under the lash in lands that were under official British rule. Displaying the products of these colonial outposts, such as a tobacco leaf or cocoa pod, was the more palatable expression of Imperial power; shocking was the spectacle of the so called 'human zoo' that denied the humanity of colonial people. Lauded English explorers brought pygmies from the Congo and placed them in recreated African villages, simulations of their natural habitat so that a gawping audience could engage in a racial freak show.

The association of Black people with animals runs deep in the western psyche. When The Real Thing sang of life in a concrete jungle on 'Children of the Ghetto' they were railing against a harsh urban environment that oppressed Black people in Liverpool, and other British cities, but also referring to a dehumanising history that involved violence and abuse, planned disadvantage and marginalisation. It was a question of keeping all those 'coons' in their place, confining them to the 'shady part of town'.

The inhabitants of such ghettos were perceived by the majority white population as aliens, outsiders or interlopers, at whom the taunt of 'Get back to your own country' was often hurled. One of the main contexts of my study is the hardening of attitudes towards ethnic minorities in this period. This included the phenomenon of the SUS laws, institutional police racism and the rise of far right political parties such as the National Front.

Against this hostile backdrop, and as an expression of resistance to it, people of colour made an uplifting creative response. *Children of the Ghetto* sets out to cover as many as possible of the significant artists making Black music between the late 1960s and early 1980s, a period which is marked by countless songs that have thought-provoking political content as well as stylistic ingenuity that is sometimes oriented to the dance floor and sometimes requires deep listening in solitude. Between them compositions such as 'Police on my Back', 'Woyaya (Heaven Knows)', 'The Message', 'Wipe Them Out', 'Brother Louie', 'Sonny's Lettah', 'How Cruel', 'Dole Age', 'The Boys in Blue' and 'Ghost Town' provide an insightful, timeless commentary on the lived experience of Black people in Britain who had to endure both state and non-state violence, a media that offered an unfiltered anti-immigrant rhetoric and the belief in many of the nation's schools that the offspring of the Windrush migrants were of a lesser intelligence than their white counterparts and much more inclined to criminal behaviour. It was a period when institutional racism took root in many of the UK's national bodies, state-run or private.

Watching footage of pitched battles between young Black teens, many with dreadlocks like black snakes swishing through the air, and uniformed police, clinging to their helmets as if they were charms to protect them from the onrushing Medusas, is a vivid reminder of the moments when daily antagonism boiled over into a open combat. War inna Babylon, for sure. The recordings of such scenes at carnival, where the forces of law and order planned a military exercise to constrict what should have been a joyous celebration are important testimony of that oppression, but so too are the recollections of those who were actually there. The eagerness of the police to raise their truncheons during Mas was a continuation of their weekday 'nigger hunting' under the protective cover of a badge and uniform. When Black and white kids lined the Westway of Portobello road, a key stretch of the carnival route, and they puffed on joints before the floats rolled up, as youth will when they seek the first thrills of an illicit substance, the police arrived in numbers and nicked only the Black kids.

The riots that exploded up and down the country in 1981 made it clear that Black communities saw the veracity of the proclamation 'Inglan Is a Bitch', and would not be repressed, despite the attempts of the state to silence them by discriminatory rates of incarceration. But it is also important to record that artistic creativity hit a peak.

The author of that forthright patois phrase, Linton Kwesi Johnson, was developing an ingenious genre known as reggae poetry or dub poetry, matching highly rhythmic verse to the sensually heavy drums and bass of Jamaican music to craft urgent and empowering social commentary. All of the other songs mentioned above come from singers and groups who made music of an immense heterogeneity that says much about the unpredictable, kaleidoscopic nature of the artistry of Black Britain in this period. This is unsurprising when one considers that these musicians benefited from the eclectic tastes of their parents, who were drawn to African American, African and Caribbean sounds. It meant that Black Britain as an emerging cultural phenomenon could not be seen as a single, easily defined entity. Not least, Black British artists, as individuals, proved consistently adventurous.

There are composers, producers and multi-instrumentalists who had strong visions, notably Eddy Grant and Dennis Bovell; singers-lyric writers, including Joan Armatrading, Linda Lewis, Labi Siffre and David Hinds, who told personal yet universal stories; and there were the groups, the assemblage of many talents bound by common cause, who displayed the kind of collective energy, that has produced outstanding results. A cursory roll call includes such as The Equals (with Eddy Grant), Osibisa, Demon Fuzz, Matumbi, Cymande, Hot Chocolate, Aswad, Steel Pulse, Misty in Roots, Talisman, Rip, Rig & Panic, Light of the World and The Specials to name but a few.

This inventiveness is matched by a continual reinvigoration of genres and sub-genres. Jazz, R&B, soul, funk, Afro-rock, rocksteady and roots reggae all speak of an unceasing evolution of ideas as well as high standards of musicianship. At the core of this book is my attempt to chronicle new forms of expression that are inherently Black British, whether the reggae poetry of Linton Kwesi Johnson or the lovers rock of Janet Kay. In each case the music, shaped as its foundations may be by the Caribbean, became *something else* when it acted as a vehicle for expressing the full range of experience of young Black people during the cold comfort of the Thatcher years, from early political awakenings to first romantic yearnings.

While the musicians mentioned above are rightly afforded legendary status today for their enduring work, they were all part of larger movements or scenes that existed the length and breadth of the UK. As was the case with *Don't Stop the Carnival,* I am interested in Black British music as a *national* rather than just a metropolitan phenomenon. The breakthrough of important regional artists, such as Liverpool's The Real Thing is a central theme of *Children of the Ghetto*. The talent that emerged from Birmingham, Bristol, Coventry, Leeds and Manchester made it clear that London was not the only creative hub for Black British artists.

Another theme is the musical link between Black Britain and Black America, which reaches back to the 18th century, in the times when ex-slaves fleeing the wars of Independence, set foot on British shores, often with fiddles or tambourines as part of their scant worldly goods. In the period this volume describes, there were continuing arrivals, such as the vocalists, the Wilder brothers, Keith and Johnnie, both ex-servicemen, previously stationed in Germany, who went on to make Heatwave one of the most successful acts in disco-soul. This band also exemplified the conspicuous multi-racialism of Black music in Britain, which should have been a model for society as a whole. The song-writing engine of the group was the gifted white English pianist, Rod Temperton, whose body of work caught the ear of legendary artists across the Atlantic, and with other members drawn from Switzerland, the Czech Republic and the Caribbean, Heatwave embodied the ideal of the international band of brothers.

If the West Indies and Africa were key sources of Black migration to Britain in their impact on music, then India was also important. In the 1960s, the collaboration of Calcutta-born violinist-composer John Mayer and Jamaican saxophonist Joe Harriott was a landmark moment in UK cultural history. In the period this volume covers, parallel to the emergence of new music born of the experience of their African and Caribbean counterparts, British Asian youth also created something unique in the form of bhangra, which I discuss, and I also chronicle the songs of brown-skinned teens who, against cultural expectation and emboldened by the political movement Rock Against Racism, formed a punk band. Indeed, the courage to face down NF thugs and skinhead boot boys was an integral part of the times.

I'm also interested in the mavericks who went against the grain and did not do what Black musicians were expected to do: make guitar-led rock under the inspiration of Jimi Hendrix? Become a pop star big enough to fill stadiums far from the turbulence of a childhood of rejection? Step forward a half-Guyanese Irishman called Phil Lynott. The focus on the front man of Thin Lizzy in *Children of the Ghetto* is apposite for a number of reasons. He widens standard definitions of Black Britain, for though his nation was Ireland, the connections between Britain and Ireland are no less colonial than those between Britain and Jamaica, and Irish migration to Britain continued strongly in the 'Windrush' period. Lynott exemplifies the presence and cultural contribution of people of colour in parts of Britain with which they are not readily associated, even though as individuals they may claim a strong sense of belonging to the place in question. Dublin *is* part of the African-Caribbean Diaspora regardless of what prevailing images, from Joyce to Guinness, might lead us to think, and the fact that Lynott was able to express his blackness, his interest in race relations, his political consciousness, all the while being unapologetically Irish rather than British, says much about the complexity of the lived experience that underpins the history of Black music made throughout the United Kingdom. Then again, to hear members of The Real Thing speak in sharp scouse, Joan Armatrading in deep Brummy, Edward Lynch in broad Yorkshire or Brinsley Forde in lively West London is to witness the evolution of Black Britishness from the moment in 1948 when 'coloured colonials' were identified by the accents of distant parts of the Empire. By 1977, to be Black and sound British was simply a birthright. The fact that urban white English youth were beginning to talk like their urban Black peers, triggering a moral panic among those who were doggedly attempting to protect a 'pure', restricted version of white Englishness, shows that influences always move in more than one direction.

Several millennia into the existence of Black people in Britain, with the earliest arrivals reaching right back to the Roman empire, it is impossible to encompass the sum total of all the lived experience, all the words, all the sounds, all the songs. We grapple with not so much the genie as the genies that are impossible to squeeze back into even the biggest of bottles. The discographies of Black musicians lend themselves to many interpretations, according to the sensibilities of a given audience or commentator, so Black British music is only one possible umbrella term, but so is British Black music. Arguing which term should be foregrounded is a self-defeating exercise. The word order is not as important as their very existence and conjunction. They point to an encounter, an intermingling and entwining of peoples, places and nationalities, a concept that has always been more ambiguous than the letters and numbers on a passport.

I chose the subtitle Black music in Britain to be as open and inclusive in my enquiry as the subject at hand. Black music that is made in Britain. Black music imagined in Britain. The shuddering rhythms, noble melodies, gilded harmonies, soaring vocals, enticing instrumentals, righteous praises to the Lord, tales of hedonistic and carnal indulgence, deeply felt affairs of the heart, rabble-rousing chants of resistance, rib-tickling stories of fun and frolics: these are the things that come to my mind when I think about the myriad sounds I have investigated in writing *Children of the Ghetto*.

I am much more interested in how the music is made than how it is sold. The record industry, with its dense undergrowth of legal machinations and infamous disputes that, as a famous artist once contended, made him a slave, is worthy of investigation, but the richness of content of the songs of Black Britain does not make that a priority for me. What singers and players do to create that magical string of notes and tones that draw a response from us, whether physical, emotional or intellectual, is the principal road of analysis down which I travel. There has been no end of music that makes us think, feel and dance in this country and whoever is minded to lend an ear will have no shortage of material to discuss. The question is how hard we might care to listen.

Given the seemingly infinite amount of music that has come to light, and continues to do so in the Internet age, it is unwise to claim that we have heard and know *everything* about a given style. The rarities, the holy grails, the previously unissued tracks and 'lost' albums pop out of the woodwork on an almost weekly basis, which means that a truly comprehensive account of all the genres developed in this country from African,

African Caribbean and African American sources is impossible.

Yet it is precisely the multi-faceted and complex nature of the development of Black music in Britain in the 1970s and 1980s that makes it a fascinating subject, which deserves detailed examination and close, attentive engagement with the music makers. Nothing challenged and excited me more than diving into this ocean of sound when writing *Children of the Ghetto*, but the great generosity of the artists who gave willingly of their time to explore memories of songs that were created decades ago was truly uplifting. It is one thing to listen to a historic, perhaps highly influential piece of music and reflect upon its conception, construction and legacy, and it is another thing to learn about the life of the artist in question, to gain a sense of who they are as individuals and what they experienced that drew them to make a statement that affected and continues to affect others.

The singer is the song, the player plays what they live. It has been my pleasure to hear their stories. This is not just about being 'conscious' through music, or attempting to send a message to one's community and the wider society through a thought-provoking lyric or a melody that is laden with feeling. In every conversation I was privileged to hold with artists for *Children of the Ghetto* there was a distinct sense of *necessity* in the music-making process, of the weight and urgency of a calling that would take them down a creative road, whether that yielded escapist entertainment and tunes for good times, a reality poem that charted trials and tribulation, or offered a eulogy to a fallen hero. In many cases, making music was a sanctuary for Black youth because the basement studio, or practice room of a school or church hall could provide solace away from hostilities in the playground or high street. This is why, on occasion, I choose to highlight lived experiences shared by artists across genres. Although they were stylistically different, reggae and soul were more politically linked than is often reported. *Children of the Ghetto* is thus about a generation, or rather successive generations of kids who met momentous challenges. They were born Black *and* British, straddling two apparently incompatible states of existence, a dilemma which had been identified by sociologists and observers in the late 1940s, none more so than the pioneering *Checkers* magazine, that deemed it an impossibility, and was aware of DuBois's 'double consciousness'. Being one thing and looking another really was the blues.

The sons and daughters of a nation should feel a sense of solidarity with a population that has a fundamental bond through a shared language. The children of the ghetto shared the same mother tongue as other citizens of the United Kingdom, but they were singled out, defined, disenfranchised and derided as foreigners who did not have the same right to belong as *real* English, Scottish, Welsh or (to a lesser extent) Irish who were perceived as legitimate, on the grounds of race. The artists who emerged during this period, who refused to be silenced, who gave voice to marginalised communities, performed acts of subversion and rebellion by their very existence. In the process, they were changing British culture. They were providing members of the white population with gifts they could not resist, even if they signed up to the Far Right on the back of reggae beats and a pair of braces JA style.

The music kept coming, regardless of all the paradoxes, persecutions, traumas, cultural and mental pressures that afflicted people of colour in Britain during the tumultuous period discussed in *Children of the Ghetto*. The time span of this volume is significantly shorter than the several centuries covered by *Don't Stop the Carnival*, though the length of the text is more or less the same. There is a simple and logical explanation. The output of music in the 'Ghetto years' was simply immense. There was such a plethora of groups and songs to consider that it would have been wrong, from a historian's standpoint, to skim over this key, formative chapter in the cultural history of Black Britain without considering the minor as well as major figures who made important personal statements.

I do not claim to have written a definitive account of Black music made in Britain in this period, but I have endeavoured to chronicle the artists who, I believe, produced work of breadth of imagination and depth of feeling, and in many cases provided an essential mouthpiece for people who needed champions. The Real Thing, proud sons of Toxteth, wrote a timeless anthem in 'Children of the Ghetto' but they also spoke for their peers up and down the country, in Birmingham, Bristol, Leeds, London, Manchester and Nottingham who related to their lives as well as lyrics. The creators of the song *were* the children of the ghetto and the music they made amounts to an invaluable document of cultural evolution.

At the end of Empire, the colonies gained independence and the United Kingdom began a transformation into an increasingly multiracial, multicultural society. For all its inhabitants this entailed learning new songs. 'Children of the Ghetto' is just one of many.

Seven Sisters, London, 2023

1. SURE IT WAS AMERICAN

We were the top-earning band in the UK in the late 60s and early 70s, as stated in *Melody Maker*. We had a very good showing anywhere we played. Manchester was another stomping ground for us.
– Root Jackson, born in Carriacou, emigrated to Huddersfield, early 1960s.

A Town That Talks
In English popular consciousness, the latter half of the 1960s was largely defined by the afterglow of the nation's World Cup victory and a global media fascination with 'swinging London'. Yet, for all the excitement around a Carnaby hegemony in the world of style, it was a different story in music. Even as the Beatles made songs of indelible charm and imagination, UK record buyers sent easy listening or novelty singles to the top of the charts. And America, having survived the 'British invasion', had a formidable weapon to fire straight back over the water. It was called Black music.

Whether from Chicago, Detroit, Memphis, Atlanta or New York, scores of Black artists, exponents of jazz, blues, soul and hybrid forms of R&B (including the psychedelic or spaced out variety), exerted a deep influence on the tastes of both audiences and artists up and down the UK. It was music that touched hearts and minds and also made bodies move. People may have wanted to sing Lennon & McCartney, but they also needed to sound like Ray Charles, Etta James, Aretha Franklin and Otis Redding, prophets who gave faithful followers of popular music what they always demanded: a brand new beat.

Jimi Hendrix, during his sojourn in Britain, revolutionised rock and carved out a new role for the guitar in it. Herbie Hancock wrote one of the great film scores of the 1960s for Antonioni's London-based celluloid circus of media, fashion, liberated sexual mores, reality and illusion: *Blow Up*. While that soundtrack used cockney vernacular in the song titles, such as 'Bring Down the Birds', what caught the ear was the force of a Hammond organ drawn from the hallowed traditions of the Black church, rather than a 'Joanna' from a pub in the East End. The Yardbirds, an integral part of the vanguard of UK pop, were also in the movie, thrashing out an aggressive piece of proto hard rock called 'Train Kept A-Rollin'. However, if this showed the virtues of London-based talent, the tune was anything but homegrown. It was a cover of Tiny Bradshaw's enduring 1950s R&B classic. The jump-blues drummer from Ohio was having his music electrified by boys from Richmond.

This was part of a pattern of white British and white American artists covering Black music from America; key examples included the Beatles, Rolling Stones, Lulu, the Animals and others. The challenge was the unmatched performing skills of the originators. To sing a song made across the Atlantic by an artist who stood on the other side of the racial divide was one thing, but to bring it to life on stage, to give bodily, dramatic meaning to the words, to achieve exactly the right split-second timing to every thump of a bass drum and thwack of a snare, to create the precise harmonic shade for every guitar or piano chord or to nail the brass lines of every 'shout chorus', was something else.

Stax, King and Motown were US record labels that took some time to win mass audiences either in the USA or Britain. But the quasi-religious devotion that their artists inspired when they materialised in concert halls in the UK was an important reminder of star qualities that transcended racial boundaries, as much as it was part of a historic fascination with the Black body as well as the cultural revolution it conveyed.

In the mid-1960s, the Motown revue came to Britain, featuring the label's marquee names – Smokey Robinson, Martha Reeves & The Vandellas, The Supremes and Stevie Wonder. Motown artists were highly esteemed because they displayed a combination of fabulous choreography, immaculate attire and songs that defined a new sophistication in R&B, courtesy of writers such as Holland-Dozier-Holland. There was also a peerless house band featuring pianist Earl Van Dyke, drummer Benny Benjamin, percussionist Jack Ashford and bass guitarist James Jamerson.[1]

But if the audience turnout was not as high as promoters had hoped, primarily because Motown records did not have the kind of national distribution necessary to reach consumers, the artists made a mark on British musicians who could not fail to recognise their brilliance. Dusty Springfield, an eminently talented vocalist, whose material fell carefully between the lines of emotive R&B and swish orchestral pop, hosted a television show, *RSG Sound of Motown*, that featured acts from the Revue, while among those who attended the concerts were the Rolling Stones' guitarist Ronnie Wood, who gushingly confessed that seeing Wonder and Reeves was a vital experience. As for the visiting African Americans, they marvelled at the wonders of warm beer and newspaper-wrapped chips.

Diana Ross and The Supremes' concert at The Talk of The Town in London in 1968 was billed as the 'show business event of the year'.[2] It was noted for the presence of pop A-listers such as Paul McCartney, as much as for the range of scintillating dance steps performed by Motown's first ladies. Critics recognised that these African Americans had stagecraft that was hard to match, that they did much more than lift their voices and sing, that they knew how to work an audience and brought a verve to a performance that was beyond the capacity of their British peers. This was given further credence by Black American expatriates such as Geno Washington.

As noted in *Don't Stop the Carnival: Black Music in Britain Volume 1*, Washington (a former member of the US military, like Hendrix) was one of the most dynamic performers on the live UK circuit in the mid-1960s. His volcanic stage presence and eruptive vocals won him a substantial national following, to the extent that he regularly stole the limelight from artists with bigger names. Washington & The Ram Jam Band only ever enjoyed moderate chart success, but they made it clear that R&B had become an integral part of the post-Beatles British pop landscape and that it was one of several idioms that prospective artists embraced. One of the great showmen of the 1960s, a quasi-Otis Reading who could be seen on the streets of London rather than Memphis, Washington saw his reputation limited by being a 'covers' artist rather than an exponent of original songs, but he was nonetheless a source of inspiration to any pretenders to what could be called British R&B based on an American model. Certainly, many of the tastemakers and powerbrokers working in pop were smart enough to know that what sounded Black could well become gold.

Up from the Basement
The popular music and entertainment industry offered job opportunities with the organisations controlling the means of production, such as record labels, in the professions of A & R (Artist & Repertoire) and management, and directly to those providing services and product, namely singers and musicians. The first two groups were largely white and middle or upper class, and the latter largely working-class kids of white British, West Indian or Asian heritages. Those who played instruments and found others with similar musical tastes coalesced into bands, and then began the often thankless task of sending out demo tapes to the talent scouts, and other Svengali figures in the music industry.

Disc jockeys, as they were formally known, were key targets. BBC Radio One, which launched in September 1967, became a key outlet for youth culture, with shows that were intended to grab a piece of the listenership created by independent radio stations such as Caroline and Luxembourg. Radio One presenters such as Tony Blackburn, Alan Freeman and Dave Cash became stars. Another influential presenter was Chris Denning, the host of a Saturday afternoon show *Where It's At*. He also freelanced in the record industry and wrote the sleeve notes for *From the Foundations*, the 1967 debut album by The Foundations. He made a point of stating who they were and what they represented, writing, 'The Foundations, who got their name after literally starting from that level (playing the basement coffee bar beneath the office of Westbourne Grove, London record dealer Barry Class, who discovered them), are made up of seven boys, who in themselves comprise a miniature United Nations!'

> Three are Londoners and the other four come from, respectively, Jamaica, Trinidad, Ceylon and the Dominican Republic. But although the group hasn't been around for long, unlike the United Nations, the boys sound as solid as if they'd been together for years.[3]

Whilst Denning's plug for the band's ethnic diversity is almost a pre-Benetton sales pitch, the cynical barb thrown at the UN's apparent dysfunction is ironic, given that the former crown colony of Ceylon, scarred by the divisive legacy of British rule, was suffering extreme civil strife during its evolution into Sri Lanka. The vexatious history of British imperialism, with its corollaries of immigration rights and racist fears, two of the tributaries that would flow into a river of social unrest, is neatly dammed off by this snide swipe at internationalism.

Witless observations notwithstanding, Denning's message about the band's exotic origins is also underscored by a stylish portrait on the album sleeve, where the range of skin tone and hair texture is enhanced by a rainbow of fabrics evoking the height of Carnaby Street fashion. It is interesting that no reference is made to the individuals themselves or what they played. By accident or design the omission of names has a kind of distancing effect, as if there was no need for any would-be fans to know exactly who the individuals were, and if this enforced anonymity suggests the power held by 'star-makers', then Denning compounds that by stating that the group's breakout hit 'Baby, Now that I've Found You' is 'written, arranged and produced by old friends of mine, Tony Macaulay and John MacLeod',[4] a claim borne out by the abundance of Macaulay's writing credits. Indeed, band members later claimed that the men in the control booth vetoed material they had written themselves.

Though Denning's introduction suggested that band members didn't matter as much as composers and talent scouts (who, as Denning did, complained of the endless stream of demo tapes clogging their letter boxes), there are contrary points to make about The Foundations. They were a mixture of experienced musicians such as the two saxophonists, Jamaican-born Mike Elliot and Englishman Pat Burke, and Dominican trombonist Eric Allendale, who had played with established jazz and pop acts, and part timers who had other sources of employment. Trinidadian singer Clem Curtis was a boxer and painter-decorator; Ceylonese (Sri Lankan) keyboardist Tony Gomez was an office clerk, and English bassist, Peter Macbeth, a teacher.

What was really important was that 'Baby, Now That I've Found You' fulfilled all the criteria of successful mid-1960s R&B: sturdy mid-tempo backbeat; yearning melody mapped out on guitar, and piano licks that are nonchalant rather than dynamic but offer effective support to the lead vocal; precise interjections by backing singers of 'ooohs' to enrich the theme; and horns that provide short, compact but memorably potent phrases that complement the central verse and chorus. These elements are the hooks onto which any listener can latch. Here was a clear application of the model developed by Motown. 'Baby, Now That I've Found You' could easily have been an outtake from a Four Tops or Smokey Robinson & The Miracles session, and there was no attempt to conceal that fact in the way The Foundations were marketed, for, as Denning admitted in his sleeve notes, the 'Hitsville USA' model set a high bar that was not easy for outsiders to reach. 'They are the first British combo to capture that elusive (for want of a better word) Detroit sound. In fact, the first time I heard "Baby, Now That I've Found You", I was absolutely sure it was American.'[5] There was no greater praise for non-American artists.

This comment provides an accurate summary of the complex unfolding of Black music between America and Britain, and the challenges faced by British exponents of a genre such as R&B, which had been defined by innovative artists whose talent had made them worldwide stars. It was inevitable that the originals would cast a long shadow on contenders across the water. As a result, there was no option but to sound like the 'real thing', and because of its convincing approximation of a Motown beat, 'Baby, Now That I've Found You' was a much easier product to bring to market. It spent a fortnight at number one in the UK singles charts in November 1967, and later entered the top 20 in Belgium, Holland, New Zealand and the top 10 in South Africa and Norway. The song also topped the charts in Canada and, perhaps most impressively of all, peaked at number 11 in the coveted Billboard Hot 100 in America.

The Foundations maintained that momentum with another hit 'Build Me Up Buttercup', which saw them raise the feel-good factor even further. Again, in the patented Motown groove, this was prime fodder for any dance floor or radio show where the emphasis was on creating a sense of release for listeners. Lyrically, the song lacked any real invention and the tale of lovesick teenager pleading with his paramour to not 'break my heart' was all too familiar. But that mattered little. Rhythmically and melodically the tune was catchy as hell. It beckoned listeners to loosen up and throw some shapes. All they had to do was feel the beat from the 'authentic' side of the Atlantic.

Further success came with later singles, but there were changes in the original line-up, wrangles over artistic direction and question marks over how The Foundations should plot the subsequent stages of their career.

They toured America with big names such as Solomon Burke but in the late 1960s they passed up offers of more dates in order to support The Temptations at the glamorous Copacabana club. Sadly, the residency flopped because they were overshadowed by one of the best vocal groups in the world, and they crawled back to the UK with tails between proverbial legs. They had one more minor hit in 'My Little Chickadee', and then broke up.

Dem Yorkshire Blues
Whether The Foundations crumbled because tough American audiences saw the Brits as an inferior facsimile of the real thing, or because their music lacked the edge of sophistication that defined Motown's finest, the story was really something of a cautionary tale, a warning of the unforgiving vagaries of the pop world and an increasing competitiveness in the marketplace.

While young West Indians, white Britons and Asians based in London were having a tilt at US-inspired pop, Black artists based outside the capital were also emerging. Huddersfield in Yorkshire would play host to another intrepid contender for the R&B crown. This was Root Jackson, born in Carriacou, the largest of the string of very small islands in the Caribbean known as the Grenadines, who settled there at the dawn of the 1960s. At his parents' behest he had come to the UK to join his sister and finish his education. It is still worth reiterating the intensity of the culture shock that awaited Jackson: from the freezing winter temperatures to the frosty reception at the local labour exchange that sent him to a textile mill when he had expressed an interest in accounting. 'I was somewhat disillusioned with what I encountered when I got here to be honest,' he would recall several years later.[6]

Inauspicious beginnings aside, Huddersfield, the town that had given a home to the expatriate blues legend Champion Jack Dupree, enabled Jackson to launch a career in music while he was completing a college course. Rhythmically savvy because of time spent playing in steel bands in Carriacou and blessed with a strong voice, Jackson gravitated towards some his fellow compatriots. He sat in on drums with Bob Adams & the Echoes and eventually joined a band called The Black Diamonds, which started to attract a youthful audience. As word spread of their high energy R&B, they landed gigs at working men's clubs in the area, most notably the Miner's Welfare Hall in Barnsley.

Then, in the mid-1960s, Jackson and co attended and won an audition at Bradford University, held by a promoter who was looking for British bands to fulfil a residency in Gelsenkirchen, Germany. With a demanding schedule of three to four shows a night, the Black Diamonds attained an enviable level of professionalism and Jackson graduated from playing drums to handling lead vocals. He saw a career path open up in front of him that had hitherto not been possible. 'We were getting paid at the end of the month. I didn't realise you could play music and make money.'[7] Six weeks in Germany turned into three months, then after a brief return to Huddersfield, the band were contacted by the same promoter who asked them to fulfil an engagement near Frankfurt, where there was a U.S. expatriate audience that needed entertainment. 'There was a club there where a lot of the Americans, the G.I.s, used to hang out; we got know them, so we ended up doing a lot of the American bases as well.'[8]

It was an invaluable learning experience because the soldiers had the latest vinyl imports by such as Otis Redding, Wilson Picket and The Impressions, and they generously gave them to Jackson, whose head was turned by this new wave of Black popular music. Jackson then made a significant change in the make-up of the band. Because of the popularity of female singers in Germany, he offloaded the Black Diamonds' male lead vocalist and enlisted his cousin Monica. They had an offer of management in Huddersfield and were rebranded as Root & Jenny Jackson & The Hightimers. With a good agent, Danny Pollock, championing their cause, they gigged regularly and amassed a sizeable local audience, reflecting the demand for Black music in northern cities such as Leeds and Sheffield. 'We were the top-earning band in the UK in the late 1960s and early '70s, as stated in *Melody Maker*. We had a very good showing anywhere we played. Manchester was another stomping ground for us.'[9]

Jackson's story is important because it makes the point that the interest in Black music in Britain was on a national/regional rather than just a metropolitan scale and that by criss-crossing the country with a reputation for delivering the goods on stage, a band could thrive. Root & Jenny Jackson went down well in a long list of venues: Plebeians, Halifax; Whisky A Gogo, Newcastle; Mojo, Sheffield; Twisted Wheel, Manchester; Reading University; and the All Star club, the Cue, the Flamingo, all in London. At this point, the group was commanding a fee of £250 a night, doing up to four performances a week between the college circuit and clubs of varying sizes. They went on to record several singles for a small independent label, Beacon, which saw the strong vocalists perform well over very well-marshalled horn and rhythm sections. The material is fascinating insofar as it points to a clear cultural duality. On one hand, pieces such as 'Save Me' and 'Let's Go Somewhere', reprises of songs by Aretha Franklin and R. Dean Taylor, respectively, consolidate the US blueprint Root had no qualms in implementing. On the other hand, the beautiful 'So Far Away' is a smart melding of calypso, pop and R&B that frames Root & Jenny's voices with a barrage of jangling percussion and assertive brass. The song underlines how the band credibly occupied an interesting stylistic space shaped equally by West Indian and American musical vocabularies, making the most of the effervescent rhythms that marked Root's formative years in steel bands as well as the energetic drive of his role models from cities such as Detroit and Memphis.

'We were mixing our own vibe with the American vibe,' says Jackson. It is a statement that foretells the future of Black music in Britain, where myriad cultures – Caribbean, American and British – would enter into a complex, fluid and evolutionary relationship. However, in the late 1960s, the pressure to do in-demand US covers on the live circuit was perhaps strongest.

Root and Jenny never recorded a full-length album following the release of the 45s, and Jenny wanted to spend more time in Italy where they had a substantial following. With Root intent on pursuing other musical directions, they parted ways. As we will see later in the book, he continued developing as an artist.

Organised Religion
The Jacksons were not the only West Indians who made their mark on the British R&B scene. Ram John Holder, a versatile Guyanese entertainer who appeared in films such as *Two Gentlemen Sharing*, a thought-provoking dramatisation of the burgeoning reality of a multi-cultural Britain, was also a singer who did a smart line in humorous blues numbers that detailed the none too glamorous reality of life in the 'mother country' for immigrants. There was also Errol Dixon, a Jamaican who had come to London to study music and taken a detour into performing and recording when people heard his powerful delivery and skilled piano playing. As well as doing decent covers, he also wrote passable original material and his 1968 solo album *Blues in the Big City* lives up to its title, blending potent reprises of classics such as 'Back at the Chicken Shack' with new tunes such as 'Dixon Bounce', both songs underpinned by rollicking, walking basslines and the forceful vocal delivery that were staples of post-war R&B.

But it was Dixon's compatriot, Jimmy James, who made a bigger impact. Born in Kingston he, like countless other vocalists, began recording with Coxsone's Studio 1 and chalked up a local hits such as 'Bewildered and Blue' and 'Come to me Softly' before relocating to Britain in 1964, after receiving an offer to tour the UK for six months as lead singer with The Vagabonds. The dates were so successful that the group was offered more work and subsequently decided to stay on a permanent basis.

Dubbed 'the band with the golden sound', The Vagabonds were significant insofar as they were one of the first bands to record Jamaican music in Britain, as the title of the album *Ska-Time* made clear. Although the arrangements of this well marshalled combo produced a richly layered sound with its horn and rhythm sections that was very much in the ska mould, their repertoire was varied and included jazz standards such as 'Stardust' and 'Watermelon Man' as well as the Afro-Cuban anthem 'La Pachanga', and the enduring Irish folk song 'Danny Boy'. The Vagabonds made ska from any kind of tune taken from anywhere.

Also interesting was the fact that the band represented the Asian Diaspora in the West Indies, having been formed by Colston 'Coley' Chen, whose grandparents emigrated to Jamaica from China as indentured labourers, along with almost a quarter of a million Indian labourers to work in the post-slave sugar economy of the British colonies. Joining bass guitarist-bandleader Chen were his brother, rhythm guitarist Phil Philco Chen, percussionist Rupert Bali Balgobin, of Indian origin, drummer Carl Grog Griffiths, saxophonist Carl 'Broadback' Noel, organist Wallace Gisty Wilson, emcee Sparrow Martin, vocalists Count 'Prince' Miller and Jimmy James. The Vagabonds were a symbol of the rich ethnic diversity of Jamaica, a model of the island united through sound. Out of many people, one band.

Like the calypso pioneer Lord Kitchener, who arrived in Britain on the *Windrush* in 1948, these musicians travelled by boat, the SS *Ascania* in April 1964, and docked two weeks later in Southampton. There is, though, no record of anybody singing 'London is the Place for Me' while descending the gangway in the full glare of BBC cameras.

The Vagabonds had plied their trade in hotels in Jamaica where they were expected to be able to play across the board stylistically, but with showmanship in the bargain. Count 'Prince' Miller played the multi-faceted role of vocalist, emcee and dancer, providing a strong focal point with vigorous moves and the switched-on stage presence of what is known today as a 'hype man', ready to raise the spirits of even the most docile of audiences.

James, too, was known for his charisma as well as his vocal power, while the ability of the group to bring dynamism to their performances struck a clear parallel with Geno Washington & The Ramjam band. It endeared them to established stars such as The Who, who lent them equipment, and also helped to build an audience. James & The Vagabonds first started making waves at a venue in Portsmouth called The Birdcage and worked their way up the pecking order on the live circuit, eventually graduating from support slots with the Jimi Hendrix Experience, The Beatles and The Who to headlining at The Marquee. They also appeared in Hungary, thus becoming first ever western group to play behind the Iron Curtain, which is a notable fact in Cold War history of which Jamaicans can be proud.

Vinyl releases followed. Their debut long player was actually shared with another band; one half of the album was allocated to James & The Vagabonds and the other to The Alan Brown Set, an interesting group that straddled pop, blues-rock and psychedelia. The album really enshrined the importance of the club scene as both groups were recorded at London's top venue and the whole package titled *London Swings at The Marquee*.[10]

James & The Vagabonds delivered exactly what was expected of a well-drilled soul combo with a powerful frontman. Covers of the American hits of the day – Otis Redding's 'Can't Turn You Loose' and 'Ain't Too Proud to Beg' established their credentials, while 'That Driving Beat' was the standout dance tune on offer. All this music was delivered with a zest and lack of restraint that resonated with British audiences.

Music as a form of testament was the subtext of James & The Vagabonds' studio debut, *The New Religion*. The big difference from the live set was the presence of a string orchestra in addition to the already potent horn and rhythm sections, and with this new resource, which was well arranged by Anthony King, the band was able to draw directly on the polished vocabulary of Motown and the Chicago R&B epitomised by the legendary Curtis Mayfield. Indeed, the reprises of Smokey Robinson & The Miracles' 'I Gotta Dance to Keep From Cryin'' and Mayfield's 'People Get Ready' reflect the value of the American model in Black British pop, and James & The Vagabonds were not about to deny this. The sleeve notes of *The New Religion* struck an unequivocally deferential chord: 'This LP is our own "New wave R&B" tribute to Curtis Mayfield and his arranger Johnny Pate, for in popdom no other team has produced more.'

Apart from the linguistic quirk of 'New wave R&B', the statement is thought-provoking insofar as it raises the question of whether any exponents of this sound who were born outside of America could define themselves on their own terms. Such was the demand for the original model, the likes of James or, as previously discussed, The Foundations, had little option but to adhere to their master sources of inspiration. Even so, there was a still nascent originality in the midst of the application of the template. In addition to being a singer with the mighty roar and shout of Redding and Pickett, James was also a composer. He had written his own songs as a boy in Jamaica and had demonstrated a gift for melody on what became his signature tune, 'Come to Me Softly'. This quite beautiful love song was a highlight of *The New Religion*, but, tellingly, producer Peter Meaden chose not to mention it in the sleeve notes, suggesting perhaps that there was little currency in the idea of a Jamaican artist writing his own material within the context of an album that was conceived in deference to American R&B.

There is no denying the beauty of the theme of 'Come To Me Softly', or the finesse with which James sang it, though the blues-gospel quotient of the string-drenched arrangement is relatively low, reminding us that there was also a lineage of black performers who stood firmly in pop-crooner territory, such as Johnny Mathis, though the jazz-inflected doyen was Nat 'King' Cole, an artist who was hugely popular in the Caribbean and whose songs were staple listening in many Caribbean households in Britain. This more sedate form of music fulfilled an important role as the soundtrack to affairs of the heart. The romanticism, the sentimentality of the down-tempo tune, offered a more contemplative alternative to the hot thrill of dance music. As James professed, 'I always try to get something across to the kids, particularly when we do slow songs. I don't think it's necessary to pull weird expressions. All I do is close my eyes. I do this a lot and it makes me feel really warm inside when I open 'em and see all those wonderful kids out there in the audience open mouthed.'[11]

James & The Vagabonds would go on to enjoy further success in the late 1960s with a cover of Neil Diamond's 'Red Red Wine', which was also given a similarly gentle touch and became a sizeable hit. The original band would break up and James didn't record again until the mid-1970s.

Hang on Sloopie
Like every singer, Black or white in Britain, who looked to America to discern the direction of travel of R&B, James was well up on the releases from Motown. The other key label was Stax and in 1967 the Memphis imprint released a compilation of cutting-edge music performed by artists who went on to achieve legendary status, such as Wilson Pickett, Ben E. King, Solomon Burke, Carla Thomas, Sam & Dave, Eddie Floyd, Aretha Franklin and Otis Redding. The marketing department chose a very specific, memorable title. The record was *This is Soul*.

Owning that album became essential for anybody who was aspiring to be part of the 'in' crowd'. Soul was both a genre of music and a cultural force, a kind of buzzing energy that did not have a precise textbook definition but carried a more abstract, ineffable quality of personal fulfilment, if not freedom. You had to have soul right down to your inner being. You had to feel soul. You did not have to explain it.

Redding's seminal album, *Otis Blue/Otis Redding Sings Soul*, confirmed that the new term was becoming a mandatory description not just for the music formerly known as R&B but for the attitude, the stance, the sense of individuality and community among African Americans. When James Brown sang 'Soul Power' he consolidated those very ideas.

Unsurprisingly, the idea of soul was readily adopted in Jamaica; the word appeared in singles by Joey & His Group – 'Soul Love' and Radcliffe Butler's 'Soul Power' and in the group names Soul Vendors, a super group that was led by ska legends Roland Alphonso, Johnny Moore and Lloyd Brevett. Assembled by producer Sir Coxsone Dodd, the band toured Britain in 1967. The year after, a combo of West Indians based in London also contributed to the new lexicon: Soul Buster. The conjunction of the words is purposeful, clearly focused on the image of music that can do something to an audience, whether it makes them holler in ecstasy or throw up their hands because they are feeling something. Soul busts. It breaks through. It hits you. Cures you. Or maybe this particular offering is capable of busting soul, breaking previous boundaries set by others for the genre. Either way there is a promise of a journey not to be missed.

The album came from Joe E. Young and The Toniks, and even the artwork of the record was a brilliant depiction of the transcultural reality of Black music in Britain. If *Soul Buster* had a distinctly American resonance, rhyming as it did with the classic 'Soul Finger' by the Memphis group, The Bar-Kays, then the sleeve in which *Soul Buster* appeared was all London: a red double-decker bus with the faces of six Black men, the band-members, peering through the windows of the upper deck, with the twisting body of the lead singer seen on the lower. Instead of getting on board a soul train, listeners could hop on a soul bus, and if that metaphor didn't touch them, then Joe E. Young's music was liable to get them moving. Highlights of *Soul Buster* such as 'Got That Feeling' were clearly predicated on Motown-Stax models, but as was the case with The Foundations, there was a sufficiently high standard of musicianship to ensure that the songs, though executed in a patented U.S. style, were not sub-standard pastiche. The music was familiar but not by any reckoning inferior.

In fact, the link with The Foundations was a direct one insofar as Joe E. Young's vocalist, the Barbadian Colin Young, would go on to join the former after the departure of Clem Curtis. Also noteworthy is that the arrangements on *Soul Buster* were credited to Pete Gage, the founder of Geno Washington & The Ramjam band, and if there is a passing similarity in the sound of the two outfits – though Young has a brighter tenor sparkle than Washington's throaty basso – that may be because of the distinctively dark swoon provided by a horn section comprising two tenor saxophones instead of one reed and one brass.

The documentation of the activities of groups such as Geno Washington and Joe E. Young & The Toniks shows how much they were part of wider social changes. In 1968, there was a small news story in the leading British music magazine *Melody Maker* about the intense fervour inspired by Young while on tour in what was becoming the prime destination for UK tourists who were embracing the jet age and the novelty of a sun-kissed foreign holiday. *Melody Maker* reported: 'Just back from Sloopie's discotheque in Majorca, Spain after performing for two months, hundreds of fans left the airport in tears after seeing them off. We have had several letters from fans who have remarked that listening to Joe & The Toniks is like listening to Sam Cooke backed by Booker T and The MGs.'[12]

Inevitably, the yardstick of the American originals is hard to escape and there is a tendency to dismiss other contenders in the soul arena because they were not American, but that perspective can be too narrow. The prevailing culture of the cover version necessitated the reprise of the material of other artists and Joe E. Young & The Toniks passed the test with a fine version of the Darrell Banks' anthem 'Open the Door to Your Heart'.

While Geno Washington, Joe E. Young & The Toniks, Jimmy James & The Vagabonds and The Foundations all have pride of place in the pantheon of British soul, there were other less well-known groups such as The Grenades, Heart and Souls, The Rick 'n' Beckers and the Blue Aces. Rarely recording, these outfits worked the live circuit as industriously as possible and if they were lucky might have a residency at a popular venue in London. All areas of the city, from east – the New All Star, near Liverpool Street station – to west – the Cue Club near Paddington – to central –the Roaring 20s in Soho – and south – the famous Ramjam in Brixton – had their small cathedrals where excitable soul disciples would gather.

There was indeed a kind of frenzied transit that defined the live circuit in the mid-1960s as bands did two or more sets in the same establishment and then hot-footed from one venue to another on the same night, sometimes in different cities. Diehard punters would play 'follow that band' if they had the time and the wherewithal to negotiate the necessary routes. In London, that could mean starting the night at the Ramjam in Brixton before travelling 'up west' to hear the same artists again. Or there could be one gig at the Ramjam and another at the Starlight in Sudbury. When groups were really putting in the hard yards on the road, they could start the evening at a venue in Birmingham and then do a midnight show at the Flamingo in London, and in between there was a set at a venue in Dunstable in Bedfordshire, which became something of a R&B and pop Mecca. This was The California Ballroom. The idea of a supposedly sleepy market town in the home counties becoming a hotspot for the best bands in the country may seem unlikely, but the listings for that establishment's peak years reveal that this was no fantasy. Between 1967 and 1968, the likes of Washington, James, Herbie Goins & The Nightimers, The Foundations, Madeline Bell and Zoot Money were among the British blues/R&B/soul contingent, while rock headliners included John Mayall, Pink Floyd, The Move, The Troggs and The Who. As for American acts, they included legends such as Bo Diddley, John Lee Hooker, Jimmy McGriff, Junior Walker, Ben E. King, Lee Dorsey, Ike & Tina Turner and Stevie Wonder. These groups and individuals marked out many key staging posts of popular music in the decades to come, in terms of instrumentation, composition and vocal performance. No doubt there are those who treasure the sight of a teenage Wonder, singing high and playing hard in the mists of time at the California Ballroom in Bedfordshire. For all the glam and glitz of 'swingin' London' there was 'swingin' Dunstable'.

Furthermore, The California, despite the concession to Americana in its name, maintained a link to another strain of popular culture that enabled it to ensure regular revenue streams by attracting a different kind of audience. On the nights when there was no music, the venue would put on men's or women's wrestling, with tickets for the latter being more expensive. This was not so outlandish when one considers that other venues had bills that featured modern jazz artists, comedians and muscle men.

Testimonials to the heady days of The California include memories of callow youth manning up to withstand Watney's Red Barrel beer and 'rolling around with a girl' on nearby Dunstable Downs at the end of the night. If the hedonism of the nightclub experience was alive and well in Bedfordshire, so was the ignominy for punters from Luton having to walk several miles home or hitch-hike down the M1 after missing the last bus. Yet the irresistible appeal of the live gig made the spirit willing even if the flesh was weak.

Premium Bond

Six to eight piece groups, adhering to the established model of the powerful 'front man' and skilled accompanists, were prevalent in British soul but there were also occasional exceptions to the patriarchal rule. A Jamaican woman singer of the period, who also emigrated to Britain after starting her career on the island, was Joyce Bond. She cut an album, *Ska and Soul*, in 1967 and after generating interest through a number of singles the Portland-born youngster – just twenty-two when she made the journey to London – went on to cut 'Wind of Change' with a British band, which was, to catch the tenor of the times, re-titled 'Soul of Change'.[13] At first sight the album conforms to the model of using known hits. There are reprises of songs by successful pop artists such as The Young Rascals ('People Got to Be Free') and the Beatles ('Oh! Darling') and soul singers who had not made a breakthrough in the mainstream, such as Bettye Swann ('Make Me Yours') and Erma Franklin ('Piece of My Heart' – also covered by Dusty Springfield). In other words, the material Bond used showed a commitment to a high standard of song writing drawn from disparate sources, including both megastars and more obscure figures who were nonetheless held in great esteem in 'specialist' circles. This embrace of dozens of songs issued on small independent labels with limited distribution was vital to the growth of Black music beyond its American heartland into the Caribbean and Britain.

Even so, the significant individual on *Soul of Change* was a Jamaican producer and composer, Keith Foster, who would go on to record under the name of Tito Simon. Foster contributed several original songs to the album that (as was the case with Jackie Edwards and the Spencer Davis group, discussed in Volume 1) made it clear that there was an intriguing and complex relationship, a dynamic of synergy and exchange between different parts of the Black Diaspora.

Foster takes his cue from masterful African American purveyors of melody such as Otis Redding and Smokey Robinson, yet it would be wrong to dismiss him as a facsimile. On a piece such as 'You Don't Stand a Chance' he sets a busy, bustling theme against a punchy underlying backbeat well-bolstered by stabbing horns, to which Bond lends a spirited performance that no doubt found favour on dancefloors packed with listeners alert to the gospel undercurrent in the song. It tells a tale of forthright, unapologetic female desire. That confidence and candour are integral elements in both the history of Black music and the identity of its exponents. While Bond did not have the extraordinary range of her role model, Aretha Franklin, as few singers did, she conveys a sufficient sense of self to make her performance convincing.

Soul of Change is an interesting record because it points to both the relentless pace of change in post-war Black music and the expanding chain of artistic communication that bound America, the West Indies and Britain. Sounds and ideas travelled between these territories, and countless singers and players continued to transit from ex-colonies to Britain to develop their careers. Whilst Bond's work on stage remained of importance because appearances at clubs helped to build a fanbase, there was other media to consider. A subsidiary operation of BBC Radio 1 was called Radio 1 Club, launched in 1968 by executive producer Derek Chinnery in order to cement the relationship between stars and fans through the new portal of the transistor radio, which was increasingly within teenage budgets. Chinnery, though, envisioned something other than disembodied voices and invisible instruments flooding into British homes. He wanted audiences to come out and be part of something that would be more memorable than a weekly on-air programme. A 'Club date' would take place at a packed venue, and the set aired live on Radio 1 at lunchtime, hosted by one of the new crop of personality DJs. Short gigs were held in London, Birmingham, Manchester, Glasgow, Belfast, Bristol, Plymouth, Bournemouth and Swansea. It was an access all areas affair.

Bond was able to build a substantial following through this new format, in addition to concerts throughout Europe. This 'diminutive bombshell of a woman' was the latest in a long line of Black artists who combined talent with flamboyance and strength of character, and she proved able to deliver the kind of performance that had a suitably explosive effect, suggested by this description her label saw fit to include on the back of her albums.

Listening to the original Radio 1 Club jingles, it is clear that the producers set great store by what they hoped would be the thrill of real-time performance: 'Happening live from now til 2!', for which it was appropriate if not mandatory to draw on the vernacular of Black America, as epitomised by soul artists. Hence the use of terms such as 'And the beat goes on!', promising rhythmic dynamism, and the vivid exhortation 'Oh go on, really sock it to me!' Here was not just the sound but the idiomatic imagination of soul, as signalled by a tune such as Rex Garvin's 'Sock It to Em J.B', or the fade out chants of 'Sock it to me, sock it to me, sock it to me' that crowned Aretha Franklin's 'Respect'. This was an influence on British pop culture that was simply impossible to resist. With the sound of Black America came the speech of Black America, a dual force of rhythm and rhetoric that did not fall on deaf ears.

Notes

1. The revered Funk Brothers band was the architect of the Motown sound and exerted a huge influence on 1960s and 1970s pop, more generally.
2. Sleeve notes of Diana Ross and The Supremes *Live at London's Talk of the Town* (Tamla Motown, 1968).
3. Sleeve notes of The Foundations' *Baby, Now That I've Found You,* (Uni, 1968).
4. Ibid.
5. Ibid.
6. Black History Month 2020: Root Jackson podcast Calderdale Council, Oct 28, 2020.
7. Ibid.
8. Ibid.
9. Ibid.
10. Jimmy James & The Vagabonds and The Alan Bown Set, *London Swings at the Marquee* vaguely echoes the title of Alexis Korner/Cyril Davies 1962 classic *R&B at the Marquee.*
11. Sleeve notes of Jimmy James & The Vagabonds, *The New Religion* (ATCO, 1966).
12. See garagehangover.com site with concert listings for 1960s bands.
13. Joyce Bond, *Soul of Change* (Windmill, 1972).

2. THE PROPERTY OF THE NEGRO RACE

> Even people with no overt racial prejudice thought that it was daring to promote a mixed race boy-girl image to the British teenage market.
> — Simon Napier-Bell, manager of Diane and Nicky

A Concert of Hostility
The use of African American idiomatic expressions on BBC Radio One may have been a no-brainer for presenters who realised that the music industry had to keep abreast of the fast-moving area of youth culture, but there were still difficult conversations to be held over other more unsavoury responses to Britain's shifting demographics. This was not so much about the arrival of migrants from the formerly colonial world – the Commonwealth Immigration Act had put a stop to that – but about the growing awareness that Black and Asian settlers were here to stay. Action had to be taken. Drawbridges had to be pulled up. The prevailing racist rhetoric was about sending those people back 'home'.

This fear of change fuelled a belief among some that the 'green and pleasant land' had to be defended. Those who could claim a birthright to reside in Nottingham or Notting Hill, Buxton or Brixton, had to do something to protect white Britain. That fear was vividly and explosively channelled into Enoch Powell's notorious 'Rivers of Blood' speech of 20 April, 1968 at the Conservative Political Centre in Birmingham. The irony of a white Tory warning of a time when the black man would have 'the whip hand' in a city with munitions factories once manned by West Indians to help 'our boys' defeat Hitler in the Second World War may well have been lost amid the ensuing uproar.

Powell was roundly condemned by politicians of all stripes, but his tirade nonetheless struck a chord with many who praised him for having the courage to say aloud what they were thinking. He became a mouthpiece. Conservative MP for Wolverhampton South West, Powell quoted his constituents, such as 'a middle-aged quite ordinary man' who said the possibility of invasion and subjugation by immigrants would be so complete that whites would be 'strangers in their own country'. Powell attacked the Race Relations Act of 1968 (an updating of the 1965 Act) as 'dangerous and divisive'. Throughout the speech he invoked the people of the Midlands as if he was a quasi-folk hero speaking for a silenced proletariat who had no effective voice in parliament. In one of his most vivid rhetorical flourishes, Powell described a woman being followed in the street by 'charming, wide-grinning piccaninnies', a corrosively racist term that would find a grim echo decades later in ex-Prime Minister Boris Johnson's tableau of 'flag waving piccaninnies' as he argued that post-colonial Africa had slipped into chronic decline because 'we are not in charge anymore'. Nostalgia for empire where whites ruled the world and Black people were unseen thousands of miles away has remained a poison in British society.

The 'Rivers of Blood' speech had an impact on outlooks and attitudes in many quarters. Black and Asian immigrants had encountered racial discrimination from the moment of their arrival, but as witnesses of the time recall, Powell's speech legitimised bigotry to take more open forms. For example, the Tanzanian author, Abdulrazak Gurnah, who came to London as a refugee at the age of twenty, said, 'There was an atmosphere being generated by the press, politicians, trade unionists who claimed plane loads of people were arriving from Kenya, from Pakistan. There was a concert of hostility at the top level and also at street level.'[1] Gurnah overcame such inauspicious circumstances to make a successful career as an academic and novelist, winning the Nobel Prize for Literature in 2022, but his path was closed to the mass of Black Britons whose priorities had to be survival in a climate where discrimination in jobs and housing, and racism on the street at the hands of the police and far right groups was a daily experience. Even so, and not just amongst Black intellectuals, there were more existential matters to debate, matters of self-definition, of how one might see oneself in a harsh, judgemental world, the extent to which you, and even more so your children, remained the same people who had left the West Indian islands or India and Pakistan. For younger people, the concern was what might one do with one's life. Many of the first arrivals had been forced to accept work that did not match the qualifications they held. As a result, there was an absence of Black role models in white-collar jobs, such as broadcasting and teaching – as exemplified by E.R. Braithwaite's struggles, so powerfully documented in his novel *To Sir, With Love* (1959). One can argue that it was this situation that made the draw of popular music particularly strong for young Black people who arrived in Britain at the end of the 1960s. It was a field in which they could possibly succeed, especially if they were able to make the right connections in the increasingly hierarchical record industry to realise their talent. In addition, while the Windrush generation consisted of many young West Indian men and women who had attended school in the Caribbean before travelling to the 'mother country', there was now a cohort of boys and girls who arrived after their parents had settled and completed their secondary education in cities and towns all over the UK. They were thus born into one culture and grew into another. They were caught between worlds. Negotiating this border was a challenge.

Music (and sport and the arts in general) had long been one of the areas of civil life in which there was at least some contact between the races, though inequalities of power and access still existed, but it was not as intensely problematic as the experience of Black people in white churches, or in white-owned pubs and barbershops where rejection stimulated the creation of Black-led churches and local businesses. In popular music there were clear instances of the influence exerted by the ethnic minority on the majority, which went far beyond the use of rhythm. The most striking case of white adoption of Black aesthetics was the decision by Noel Redding and Mitch Mitchell to puff their straight hair into something resembling the Afro sported by their bandleader, Jimi Hendrix, as if to endorse his status as more than a significant new musical phenomenon. Some artists evidently wanted to go so far as to look like a Black man in addition to playing the songs of Black folks. This is ironic given the contempt the Victorians had for 'the bestial fleece' of the Negro and the sorry spectacle of 'blacking-up'. The voluminous, rounded coiffures of English rock musicians, not to mention the adoption of African American vernacular and choreography may not have sent people scurrying to read Norman Mailer and ponder what the term 'White Negro' meant in Britain, yet it was clear that blackness, in concrete and abstract terms, had substantial counter-currency to the long history of physical caricature, such as Laurence Olivier blacking up in the screen adaptation of Shakespeare's *Othello*, a casting decision made more crass by the fact that Paul Robeson had brought such gravitas and indeed authenticity to the part as an African American actor years prior. The fact that no actor of colour was considered for the role – Black Britons such as Earl Cameron and Cy Grant did not have Olivier's reputation or box office appeal but they were nonetheless immense talents – underlined, along with the lack of questioning by the production team of the possible offence of making a Caucasian become 'burnished mahogany' (as Olivier himself recalled), that the representation of ethnic minorities in the mainstream could still lack sensitivity and respect. Recognition of what might shock Black people was not in the script. It would have been interesting to hear what Jimi Hendrix might have said about Olivier as Othello. Although there are no lyrics in his songbook in which he talks overtly about Blackness or racism, he did make it clear to at least one journalist that he knew that Europe was anything but some kind of multi-cultural utopia, even if it lacked US-style segregation laws.

Nowhere was this more apparent than in the BBC's ongoing commissioning of *The Black and White Minstrel Show* and its staunch defence of it when objections were raised about its grossly offensive nature. Faced with a petition against the programme by the Campaign Against Racial Discrimination in 1967, the Corporation issued this quite astonishing counter-argument: 'The show is not about race.'[2]

Hard as it may have been to imagine such a debacle in pop, where Hendrix's band embodied unity across the colour line, it is worth noting that Eric Clapton, a guitarist given God-like status by some fans, peddled the most hackneyed caricatures of Black musicians in interviews. This was not even in the immediate aftermath of the Powell speech when dockers and meat-market workers marched in support of the sacked Birmingham MP. When Clapton talked of British audiences falling for 'a spade with a big dick' and directly equated 'that magic thing' with Hendrix, he laid bare deep-set historical prejudices that reached back to the Victorian era. Clapton, who had made his name playing Black music, and who had shared the stage with Hendrix and the expatriate blues legend Sonny Boy Williamson – though it's unlikely that he used the word 'spades' in their company – made it an inconvenient truth that whites playing Black music did not necessarily mean they had a real understanding of and respect for its originators.

So Much Feeling
Debates on exactly what constituted the unquantifiable quality of the sounds produced by the descendants of enslaved African people became more feverish in the late 1960s, a period which, it should not be forgotten, was still relatively close to the history of plantation slavery in the Americas and the abominable racist pseudo-science it espoused.

There was no escaping the association of Black music and Blackness as racial identity, something casually expressed in descriptive terms such as 'coloured soul singer' (Jackie Edwards) or 'eight-handed coloured band who played Rock & Roll Soul' (Jimmy James & The Vagabonds), and, as argued in the previous chapter, this became prominent in the rebranding of rhythm & blues as soul. The idea that the new genre of the music was something intrinsic to African Americans stemmed variously from notions of the lived experience of 'the Negro', subject of suffering and totem of resilience and in the 1960s militant resistance. But there was also the much more contentious question of innate gift, and that focused on the voice.

If some of Stax's British fans had been dumbstruck at the sight of the white guitarist Steve Cropper on stage playing so beautifully, they may well have been tongue-tied had he opened his mouth and started to sing soul, for while there was recognition that whites could play jazz, probably because there was the material proof throughout Britain in the form of musicians inspired by 'Negro' legends from Louis Armstrong to John Coltrane, there was still a deeply held belief in the inimitable quality of African New World voices, whether from North and South America or the Caribbean.

When Marble Arch, a subsidiary of Pye, the imprint that had grown from radio and television manufacturer, issued a compilation in 1966 titled *Blues and Soul*, featuring relatively obscure but highly talented African Americans such as Joe Tex, Mitty Collier and Little Milton, it offered fulsome praise their 'freedom of phrasing' on one hand and on the other placed the abundant talent in a clearly defined racial framework:

> Soul and blues have always run side by side, hand in hand. It's basically Negro music, stemming from hearts burdened by deprivation and struggle and a constant search for artistic freedom. Sure, it has now taken on a commercial appeal but this in no way reduces the authenticity, the authority of the performers.[3]

In the 1930s, West Indian musicians in Britain played with some English counterparts who were convinced that you had to be Black to play jazz. Now, decades down the line, the idea took hold that you had to be Black to sing soul. Journalist Roger St. Pierre stated: 'They used to talk about people singing with heart, now the catchword is "soul". It's a property which seems particularly to be the property of the Negro race, an intrinsic inborn quality which makes their music so exciting, so warm, so emotional, so moving with its tinge of anguish and bitterness.'[4] Studious avoidance of the possible reasons for such resentment aside, the text spells out the entrenched belief that soul was an immutable racial phenomenon. Yet this was part of St. Pierre's presentation of Chris Farlowe, the white English vocalist who emerged in the early 1960s and recorded and gigged regularly throughout the decade. To bolster the contender's credentials, he quoted the R&B organist-vocalist Georgie Fame who said, 'Chris is a natural. He sings like a white Negro. It's what we have all been arguing about for years, getting that authentic rhythm & blues voice. His voice has so much feeling and it's unique.'[5]

The Maileresque language is jarring to say the least, but the comment effectively underlines how uncomfortably conflated race and culture can become. Soul is Black because Blacks have soul, but whites who sing soul must be some kind of miraculous transracial entity that achieves authenticity, becoming the 'real thing' to the astonishment of all. Black man born in the wrong body or white man born with the right, but another's voice, amounted to a glib formula that laid bare reductive and essentialist obsessions with supposed racial identities and reinforced race-related musical borders rather than opening them up. If 'blue-eyed soul' was a newsworthy phenomenon, did that mean that it had a counterpart in something called 'nappy-haired classical', because it was assumed that the European orchestral tradition was outside of the Negro's ability? While Farlowe hit peaks of popularity, posters for club nights, both in London and the regions, advertised headliners as well as 'local coloured soul or R&B bands', because of the lingering expectation of what band members had to look like. Nobody talked about the 'all white Philharmonic ensembles'; that would have been a patronising tautology. What is lost in these convolutions is the key element of any pertinent perception and understanding of soul music. It is an art. No amount of gifts from god can alter the need for commitment to the development of a voice so that it becomes an instrument capable of beauty that must be carefully maintained, and astutely deployed. Not all black people are born soul singers. Some just can't sing. They do other things.

Listen carefully to soul's founding fathers and mothers, from Sam Cooke and Rosetta Tharpe to Aretha Franklin and Otis Redding, and the inescapable conclusion is that the 'natural' richness of tone is only a part of their aesthetic. There is the regulation of delivery, the dynamics, emphasis, understatement, subtleties of phrasing and finesse of articulation, pacing of energy, control of pitch and shadings of timbre. The 'cry' and 'shout' are not the only weapons in the singer's arsenal.

It is commonplace to note that these soul legends took their first musical steps in church, but that setting is also where singers and musicians learn their craft, rather than simply awaiting divine inspiration to swing low and lift them up to greatness in a sweet chariot. It may well be true that certain Black people are born with extraordinary voices, but the fulfilment of their talent does not preclude an immense amount of dedication to specific techniques. Church bands don't abide backsliders. Soul singers are not half-steppers.

Imitation is part of the tuition – as well as sincere flattery. The availability of recordings made it possible for Black and white artists to approximate to varying degrees the work of the pioneers of African American music, and the obvious wider context to the case of Farlowe is that there was a whole generation of 1960s white British singers who took their cue from the blues, with the likes of Mick Jagger and Eric Burdon being the most high profile and Rod Stewart and Joe Cocker the most accomplished. They were all liberated by the sound of Muddy and co. They bought the albums. They listened hard. They learned the lessons.

Quite ironically, St. Pierre made a case for Chris Farlowe as a soul singer on the album *Stormy Monday*, which was really a blues/R&B set (with covers of songs by icons such as T-Bone Walker, Chuck Berry and Big Mama Thornton) that doesn't feature any Stax or Motown material, thus negating the dominant idea of soul as a new repertoire in Black popular music. Farlowe also worked with Mick Jagger, who produced his version of the Rolling Stones' lugubrious 'Paint It Black', which was brilliantly re-imagined as an orchestral piece with a swirling Russian folk feel. It is just one of many highlights of a large discography that was consistently of a high quality. Farlowe was held in great esteem by his peers, above all

Geno Washington as well as Jagger, and he notched up hit singles such as 'Out of Time' but sadly never quite reached the level of success his talent warranted. Which is also something that can be said of a great many artists of the time, be they black, white, or black and white.

Wasn't the Right Class
If the connections between race and genre were matters of confusion of thought, what was undoubtedly real were the structures of power inside the popular music business. The 'insiders' – people employed in the A&R departments of labels or for the management companies that oversaw an artist's career – were able to witness at a close and personal level the many spheres of influences that held sway, and the thought processes of those at executive level. For example, Simon Napier-Bell, who started life as a trumpeter with the John Dankworth jazz band before becoming a versatile writer-producer-manager, was all too aware of how sensitive the question of interracial relationships was when he put together not just a 'mixed' group but a boy-girl duo that comprised two accomplished singers, the white Englishman Nicky Scott and Black Trinidadian woman, Diane Ferraz. As Diane and Nicky, they carved a niche as purveyors of soulful love songs. Napier-Bell recalls, 'Even people with no overt racial prejudice thought that it was daring to promote a mixed race boy-girl image to the British teenage market... I had photos taken that emphasised Nicky's paleness, Dianne's darkness, and their attraction to one another. There was no question about it, the best way to get publicity in the music business was with relationships that could be talked about.'[6]

By Napier-Bell's candid admission Diane and Nick's debut 'Me And You' was a rip-off of Rolling Stones' 'Get Off Of My Cloud' (itself an engaging composite of several blues numbers including The McCoys' 'Hang On Sloopy' and Howlin' Wolf's 'Smokestack Lightnin''), but more important is Napier-Bell's awareness of the degree of unease that was fostered by love across the colour line as a sign of prevailing British attitudes to race. Miscegenation remained a subject of controversy, if not scandal.

Indeed, the case of Diane and Nicky is also a rejoinder to the question of blue-eyed soul, and the phenomenon of white singing black. Had punters not seen the photograph of the duo and only heard their records, would they have assumed that one was Black and the other white? Diane and Nicky enjoyed minor hits but one can speculate on whether they would have been more successful as an act that was either all Black or all white, and deemed a 'safer' product to sell to a mass market. But if a Black and white couple in music was challenging in the late 1960s, then a major white star going black also posed problems. Napier-Bell learned from credible sources about the veto slapped on Tom Jones, following the monster success of singles such as 'It's Not Unusual' (many thought he was black on hearing his big booming baritone), when it was suggested that he record with Motown. Decca, to whom Jones was then signed, baulked, even though Motown boss Berry Gordy was keen for it, presumably because he saw 'greenbacks' in the union. Decca's general manager Bill Townsley said no. There was also talk of Decca giving Motown a distribution deal, but again there was a rebuttal from Townsley who is reported to have said 'this Motown stuff' would never sell. Years later, when reflecting on what the whole episode said about race in the British music industry, Napier-Bell did not mince his words: 'Class distinction was still rife within major record companies and as far as Sir Edward Lewis was concerned, black music wasn't of the right class. Company bosses thought not only of profits but endearing themselves to the establishment.'[7]

For all the embrace of the blues, for all the Bentleys sent by pop stars to visiting African American revues, for all the gushing royal receptions granted singers from 'the coloured section' of Detroit, question marks persisted over exactly where ethnic minority artists should be placed in the cultural pantheon. There is no reason not to believe Napier-Bell's account of glass ceilings in the music industry, which reflected other social hierarchies in Britain. For the most part, decision-makers, powerbrokers, career- shapers tended to be 'of better stock', while the artists in pop were drawn mostly from the lower orders. Black representation at executive level was non-existent. And yet musicians of colour continued to emerge, sometimes in successful bands that were interesting for both their choice of songs and the roles that were allocated to individual members.

The Other Merseysider
Three young hopefuls are on the sleeve of an album. They have been deftly styled, the fashion of choice being black, crew-neck sweaters and Staprest trousers, the classic mod look with more than a dash of 007 cool in the casually confident poise. You might assume the man in the middle, the focal point of the image, would be the frontman of the band, very possibly the lead singer, while those who flank him might be the rhythm section, just as was the case with the Jimi Hendrix Experience. The two combos had the same black-white ratio, but your assumption would be wrong. The name of the band was The Peddlers and the Black man in the middle was not the singer. His name was Trevor Morais, and he was a drummer who had played an important role in the development of white 'Merseybeat'. Born in Liverpool to Trinidadian parents, he started young and became a member of a group that was considered one of the most promising on the local scene, Faron's Flamingos, before moving on to Rory Storm & The Hurricanes after Ringo Starr left to join The Beatles. Rather than just being linked to the Fab Four, Morais could have been

one, given his reputation among Liverpool's young bands. According to Bob Wooler, the MC and DJ at the Cavern, who had clout on the local scene, Morais' hopes of landing the gig were dashed by the fact he had a bit too much eye-catching, limelight-stealing flair on stage. 'He was an attraction and they [The Beatles] didn't want all the showmanship.'[8] There are claims made by countless other drummers about almost joining the Fab Four, it should be pointed out, but apocryphal as the story may be, one can only imagine the impact on race relations had Morais actually joined the Beatles. Could it have led to more tolerance for ethnic minorities or could it have been a hindrance to the group's global success given their predominantly white following? God only knows.

Beatle manqué or not, Morais continued to play professionally and joined Ian Crawford & The Boomerangs and gigged mostly in the north. Then, in 1964, he became a member of another band with whom he would record a substantial body of work during the rest of the decade. Initially named The Song Peddlers, the group simply became The Peddlers for the release of its debut single 'Rose Marie'. Consisting of Newcastle-born bassist, Tab Martin, organist-vocalist, Roy Phillips, who hailed from Poole, and Morais on drums, the trio gained sufficient traction from its first round of gigs in the regions to be offered residencies in London, which gave them their only real hope of clinching a record deal. The Peddlers were signed, first, to Phillips and later to Columbia.

One of the group's significant early champions was Annie Ross, a highly talented English jazz singer who had lived in America and found fame as part of the superb vocal trio Lambert, Hendricks & Ross. The club she founded in London in the early 1960s, Annie's Room, became a hotspot in the West End, thanks to bookings that included major U.S. stars such as Errol Garner, Blossom Dearie and Nina Simone. The Peddlers were booked there in the mid-1960s, and their other notable appearances included The Scotch of St. James, where the Jimi Hendrix Experience made its debut, and The Pickwick, an upscale honey pot that buzzed with the great and good of pop and film, thus becoming one of the places to be seen and network. The Peddlers recorded a gig that was issued as *Live at The Pickwick*, complete with an effusive introduction by Pete Murray, then one of the increasingly influential radio DJs. Such endorsements were priceless.

Not a Cloud in the Sky
In three busy years, between 1967 and 1970, The Peddlers released no fewer than five albums and carved a solid reputation for themselves as a live act. Recordings such as *Freewheelers*, *Three in a Cell*, *Birthday* and *Three For All* make it clear that the trio is rooted very solidly in the earthy blues and R&B that was also being successfully ploughed by Georgie Fame and

the Blue Flames. Roy Phillips had a powerful tone and well-paced delivery as well as a command of the organ that draws on the vocabulary of jazz greats such as Jimmy Smith and an R&B pioneers such as Booker T, both of whom made the instrument a key element in those genres, while Trevor Morais and Tab Martin were a flexible drums and bass axis that could move effectively from a subtle, understated pulse on sensual ballads to tough, driving backbeats on more dance-oriented numbers. The Peddlers were a small group that could produce a big sound.

On the one hand, the band conformed to the common model of an act in the mid-1960s by covering miscellaneous material drawn from a large pool of jazz, blues and Broadway standards, ranging from 'In the Still of the Night' and 'Stormy Weather' to 'Comin' Home Baby' and 'Little Red Rooster'. On the other hand, in Phillips, the band had a skilled and mature composer who was able to craft original songs that were appealing for their blend of quirky lyrics and themes that reflected the gravitas of trailblazers such as Ray Charles,[9] an unavoidable reference for artists who recognised the blend of the sacred and secular in African-American culture. 'The Lost Continent' is a prime example of Phillips' achievement as a writer. Following an extended introduction in which he evokes the mythical image of 'sirens' and the 'sea's frightening scent', over heavily sustained, quite funereal minor organ chords, the tune skips into a 3/4 beat that is tightly marshalled by a tingling ride-cymbal, pinched, staccato stabs on the keyboard and a luscious sweep of strings. If there is something cinematic about the piece then that makes sense because it was the main theme of a film of the same name, a ludicrous tale of travellers washed up on a monster-inhabited land that time forgot, released by the Hammer studio. The music, not the movie, is the star attraction here.

'Birth' had a slight yet affecting gospel flavour, while 'Girlie P.S. I Love You' is another demonstration of how skilled a keyboard player Phillips is. His hissing, almost simpering vibrato effects on the organ infuse the piece with an undercurrent of tension that is very effective against the predominantly serene containment of the rhythm, which he then galvanizes dramatically after unexpectedly switching to piano around the two-thirds mark of the lengthy arrangement (6.33). He starts to swing before teasingly drawing back down to ballad pace. The piece is one of the Peddlers' clearest indications of their kinship to the jazz aesthetic, even though they retain the hooks so essential in pop. 'Just A Pretty Song' celebrates music that makes no claim to being profound but nonetheless holds the interest for the way in which Morais's pounding cowbell patterns impart a calypso resonance to the bright bossa nova on which the piece is built. As for 'Nobody Likes Me', it has a jaunty, nonchalant theme whose harmonic foundation is really an astutely oblique reference to Duke Ellington's sublime 'Satin Doll'. With Tab Martin's bass guitar, which he held vertically in the manner of a double bass, propelling the groove, The Peddlers showed themselves to be more than adept at lively tempos, yet they came into their own when they took the bpm down. There was something very enticing about the way Phillips' assertive, leonine voice blended into the shimmer of the keyboard, again a lesson learned from Ray Charles, while the supporting bass and percussion provided light and shade by a range of accents on and off the beat. The band had measured energy.

'On a Clear Day' was a crowning glory in this respect. The title track of a 1965 Broadway musical written by Burton Lane, the song was given a gospel-inflected rendition by organist Shirley Scott in 1966, but The Peddlers' version is all languid control. The rhythmic foundation is a repeated bassline with an assured leap through an octave, which keeps the movement as steady as in a James Brown record, while the accompanying rhythmic patter on the ride cymbal contributes to the sense of fluency, almost like a cool breath streaming into the solid heat in the low register. From the organ, come purring tremolos that are then offset by stark, bright eighth notes, delivered with sufficient precision to create a minimal but perceptible jolt in the steady tranquillity of the pulse. While there is nothing frenetic in the way these various elements come together, there's a subtle drama in the performance. Morais and Martin's stealthy handling of the beat and Phillips's colour palette on the organ juxtapose lightness and heaviness, a neat spike of aggression amid the softer vibrations. According to the blues vernacular, the band is strollin' or struttin', but there is still a fleeting tension that pierces the regulated composure. Phillips sings his way confidently through the verse, and strings pad out the melody to give a decidedly romantic undercurrent to the arrangement, especially after a ripple of harp at the halfway mark, before Phillips takes a solo in which he plays a series of busy, choppy riffs that inject adrenalin rather than wildness into the groove. There is a real magic in the opening bars of the song, with its woozy, blissfully cajoling atmosphere, its sense of carefree and casual movement. Decades after the song was recorded, DJs and producers fell under the spell of 'On a Clear Day', the track being sampled over a dozen times, making the point that The Peddlers crafted sounds that would speak to the era of 'loops and breaks'. In fact, the group's influence became even more explicit in 2001 when the group, Zero Seven, hugely successful exponents of the kind of moody, often electronically inflected downtempo music synonymous with the 'chillout' room of the new superclubs, covered one of its songs, 'I Have Seen', a beautiful composition built on a similarly leisurely yet charged ambiance to 'On a Clear Day', with a concise, resonant lyric about the march of time and the pull of nostalgia. Adding further distinction to the piece are the sumptuous strings of The London Philharmonic Orchestra. They appeared with the trio on *Suite London*, an ambitious blend of pop and classical music that contained some of Roy Phillips's best writing, though the arrangements by keyboardist Peter Robinson[10] are also excellent. Released in 1972, it would be The Peddlers' final album with the original line-up, as Trevor Morais left soon after. A new drummer came in and two more live albums were made.

No Chart Smash, No Problem
The metrics of success in popular music have never been set in stone. While there may be a not unreasonable consensus that an artist without hit singles will not be able to grow an audience to the same extent as one who has, there are bands that nonetheless managed to enjoy relatively fulfilled careers, even without any extensive radio play.

No doubt, The Peddlers endured frustration. They released many well-received singles as well as albums, but none ever sold in large quantities. Yet the trio had an enviable visibility in the media, with numerous appearances on television, including on Simon Dee's show, which ensured a steady flow of live work. 'People see us cropping up all the time and assume that we must be stars anyway, so we really do the business at the clubs and in cabaret,' Morais reflected in an interview in 1966. 'Not having a hit record doesn't affect us in the amount of work that we get, or the television, or the fact that we're getting top billing.' That was no exaggeration. They gigged regularly in Europe and had the distinction of being the first British group to play in Las Vegas; they also toured Australia, where only the name of a megastar like Shirley Bassey was above theirs on posters. It is possible that at several junctures in their career, The Peddlers had a bigger following abroad than they did at home.

They continued to work into the mid-1970s before winding down, but they remain one of the most interesting bands to have emerged in Britain at the end of the 1960s. They plotted a smart course through pop, retaining elements of both jazz and classical music at a time when the bulk of their peers were moving away from those genres. Having the organ at the centre of the group's sound also went against the grain of the ascendant guitar-led, post-Beatles-Stones rock-pop groups of the time. Yet soulful as they were on occasion, The Peddlers were quite different from the US-derived UK soul acts discussed in Chapter 1. Blurring the lines between R&B, pop and jazz, they managed to carve out a musical identity that embraced excellent large-scale orchestrations, the highlight being *Suite London*. Recent reappraisals of their work have been positive, and though they did not sell huge numbers of records, they made good ones that now change hands for large sums of money.

The presence of a Black Liverpudlian drummer, Trevor Morais, at the heart of the band is important because it highlights the range of activities that musicians of West Indian origin were engaged in at the time, and also flags up the important heritage of Black music in the north of England. Morais was often in the middle of press shots of the band, but he was not the lead singer, and he certainly didn't speak as if he was born within Bow Bells. These marks of distinction are to be celebrated, not bemoaned.

A Discussion about Immigrant Communities
Regardless of the achievements of Black musicians around the UK, the sense of unease over the treatment of Black immigrants in mainstream British society had been growing, even before the grim watershed of 'Rivers of Blood'. The presence of African American Civil Rights activists such as the writer James Baldwin and comedian Dick Gregory in London, addressing a group of West Indian Students was important, as was that of 'Black Power' activists such as Malcolm X, who visited Smethwick, Birmingham, to lend moral support to Asians and West Indians in the aftermath of the infamous Conservative Party's 'If you want a nigger for a neighbour' 1964 election campaign. Dr. Martin Luther King Jnr was another important visitor. When he stopped over in London on his way to Stockholm to collect the Nobel Peace Prize, he met with a number of activists including the Trinidadian novelist/pacifist Marion Glean (aka Marion Patrick Jones); her compatriots, historian-writer C.L.R. James and educator-politician Jocelyn Barrow; English barrister Anthony Lester and Indian academic Dipak K. Nandy. Amongst this group were those who went on to found the Campaign Against Racial Discrimination (CARD), which was to lobby for real progress in legislation for race relations.

Although it had wound down by the end of the decade, CARD has a notable place in history for both its stated intentions as well as its limitations. Perhaps its greatest achievement was the national focus it brought to the debate on discrimination, particularly in employment and housing and the need to counter it. According to statistics, in the mid-1960s the UK was home to some 800,000 'coloured immigrants', a term which clearly evinced an awareness of foreigners who were not white. CARD tried to mobilise a mass movement to improve their lot. In an article in *The Observer*, one executive member stated: 'There is a discussion going on in Britain about the immigrant communities, in which they have played no part. Our aim is to enter into the discussion.'[11] Yet the same piece also pointedly suggested a need for forbearance and moderation: 'We don't want to raise anger or start bad feeling', a reflection of the lack of power that Black people felt they had at the time. They dared not rock the boat. Even more revealing was the comment of another member who stated: 'CARD will have failed if enough white people don't join', which begs the question of how community action could progress when Black people in Britain did not feel confident enough to shout for themselves, and needed to seek the endorsement or solidarity of the white mainstream.

It would be wrong, also, to imagine that popular music was an exception to the problematic nature of black-white relationships within civil society. Young white audiences might have embraced African American R&B and soul, but as was argued earlier in this chapter, if the presentation of a multi-racial vocal duo could raise an eyebrow, there were also more overt, even brutal instances of racism directed at Black musicians. For example, Derek Thompson, a white organist who played with jazz and R&B bands in a variety of venues in Greater Manchester, recalls a shocking incident at The Market Hotel in Oldham, following a residency he had completed with the Ghanaian drummer, Sammy Nelson.

'We'd done a week there; we got our wages and then the landlord started kicking off. He didn't want Sammy to come back! He said he'd have me but don't bring that fella, because he was black. It was the first time that I'd come across that,' Thompson told me in 2022, his voice cracking at the memory.[12] 'I said he's a great player; the landlord said he just didn't like him, because he was black. I was on Sammy's side, trying to calm things down, and this fella was really kicking off, but Sammy seemed to take it in his stride and said there are people like that. And Sammy was driving as well. I didn't have a car at the time.'

Thompson pointed out that the working man's club circuit, in which he also worked, was decidedly mono-racial, though there is also evidence that Black artists, like Root Jackson, discussed in Chapter 1, met with entirely approving audiences on that same network. However, the comedy scene, which also booked bands, featured stand-up performers with notoriously racist material, like Bernard Manning, whose following catapulted him to success on national television, revealing the extent to which ethnic minorities were still perceived as fair game for ridicule. 'I realised that some people wanted it be to be all white,' Thompson said of the venues he knew.[13] Equally, if bands were multi-racial, that did not mean the case for wider integration had been won, especially if a club owner felt entitled to uphold a colour bar, knowing that, despite the various race relations acts passed in the 1960s, similar attitudes were shared by patrons cradling their pints, as well as by those powerful record label executives who sat in judgment on the nation's tastes.

Notes

1. Newspaper interview with Abdulrazak Gurnah by Max Liu, 16 December 2021.
2. Official response from the BBC to the charge that *The Black and White Minstrel show* was racist.
3. Sleeve notes to Various artists *Blues & Soul* (Marble Arch, 1966).

4. Sleeve notes to Chris Farlowe & The Thunderbirds, *Stormy Monday* (MFP, 1966).
5. Ibid.
6. Simon Napier Bell, *Black Vinyl White Powder* (Ebury Press, 2001), p. 62.
7. Ibid, p. 75.
8. David Bedford and Gary Popper, *Finding the Fourth Beatle* (Tredition, 2018).
9. The influence Ray Charles exerted on the 1960s British pop revolution is often overlooked. His vocal style and organ playing can be heard from everybody from the Beatles to Steve Winwood, Georgie Fame, and The Peddlers.
10. Robinson also worked with artists in pop, classical and jazz, from David Bowie and Andrew Lloyd Webber to Lenny White and Al Jarreau.
11. Colin McGlashan, *The Observer*, 24 January 1965.
12. Interview with the author, February 2022.
13. Ibid.

3 ALL MEN ARE CREATED EQUAL

There is this sort of hard man cult that exists among the lower ranks, and this requires a young man to prove himself in many ways, mainly by the number of arrests that he makes. The old tradition would be that the coloured man is not as fully aware of his rights as a white man would be and on this assumption, I suppose he would be more vulnerable.
– Testimony of a former Metropolitan Police officer.

'What have I done?'
'Police On My Back' by The Equals.

Plain as Black and White
In spite of the challenges posed by racism and limited access to jobs and housing, West Indians continued to migrate to Britain throughout the 1960s, convinced that greater financial security lay ahead of them. Many, though, were leaving behind something quite priceless. Certainly for some people from rural areas, the Caribbean had an environmental beauty – from rivers and streams to fauna and flora – that offered a quality of life that could be seen as experiential wealth. Eddy Grant makes that clear when discussing his earliest memories of Guyana. He was growing up fast and growing up good.

> I did a lot of things before I came to England. A child of eight years old in Plaisance is like a 24 year-old in England because you have very little, but you have a lot of space and that space gives you a lot to extemporise on, to make a lot of mistakes, but you're learning a lot. And you're getting strong. I noticed how strong I was compared to boys in this country. At 12, I could do anything... not many people in this world have climbed a coconut tree. If I needed a coconut I could climb the tree; you put the belt around your feet and go like crazy.
>
> I swam in every trench, every canal, every waterway that surrounded Plaisance. Sometimes, we were chasing birds. You don't have much, but what you have is nature in the most unbelievable way. When I say chasing birds, I mean the birds were so beautiful you really wanted to be in their company... the colours. You run after them so you end up miles away from where you live. You had massive areas of land... where we played. I had a fantastic childhood. When I came here, I just thought...

what am I gonna do? Where am I gonna play? So you played in the street, that freedom to be able to try things was crucial.[1]

Relocating to the constrictions of Kentish Town, north London, in 1960 to join his parents was such a culture shock for the twelve-year-old Grant that his desire was to gain skills and then return to his country of origin, a feeling not uncommon among other members of the Windrush generation. Grant had suffered from diphtheria as a child, and in Plaisance he had seen some of his peers die of that condition. This traumatic event gave him a purpose in life and shaped his vision: "My whole thinking was to go to England where there's going to be an opportunity for me to learn medicine and come back," he said emphatically. "I was not interested in being in England."[2]

The advantage of accelerated maturity given to him by his childhood in Guyana also underpinned his ambition to become a musician, partly because his father, an accomplished trumpeter, had declared it his own pipe dream. Grant also played trumpet as a boy, falling under the spell of trad hero, Louis Armstrong, and modernist pioneers Miles Davis and Lee Morgan, before gravitating to a taste for pop music. Grant's arrival in London caught the tail end of the skiffle craze, the rise of the Beatles and the Notting Hill riots, where, in his own words, 'the whole race thing reared its ugly head.'[3]

Grant went through a number of stages in becoming a professional musician. He joined the horn section of the Acklam Burley secondary school orchestra, learned to sight-read and transcribe songs, *made* his own guitar in woodwork classes and, perhaps most importantly of all, saw rock & roll legend Chuck Berry at the Finsbury Park Astoria. It was an education. Armed with Berry's riffs, Grant took on all pretenders at jam sessions, 'cowboy showdown style' and also, after meeting more and more musicians who worked in a variety of genres, realised that the bulk of West Indians who aspired to play jazz ended up huddled next to paraffin stoves in freezing basements and did not enjoy financial rewards in line with their talents. This fact strengthened his resolve to make the kind of music that would spare him such indignities.

To that end, he and many of his peers pursued the path of the R&B-informed pop opening up around them, and it was a jam session in a schoolboy's house in Highgate, where an accommodating mother made sandwiches for noisy budding stars, that laid the foundation for Grant's first band, The Equals. They would go on to become an integral part of British musical history. Comprising three black kids – two Jamaican twins, guitarist Lincoln Gordon and vocalist Derv, Guyanese lead guitarist Grant, and two whites – drummer John Hall and guitarist Patrick Lloyd – this five-piece formed in the mid-1960s. They hailed from a council estate in Hornsey, north London, and encapsulated the democratisation of popular culture of the age. Like other working-class boys, they took up instruments such as the guitar because the six string was cheaper than a piano and perhaps less intimidating to learn for those who had not been weaned on the 'proper' ways of classical music. Grant, more than a touch mischievously, remembers being unimpressed by many of the new bands also vying to make a name for themselves.

If there is a degree of cocky temerity in that statement, then it is worth remembering that the name chosen for Grant's group made its personnel a political statement. As Grant recalled: "John said we should call the band The Equals, and I interpreted that as because we were black and white, and he said it's equal votes."[4] While the group emerged before the Powell's 'Rivers of Blood', the electoral slogan "If You Want a Nigger for a Neighbour Vote Labour", had been used just a year before the Equals were launched. The R&B combo, The Foundations, discussed in Chapter 1, was described as a mini-United Nations; The Equals, as a guitar-led group, broke with the Beatles-Stones white boys model. Grant made that clear when he looked back:

> You're right, you couldn't help but see the difference (racially in the band) with all that was going on with the Enoch Powells and what have you. We had five days on the BBC Play School. So, we were seen. It was in your face with us! (And yes, I believed in us). I wrote the songs, produced the records. I was at school whereas the other guys were at work. I had time to go down and interface with the agents, people in the West End. I was very vociferous and braggadocious... All 'my band is the best band in the world'. It's also the time of Cassius Clay.[5]

Surprise Partie
Crossing the colour line was one thing, but Grant and co also had a sharp eye for new fashion trends that would attract attention. The Equals sported extravagant threads that rivalled those of the Jimi Hendrix Experience and other acts that embraced the wave of psychedelia when smart tailoring and careful colour co-ordination was upended by a rainbow of clashing hues, outlandishly patterned materials and a camp flourish that marked them out as anything but conservative.

From the sleeve of their 1967 debut, *Equals Explosion*, to that of their 1970 album, *Equals at the Top*, there was a dramatic change in sartorial style and accompanying artwork. Modestly cut jackets and ties photographed in clearly lit studio gave way to wing collars, sideburns and Afros that were bathed in iridescent shades, thanks to the wonders of post-production. Most strikingly of all, Eddy Grant, on the cover of that last record, wears a halo-like blonde mop top whose fringe, covering one eye, makes him look like a cross between a high-seas buccaneer and a drag artist who is too drunk to wig up with accuracy.

The effect this had on record buyers at the time is hard to know. Whether charmed or alarmed, they would not have been able to ignore Grant, and it was that daring, unrestrained flamboyance that placed him in the long line of theatrical African American performers that included Little Richard, Screamin' Jay Hawkins, Sly Stone, Jimi Hendrix, George Clinton and Bootsy Collins – performers who influenced Prince in the 1980s and Andre 3000 in the present.

Grant can also be seen as a West Indian carnival figure, a masquerader who knows that audacity is a valuable currency. Bravado meant risking ridicule. Indeed, the Guyanese bleached his hair in response to the jibe that 'black boys just don't have bottle.' The peroxide transformation occurred in full view of an open-mouthed barbershop clientele, followed by gasps of disbelief from passengers during a long bus ride home. Even without his guitar Grant still found an audience.

But beyond sartorial flamboyance, it was the unforgettable gigs The Equals performed that drew fans into their orbit and gave them an advantage over rivals who lacked their firecracker energy and showmanship. They sang and danced vigorously with eye-catching movement and gestures that enhanced the songs they played. Appearing on the French TV pop show, *Surprise Partie*, in 1968, The Equals were imperious, with Grant stealing the show when he took a deeply bluesy, extended guitar solo on 'Equality'. Sporting a close-cropped, corn yellow Afro and a loose-fitting, double-breasted orange jump-suit, he looks like a surreal urban spaceman, the brother from another planet who has somehow time-travelled from moonscape to catwalk and landed on a higher plane of a very weird pop culture fantasia. He also played the instrument with his teeth, a la Jimi.

There could be no greater advert for The Equals as a live act that ticked every box required for success in the pop world of the late 1960s. Image as well as talent was important, and the clips of their performances, along with their publicity shots, make it clear that this is a group with colour in the literal and figurative sense. Skin, hair, clothes, stance, moves, attitude. It is all very much in line with what would become known as glamrock, and Grant certainly had a peacockery to match the likes of David Bowie, Marc Bolan and Elton John. The failure to recognise this is one of the shortcomings of much British pop historiography.

More importantly, The Equals had a phenomenal output during their relatively short lifecycle. Their debut single 'I Won't Be There' was issued in 1966 and within 18 months several 45s also hit the market, along with three albums, whose titles, *Equals Explosion*, *Unequalled Equals* and *Sensational*, convey the kind of sparky, zestful self-confidence of young men on an expressway to stardom. A songbook of just under 40 entries makes it clear that Grant and bandmates were adept in the art of the three-minute pop tune in which strong instrumental riffs and vocal hooks are used to great effect. Unconventionally, the Equals had no bassist (though Grant occasionally played bass in the studio) so there was an emphasis on heavy chords and swells and squalls of sound to cover the low register. Grant's lead guitar, often put through a hail of distortion or thicket of fuzz, so that the notes were studiously dirty, provided a vital frame for Derv Gordon's raspy vocal. But The Equals could also be sunny as well as heavy.

Law of the Land
Grant's Guyana to GB trajectory offers a fascinating example of the immigrant experience in responding to a dramatic shift of environment – from spatial freedom to constraint, the replacement of the rural world by an urban milieu and the impact of new sights, sounds and forms of speech. While western pop became Grant's lingua franca, there were still clear echoes of the music of his childhood in his rhythms and melodies. The most emphatic 'Caribbean retention' in The Equal's songbook was the band's breakout single, 'Baby Come Back', which was a B-side to 'Hold Me Closer', before it graduated to the A-side due to popular demand, being rereleased and topping the UK singles chart in 1968.

Grant wrote the central guitar riff when he was walking home one day from the West End in central London, to Kentish Town in the north of the city. As he skipped along the pavement, the rhythm of his feet suggested a six-note phrase which had a swaying momentum that conveys the rousing, liberating energy of a calypso group or steel band. With its *jump-up* feel and R&B/rock instrumentation, 'Baby Come Back' reflects the wide range of Grant's formative influences, particularly the legendary singers who defined the popular music of the Caribbean. As he explained: 'I love the Mighty Sparrow. (Yes) Sparrow was my god… Here's me who wants to hear (his great anthem) "Jean & Dinah". I can't hear it so when I started playing, I say *well, ras*, I really want to hear it so I tried to interpolate calypso in any way I can.'[6]

Given these foundations, and the need to sell records to a predominantly white audience, it was perhaps inevitable that Grant and The Equals would build towards a form of popular music with cross-cultural content that is sometimes emphatic and sometimes understated. 'Laurel and Hardy' is firmly in the tradition of *kickster* calypso, complete with lyrical highjinks and teasing groove, while 'The Skies Above' and 'Butterfly Red, White and Blue' are both tough, tense rock songs which the likes of Hendrix, The Stones or The Kinks would have been proud of. 'My Life Ain't Easy' is a piece of vigorous R&B built on hearty, punchy vocal refrains in the mould of Don Covay's 'See Saw'.

'I'm A Poor Man' is another highlight of The Equals catalogue. The stomping backbeat is premium Motown, but Grant's brash, brawny guitar has a menace that would have cooled the ardour of any Four Tops fan looking for a love song. The lyrics are a stark confession of the pain of a working-class boy who is the laughing stock of 'rich friends'. Towards the end of the piece Derv Gordon's takes an impassioned vocal solo, forgoing words for yelps of anguish. He unleashes a bluesy scream, but as Grant starts to improvise on guitar, the singer leaves behind the soulful 'Aoow!' and 'Yeah baby!' and switches to a double time ska-style lick of 'Bring it up! Bring it up! Bring it up.' The cultural shift is fleeting but striking. The vernacular of Levi Stubbs has been vividly complemented by that of Prince Buster.

That strategy was also used in 'Baby Come Back' where the percussive 'chekeh' vocal effects, and rugged hollers of 'Rude boy!' on the outro, further push the song away from America and deeper into the West Indies. In their use of concise, Creole phrases, The Equals opened the door to a future when the Black Caribbean as well as, or rather than, Black America, might become the central reference point for popular music made in the 'mother country'.

They were rewarded by having a success that was international rather than just national. 'Baby Come Back', reached the top ten in France, Canada and Zimbabwe, proving that there was a market for pop that was born of immigration to the UK, and which reflected the pool of talent that had arrived there from former outposts of Empire. Yet if 'Baby Come Back' showcased Grant as a songwriter with a gift for a melody that had a feel-good factor, he also revealed a sharp political edge in compositions such as the brilliantly titled 'Black Skin Blue Eyed Boys'. Set to a taut, belligerent backbeat, enhanced by crisp percussion and a stinging funk guitar, the song was an ode to racial harmony that foresaw a world in which multi-racialism – expressed in the then commonplace though now offensive term 'half-caste' – would prevail. The message was one of unity beyond nationality, religion and race. As a song against bigotry, it also conveyed a marked anti-war sentiment, at the height of the USA's engagement in Vietnam. This was a long way from 'Baby Come Back', and for some it was problematic.

As Grant recalled:

> 'Black Skin Blue Eyed Boys' was really an anomaly. The record company I was with, President... the boss didn't like the song because it talked about black, black, black... As far as he was concerned that really wasn't the thing for the jolly Equals to be doing. And I thought, you know what, I'm going to write the song for the time. And the song for the time was *who* we were. *We* were black skin blue-eyed boys. We were our mother's blue-eyed boys and we were black as hell, and the other boys got it by when you cross pollinate, they got that, I mean John (Hall) danced like a black man.[7]

As far as Grant was concerned, the onus was on him to negotiate between his two worlds. Officially, Grant was a pop star. But culturally he was the son of West Indian immigrants and there was an inevitable discrepancy between the trappings of success and the prevailing image of *his* kind, which did not escape him when he reflected on the period. 'If you can imagine in the '60s a couple of black boys running around in Aston Martins… only Prince Charles was doing that and even he may have had a small one. It was a total conflict with what was expected at the time.' Riding in luxury motors fit for royals and movie stars was no doubt a thrill for a Guyanese teenager with a phenomenal talent as a songwriter and musician, yet Grant did not retreat into an luxury mansion whose high walls made him oblivious to the indignities suffered by those less fortunate than himself. One of the key songs in The Equals repertoire, 'Police on My Back', addressed head on the issue of police persecution. It casts a heavy subject in a relatively light, upbeat musical setting, perhaps a subterfuge, so by its relative jocularity the performance could reach a wider audience than would a more dirge-like number. Clocking in at just over two and a half minutes, 'Police on My Back' was a short piece with a vigorous R&B stomp as its core rhythm, crashing guitars and a lyric that presented the narrator in a desperate situation, trying to evade the boys in blue in hot pursuit:

> Runnin' down the railway track
> Could you help me, police on my back?
> They will catch me, if I dare drop back
> Won't you give me, all the speed I lack?

The chase is a never-ending one, unfolding over an entire week, from Monday to Sunday, words that are repeated over a repetitive rhythm, cycling round and round on just a few chords, adding to the impression that the fugitive has no option but to keep on the move. In African Diasporan history, the scene could be equated with the runaway slave mercilessly tracked by vicious dogs, or the Windrush arrivals chased by Teddy boys and fascist thugs on British streets. There is no explicit mention of race in the verses, but the use of the simple yet resonant interrogative would have struck a chord with any Black migrants who had been victimised by the police. 'What have I done?' sings Derv Gordon. We are left to wonder. Forty years prior, one of Grant's early influences, Louis Armstrong had sung: 'What did I do to be so black and blue?' The question lingered.

Unequal not unchallenged
In 1968, just a year after The Equals released 'Police on My Back', Richard Taylor made a film called *Equal Before the Law*, which consisted of first-hand testimonies of police persecution from young white

and West Indian men, which was then followed by a studio discussion between senior officers of the Metropolitan Police and Black and white activists and campaigners. They included the Trinidadian activist, Darcus Howe and Ian McDonald, who was a Scottish barrister, Geoff Crawford of The West Indian Standing Conference (WISC), an organisation created to further the interests of Blacks in Britain in the wake of the 1958 Notting Hill and Nottingham riots, and Tony Smythe, Secretary of the National Council for Civil Liberties (NCCL).

Given that the Metropolitan Police tried to have the footage banned for fear of the damage it would do to public confidence in them, it is hardly surprising that its representatives were adversarial during the exchange with the community leaders and legal representatives. The testimonies were overwhelming, particularly the tales of 'driving while black', when West Indians were stopped at the wheel of a car if the vehicle was deemed to be too 'flash' – which was a surefire indicator of criminal activity because 'spades' could only afford a top of the range 'motor' if they were 'poncing'. The belief that people of colour were wont to live off immoral earnings was deeply rooted. This was made clear in the statement of an ex-police officer who spoke with commendable candour about the endemic bigotry at the heart of the force. As he told a BBC reporter: 'You might find a certain number of police officers might be prejudiced against taxi drivers, bus drivers, or against Jewish people, but I think colour prejudice is virtually absolute, in other words it extends probably to 99%.'

When he was asked if any attempts were made by senior officers to counteract this, his reply was instant and utterly damning. 'None at all, either they're aware that it exists or else they just choose to ignore it. I suppose they're looking on them as an inferior people.' He made other revelations about the Met's behaviour. 'There is this sort of hard man cult that exists among the lower ranks, and this requires a young man to prove himself in many ways, mainly by the number of arrests that he makes. The old tradition would be that the coloured man is not as fully aware of his rights as a white man would be and on this assumption, I suppose he would be more vulnerable. But I think generally the prejudice that exists would make him more vulnerable.'

Against such a backdrop, the lyrics of The Equals' 'Police on My Back', particularly the line 'the victim won't be coming back', take on a greater force than a casual listener might imagine. *Equal Before the Law* was a powerful programme because the actions of the police, a key pillar of the British establishment, were comprehensively exposed as racist and corrupt by detailed and compelling first-hand accounts from those who were within as well as outside the organisation.

Down by the River
Following concerted protest movements against 'colour bars' in Bristol and Coventry, the Race Relations Act was passed in 1965, and it was amended just three years later, a sign that laws had to be refined in a still changing British society. The nebulous language of the new statutes fostered ambiguity if not confusion. How exactly were the races supposed to manage 'relations' both on practical as well as emotional levels? The ideal of fairness and the absence of disadvantage based on ethnicity, had to be matched by the means to achieve those goals, or what those who drafted the legislation called the 'strength' of its procedures for enforcement. The later 1968 bill thus specified what was to be deemed open to prosecution in everyday life:

> Discrimination on grounds of colour, race, ethnic or national origins is made unlawful in all the major areas of conduct in which it is a social problem: in the provision of goods, facilities and services, in employment, by trade unions, employers and professional organisations, in housing and business premises, in advertisements and notices. This is subject to important and controversial exceptions.

Conspicuous by its absence was any reference to the police. This made the Act liable to the whims of both the force as an organisation and those politically responsible for it, and made it almost impossible to hold them to account. The dire victimisation of David Oluwale, a Nigerian migrant persecuted by the police in Leeds, should have found redress within the Race Relations Act, but nobody seemed to be watching. Oluwale's is one of the most shameful cases in the annals of British policing. Over an eighteen-month period, the Nigerian tailor, who had been mostly unemployed since arriving in Britain as a stowaway, and who suffered from mental health problems, became a target for the police in Leeds, where he had been living on the streets. He had no support structure. On several occasions Oluwale was beaten by officers, who used racist language towards him, referring to him as a 'lame darkie' before ratcheting their hostility up to a full-scale a campaign of intimidation which culminated in a chase, according to witnesses, along the banks of the River Aire, during which the homeless man ran for his life. Oluwale's body was fished out of the water on April 17, 1969. The Equals' 'Police on My Back' had the most hauntingly prophetic of lyrics. *The victim won't be coming back.*

Two years later, two officers, Geoffrey Ellerker and Kenneth Kitching, were convicted of actual bodily harm but found not guilty of the more serious charge of manslaughter, raising the unavoidable issue of how a Black life could be defended within the existing legal framework. Perhaps most alarmingly, the judge at the trial, Justice Hinchcliffe, termed Oluwale 'a dirty, filthy violent vagrant' and actively *encouraged* the jury to clear the officers of the charges against them.[8] To say the Nigerian needed shelter came to mean from more than Britain's notoriously bad weather.

A New Dance (Again)
In the late 1960s, outright discrimination in the area of housing still haunted many people of colour. White property owners who put a house on the open market could, and to this day, still can, refuse offers without stating on what grounds. Further, for many in Britain's Black and South Asian population, mortgages and loans from building societies and high street banks to buy houses were hard to come by. As a result, many West Indians set up their own credit unions or clubbed together in order to gain a foothold in the housing market. Black people had to take matters into their own hands and be proactive and tenacious to have any chance of becoming property-owners. This goal had become ever more important as the Black community put down roots and deferred dreams of a return to their islands. Trinidadian writer Sam Selvon, who brilliantly chronicled the lives of Windrush migrants in his 1956 novel, *The Lonely Londoners*, directed his penetrating, and humorous gaze on the issue in his 1965 novel, *The Housing Lark*.

In any case, the desire for permanent rather than temporary residence inevitably lent further weight to the development of cultural norms and recreational activities among the Black community in the face of a hostile Britain. One focal point of West Indian social life was the informal gathering at a private residence that became known as a 'blues'. The 'blues dance' is essentially a house party in the lineage of the 'shebeen', but where the latter might offer a pianist or small group of musicians, in a private residence the entertainment was provided by the latest 45rpm singles imported from *yard,* rather than a live band.

Here, the story was the rapid pace of creative change in the music that made its way to Black Britain from the relentlessly shifting sound of the Caribbean, above all Jamaica. If the commercial peak of ska in Britain (until its re-emergence in the 1980s) was Millie Small's 1964 hit, 'My Boy Lollypop', by a year or two later, the genre started to fade from view. Rocksteady was the latest beat to move the crowd. Vibrant, sensual and seductive, its leading lights included male solo singers such as Derrick Harriott, Pat Kelly and Ken Boothe, as well as harmony groups such as The Paragons, The Melodians and The Gaylads, all of whom released singles marked by the beauty of the vocal performance as well as the leisurely enticement of the musical accompaniment. The players, of whom guitarists such as Lynn Tait and Ernest Ranglin were important pathfinders, had constructed a new model that broke with the older style by altering its tempo. They left behind ska's nervy, jittery frenzy and opted for a much more relaxed, legato approach that sometimes made the melody hang in the air, as epitomised by the way the legendary Alton Ellis wooed the listener with memorable rhymes that matched irresistible rhythms, leading to a physical response to a song, step by step: *Better get ready, come do rocksteady, you've got to do this new dance.*[9]

Colour of Velvet

While Ellis and scores of many other Jamaican artists found huge favour amongst the West Indian community in Britain, where their records were staples at blues dances up and down the country, two rocksteady 45s made a huge dent both in the UK and international record market that challenged its limited status as a 'specialist' ethnic product. In 1968, Desmond Dekker & The Aces scored a number one in the national UK singles chart with the masterful 'Israelites',[10] a song that was imperious in its foregrounding of the Jamaican voice and accent, while The Upsetters' 'Return of Django',[11] peaked at 5. Between them, the two cuts confirmed that JA instrumental as well as vocal music had an appeal for mainstream audiences far, far away.

Produced by the visionary Lee Perry, who would shape modern music for decades to come, 'Django', was a brilliant example of the art and science of building a series of curt, clipped phrases into a body of sound that had exactly the right push and pull between horn and rhythm sections, because the written parts have such measure and balance. Everybody plays enough yet nobody plays too much. Providing a solid yet supple backdrop to Val Bennett's saxophone are drums, bass and guitar, all marshalled with an iron grip, creating a deliciously maintained heat, a pot that simmers rather than boils. It is not just that these elements are accurately assembled around the central pulse, with its relaxed, rush-free, rocksteady pattern, it is that there is a perfect alliance of poise, precision and concision in how the piece is performed. The sharp rimshots that fill the space at opportune moments offset the gaps and rests left elsewhere. One electric guitar provides a deft chordal anchor, the other, finger-picked, has the rhythmic finesse – thin and wiry yet impactful – that would become an emblematic feature of many classic rocksteady recordings. Listening to 'Django' it easy to see why the new genre captured the imagination of teenage dancers at youth clubs, or 'mods' who had previously revered soul heroes like Booker T & The MGs and Jimmy McGriff.

Unsurprisingly, the dynamism of Jamaican music added to the interesting alterations in British pop that The Equals had ushered in. True to form, Eddy Grant penned a brilliant rocksteady tune for The Pyramids, a UK-based West Indian band originally called The Bees, who had supported the legendary Prince Buster. 'Train Tour to Rainbow City' used the joyous slip and slide of this latest Jamaican groove to riff playfully on the outsider status of people of colour in Britain. The journey of the title evokes a tragic end for juvenile delinquency (a 'dead rude boy'), the artistry of Buster and master saxophonist Roland Alphonso, and the dangerous charm of Caribbean sexuality in the form of 'big black bad women.' Rather than being sung, the lyrics, freighted with socio-political substance and spicy humour, are delivered as an off the cuff, conversational speech, but it is the insistent chugging of the offbeat, like a locomotive at half speed, that gives the song such appealing languid motion.

In short, the new rhythmic vocabulary from the former British colonies was too rich to ignore, and in the late 1960s there emerged a number of interesting bands that alternated between rocksteady and soul and also produced hybrids of the two. Beacon, an independent London label, was a key purveyor of much of this product, releasing songs by UK based West Indians such as Root & Jenny Jackson and Ram John Holder, both of which were eclectic, wonderful oddities that reflect this confluence of sounds. One Beacon disk, 'Dance of The Clangers', by The Clangers, an obscure, one-off session group, was a tribute to the enchanting organ anthems of Jamaican legends Jackie Mittoo and Harry J's Al Stars, creator of the swooning, mesmeric 'Liquidator'. Then there was the London-based, Jamaican-descended Coloured Raisins, whose members included organist Peter Nelson and vocalist Brian Clark. Their debut single 'One Way Love' was an appealing, smartly executed piece of rocksteady that compared favourably to any JA favourite. Later, the band changed its name, firstly to The Raisins and then to Black Velvet and in that formation continued to epitomise the open-minded outlook that led to artists producing varied output.

Whilst they upheld the eclectic legacy of a group such as The Equals, there was a major difference in sound palette between the two, with Black Velvet sometimes opting for swirling orchestrations that effectively supplemented Clark's voice. Eddy Grant wrote Velvet's 'Peace and Love is the Message,' a yearning guitar-led rock ballad with a pacifist message, denouncing the Vietnam war amongst other acts of folly, while 'Clown' was a quite astounding piece of hazy, trippy psychedelic pop built around a trundling fairground organ motif that is as disturbing as it is intriguing. Most interesting of all is 'African Velvet', which suggests a wholly organic mash-up of Wilson Pickett's 'In the Midnight Hour' and Toots & The Maytals '54-46 Was My Number'. You could call it rocksteady soul or soul rocksteady, but that still doesn't adequately define the resulting sound. However, that was the point. It was its own *ting*.

While all these songs display the genre cross-fertilisation and the start of a sustained *permeation* of British pop by Jamaica, what is also interesting was the response of Jamaican musicians to the 'mother country' when they either travelled here to record or promote music, as Prince Buster did, or if they got wind of the specificities of life in England. Adapting the melodies of the Beatles tunes was one thing, but absorbing the colloquialisms of Blighty and funnelling them into rocksteady was another. Nowhere was that more salient than in Max Romeo's 'Wet Dream', a song that gripped Jamaican and British adolescents by daring to describe budding sexual desire in a way that alarmed moral gatekeepers vexed by its explicitness.

The would-be censors may have missed the point. In the reedy, if not tinny sound of the organ melody of the song's opening bars, there was a child-like mischief as well as sauciness, reinforced by the easy fluidity of the rocksteady rhythm, over which Romeo's honeyed voice floats. *Every night me have wet dream*, he sings. Here is a very dirty lullaby. The irresistible chorus – *Lie down gal let me push it up* – confirms that while the whole premise of the song may be youthful lust, the real intent is wish fulfilment. Max wants to do much more than dream. After another short scratchy keyboard solo, the cup of horniness starts to run over, and Romeo intones what is an emphatically smutty lyric:

> Look how you big and fat, like a big, big shot
> Give the crumpet to bigfoot Joe, give the fanny to me.

This is a fascinating encounter of cultures. On the one hand, the reference to the woman's body betrays a distinctly Jamaican mindset insofar as a plus-sized female is not viewed as any less attractive than a size zero. But Romeo also makes a dramatic geo-linguistic shift by using common English colloquialisms to designate sexual attractiveness and private parts in the form of the relatively innocent 'crumpet' and the distinctly less innocent 'fanny'. He has somehow slipped into the language of lascivious geezers prattling in a British pub. The bawdy journey into schoolboy sexual fantasy starts inna Kingston and ends up in London.

Numerous readings can be made of the choice of vocabulary. Romeo may have forsaken the Jamaican slang of 'pum pum' to avoid censorship on the island, or perhaps there is another simpler explanation. Romeo is employing words that are foreign, dare one say exotic to *him* as a Jamaican and thus exercising the right to reference, though he stops short of mimicry or mockery. He is reflecting an ongoing musical relationship between the Caribbean and Britain that would continue to evolve as artists in each territory found forms of expression in the other that appealed as having novelty. There was an adoption of words that built into an evolving lexicon, a fluid vocabulary that revealed engagement by migrants with what they heard 'inna foreign' and an ability to apply such data to their own singular depictions of universal themes, such as sexual awakening. This cultural exchange was interesting, and set to continue.

Notes

1. Interview with the author, September 2023.
2. *Blues and Soul,* Online magazine, issue no. 1008.
3. Interview with the author, September 2023.
4. Ibid.
5. Ibid.
6. Ibid.
7. *Stars Cars Guitars*, 11 March 2021.
8. The case of David Oluwale is chronicled in Kester Aspden's Book *Nationality: Wog, The Hounding of David Oluwale* (Vintage, 2007) which was made into a play by Oladipe Agboulaje and performed at the West Yorkshire Playhouse in 2009.
9. Alton Ellis, 'Rocksteady' (Studio One, 1967).
10. Desmond Dekker, 'Israelites' (Pyramid, 1968).
11. The Upsetters, 'Return of Django' (Trojan, 1968).

4 ONLY THE BLACK MAN UNDERSTAND IT

Reggae afforded us our own independent cultural identity. We were rejected by the wider society so this was our music, this was our culture. My generation... we were the rebel generation and we refused to tolerate the things our parents tolerated.
— Linton Kwesi Johnson, British Black Panther Movement and Race Today Collective.

My father would not hear of me speaking with a Jamaican accent! If I ever went home and said 'Wh'appen, Daddy?' he would be... 'Who you think you talking to? You think you talking to your friends outside? You forget yourself?' My mother and father have not shifted their Bajan accents after 60 years of being in the UK.
— Dennis Bovell, founder of Matumbi, who came to Britain from Barbados at the age of 12.

Wha' yuh say, sah?
— Errol Brown, Hot Chocolate Band.

Touch the Untouchables
While the success of 'Wet Dream' and other rocksteady classics reflected the burgeoning demand for Jamaican music in Britain, product distribution remained a challenge. Chris Blackwell, who issued Millie Small's seminal 'My Boy Lollipop' on his own Island imprint and Lee Gopthal, founder of Beat & Commercial and purveyor of the numerous 7" 45 rpm records being made in and shipped out of Kingston, struck a deal to found Trojan Records. This label created an important outlet for scores of new West Indian artists, including those either based in or visiting the UK.

Trojan referred to both the famous truck that carried the equipment of legendary producer/sound system operator, Duke Reid, and the emblematic conflict of Homeric mythology, in which men were driven to folly by a beautiful woman. With a warrior's feathered helmet as the logo, the label did not need a wooden horse to force open the gates of a mainstream record industry, which remained convinced that there was no market for Jamaican music outside the West Indian community. Trojan found listeners among British youth, Black and white, who were eager to hear 'island' sounds that captured the imagination, just as American urban blues had done back in the 1950s.

Given the enormous volume of new music recorded and issued on a large number of small labels in Jamaica, there was no shortage of tracks to be discovered. Initially, Trojan acted mainly as an international distributor, licensing work produced by the likes of Reid, Leslie Kong and many others. Then in line with the strategy of American independent labels such as Motown, Stax and Atlantic, Trojan began to release compilation albums, usually featuring a dozen songs by various artists. This was a very shrewd move since it mitigated the distribution problems for 7" singles encountered by smaller operations like Chris Blackwell's,[1] but also provided listeners with a valuable overview of the rocksteady genre

Tighten Up was a series of compilations that featured a cornucopia of songs, with Val Bennett, Derrick Morgan, Ken Boothe and Jimmy Cliff among the standouts. They had eye-catching artwork. On the sleeve of Volume 1 is a Black woman with a large red headwrap, gold hooped earrings and a low-cut orange feathered dress that exposes her bare shoulders against the glare of the sun over an expanse of white sand and the leaning trunk of a palm tree – a conflation of Afro-centricity and sexuality.

Subsequent instalments went further down the road of titillation. Volume 2 had a close-up of the bare midriff of a white model with the title *Tighten Up* daubed in red crayon around her navel, while Volume 3 featured the face of a Black woman with a song title, 'Freedom Street' (Ken Boothe) written just under her collarbone. Further eroticism was delivered by an accompanying poster which showed the model naked, down on her bended knees, with an arm strategically placed to obscure her nipples, but with other song titles – 'Herbsman', 'A Little Bit Longer', 'Barbwire' – clearly visible on her body. Was this just a recognition of the essential sexiness of rocksteady as a dance, or the shameless, sexist use of female beauty as a means of enticing the male consumer? The fact that Black women were not involved in record label management and the key decisions on the marketing of product suggests the latter. Carnal desire was a very openly embraced element in Caribbean popular music (much more so than in 1960s white rock music), not least the ubiquity of double entendre and tales of steamy attraction in genres like calypso, but it is impossible not to acknowledge the objectification of women in many calypso and rocksteady lyrics, however great the tunes and voices, however inventive the wordplay.

Trojan's marketing was absolutely in keeping with the times. Similar strategies were employed by mainstream pop imprints such as MFP (Music for Pleasure)[2] whose collections of the latest hit singles played by anonymous studio musicians were packaged in sleeves of women in various states of undress, the nadir of which was a bikini-clad model, or 'dolly bird' lasciviously swinging a cricket bat. It was more middle than top shelf, but nonetheless still a sign of the misogyny that ran right through a male dominated pop industry.

Another series of compilations was produced by the Pama label, founded by the Palmer brothers (Harry, Jeff, Carl), which also distributed Jamaican music in Britain. Pama also used similarly x-rated artwork. *Straighten Up* featured fine music by the likes of Owen Gray, John Holt, The Viceroys and The Versatiles, but male consumers may have been drawn to the sight of a naked Black woman on the cover, kneeling and cradling a turquoise lamp. She was hard not to notice.

Then, just as rocksteady supplanted ska, the songs pouring out of the Kingston studios of the 1970s saw the birth of another new style known as reggae. This again displayed a wealth of musicianship and the dynamism of the local vernacular. The word itself was a loose derivation of 'regular', denoting the steadiness of the beat, and like rocksteady it also signalled a new style of dance, as was made clear by the exhortation 'Do the Reggay'. Indeed, Trojan provided a set of illustrated instructions on how to master the latest Jamaican steps for unschooled white British teenagers.

Reggae had a sound palette that like ska and rocksteady acknowledged the US rhythm & blues lexicon but alchemised its elements into something distinctive with its own vocabulary. The offbeat accents that imparted to the undercarriage of the music a kind of jockeying, slightly mesmeric sensation were enhanced by skilful pauses and curt phrases, so that the rhythmic motion was not dissipated by wildness or frenzy. Some reggae tunes had higher tempos than others, but in all cases, there was a sense of composure, of ease in the unfolding and negotiation of time that imparted to the music a thrilling ramification of sensuality. With more prominence given to electric bass, a steely quality in the rimshot of the drums, a slightly harder attack from the guitar, and a general sense of weight in the production and mix, reggae was an altogether heavier proposition than rocksteady, and the new music increasingly acquired a post-colonial political dimension that explored the fact that though independence had come, not much was changing in the life-opportunities of Black Jamaicans. When the Trinidadian photographer and filmmaker Horace Ove[3] made a compelling documentary about the music in 1970, he filmed a gala concert at Wembley stadium, London, featuring Nicky Thomas, Desmond Dekker, Millie Small and The Pioneers among others, but more importantly he canvassed the opinion of the audience about the meaning of the music. The fact that Black and white teenagers talked about 'the beat' which was 'good for dancing', and that both spoke in cockney accents made it clear that reggae provided them with common ground. What was even more revealing was the response of the parents of Black youth. One older gentleman, with what sounds like a middle-class Jamaican accent stated, 'Well, it's fantastic really... it's something that's from the heart. It came from the mother country, Jamaica', which reverses the paradigm of England as the mother country, as sung by Lord Kitchener in 1948. If this marks a clear shift from the outlook of the Windrush generation, then another interviewee with a broader working-class Jamaican accent is even more emphatic: 'Reggae is a sound… that is only the black man understand it!' A previously unheard sense of ownership and empowerment is expressed.

Perhaps, even more than had been the case with ska and rocksteady, the lyrics of reggae were strongly embedded in Jamaican patois. This creolised "nation language" had both linguistic and social meanings. With a lexicon and grammar distinctive from standard English, it had its own flavour, vitality and a sense of musicality that would make cadence and inflection important in the shaping of songs. Socially, it was primarily the language of Black people (though shared by Jamaicans of all ethnicities) and its distance from standard English (if pronounced in a Jamaican way), tended to point towards those who were at the bottom of the social scale and those whose culture was most Afro-centric (often the same people). Hence, patois in lyrics was itself a sign of the rejection of the Eurocentric norms that still dominated official Jamaican culture and signalled a subversive identity. When Dandy Livingstone rhymed 'reggae' with 'jeggae' he expressed a Jamaican colloquialism that stood in a long lineage of black Diasporan linguistic invention. African American jazz musicians had done similar things back in the 1920s by locking 'heebie' to 'jeebies' or 'jeepers' to 'creepers'.

The singers of Kingston no longer made such mundane statements as 'I don't want any trouble', but used the ripe, boldface rhyme of 'Mih no wah no cuss cuss/ Mih no wah no fuss fuss'. Black Jamaicans, wherever they were in the world, could hear themselves and their increasing race-consciousness in such words, 'improper' as they may have been to the ear of the establishment. Only the Black man understand it because the Black man is talkin' black.

To the sounds of Jamaica was added the sight of Jamaicans on the big screen. The film, *The Harder They Come*, brought black people to cinemas in large numbers when its distribution was widened from Jamaica to Britain on its release in 1972. For Jamaicans, there was the chance to see something of themselves in dramatic roles that had autonomy, defiance and courage rather than timidity, subordination or servility. The themes of endemic poverty, rural-urban conflict, music industry exploitation, police brutality and the staunch resistance of the individual to oppression struck a chord with Caribbean youth both 'at home' and in Britain. They identified with the 'sufferer', Ivan, brilliantly portrayed by the legendary vocalist and composer, Jimmy Cliff. He was a gunslinger, fighter, sharp-dresser, charmer, lover and singer, and his contribution to the film's glorious soundtrack, alongside the likes of Toots & The Maytals, Scotty, Desmond Dekker and The Slickers, further anchored reggae as the music of the disenfranchised who would not bow to any form of injustice or be denied their dues.

Inevitably, the genre resonated with a groundswell of Black, grass-roots political activity in Britain. The case of the 'Mangrove 9', with its exposure of police corruption and the concerted persecution of West Indians in their own recreational spaces, was part of a growing realisation that the attitudes that underpinned the targeting of Black activists and community leaders were deeply entrenched in the upper echelons of the British political establishment as well as in the ranks of the police. Rather being recognised as a legitimate part of the struggle for racial equality, Black radicalism was characterised in the right-wing media as an attempt to overthrow the state and destroy British values and way of life. This was what legitimised the police to put Caribbean restaurants under surveillance. Ian McDonald, the Scottish barrister who represented the 'Mangrove 9', had warned just a few years before that for the elite, Black people had come to embody a kind of danger to polite society, and that the policeman on the beat thus took it upon himself to fabricate evidence in order to 'take them down' at all costs. McDonald noted that 'after West Indian dances, you get the police there and they're trying to pick up a few people for insulting behaviour or having offensive weapons. There was one case where we had two witnesses who actually saw the police take a piece of wooden fencing off a fence nearby, they then got up in court and said this particular black person had been waving this vicious looking stick around.'[4]

Inevitably, organisations sprang up in the name of civil liberties. As previously mentioned, CARD (Campaign Against Racial Discrimination) was relatively short lived, lasting from the mid to late 1960s, but in its wake came other initiatives. The Institute for Race Relations (IRR) was founded as an academic, university-focused think tank in London, but evolved into a campaigning hub with a significantly more radical agenda, when its offices relocated from Bloomsbury to King's Cross to Brixton, where it found itself at the heart of the West Indian community *and* the squatters movement, in which it also came to play a major role. Out of this shift in focus came *Race Today* magazine which had a strong Marxist leaning, largely inspired by the pioneering Trinidadian intellectual C.L.R. James, the author of seminal texts like *The Black Jacobins*. Other groups were influenced by African American radicalism, such as the British Black Panther Movement and Black Unity and Freedom Party. Prominent figures emerged out of such groups, such as Obi Egbuna, Darcus Howe, Farrukh Dhondy, Leila Hassan, Olive Morris and Althea Jones-LeCointe – amongst whom were skilled journalists, editors and playwrights – along with countless other activists determined to mobilise the black community in Britain to collective action.

Egbuna, for instance, was arrested for allegedly inciting the murder of policemen in a pamphlet entitled 'What to Do if Cops Lay Their hands On a Black Man at Speaker's Corner', in which he vividly encouraged 'the Black crowd to surge forward like one big black steamroller... to catch up with the cop 'til the brother is rescued, freed and made to flee at once.'[5] Dhondy recalls the hardening of race prejudice at this time, so that 'Whenever there were any gatherings of West Indians and blacks the police assumed that there was either some kind of drug peddling or prostitution going on.'[6]

Amongst those who were either born in Britain in the mid- or late-1950s or who had come to Britain as teenagers in the early 1960s, there was an evident change of mindset and determination to realise other possibilities that marked them out from their elders. The idea of acceptance of a lower social status was being replaced by one of defiance and dissent. Here, Linton Kwesi Johnson, who became a pivotal figure at the crossroads of music, poetry and politics in the late 1970s, epitomised this new mentality. A member of the British Black Panther Movement and the Race Today collective, he saw how the outlook of younger West Indians changed and how a spirit of resistance to the status quo came to resonate with the latest evolution of Jamaican music:

> What we did reject was the caution and the restraint that our parents had in a hostile racial environment. They were limited in the ways that they could fight against racial oppression. They had responsibilities, they had to put kids through school, they had to put bread on the table, send money back home to their families and so on. Reggae afforded us our own independent cultural identity. We were rejected by the wider society so this was our music, this was our culture. My generation... we were the rebel generation and we refused to tolerate the things our parents tolerated.[7]

Given such convictions, it is easy to understand why the sparky intensity of Toots & The Maytals' 'Pressure Drop', with its soulful vocal exhortations and promise of retribution for wrongdoers, appealed to anybody who refused to be marginalised or show fear in the face of adversity. As Jimmy Cliff would say, the harder they come is the harder they fall.

Yet for all the business acumen displayed by Trojan records and the success of Toots, Jimmy Cliff and Desmond Dekker, there remained a substantial wall for Jamaican artists to climb, and that was national radio. Despite all the interest in what was being produced in Kingston, the commercial progress of reggae in Britain was being held back by the staunch refusal of disc jockeys on the primetime shows at the BBC to embrace the genre. The exponents of Black diasporan music did not see themselves as parochial or marginal, whatever the white gatekeepers of the day thought. Unwilling to remain silent on the prohibition they endured, Jamaican artists voiced their resentment, most resonantly Nicky Thomas in his song

'B.B.C.', which detailed his long walk to the Corporation to attempt to overturn its restrictive policy.

Being denied access to prime-time pop programmes was a substantial obstacle, but Jamaican culture had already developed a form of independent and informal means of distribution and communication that had its own vital broadcasting function: the sound system. Giant stacks of speakers and a disc jockey with an endless supply of the latest recordings in the dance hall had been the means of connecting artist and audience in the West Indies for many years.

In the UK, post-Windrush 'sound men' such as Duke Vin and Count Suckle had taken their operations all over the country from their London base, but soon there were no end of acolytes who came to prominence in the regions in the early 1970s, providing important platforms for new 7" singles as well as an opportunity for local Black youth to socialise.

In Jamaica, the 'selectors' often set up outside, since dances were held in the open air so there were fewer spatial restrictions, but the use of indoor venues in Britain entailed practical problems such as the need to take doors off their hinges to move in the equipment. In East London there were clubs like the Four Aces in Dalston, which gained iconic status as a hub for both soundmen and live bands; in Manchester, Persian would set up in Moss Side pubs to spin records and later in the decade there was Kilowatt; dances in Leeds were run by Maverick Sound, and Birmingham, too, boasted a particularly fertile scene. And there were revered figures such as Count Shelly, Coxsone or Neville the Enchanter who gigged all over the country. The pioneers often had aristocratic names like calypsonians – Duke Neville, Duke Sunny, Duke Wally, Count Flash, Count Ryan, Count Sugar, Lord Callie, Lord Monarch, Lord Pluto – and their successors went for grandiose wartime handles such as Bismark or denominations with a decidedly technical slant, such as Sanatone or the mighty Studio City, which acquired legendary status.

If you dig deeper into sound system history in Birmingham, it becomes clear that the selectors covered a large amount of ground, so that localities such as Smethwick and Small Heath hosted dances, as did makeshift spaces near West Bromwich football ground. Furthermore, testimonies from the era suggest a quasi-democratic mindset amongst those who acquired speakers and played records to anyone who cared to gather and listen in a way that looked forward to file-sharing in the internet age. As the following recollection by Glen Ranking makes clear, there were 'junior selectors' who showed considerable gumption to start spinning, regardless of how much homework was on the table. 'Back in '72, I was a 1st year in school, I brought my set and played to Victoria Park youth club. I call my ting Stone Mafia Sound.'[8]

Beyond sound system culture, the growth of reggae in Britain was fostered by the appearance of Jamaican artists who came in to perform for their fans, whose adulation was often expressed in the ritual of trekking to the airport to greet their heroes. Inevitably, Black musicians living in the UK, well aware of changes in style, began to make reggae rather than simply listening to it, to produce and not just consume. The transition towards home-grown reggae was gradual rather than immediate and has to be seen in the context of artists, epitomised by The Equals, discussed in Chapter 3, who retained a strong Caribbean slant in much of their material, essaying many genres, including calypso. In any case, even within Jamaican produced reggae, there remained as much emphasis on transforming 'cover' versions as on writing new material, of giving a new character to melody and rhythm when a song in one style is remade in another. Jamaican reggae artists had reprised American soul, particularly Motown, as well as British and European pop, but there was a particular audacity of a South London-based R&B group, called Hot Chocolate Band, doing a reggae version of a pop anthem like The Beatles' 'Give Peace A Chance' in 1970. It is one of the most intriguing entries in the canon of modern British music.

The song starts by placing the voice of the lead singer, Errol Brown, in the spotlight. Born in Kingston, Brown came to London in 1955 at the age of 12 and grew up in Brixton, yet his Caribbean identity is emphatically expressed in proper yard style, as he produces a loud, crisp steupse before he proceeds to wax rhetorical in an undiluted JA accent, thus laying claim to have given the world possibly the first ever kiss-teeth on vinyl. The speaker then breaks out into lively patois: Wha' yuh say, sah? John and Paul never did that.

As the piece unfolds, the singer utters a series of emphatic rhymes that detail the alarming state of the world, reflecting the concerns of people of colour who, in the aftermath of Enoch Powell's grim soothsaying, were sensitive to the real possibility of being sent back to 'where they came from'. Brown evokes a sense of impending doom because of these culture wars and even calls out the UN as an ineffective think tank: 'Everybody taking 'bout religious separation,/racial segregation, repatriation,/ bring the United Nations to mek conversation. Rubbish!'

Hot Chocolate Band's cover of 'Give Peace a Chance', was, with some trepidation, sent to the Beatles' label Apple, because the Londoners had taken the liberty of adding new lyrics, but the Beatles gave a thumbs-up to their efforts. Maybe it was because they had also changed the beat.

'We made a kind of reggaefied version of it,' Brown explained years later. 'I got the call, saying that John Lennon had heard it and how he'd loved it and wanted to put it out, which is amazing for some guys who were just, you know, trying something.'[9]

Keen as Brown may have been to play down the Jamaicanised take on Lennon's tune, which has a subtle rhythmic slant and choral richness that evokes a folk song such as 'Rivers Of Babylon', says much about the way that Black and multi-racial bands in Britain could move across genres as well as defining themselves in one, as Hot Chocolate eventually would – soul.

One musician who remembers the group right from its earliest incarnation is Dennis Bovell, a multi-instrumentalist, engineer, composer and producer who would go on to found one of the first significant acts in British reggae, Matumbi. Bovell arrived from his native Barbados in 1953 at the age of 12 and attended secondary school in Wandsworth, south London, where he fell in with a group of other boys who were interested in playing music. He formed his first group, Road Works Ahead in 1968 and after its demise a few years later he launched another outfit by the name of Stonehenge. The question of career paths for Black youth was a thorny one. Bovell's parents were aware of the pitfalls of the music industry, with its list of artists who did not succeed being much longer than the list of those who did, and they were not keen for him to leave school as early as he wished. Yet other daily hazards were on the radar, such as the police.

'In the basement of our house I had drums, keyboards, bass and guitar amps,' Bovell told me in 2022. 'The group was allowed to rehearse at my house. Dad didn't mind that. What he minded was me going out into the streets and being fodder for the Old Bill, or falling in with the wrong company and just being a street boy.'[10]

As far as Bovell was concerned, groups such as The Equals and Hot Chocolate were important role models because, including both West Indian and white English musicians, they embodied the reality of multicultural London as he had experienced it, given that his classmates were Black, white, Indian and Chinese. The other major influence he claimed were the American soul stars Booker T & The MGs, who, as a multi-racial combo, also helped to break down barriers in the Civil Rights era. Bovell had an interest in a wide range of Black music, but he also felt that a significant shift in taste was underway, and that artists arriving on the scene such as himself had to make choices. He explained:

> It was a toss-up between playing reggae and playing calypso, and reggae kind of got the edge because there were more people tuning into that, there were more Jamaicans. So to play to a black audience who would probably be predominantly Jamaican you had to play some ska or rocksteady; reggae wasn't quite there yet but you'd have to play Toots & The Maytals, you'd have to play The Pioneers, you had to play Dandy Livingstone, Desmond Dekker. So we thought, yeah that music is what we want, that's what we want to do to portray ourselves as West Indian musicians in the UK.[11]

Bovell was well aware of the real barriers to the wider exposure of reggae mentioned earlier, but he took heart from the fact that Jamaican artists still met with success:

> A lot of people believed that reggae would not be around for too long, and that it would soon die out. Because of the patois and the lack of understanding from Radio 1 DJs they wouldn't play it, because they wouldn't know what the guy was saying and they were all afraid of being told 'Hey there were some expletives in there.' I was inspired by my friends in Greyhound [a British reggae band formed in 1970, who had a top ten hit with 'Black and White'], the bass player, Glen, was the son of a family friend so we moved about together. When they made it big with 'Black And White' that was a sign that you could get to the top, and that it was time to say reggae is here to stay.[12]

Indeed Greyhound, who were formerly known as The Rudies, were part of what might be called 'the first wave of British reggae', a cohort of bands comprising young Jamaicans who had settled in London and saw the capital as their home even though they maintained strong links to the mother country. The other main players here were Symarip, who were lionized by one of the youth cults of the early 1970s, the 'skinheads' and reflected this affinity by way of jaunty, joyous songs such as 'Skinhead Moonstomp', 'Skinhead Jamboree' and 'Skinhead Girl'.

A less well known but nonetheless important group was The Cats, whose line-up underlined the African as well as West Indian presence in Britain. The group came together when two teenagers, guitarist John Kpiaye, born to a Nigerian father and English mother in Bethnal Green, east London, and his cousin, drummer Michael Okoro heard that a keyboard player of Jamaican heritage called Tyrone Patterson lived in their local area. 'He was just round the corner so we went and knocked on his door to see of he'd want to play. He was up for it. He said he knew a bass player. We had a few rehearsals, and that was it, we were The Hustling Kind,' Kpiaye told me in 2022.[13] 'We gigged around local pubs, I remember doing Christmas parties. In them days companies would hire bands to come to the factory. We did a load of those things, but we never recorded. In early '68 we had a residency in Germany that didn't go well and the band split up for 3 or 4 months. We got back together as The Cats.'

Like many of their peers, the band cut its teeth on covers of rocksteady and soul hits, so they learned to play Harry J & The All Stars' 'Liquidator' and Booker T & The MGs' 'Green Onions', and an occasional calypso tune. What was significant was their commitment to instrumental music, because they also drew inspiration from the work of American trumpeter Willie Mitchell and the Jamaican organist Jackie Mittoo. Kpiaye, whose Nigerian heritage felt restricted by the small numbers of Africans in Britain at that time – 'My father said you could walk for hours in London and not see any countrymen' – was drawn to all genres available to him, so, in addition to reggae, he heard jazz on a crystal-set radio that brought him solace at night when his severe asthma kept him up wheezing. His interests became broad, and that open-mindedness led Kpiaye to discover other genres that would have a significant effect on his musical development, beyond his unerring devotion to Bert Weedon's *Play in a Day* guitar manual. He recalled, his voice grainy due to his medical condition:

> My mother at the time was working in Woolworths at the top of Bethnal Green Road. They used to do clear-outs of old stock, and she bought a whole bunch of records on this cheap label Pickwick – it was mostly classical and jazz. At that time, any record was gold dust to me. I remember playing Tchaikovsky's 'Swan Lake' and I just fell in love with the melody, so I worked up a kind of arrangement. This was the end of the rocksteady era, so my 'Swan Lake' was more rocksteady... we rehearsed it up and recorded it. That went in the charts at about number 47 with no radio play, it was just word of mouth. It was a big thing for us at the time. We financed it ourselves, set up the label, got a new manager... that was the start of The Cats. It was a big tune with the early skinheads. We were together for about two years, the first chart entry of a reggae tune recorded in Britain after 'My Boy Lollipop'.[14]

A key entry in the canon of Black British music, The Cats' 'Swan Lake' is fascinating from many points of view. The arrangement retains all the languid, leisurely charm of rocksteady, with Kpiaye's chords a floating, ethereal presence in contrast to the hefty punch of the bass, in keeping with the growing importance of the low end in Jamaican sonic aesthetics. The song was also a union of West Indian popular culture and European high art that echoed the development of the steel pan in Trinidad decades before. The earliest pan groups played the music of composers such as Tchaikovsky, Rossini and Strauss, whose concertos were studiously learned by ear, and it is uncanny that a group of aspiring British reggae musicians would do the same albeit in a very different setting. It was a case of Black creativity embracing and engaging with white history. Kpiaye, by his own admission, was keen to play any kind of music at that time, and he would go on to become a musician of enormous stature on the session scene in the decades to come, making vital contributions to the recordings of many great British reggae artists.

While The Cats may have disappointed skinhead fans when they disbanded, another group in whom they could take solace was The Cimarons. They had a wonderful singer by the name of Winston Reedy and a razor-sharp rhythm section. Like other musically accomplished British groups they were often called on to back visiting Jamaican singers who did not always travel to the UK with a full complement of their own musicians. The Cimarons supplied the beat for successful artists such as Jimmy Cliff, Nicky Thomas and a young Bob Marley, while Matumbi extended the same courtesy to Johnny Clarke, Pat Kelly and Ken Boothe.

And just as was the case with sound systems, there was a burgeoning national network of West Indian clubs that offered a touring circuit. Peckham in southeast London had Mister Bs, Birmingham had Santa Rosa, Manchester had The International, and Bristol had The Bamboo. Successful live shows at such places, rather than royalties generated by radio play, especially with the BBC's unofficial blanket ban on reggae, was a major source of income. Recording was nonetheless important to give bands product to promote, and Trojan used a studio in Chalk Farm, north London, though occasionally groups were sent to Jamaica for sessions. Dennis Bovell recalls a humorous bout of friendly rivalry when the new 'Brits' found themselves back in the 'yard' and crossed paths with local artists.

'The Cimarons did a version of Bob Marley's 'Talking Blues' and it became a bigger hit than Marley's version,' Bovell chuckles heartily. 'And Bob said to (Cimarons singer) Winston Reedy, so w'happen? Now de yoot dem a sing my tune!'[15]

Charming as the anecdote is, it makes a serious point about the complexities of the cultural continuum that bound Britain and Jamaica as music transited back and forth between the two territories. With the Jamaican paradigm of producing 'versions galore' of a single melody or rhythm, increasingly, influences moved in two directions across the Atlantic. The fact that a band based in Britain could outdo in popularity a real JA artist with his own song underlined how reggae made in Britain was coming of age. Bands in the UK were creating music that became another line of demarcation between young Black kids and their parents. As Dennis Bovell states, 'In the days when people would go on stage and say, 'Good evening ladies and gentlemen', we would come on and go, 'Wha' gwan?' A lot of parents didn't want their children to have that accent; they wanted them to speak the Queen's English… so when we started to do that at first people were frowning upon us. But then they grew to it and we able to speak patois, our lingo from the stage. We just spoke like we'd come from Kingston and occasionally, when there was a predominantly Bajan audience, I'd break out my Bajan or my fake Trini.'[16]

Bovell guffaws heartily at that admission, yet he was putting his finger on the extensive scrambling of identity that unfolded during this time, because as much as he was rejecting the conservatism of his elders, he was also acknowledging the growing dominance of the Jamaican vernacular over that of other Caribbean islands, as well as the advantage of being able to alternate between them. Not everybody was impressed.

'My father would not hear of me speaking with a Jamaican accent. If I ever went home and said 'Wh'appen, Daddy? he would be… Who you think you talking to? You think you talking to your friends outside? You forget yourself?' My mother and father have not shifted their Bajan accents after 60 years of being in the UK. They still have strong Bajan accents. I let mine go. I was fed up with people going 'Wha' you say?' There were more Jamaicans than Bajans, so instead of trying to get them to understand me I found it easier to become one of them.'[17]

Embracing the vernacular of Kingston was one thing, signing up to the credo of Rastafarianism was an altogether more audacious undertaking. And that is exactly what Matumbi did in the early 1970s when they released a magnificent single called 'Wipe Them Out', which had bubbling piano and organ riffs that were reminiscent of Dave & Ansel Collins' 'Double Barrell'", over which came a lyric that spoke of the 'fruitful fields of Ethiopia' and the redemption offered by a return of the black man to Africa. The b-side of the 7" was a tune called 'Go Back Home', which offered a pointed challenge to Enoch Powell's hateful rhetoric. Matumbi were asserting the need for resistance to racism in the UK while announcing that Rastafarianism, a belief system that was a radical alternative to Christianity, had much to offer Black people. It was gaining currency in Jamaica, despite the fierce opposition of the ruling class, and its influence was increasing in Black Britain. One of its key evangelists, Bob Marley, had come to 'Babylon' to promote his music, but he was still a small axe at the time.

Notes
1. Interestingly, Chris Blackwell was an extra on *Dr. No*, the debut James Bond movie set in Jamaica.
2. MFP was a budget label.
3. Ové spent time in Rome as a artist and film extra.
4. *Equal Before the Law* (part of the series *Cause for Concern*).
5. Bryan Knight, 'They were afraid of us: the legacy of Britain's Black Panthers', http://www.aljazeera.com/7 December, 2020.
6. Interview with the author, January 2022.
7. Featured on *Reggae Britannia*, BBC.
8. *Lardsah*, 22 Sep 2020.
9. Interview with Errol Brown, featured on http://www.celebrityradio.biz/
10. Interview with the author, February 2022.
11. Ibid.
12. Ibid.
13. Interview with the author, July 2022.
14. Ibid.
15. Interview with the author, February 2022.
16. Ibid.
17. Ibid.

5 WHOLE LOTTA CONSCIOUSNESS

We were looking for heroes at the time. I didn't have any role models, I didn't have any inspirational figures.
– Vanley Burke, Jamaican born, Birmingham raised photographer.

Salad Days
Pictures of the famous before they were famous have an appeal to those who know how their destiny will unfold, particularly if it shows somebody unremarkable and ordinary, an everyday pre-icon to whom worshipping fans can relate, thinking perhaps that the superstar is really just one of them. Every god starts as a mere mortal.

Two young Black singers are sitting on stools in the gymnasium of Peckham Manor School, south London in 1972. Both are dressed in dark shirts and jackets and they cradle acoustic guitars. One has a medium sized Afro, rising like a halo over his head, the other sports a striped, crocheted tam, from under which sprouts an infant growth of dreadlocks. The former is American, Johnny Nash, the latter Jamaican, Bob Marley. They are seated in front of rows of teenage heads, the bulk of whom have the same orb-like hair as Nash, but one of the focal points of the photo is a rogue yootman who has turned round to lock eyes on a classmate behind him. He seems to be sharing a kind of conspiratorial joy, hearing Nash, a superlative songwriter, and one of the first Americans to recognise the value of reggae and endorse its artists. The schoolboy does not yet know that Marley would make the music into a global force to be reckoned with, in a few years' time appearing in places where they did not have basketball hoops on the wall. Even more charm radiates from a post-show shot of Marley walking through the playground, smiling broadly as one of the boys chests a football high into air. The man from Trenchtown had a passion for the beautiful game and often took part in friendly matches with the bredrin during downtime between gigs. Everyday people doing everyday things.

Yet the reason why Marley was at a school reflects the struggles he encountered in his early career, when there was little interest in such masterful songs as 'Soul Rebel', or 'Stir It Up', with versions recorded by him and by Nash. Such tunes gained little airplay beyond the specialist circles out of which they were attempting to break. This situation made for greater accessibility of musicians to fans when entourages weren't as big and security not as tight as is the case today. It was the Peckham Manor School's art teacher, Keith Baugh, who met Nash and Marley at the Bag O' Nails club in Soho and invited them to do an impromptu set in the games-hall the next day. For the Black kids at the school, many of whom were of West Indian origin, it was an opportunity to see a reflection of themselves in the two guest singers, even though the Rasta religion embraced by Marley had as yet very few followers outside Jamaica. Marley had to remove his beanie and carefully explain what locks were to his young audience.

Had he had the chance to travel beyond the capital, Marley could have impacted other school children. For examples black families in Birmingham had to confront the same demoralizing challenges as their counterparts up and down the country. One person who was able to chronicle the wider experience of Black families in the city was photographer, Vanley Burke. His pictures of the West Indian community are an invaluable document of how his peers and elders lived at the time. With a sharp eye for detail, he captured a sense of what people thought and felt as well as where they were and what they did. When I asked him in 2022 to speculate about what the magical day at Peckham Manor would have meant had it taken place at his school in the Midlands, Vanley was forthright:

> If Johnny Nash and Bob Marley had come to our school I think it would have been the same as [the joy] you see on the faces of those kids in the photograph! I mean we were looking for heroes at the time, I didn't have any role models, I didn't have any inspirational figures like that available; we just had to sort things out on our own. The majority of us at the school were black... I think there were dynamics being played out between different racial groups at the time. And there was the usual stuff going on with the teachers, I mean the usual kind of racist attitudes. For example, prior to a meal you were supposed to wash your hands because that was the rule, and a teacher would say 'I wouldn't know if it's clean anyway'.[1]

Arriving in Handsworth, the central hub of Black Birmingham in 1965, Burke lived with his parents above the grocery shop they ran in Grove Lane. As one of six boys he found his home was cramped and constraining, which led him to spend a great deal of his childhood outdoors, on the streets or in local parks, and these spaces became the scenes for countless of his striking photographs that present black people as he encountered them.

Because his family ran a small business that attracted primarily Black customers, Burke early gained a strong sense of where hearts and minds were at in situations that involved more dark than light. As he later recalled, 'I had overheard conversations in the shop of factory workers who were disillusioned with England.' He was equally, 'quite conscious of the negative aspects of the representations of black people in the mainstream press.'[2]

In addition to discrimination in employment and housing and police harassment, discrimination in education was no less of an issue, particularly because of low rates of attainment reported for Black children who went through the primary and secondary systems. John La Rose, a poet, publisher and activist from Trinidad, emerged as a leading figure in the drive to secure equality for Black pupils and to resist attempts by the state to automatically place them in the lowest rankings of intelligence or 'bands' that significantly reduced their life chances. A one-time chairman of the Institute For Race Relations, La Rose founded the George Padmore Supplementary School to offset the lack of adequate provision for Black children in state schools, and the Black Parents Association and also helped to create the Caribbean Education and Community Workers Association, which published Bernard Coard's *How The West Indian Child Is Made Educationally Sub-Normal in The British School System*.[3] With factual evidence, the book articulated truths that had been known in the Black community for years, namely the education system's assumption of the inferiority of people of colour and the discriminatory behaviour of white teachers, which together closed down the possibilities for ethnic minority children. The advent of the 'Saturday School', where Black teachers and parents offered weekend tuition to their children, was pivotal in countering these disadvantages. Such experiences permeated the consciousness of a new generation of Black children born in Britain, blighted by marginalisation which induced in some a sense of worthlessness and in others a rebelliousness that would produce songs of great significance when the musicians among them effectively channelled that resentment.

Supermen from the Motherland
Vanley Burke recalls that reggae was the dominant soundtrack of his youth and that sound system dances, blues parties and clubs such as Santa Rosa became the centre of his social life in Birmingham. Exponents of jazz, such as the Jamaican saxophonist Andy Hamilton, also resident in the city since the late 1940s, were largely unknown to him. Hamilton had neither the rebel cool nor new beat of Bob Marley.

Reggae and soul were at the cutting edge of Black music in Britain in the late 1960s and early 1970s, but it would be wrong to overlook the continuing presence of what had preceded them – the 'mother genres', namely the African American styles of R&B and jazz. In Britain, as in America and Europe, jazz could not compete with the various genres of popular music as a commercial force, but it still had considerable vitality, because several gifted soloists who had debuted in the 1960s kept producing excellent work, despite their precarious financial circumstances. One obvious example was the Barbadian trumpeter, Harry Beckett, whose albums such as *Flare Up* and *Warm Smiles*, proved that at the age of 36, he was very much in his prime.

Furthermore, South African players such as Dudu Pukwana and Harry Miller, also hit creative peaks, recording mostly for the independent Ogun label set up by Miller and his wife Hazel. But it was the arrival of the trumpeter and staunch anti-apartheid activist, Hugh Masekela, in London in 1972, that yielded one of the era's seminal recordings. His presence also signalled that London remained an active international hub to which players travelled in order to fulfil their creative desires. Masekela's *Home Is Where the Music Is*[4] was an album that conveyed angst as well as joy, in line with the cleverly formulated title that made the point that black South Africans could not lay down roots where their heart was, namely in racist South Africa. In every note they played, they resisted the war waged on them by apartheid. The recording sessions for this album took place at Chris Blackwell's Island studio in west London in 1972 with a transatlantic band of grade A players: Puerto Rican-American double bassist Eddie Gomez, African American pianist Larry Willis, and two South Africans, Makya Ntshoko on drums and Pukwana on alto saxophone. In the producer's chair was Stewart Levine, whom Masekela had met when both were students at the Manhattan School of Music before they jointly set up the Chisa label. Another talented South African, Caiphus Semenya did the bulk of the writing and his hauntingly lyrical pieces such as 'Nomali', 'Maesha', 'Part of a Whole' and 'The Big Apple' defined a sound that reflected his deep immersion in the choral and folk traditions of his homeland, as well as the history of American jazz. More than any knowing attempt at a hybridisation or fusion of styles, the music presented a captivating language that was both rugged and sophisticated, alternating the hard edge of the blues with the lighter sway of township swing to reflect the life journeys of Semenya and Masekela, both of whom had relocated to Los Angeles, where the latter was for a time placed under surveillance by the F.B.I. for his supposedly un-American activities.

What stood out on *Home Is Where the Music Is* was the regal melodic content and searing improvisations, as well as the compelling emotional narrative of each composition. In some there was a fraught tension, if not a sense of dread. This was most evident on 'Inner Crisis', a shadowy Larry Willis[5] piece with clenched funky beats that set up articulate, expansive solos by Masekela and Willis himself. On other songs, such as the gorgeous lament 'Minawa', Dudu Pukwana was imperious, combining a pungently aggressive tone and phrases that sauntered and swaggered over the pulse, imbuing the music with a brash, ballsy, electrifying *joie de vivre*.

Pukwana, trumpeter Mongezi Feza, double bassist Johnny Dyani and drummer Louis Moholo, had, along with white pianist Chris McGregor, been part of the band The Blue Notes, which had arrived in Britain to great acclaim in the 1960s and continued to do excellent work throughout the 1970s, mostly for Ogun. Each member of the Blue Notes, and Miller as well, recorded solo albums that reflected their roots in a number of musical traditions, from township pop to bebop to avant-garde, and seamlessly showed the organic links or parallels between them. On the one hand, there was a marked swing in the gentler, more accessible side of South African music that was not entirely alien to American blues and gospel. On the other hand, the fiery energy of avant-garde pioneers such as Albert Ayler and John Coltrane was something to which Pukwana, Moholo and McGregor related and it was McGregor's group, Brotherhood of Breath, that consolidated this ingenuity and also presented what was a kind of united front among British jazz players who were drawn to both the experimental nature of free improvisation as well as 'straight-ahead' composition. These included the likes of Alan Skidmore, John Surman, Mike Osborne, Malcolm Griffiths and Nick Evans, musicians who had come of age in the mid- to late 1960s, absorbing the work of classic American artists and now forging paths of their own. All bandleaders in their own right, these individuals made Brotherhood of Breath into nothing less than a supergroup, a 13-piece ensemble that extended and personalised the lineage of orchestral jazz epitomised by legends such as Duke Ellington, Gil Evans and Sun Ra. Issued in the early 1970s, *Brotherhood of Breath* and *Brotherhood*[6] were landmark albums that have lost none of their appeal years later.

McGregor found a way of harnessing the resources at his disposal to bring out a rich yet nuanced tonal palette of brass and reeds that made the melodic and contrapuntal lines glow with a warmth similar to that found in South African choral music. Yet he also gave sufficient space for the soloists to express themselves. Amid all the discipline of the arrangements, there were moments of raucous freedom. By accident or design, Brotherhood of Breath also challenged any preconceived ideas about cultural borders, and not just in the sense that this was a British band with an inter-continental personnel. At moments there were echoes of the legendary 1940s Afro-Cuban orchestral sound of Machito, above all in the distinctive character of the reeds, which purred sensually over the relentless percussive drive of the rhythm section, a quite formidable power unit within the band. A track like 'MRA' typified the magic. Built on snappy, almost tick-tock, double-time drums and hissing cymbals, the piece created an irresistibly infectious energy that was enhanced by stately horns whirling around in short motifs executed with such perfect timing that they gave the impression of one continuous line that had dramatically changing contours and colours. The drive was unstoppable. As much as this was intricately scored 'art music' with its attention to detail, 'MRA' also stood unapologetically in the tradition of orchestras led by Ellington and Ra that also played dance music.

On the other hand there was music of graceful tranquillity, like 'Davashe's Dream', a quite gorgeous ballad that could lull and soothe, with its plaintive harmony and legato horn lines that seemed to swoon for an absent lover. The piece provided a showcase for alto saxophonist Dudu Pukwana whose deliciously grainy, rugged tone and scurrying phrases brought an edge to the tranquil atmosphere that made clear the creative kinship that bound him to US avant-garde pioneer Ornette Coleman. The whimsical structure of the whole piece also reflected the great impact that Thelonious Monk had made on composers of McGregor's generation.

Brotherhood of Breath was one of the most important bands in British jazz in the 1970s, because it kept alive and invigorated the big band tradition at a time when there was a prevailing fashion for small groups because financial pressures made it difficult to maintain large and experimental ensembles. BoB's changing line-up also gave it an evolutionary, quasi-workshop feel that brought together many of the most significant players on the UK scene, such as saxophone titan Evan Parker and trumpeter Mark Charig, both of whose individual approaches to their respective instruments served McGregor's imaginative writing very well.

There was arguably a greater appreciation of jazz, particularly that which leaned towards the avant-garde, in Europe than there was in Britain at the time and the live recordings of BoB at major festivals on the continent, such as Willisau in Switzerland and Toulouse and Angouleme in France, the latter, featuring excellent French players such as Francois Jeanneau, Louis Sclavis and Didier Levallet, lent further credence to the ideal of artistic co-operation across borders. McGregor's brotherhood was as wide as it was big.

Another talented South African who moved to Britain in the early 1970s was Sebothane Julian Bahula, originally from Eersterust, Pretoria. A percussionist and vocalist, he built creative bridges between indigenous rhythms and chants and western improvisation, winning acclaim for his work as part of the group Malombo with guitarist Philip Tabane, before founding Jabula within a short time of his arrival in London. This wonderful band reflected the riches of the capital's multicultural music scene as Bahula brought together his compatriots Dudu Pukwana, Mogotsi Ernest Mothle (bass), Madumetja Lucky Ranku (guitar), as well as a West Indian Frank Roberts (keyboards), and an Englishman Nick Evans (trombone). Their music was wildly explosive and deeply sorrowful, full of tears for the Africa Bahula knew and had been forced to leave for fear of his life.

The individual work of these expatriate South African artists was outstanding, but it is the solidarity between them that was notable. This was highlighted by the keen sense of loss felt over the death of the brilliant trumpeter, Mongezi Feza. Pukwana and other members of the Blue Notes recorded a sublime tribute album *Blue Notes for Mongezi*, while Jabula dedicated *Thunder into Our Hearts* to his memory.

Apart from his work as a player, composer and bandleader, Bahula became a visible symbol of resistance against oppression in Africa and a champion of the continent's artists. He began to programme a regular Friday night slot at the 100 Club in Oxford Street, in central London, giving gigs to Hugh Masekela, Miriam Makeba, Fela Kuti and others.

Conscious Mind
For the most part, British jazz musicians in the early 1970s did not develop in isolation from other genres of music. Session work in the world of pop had long been a necessity to supplement a fairly meagre income from gigs in small clubs, but it also had the outcome of an organic cross-fertilisation of styles. The transition of blues into rock in the late 1960s may have created the new genre that captured the imagination of young listeners who were not particularly drawn to jazz, but there was nonetheless a degree of exchange between the various idioms. For a start there were rock groups with jazz affinities where musicians had embraced the principle of improvising on themes and 'stretching out' beyond a verse-chorus model, creating arrangements that were longer and more detailed than those found in mainstream pop. Obvious examples here were blues graduates such as John Mayall, Eric Clapton and Jack Bruce, but others such as Robert Wyatt and Mike Ratledge were also clearly familiar with American modernist jazz musicians such as John Coltrane and Charles Mingus. When they formed the influential band Soft Machine in the mid-1960s, they didn't so much fuse genres as shape them into a creative vocabulary that was underpinned by biting satire, beat poetry and a surrealist impulse, perfectly expressed in the wordplay of *Out-Bloody-Rageous*,[7] it was a given they would have jazz musicians in the fold. Two of their most accomplished members, saxophonist Elton Dean and trumpeter Mark Charig, were also part of Chris McGregor's Brotherhood of Breath.

Although most jazz artists sold far fewer records than their rock counterparts, there was still a recognition among more imaginative musicians that elements of jazz could enhance any kind of popular song. While Soft Machine were confecting their idiosyncratic tapestries of strange words and stranger sounds, another group also formed a bridge between the conventional and the outré in early 1970s music, with improvisation as a major part of their artistry. C.C.S. was a catchy, easily retained name for a band, but the fact that the initials stood for Collective Consciousness Society caught the wind of the hippy movement that was still blowing around popular culture at the time. The use of initials recognised that having too many syllables in a three-word tongue-twister could be problematic. The group was founded by classical composer, conductor and pianist John Cameron, who had scored films such as *Kes* and worked with big names in jazz, pop and folk, from Ella Fitzgerald to Cilla Black and Joni Mitchell. When he explained the raison d'etre of C.C.S., he insisted that there was no desire to create a new category of music that could be used for marketing. 'I had a concept of a band that would have a large brass/woods line-up plus a complex and heavy rhythm section. The music should not be jazz, rock, blues, big band but use elements for its own purposes and not for the sheer sake of fusion. The result was to be a sound of its own and not just another fashionable forced marriage.'

Completing the union were two guitarist-vocalists, Alexis Korner, 'the godfather of British blues'[7] who had nurtured young rock stars of the Cream-Stones cohort, and a Dane, Peter Thorup, both of whom had been part of a beguiling band by the name of New Church. C.C.S. was produced by Mickie Most, who had enjoyed big time chart success with Lulu, and created a strong body of work. This was the result of the open-mindedness defined by Cameron as well as the quality of the additional personnel drafted in. C.C.S. used some of the best jazz musicians in the country, with the brass section including Kenny Wheeler and Henry Lowther, and the reeds Ronnie Ross, Pete King and Tony Coe. There were also two notable West Indians, Bajan trumpeter Harry Beckett, who had also been part of Brotherhood of Breath, and Jamaican flautist-saxophonist Harold McNair, who had previously worked with Cameron on the *Kes* soundtrack. Put simply, this was an all-star ensemble.

C.C.S. used its enviable resources well. A band that is more of a studio project with changing members can run the risk of having no real sense of identity or cohesion, but the group's recordings were anything but cold affairs in which hired hands turned up, played scores and then scooted off to another gig. Whether they rehearsed hard or not, the band had 'a real vibe'.

Beckett may have found C.C.S. an intriguing proposition. This was a man who, in addition to work with Brotherhood of Breath, and the forward-thinking British composer, Graham Collier, cut very good solo albums such as *Flare Up*, which featured arrangements by Collier as well as stellar contributions from BoB colleagues such as John Surman, Mike Osborne and Alan Skidmore. Beckett was a highly articulate soloist who could navigate challenging orchestrations very well, and who had played everything from calypso to high-life to jazz, blues and rock since arriving in Britain in the mid-1950s. Now he was taking part in what was a loose synthesis of several of these elements.

There was no pronounced Caribbean flavour on the eponymous C.C.S. debut, but Cameron's range as a composer did take him into the kind of Spanish folk territory that had partly informed West Indian music, on an extended piece called 'Dos Cantos', which had stirring flamenco echoes, and the heady emotional charge of 'duende'. Elsewhere, C.C.S. did what jazz artists had done for decades. It took popular songs, both underground classics and chart hits, and used them as building blocks for arrangements that steered the source material in new directions while staying true to the defining elements of the original. It was not so much about 'jazzing up' a familiar melody with strong solos but more about taking a recognised tune and imaginatively altering the aural landscape in which it had first appeared. For example, '(I Can't Get No) Satisfaction' was out of left field. The pounding backbeat and relentless snarl of the Stones' anthem was replaced by a stuttering staccato rhythm in which horns and guitar stabbed through the melody to crank up a sticky, torrid tension which was subsequently released by a barrage of electric piano from Cameron that had a similar feel to what the great Booker T. Jones drew from a Hammond organ. More surprises came. After a vocal chorus, the brass and reeds roared back into action, matched by an cascade of percussion before the rhythm section flew into double-time swing, and flautist Harold McNair imparted new energy with a piping hot solo. Another vocal chorus shifted the beat back to the jaunty, jerky feel of the opening section, before the horns then took the song home to a dizzy climax. Cameron also let his imagination run riot when he took the timeless spiritual 'Wade in the Water' and recast it in a slouchy 7/4, which then gave way to a jittery 13/8, so that the song felt very much like a series of whimsical agitations rather than the solid application of common 4/4 time. The highpoint of the album was another well-known pop anthem that again featured a stellar headline performance by McNair. This was Led Zeppelin's 'Whole Lotta Love', a version of the Willie Dixon-penned, Muddy Waters-performed blues classic, 'You Need Love'. C.C.S. replaced the brash growl of Robert Plant's vocal with the wild snarl of McNair's flute; his notes were laden with carnal exhalations that outdid the wanton sexual charge of the original. It was heavy breathing on the beat. Even more daring was Cameron's arrangement. The piece started as a gentle pastoral duet for piano and clarinet before blasting into life with heavy electric guitar and McNair's piercing woodwind, supported by a hard-hitting cowbell and the thunder of additional percussion and Hammond organ growls. Then, with a dramatic shift, the drums pounded at a brisker tempo and guitar and brass played a subtle variation on the initial riff before a swell of organ set up a new break in which the whole horn section played curling motifs that put the music right back in the big band era. This was a spiking of the lexicon of rock by its swing antecedent, before the music stopped dead to make way for an a capella vocal drenched in reverb. The band then resumed the original melodic line, complete with frenetic scrambling on organ, before playing to a fade out.

 These improvising musicians were taking liberties with the song's given harmony and structure, making the composition a point of departure for a narrative journey that had no obvious development or destination. The point about the C.C.S. take on 'Whole Lotta Love' was that at times it did not rock at all but at other times it out-rocked Zeppelin. In any case the C.C.S. arrangement gained huge exposure when it was chosen as the theme for Top of the Pops, the most important UK media outlet for mainstream pop music.

During this mercurial period of the early 1970s, when new strains of blues-inflected soul and rock were developing, TOTP held up a fascinating mirror to the way that pop musical culture inspired and beguiled during its travels from Black American heartlands to British outposts. Indeed, nothing appears more incongruous than the sight of an all-white studio audience, urged on by the notorious but as yet undiscovered paedophile, Jimmy Saville, dancing as if they have coat-hangers up their backs to the glorious, cinematic, symphonic soul of Isaac Hayes' 'Shaft'. But the sounds of the iconic Memphis label Stax, which issued the song, continued to cross borders, such was their irresistible appeal.

Also on TOTP's December 1971 edition was Deep Purple's heavy rock barnstormer 'Fireball', accompanied by the high kicks and skimpy costumes of the show's resident dance troupe, Pan's People. If white British artists were building on the foundation of Black American music with the loud guitar-led attack of 'Fireball', then C.C.S.' 'Whole Lotta Love' could not have been more appropriate as an enthralling collision of vocabularies that collapsed notions of what was old and new in the confusingly evolutionary world of pop.

And who was in the middle of it all? A Jamaican jazz flautist called Harold McNair. He had attended the legendary Alpha Boys School for underprivileged children and orphans in Kingston, and now his furiously powerful blowing was heard by millions of people watching television, a medium to which he did not have access as a child. The motto of the institution that had nurtured him and others was 'upward and onward'.

Gone Before Their Time
Tragedy struck C.C.S. while its scorching version of 'Whole Lotta Love' was given weekly national exposure on prime television as the theme tune of Top of the Pops. Did millions of enthralled viewers and a studio full of hyped teenagers realise that the man who played the flute on the piece was no more? Harold McNair died of lung cancer on 7 March 1971. He was just 39. A bright light snuffed out far too soon, the Jamaican can be placed in a long line of African Diasporan musicians who did not have time to fulfil their creative potential. There is also the irony that McNair was more widely heard in death than in life, and whilst his name did not appear on the show's credits, everybody knew the tune that introduced Thursday night's chart rundown.

The loss of McNair was probably felt most keenly by his fellow Alpha Boys School alumni who had made an impact on the UK jazz scene, notably Joe Harriott, who was reputed to have had great affection for McNair, and even those with the darkest of premonitions might not have foreseen that Harriott himself would pass just two years later. The death of two such driving forces in Black British 'art music' was a painful loss.

McNair had taken a bold step towards the world of improvised electric music, just as American visionaries such as Miles Davis and Weather Report were 'plugging in' and creating jazz-rock, which was later referred to as fusion. It is impossible to say what McNair would have done if he had continued with C.C.S., but the sound of his withering, salty flute against the loud crunch of amplified guitars suggested he could well have thrived in other new musical settings.

Harriott, who died at just 44 years of age, was widely regarded as one of the most gifted figures of the European post-war 'modern' school in improvised music. He breathed his last in Southampton, virtually penniless and surrounded by few friends. His death not widely reported. A highly gifted saxophonist, he had an astounding command of the bebop idiom pioneered by Americans such as Charlie Parker and Dizzy Gillespie, but he also developed a vocabulary he called 'freeform', which caused a storm of controversy because of its departure from song structures with a clearly stated theme and solos based on the chord sequences that underpinned it. Harriott's performance of music with open, ambiguous harmony and unpredictable, fluid arrangements, which enabled him to 'paint pictures in sound', split opinion in the 1960s. Recently there has been a major reassessment of his work, particularly of albums such as *Freeform* and *Abstract*,[8] and he has been widely recognised as a pioneer, if not a genius ahead of his time. Even so, his death points to a number of the unforgiving realities of the jazz industry, from the power of the critical establishment to the lifestyle of artists, to race relations. The Jamaican saxophonist's health faded over several years, following the onset of pleurisy, but there were contributory factors to his death: a demanding nocturnal lifestyle marked by gigs lasting into the early hours was often supplemented by heavy drinking and, perhaps most damagingly of all, chain smoking, still then a pastime associated more with movie-star glamour than the dread of ill health. Like many jazz artists of his generation Harriott was not known to take good care of himself.

Self-indulgence and neglect may not have been the only things that sent Harriott to an early grave. His personality and the attitudes he elicited are thornier questions. Never one to button his lip, he declared himself 'clearly superior' when quizzed about comparisons with other jazz musicians, a boast that would not have gone down well in a post-colonial Britain still coming to terms with entrenched racial hierarchies. In the 1950s, self-appointed moral custodians warned against the 'flashy, arrogant black man', and here was Harriott being just that and not apologising for it.

Whether his confrontational stance closed more doors for him than the challenging nature of his music is a moot question. In a music industry which appeared to set great store by the quality of African American music, and offered success to some of Harriott's peers working in pop music, such as Kenny Lynch, there were real limits nonetheless. As she was hitting the big time, Shirley Bassey was rejected by a number of film companies for starring roles because she was not white. She could not 'pass'.

Of course, white musicians who broke with orthodoxy also found themselves cold-shouldered, the most obvious example being Stan Tracey, who was much admired by visiting Americans A-listers such as Sonny Rollins, but Harriott, as a difficult man and Black may have been particularly liable to censure. Pianist Michael Garrick, who played with Harriott and other West Indians such as Shake Keane, expressed his frustration at what he saw as a kind of cartel mentality, if not forthright cronyism in jazz, that impacted on the access of particular individuals to success, although he stopped short of naming the gatekeepers. 'In those days there really were people who controlled things and you had to be in with them, and Joe had none of it. He didn't play the 'hanging in game' like others.'[9]

Had Harriott had a decent support structure, above all a strong, committed management that was able to look out for his interests, this visionary saxophonist might not have passed away at such a young age. Coleridge Goode, the Jamaican double bassist who was one of Harriott's consistent collaborators, made another point, which went to the heart of prevailing perceptions about what Jamaican musicians were supposed to play. 'There were some who thought that the thing that West Indians really should do was calypso, rather than modern jazz. It was difficult not to conclude that him not being the kind of black musician that was acceptable to some, held him back in some way.'[10]

It's the kind of assertion that is thought provoking but difficult to prove. There are no recorded statements to the effect that black players were only allowed to do what was deemed palatable to audiences who already harboured reductive expectations about them, but Goode is certainly on to something when he talks about the destructive nature of cultural clichés, which is the subtext of his argument.

Did the fact that Harriott was notoriously prickly, if not belligerent, stoke a more general prejudice against a Black man who insisted on playing music regarded as advanced to some and difficult and pretentious to others? Was he seen as a Black man who simply had ideas above his station? His death raised questions about the need for greater artist welfare, competent management and career guidance, and above all higher rates of pay for jazz musicians who lived lives that were characterised by attritional insecurity. With the passing of Harriott and McNair, and the departure to Europe of the very gifted St. Vincent-born trumpeter, Shake Keane, who only recorded one album under his own name in the 1970s (the orchestral project *Rising Stars at Evening Time*), there was a distinct sense that the Caribbean presence in British jazz had ebbed from its heyday of the early 1960s.

Even so, jazz remained an important part of soul music made in Britain, above all by way of orchestrations and improvisations. Black pop still set great store by expressive solos and ambitious arrangements, and jazz musicians reached popular audiences through their work in film, television and theatre. The success of the 1977 musical revue, *Bubbling Brown Sugar*, a celebration of legendary Harlem Renaissance composers, such as Fats Waller and Duke Ellington, showed that 'Old' African American music had lost none of its power to attract new audiences. And the casting of the excellent vocalist Elaine Delmar, daughter of Jamaican trumpeter Leslie 'Jiver' Hutchinson, was a neat link between generations.

Notes
1. Interview with the author, February 2022.
2. Ibid.
3. Bernard Coard, *How the West Indian Child Is Made Educationally Sub-Normal by the British School System* published by New Beacon Books in 1971.
4. *Home Is Where the Music Is* (Blue Thumb) was reissued on cd by Verve in 2008.
5. Hugh Masekela and Larry Willis formed a memorable duo in 2012, recording the album *Friends* and touring extensively.
6. Soft Machine, *Third* (Columbia), 1970.
7. Alexis Korner's group, Blues Incorporated, was an institution that gave opportunities to many young rock and jazz musicians in the 1960s and 1970s, notably Ginger Baker and Dick Heckstall-Smith.
8. Joe Harriott features in *Don't Stop the Carnival: Black Music in Britain* Vol.1 (Peepal Tree), 2018, pp. 305-309, 337, 338.
9. Interview with the author, 1998.
10. Ibid.

6 BLACK WOMAN AND CHILD

I was in the village shop... this woman said to me 'Oh, what a cute little pickaninny you got there'. So I said, 'We don't call 'em pickaninnies no more!' And guess what? Her daughter ended up marrying an African guy and I was the only one in the village she could talk to about it.
– P.P. Arnold on life in the Cotswolds

I won't rearrange my hair,
I won't powder my underwear
I won't stoop to shave my legs
I don't care how much you beg
– Marsha Hunt, 'Man to Woman'

Pot Heads
There are covers and covers of covers. When an artist creates an arrangement of a song that is considerably different from the original, they engage in a debate about the way a melody can be a point of departure for any number of musical destinations. Rhythm and harmony can be altered beyond recognition, lyrics can sometimes be replaced by a guitar, horn or piano. What a song once was may be tangential to what it becomes.

In 1972, a new take on 'Whole Lotta Love' was recorded. But rather than referring to Led Zeppelin's vocal version, it was made as an instrumental that owed an obvious debt to the inspired C.C.S. reinvention discussed in the previous chapter. It was by a band called Blue Mink. The groove had a pleasingly funky edge, but it was curious that this 5-piece ensemble, formed in London in the late 1960s, had two excellent singers who stood down for this song, a highlight of their album, *Live at The Talk of the Town*. One was a white Englishmen called Roger Cook, the other an African American woman, Madeline Bell, and their absence on 'Whole Lotta Love' only served to heighten their presence elsewhere. The pair harmonised beautifully on a Beatles' classic, 'Something', and Bell sang a spellbinding lead on an interpretation of 'I Who Have Nothing', the torch song that had become an anthem for Shirley Bassey, Ben E. King and Tom Jones. These covers, as well as originals such as 'Good Morning Freedom', a top ten UK single, explain why Blue Mink became a success. The group combined strong emotive themes with a high standard of musicianship supplied by keyboardist-founder Roger Coulam, guitarist

Alan Parker, drummer Barry Morgan and bass guitarist Herbie Flowers, an impressive player who freelanced extensively and was also a member of C.C.S.. Blue Mink was eclectic. They played pop, soul, and rock, very often with deft jazz inflections. They were artistic and commercial, and they had in Bell a vocalist of immense talent. As noted in *Don't Stop the Carnival*, she came to Britain in 1962 as part of the theatre show *Black Nativity* and had become a much in-demand session singer for stars such as Rod Stewart, Elton John and Joe Cocker. She also recorded excellent solo albums such as *Bell's A Poppin'* that showcased the richness of her gospel-reared voice and her stylistic versatility. Bell was as convincing on relaxed orchestral ballads as she was on the funkiest rhythmic numbers.

A Lovin' Machine with Glitches
There was a consistent idealism in the lyrical content of Blue Mink songs, particularly in numbers like 'Our World' and 'Good Morning Freedom', a quietly subversive piece about the need for everyday people to come together in solidarity. Set to a bouncy blues-rock backbeat, it features chipper guitar chords and glossy piano trills in an arrangement which astutely funnels Black music into a palatable pop sound that is catchy yet not so neutered as to be forgettable. While the lyric urges universal peace and tolerance – loving your neighbour is a real nice thing/ there's only one way to get the people to sing – it has a couplet with a much more provocative slant when Bell sings 'I'm getting bad looks from the big white man/gotta get away just as fast as I can.' As much as Blue Mink can be commended for that swipe at race-related power dynamics, the group fell down, somewhat ironically, when advocating for racial harmony. 'Melting Pot', which climbed to number 3 in the UK singles chart, has a wide-eyed brotherhood of man message, the utopian notion of people getting together in a 'lovin' machine' – in a manner not dissimilar to The Equals' 'Black Skin Blue Eyed Boys'. It was a song that would have horrified those who wanted to keep Britain white, though censure of racial mixing was also prevalent in the British Black Panther Party, which was one reason why Farrukh Dhondy decided to leave. Inter-racial marriages still attracted unwanted attention and quite widespread discussion of the implications for children of such unions, particularly when the hurtful term 'half-caste' was likely to be directed at them. As bold a song as 'Melting Pot' was in its sentiments, it also laid bare the complexities and contradictions of language and imagery in discussing race relations. Lyrically, the song has landed on the wrong side of history, with its questionable shadist notion of an ideal of 'coffee coloured people', while its use of the racially offensive colloquialisms of the 1970s – 'red Indian boy,' 'curly Latin kinkies' and 'yellow chinkies' – remain untenable whatever the good intentions. The song was penned by two white writers,

Roger Cook and Roger Greenaway, and one wonders how Madeline Bell felt about it as a Black woman, or what Chinese-Jamaican musicians such as Philip and Colston Chen, both members of Jimmy James' band, would have felt about this reprise of imperial sinophobic language? But then again the Black reggae singer, Max Romeo, reprised 'Melting Pot' with the same lyric cast over a wrangling new beat. Lyrical missteps aside, the very existence of Blue Mink as an interracial band, makes it an interesting and noteworthy part of the history of Black music in Britain. Madeline Bell's presence was important because she broke with prevailing perceptions of black female singers confined to R&B, and embraced a creative opportunity she might not have had in America. Blue Mink can be seen in the lineage of British multi-racial groups such as The Equals and The Foundations, and it's worth remembering that, proportionally, there were more integrated ensembles in the UK than in the US, where groups such as Sly & The Family Stone and Electric Flag were notable exceptions to the generality of mono-racial formations.

Above all, Blue Mink created an eclectic discography that has stood the test of time. They recorded consistently in the first half of the 1970s, making more or less an album a year, such as *Blue Mink*, *Our World*, *Real Mink*, *A Time of Change*, *Only When I Laugh* and *Fruity*. Taken as a whole, the body of work is impressive because of the consistently high standard of writing, mostly by Cook and Greenaway, and the smart arrangements of covers. With Cook and Bell forming a solid vocal partnership, alternating lead duties from one verse to the next before harmonising on choruses, the band had a powerful front line. Like many of their peers, Blue Mink acknowledged both the Britishness of the Beatles and the African Americanness that had been integral to their genesis. Blue Mink thus moved from successful originals such as 'The Banner Man', which peaked at number 3 in the UK singles charts, to reprises of the music of soul heroes such as Stevie Wonder ('You Are the Sunshine of My Life') and Bill Withers ('Harlem'), while tracks such as 'Get Up' and 'Mind Your Business' were right on the pulse of a soul-rock sound that followed other British acts such as Spencer Davis. As for 'Gidda Wadda Wobble', it was a hard-edged R&B instrumental. All things considered, Blue Mink were difficult to categorise. It is tempting to argue that they were too pop to be a soul and too soul to be pop, but the point is that they were able to straddle the boundary between many genres, or rather show the continuum between them. The softer strain of what might be called easy listening was present in the work of iconic African American stars such as Dionne Warwick or The Fifth Dimension, who could move from a polished radio-friendly sheen to a fiery 'spirituals' holler in just a few beats, and something of the same can be heard in Blue Mink.

Down in the Village

Blue Mink recorded into the mid-1970s before disbanding, after which Madeline Bell carried on recording solo. One of Bell's notable compatriots, who had also made forays into the world of rock and was similarly ready to cross genre boundaries, was another excellent singer, P.P. Arnold. She had come to Britain in 1966 as a member of the Ikettes, backing Ike & Tina Turner, settled in London and fallen in with the prime movers of the pop world such as the Small Faces, with whom she recorded the excellent single 'Tin Soldier'. Like Bell, Arnold became an important part of the UK music scene. She embodied 'real soul' as a gifted vocalist nurtured in church in the historic Black neighbourhood of Watts, Los Angeles, and she brought a great richness of tone to singles such as 'The First Cut is the Deepest', one of the seminal heartbreak ballads of the late 1960s. Arnold had what was actively sought by many British artists in thrall to African American culture – nobody more so than Mick Jagger to whom she had taught many of the latest dance steps. 'I swear that if he could have been born black, he would have,' Arnold said later.

Yet the success Arnold enjoyed in Britain did not mean that she was immune to the less savoury realities of an entertainment industry where white males held power. She became a cast member of *Catch My Soul*,[2] a 1970 rock musical staged at the University Theatre, Manchester, then the Roundhouse and the Prince of Wales, London, which was based on Shakespeare's *Othello*. It gave the flower children of the hippie generation another chance to broach the question of interracial romance. Sadly, a deep fault line ran through the multi-racial cast, as one of the singers, P.J. Proby (of trouser-splitting fame), openly indulged in crass good ol' boy Texan bigotry, right down to patting Arnold's buttocks during rehearsals. To add insult to injury, the show's producer and star, Jack Good, who cast himself as Othello, decided to black up. Arnold was understandably upset. She wrote in her autobiography,

> Even without the blacking up, Jack's interpretation was straight out of a minstrel show. This was highly embarrassing to many of us, not to say insulting. In the early 70s, black actors just weren't being given the leading West End roles they deserved and would have loved.[3]

Arnold's testimony is important because it shows that the self-flattering view that Britain was far ahead of America in terms of race relations was an illusion. And if the outwardly accepting world of the arts and music industry offered some element of comfort, it could not shield Arnold from the shock of being cold-shouldered when she tried to buy a house in Berkshire or the regularity of hearing racist remarks on public transport. Racism in America might have been more naked, direct, unfiltered and 'in your face', but the British version could be both mischievously subtle and emphatically explicit. In fact, the offensive language that Enoch Powell had used in the late 1960s was something that Arnold had to confront head on. 'I lived in Surrey and in the Cotswolds I had some nice experiences, but I wouldn't say that I was happy. I mean people would just stare at you,' she told me in 2022. 'I had a young son, Kodzo, and when I was in the village shop, this woman said to me oh, what a cute little pickaninny you got there. I was so shocked, I said we don't call 'em pickaninnies no more. And guess what? Her daughter ended up marrying an African guy and I was the only one in the village she could talk to about it!'[4]

Arnold had an auspicious start to her career as a solo artist in Britain by recording two very good solo albums, *Kafunta*[5] and *First Lady of Immediate*, both for the Immediate label founded by Andrew Loog Oldham, a minor celebrity in his own right as the manager of the Rolling Stones, who proved to be a cunning operator in the world of public relations. But Oldham's operation folded and over the next decade Arnold's life was a constant struggle to consolidate her initial success. She was clear about the problem, which she witnessed at first hand, that 'The majority of women were controlled by men. That was it.' She had even performed a song called 'Piccaninny', written by Barry Gibb, in spite of her deep discomfort with the lyric, and she bitterly regrets not being stronger and refusing to record it; such an indignity was precisely where the isolation of a black woman in a white male environment could lead. As Arnold recalls in her revealing autobiography, *Soul Survivor*, a sense of hazard reigned in her life amid all the excitement of meeting a large number of creative musicians and producers, above all because London acquired a 'dark, scary vibe' as drug culture became more widespread. There was a pressure to use the 'hard stuff' which Arnold resisted, knowing that as a sister from Watts, Los Angeles she did not have the same connections as her middle-class white colleagues to protect her if substance abuse spiralled out of control.

A series of career missteps followed. She signed with RSO (Robert Stigwood Operation), named after the powerful producer-publisher-manager-impresario who had enjoyed major success with Cream and The Bee Gees, but though he brokered writing sessions with Barry Gibb of the latter band, and a considerable amount of material was generated, the project was shelved. After this, Arnold, who had entered a relationship with Calvin 'Fuzzy' Samuels, a talented bassist with an interesting psychedelic rock combo called Sundae Times (produced by Eddy Grant), went to her hometown of Los Angeles in search of a record deal and what was meant to be a fresh start in her career. Nothing came of it.

This was the beginning of a downward spiral that resulted in bouts of depression and a lifestyle of unrelenting chaos, tragically capped by the death of her daughter. In order to get her professional life back on track, Arnold found herself mostly working as a session singer, doing backing vocals for big names such as Eric Clapton and Dr. John. What is poignant in the case of Arnold, beyond the personal tragedy, and the more general tribulations of Black women in the music industry, was the missed opportunity to fully realise her undeniable talent as a composer as well as singer. Her gifts can be heard in the melodic richness of songs such as 'Dreamin', a lavishly orchestrated mid-tempo number based on a spare but memorable theme that is repeated with minimal harmonic variation, but which builds to an effective climax through the focused power of Arnold's voice. To say that the song gives an indication of what might have been artistically is an understatement. Arnold will not play the victim card about why she did not generate more original material; she admits, 'I had no confidence in my own creativity or mc even being a songwriter'. She makes it clear that 'Being a mother and a black woman in the music industry has been really hard. My kids paid the price, I mean I lost my daughter. But having to stand up for myself was the thing that I had to and still have to do because of what went on. Where are my royalties for my work in the '60s? Where are the tracks I recorded in the '70s that were never released? Why can't I get them back? I had to go through all that.'[6] Arnold's story points once again to the absence of women in positions of power who could have offered the support that she needed.

Ain't No Such Thing As A Superman
If *Catch My Soul* had provided uncomfortable employment for P.P. Arnold, a much more notable piece of musical theatre, *Hair*, the 'American tribal love rock musical', was more genuinely interracial in its casting, and it also provided a starring role for the African American singer, actress and model, Marsha Hunt, a Philadelphian resident in London since the mid-1960s. She had appeared as an extra in Michelangelo Antonioni's *Blow-Up* and then raised her profile further by appearing nude on the cover of British Vogue, the portrait being shot by the photographer Patrick Lichfield.

Hair became (in)famous for its countercultural attitudes, extensive use of nudity and profanity, complete with risqué references to sodomy, fellatio and cunnilingus. The show was a huge success, not least because its musical score had thought-provoking lyrics by Gerome Ragni and James Rado and superb tunes by Galt McDermot, who created a masterful blend of R&B, jazz, rock, gospel and psychedelia with memorable choruses. 'I Got Life', 'Walking in Space', 'Let the Sunshine In' and 'Aquarius' all became anthems. Also striking was the talented cast. The London production, which opened at the Shaftesbury theatre, featured white English actors who went on to achieve considerable stardom in film and theatre, such as Richard O' Brien and Tim Curry, Oliver Tobias and Elaine Paige as well as Black performers of Caribbean heritage, including Peter Straker and Floella Benjamin, who would enjoy a successful career as a children's television presenter and author. She is now a peer of the realm.

Of all the Black performers in the British show, the most notable was Marsha Hunt, who stood out for her feline elegance and voluminous Afro, like an eclipse of the sun over her head. Hunt was the perfect symbol for Black womanhood in a seemingly more enlightened era, in which natural hair stood as a statement of pride and self-empowerment. At the time, the much freer use of nudity tended to be seen in that light, but hindsight suggests its use was also a sales device that cynically objectified women's bodies, whether in fashion magazines or on record sleeves.

After *Hair*, Hunt worked as a backing vocalist for blues singer Long John Baldry, and briefly became a member of the soul-pop combo, The Ferris Wheel. She then led her own band, White Trash and appeared at the Isle of Wight festival in 1969, which also featured The Who, Bob Dylan and The Nice. Her first single release was a cover of 'I Walk on Gilded Splinters', composed by the New Orleans R&B legend Dr. John. Set to an ambling mid-tempo groove shaped by a needling guitar, vibrant percussion and a trail of muffled chants, the song is really an exercise in ceremonial atmosphere rather than standard verse-chorus linearity, and the vocalist really has to tune in to the world being dramatised to make the song work. With her theatrical skill and ability to blend half-spoken and half-sung phrases, Hunt performed well. She was not an outstanding singer but used her tone effectively. On the B-side is a tune called 'Hot Rod Poppa' which is a much heavier, bluesy rocker in which Hunt lays down a far more confrontational, throatier vocal, in the mould of a Tina Turner or Etta James, and while she doesn't have quite their visceral power, she rides the pounding backbeat and funky pentatonic basslines with a level of don't-mess-with-me attitude that enables her to deliver the lyric with threatening grit. The composer of 'Hot Rod Poppa' was Marc Bolan, the English singer whose outlandish imagery and grandiose melodies gave birth to what became known as 'glam rock', and with whom Hunt had a brief but intense relationship.

Hunt's musical output was consolidated by the input of other talented individuals. Her producers were Tony Visconti, fresh from working on David Bowie's 1968 single 'In the Heat of the Morning', and Gus Dudgeon, noted for his collaborations with singer-songwriter Elton John. Over the next two years, Hunt continued to record songs and in 1971 released her debut album *Woman Child*, which provided an effective summary of her artistic journey to date. Retaining the blues-rock and soul ingredients of her debut single, the album had a string of covers from theatre and pop – 'Let The Sunshine In' from *Hair*; The Troggs's 'Wild Thing'; Bolan's 'Stacey Grove' and 'Desdemona'; Traffic's 'No Face No Name No Number', Paul Simon's 'Keep the Customer Satisfied', Bob Dylan's 'You Ain't

Goin Nowhere' and The Supremes's 'My World Is Empty Without You'. Hunt was able to pull together this breadth of material across stylistic lines – folk, rock, R&B – to make *Woman Child* an enjoyable album not least because of the consistent quality of her vocals as well as the strength of the highly eclectic repertoire.

Her next set, released in 1973, marked a significant change. She asserted herself much more thoroughly. *Attention! Marsha Hunt!* unveiled a new band, Marsha Hunt's 22, but more importantly it marked the singer's debut as a composer. She penned 'Will They Still' and co-wrote three other songs with guitarist, Hugh Burns, out of the ten on the album, which was significant because most black women artists were still expected to accept material provided by male producers. No song makes clearer Hunt's agenda than the excellent 'Man to Woman'. Over a hearty post-Motown stomp, she addresses gender relations head on, singing: 'You want me to cook at five o'clock/you want me to wash your dirty socks' – as well as calling out self-indulgent patriarchal infidelity (while also probably taking a swipe at sexual abuse within the music industry): 'You wanna sit watchin'' the telly/rubbin the belly of some young girl supplied for fun.' As the song unfolds, Hunt becomes more emphatic, stating 'I won't rearrange my hair. I won't powder my underwear/ I won't stoop to shave my legs, I don't care how much you beg' – words in tune with the burgeoning women's liberation movement of the early 1970s. She is also bluntly sarcastic: 'I ain't read a bible baby, but you sure ain't superman.' Whilst the song ends on a conciliatory note – 'We can talk we don't have to shout / We better work something out/Man to woman' – this is a rousing feminist anthem that has largely slipped under the radar. Commercially, *Woman Child* and *Attention! Marsha Hunt!*, both reissued in Germany as *Desdemona* and *Marsha Hunt*, respectively, had more success in Europe than in Britain, and the singer did not record again for a number of years, focusing on raising the daughter she had with Mick Jagger as a single parent. Unfortunately, her private life became the lens through she was largely viewed, deflecting attention from her artistic achievements. It is far easier to speculate on Hunt as the inspiration for 'Brown Sugar' than to discuss her song-writing ability.

Hunt and Jagger may have had a real mutual attraction, but as P.P. Arnold, who also had relationships with several white rock stars, including Jagger and Rod Stewart, pointed out: 'Mick used to make me laugh, I mean he was always trying to talk black and walk black, and acting all black all the time… But I knew he was never gonna marry a black woman.'[8] The perception of non-white females as exotic objects of desire was firmly entrenched in the eyes of some. Miscegenation was an issue.

Indeed, the hot looking 'spade chick', a term used in *Two Gentlemen Sharing* (1969), an important British film on race, society and sexuality, stood as a fantasy to be indulged in private rather than be recognised in the public domain. Arnold found that out to her chagrin when travelling back to England with the Stones after a gig in Glasgow. The glamour of a limo ride with white rock royalty did not cushion the emotional bumps in the road as the party rolled towards Gretna Green, a village on the border. She reports the in-car conversation: "'It's okay to go out with coloured girls", someone said and everyone started to laugh, "but you can't take them home to meet your mother." I could feel their laughter and my hackles raising all at the same time. "And you certainly can't marry one!" I guess it was meant to be amusing but I went OFF. I was all the way back in Watts in full-on Marty Cole defensive mode, cursing them all: "Fuck all you motherfuckers!"'[9]

Love Jones
The subject of interracial relationships was topical, as musical theatre hits such as *Catch My Soul*, in which Arnold had appeared, made clear. Another notable vocalist who was part of the American cast of the show, as well as that of *Hair*, was Gloria Jones, an African American singer who came to Britain in the early 1970s. Cincinatti-born and Los Angeles-raised, Jones had formed a gospel group, the COGIC Singers with the renowned organist-vocalist, Billy Preston. She also made a name for herself as a writer for Motown with an impressive list of composer or co-composer credits for several of the label's major stars, including The Supremes, The Commodores, Gladys Knight & The Pips and The Four Tops. As a performer, Jones maintained the connection with Motown and released *Share My Love*, an excellent album of material that she either wrote or co-wrote with the legendary arranger, Paul Riser, and with Janie Bradford, one of the authors of the R&B classic 'Money'. Jones had substantial melodic and vocal skills, as revealed on lushly scored ballads such as 'Old Love, New Love', which she sang with the kind of judicious subtleties of phrasing and breathing space to give pathos to the song. But despite its high quality, Jones's album made very little impact commercially, primarily through lack of promotion, because she opted to spend time in Germany in order to help her then English boyfriend to finish a record of his own. She had decided to follow her heart.

The man with whom Jones had a personal and musical relationship was Marc Bolan. Jones had sung backing vocals for Bolan at a high-profile concert he performed at Winterland in San Francisco, and then became an important member of both his touring and studio band, playing clavinet and adding rich harmonies to his idiosyncratic lead. Jones appeared on *Zinc Alloy and the Hidden Riders of Tomorrow* and Bolan's *Zip Gun*, two albums that cemented the reputation of Bolan and his band T-Rex as new stars in the British pop firmament. Bolan's material already reflected the influence of blues and R&B and Jones's input enhanced that further, lending an element of soulfulness to his often esoteric compositions.

Jones actually sang lead on a sparkly, keyboard-led T-Rex version of Otis Redding's 'Sitting on the Dock of the Bay', but it featured only on the B-side of the single 'Dreamy Lady' that was not released until the mid-1970s, several years after it was recorded. Why the song was omitted from any of the studio albums is anybody's guess, but it does hint at how Bolan's record label and management saw the place of Jones within his development. One of the few models in Britain for a white pop ensemble with a white male and black female singer was Blue Mink, discussed above. But there was no sense of sexual tension between the band's vocalists as there would have surely been had Jones been asked to perform duets with Bolan. Lest we forget, Simon Napier-Bell revealed that eyebrows had been raised when he attempted to do just that with Diane Ferraz & Nicky Scott in the late 60s. The extent to which society had moved on was ambiguous.

The Jones-Bolan union ended in the most tragic circumstances when he was killed after the Mini Jones was driving struck a tree in Barnes, south west London, and she was left to raise their son Rolan as a single mother. Later, Jones pursued an interesting path as an artist, making eclectic solo albums such as *Vixen* and *Windstorm* which contained both her own compositions and several that were co-written with Bolan. Despite that dark chapter in her life, Jones's career had redemptive moments. Her song, 'Tainted Love', made in 1964, was discovered and elevated to anthem status in the early 1970s by DJs such as Richard Searling, who would become a key figure in what was known as 'Northern Soul'. Venues such as Wigan Casino, Twisted Wheel in Manchester and Blackpool Mecca hosted dance sessions where obscure singles by African American artists that had not achieved mainstream success were particularly revered. The desire of club-goers to 'keep the faith' in this kind of sound is one of the great curiosities in the history of the appreciation of Black music in Britain. It came complete with a codified aesthetic, from distinctive styles of dress, above all tight vests and loose flares, to tribalistic badges that professed allegiance to specific venues, and highly acrobatic, adrenalin-fuelled dance steps. Appearances by U.S. icons like Major Lance, who sang to an ecstatic audience at The Torch, Stoke-on-Trent in 1971, only upped the fervour. At the time the venue deemed itself 'the best soul club in Britain.'

Live shows aside, the lifeblood of Northern Soul was record collecting, in which the rarity of a disc largely determined its desirability and price. Rubbing out the names of an artist and title on a label, so as to keep it a hidden gem (something which Jamaican DJs had done in the 1950s), simply added to the mythology around certain tunes, which ignited feverish debate. A 45" that could not be found was one that had to be heard. It was a double-edged sword. On the one hand, Northern Soul adepts were obsessive to the point of pedantry. On the other, the scene had a wealth of knowledge about Black music that unearthed several inspirational tunes over the years, some further enshrined by sampling.[10] Not least, through her 'lost' single, 'Tainted Love', Gloria Jones became a 'Queen of Northern Soul', a voice from Los Angeles that provided the soundtrack to nights of frantic dancefloor action in Greater Manchester.

Dynamite Doris
The final member of the group of African American women expatriates who became involved in British music was Doris Troy. She left her native New York for London in 1969 where she sang backing vocals for several British rock and pop superstars from the Rolling Stones and Pink Floyd to Nick Drake and Kevin Ayers. Heard by many punters, and her presence certainly felt, Troy remained unrecognised for some time. Musicians were aware of her talent and she was, like Madeleine Bell, much in demand. Her credits as a backing vocalist are substantial and include work on landmark moments in rock such as Pink Floyd's *Dark Side of The Moon* and the Rolling Stones 'You Can't Always Get What You Want'. In any case Troy was also a recording artist in her own right who had done important work prior to her arrival in the UK.

Born in the Bronx to a Bajan preacher father and African American mother, Troy initially sang only gospel because of the prohibition of blues-based music in the household, but she later moved over to R&B and soul. She was part of the original line-up of The Sweet Inspirations alongside the legendary Dionne Warwick, and she also provided backing vocals for Warwick after she went solo, as well as for Solomon Burke and for The Drifters, all stars on the increasingly influential Atlantic label. Furthermore, Troy enjoyed major success when a song that she co-wrote and performed, 'Just One Look', made the top ten of the Billboard chart, and its sumptuous melody was given further endorsement when it was covered by several talented soul and pop artists, including Major Lance and Bryan Ferry.

Although Troy did not stop working as a backing vocalist, she recorded notable solo albums, none more so than her eponymous 1970 set that was co-produced by herself and George Harrison of the Beatles, issued on their own imprint Apple and enhanced by the presence of 'famous friends', such as guitarist Eric Clapton. *Doris Troy* is a fabulous synthesis of the dominant strains of black popular music of the period, particularly because it foregrounds soul's dual foundations of gospel, in the scintillating arrangement of the traditional 'Jacob's Ladder' and the blues, in the electrifying original 'Give Me Back My Dynamite'. These two songs could not be more different in terms of conceptual premise and lyrical detail, but both exemplified the desire of Black female artists to speak their minds, as part of a lineage that can be traced back to 1920s pioneers such as Bessie Smith. While 'Jacob's Ladder' is a wonderfully joyous submission to the power of the Lord, and the long road to redemption, 'Dynamite' is a ferocious challenge to the self-indulgence and financial impropriety of a male lover who thinks he can make a swipe for Troy and her money:

> Every time that I see you/You keep comin' on strong
> Got your hand in my pocket/When you know that it's wrong

Although it has less detailed observations than Marsha Hunt's 'Man to Woman', the song shares the same current of feminist self-assertion. After all, this was a world in which casual sexual aggression, from a pat on the backside to a grope of the breast or forceful kiss, was far more 'normalised' than it is today, post '#MeToo'. The energy exploding in 'Give Me Back My Dynamite' presents Troy as a strong, resolute woman who makes it clear that any kind of serial infidelity will no longer fly, because she is 'so tired of y'all messing round'. Like Aretha, she's just asking for her propers.

Troy went on to cut other fine albums, such as *Stretchin' Out*, and added to the immense contribution made by African American women to British pop in the 1970s. She and Madeleine Bell were both backing singers on *Let It Bleed*, one of the best records made by the Rolling Stones, and it is perhaps fitting that is was another superlative soul sister, the great Merry Clayton, who helped make 'Gimme Shelter' a highpoint in the Jagger-Richards songbook through the sumptuously operatic improvisations she pulled off when she was called to a studio in Los Angeles at very short notice. The lyrical context of the song, with its ghastly disclosure that 'Rape and murder, it's just a shot away' could not be any farther away from the New Orleans church where Clayton learned how to sing, but her performance remains an important example of the ability of gospel-reared musicians to transcend the most profane setting through sheer artistry.

Perhaps unsurprisingly, Merry Clayton also played a major role on the soundtrack of *Performance*,[11] the 1970 British movie that starred Mick Jagger and James Fox, as interchangeable rock star and gangster in a twisted and sinister misadventure that sucked the life out of any hippie idealism. It was Clayton's majestic voice on the song 'Turner's Murder' that brought a redemptive light to the unremittingly chilling darkness of the story.

Between them, Clayton, Troy, Bell, Jones, Hunt and Arnold have sufficiently large discographies and stories to fill an entire book, as the latter's autobiography indicates. Pressing questions remain on why they were not given a much bigger platform for their talents, and, particularly, not allowed greater agency and decision-making power over their professional destinies. This state of affairs still exists. The imbalance has not been fully redressed.

Despite the struggles endured by Arnold in particular, there was solace to be drawn from the informal sisterhood that occasionally propped her up, as she moved between America and Britain throughout the 1970s to try and get both her life and career on track. As Arnold records, 'When I was out in LA and really unhappy and going through a lot, Doris (Troy) picked me up and took me to meet a friend in an apartment just off Sunset Boulevard. She said there's somebody I really want you to meet, and listen to. It was Nina Simone. So I sat down with Nina and Doris and they just told me about black women in the music industry being ripped off. Just listening to these two legends made me realise how hard it was. They explained about the industry, about publishing and writing, and that was a big lesson for me because I just didn't know about any of that at the time, but I needed to. I thank them for that.'[12]

Notes

1. See Loving vs Virginia, 388, U.S. Supreme Court rules that laws banning interracial marriage are in breach of the 14th amendment.
2. The 1974 American film version of *Catch My Soul* features two great singers Richie Havens and Tony Joe White. It was directed by Patrick McGoohan, the British actor famous for his role in the cult television series *The Prisoner*. McGoohan also appeared in a previous Othello-inspired film, 1962's *All Night Long*, set on the London jazz scene. His character was based on Iago.
3. P.P. Arnold, *Soul Survivor: The Autobiography* (Nine-Eight, 2022).
4. Interview with the author, June 2022.
5. *Kafunta* (Immediate) 1968 has a striking cover with Arnold looking regal in a resplendent African headdress and make up.
6. Interview with the author, June 2022.
7. Arnold also appeared in Lloyd-Webber's *Starlight Express* in 1984.
8. Interview with the author, June 2022.
9. P.P. Arnold, *Soul Survivor: The Autobiography*, p.106.
10. I'm thinking of Just Brothers' 'Sliced Tomatoes', a hugely popular Northern soul track that decisively boosted British producer Fat Boy Slim's career in 1998 when he sampled it on 'The Rockafeller Skank'.
11. The soundtrack of *Performance*, (1970), a quintessentially British movie, is dominated by American artists, from Ry Cooder, Bernard Krause and Buffy Sainte-Marie to The Last Poets, Randy Newman and Merry Clayton. Mick Jagger is the only featured Brit.
12. Interview with the author, June, 2022.

7 FUNKIN' FOR JAMAICA... GUYANA, ST. VINCENT... AND AFRICA.

Cymande is part of an old West Indian nursery rhyme. It was a nursery rhyme about a dove and a pigeon and at the end of the day the dove came out the winner, so that's how we chose the dove as the symbol of peace and love.
– Cymande bassist, Steve Scipio, on the origins of the band's name.

Every performance was accompanied by a kind of prayer to Jah, with the drums in true African roots style, mixed in with Nyabinghi, the repeating drums, the tribal sound and the kind of very African way of singing. This was what was different about their sound... and they had loud guitars with wah wahs!
– Dennis Bovell on Cymande live.

They had the bingo and you had to stop playing halfway through.
– Cymande drummer, Steve Kelly, on gigging in Whitley Bay.

Funky See, Funky Do
Throughout the late 1960s and 1970s, many Black British groups moved between different genres, perhaps for the practical reason of reaching a wider range of potential consumers as well as expressing a genuine interest in new stylistic territory, and not wanting to be pigeonholed. Not least, this was a period when innovations in Black music spread rapidly from their places of origin. Reggae, the popular music of Jamaica, was reaching the rest of the world and, as noted in Chapter 4, was giving succour to members of the Black British community as an articulation of revolt and the call for racial pride. The music was also exerting an influence on other genres. Songs such as Johnny Nash's 'I can See Clearly Now', The Staple Singers 'I'll Take You There' and Paul Simon's 'Mother and Child Reunion' made it clear that reggae's rhythmic characteristics, its particular handling of pulse and time, and its sensual atmospherics, were seeping into the vocabulary of soul and folk-pop singers. The sound of Kingston had really started to go inna foreign. Then again, there had long been a two-way influence between Jamaican and African American music. Soul was something that Jamaicans still listened to, as is obvious from the large

number of reggae cover versions of Stax and Motown singles – all evidence of the continual pace of change and interchange in Black music.

The question of what rhythm would make a crowd dance had a new thing called funk as its answer. Gifted drummers such as Idris Muhammad (1939-2014) who moved between soul (supporting Roberta Flack) and jazz (with Lou Donaldson and Horace Silver), and Clyde Stubblefield (1943-2017) who played with Otis Redding before he moved to James Brown's band, were among funk's prime originators. They had been injecting expertly timed syncopation into their snare patterns to produce a marked sense of nervy, agitated percussive energy in the central beat of a piece and gradually this became nothing less than an organising principle for visionaries such as James Brown, who introduced invigorating, overlapping polyrhythms into his music. The use of crisp, raking guitar figures, with dissonant 'chicken scratch' effects and screechy brass stabs and vocal screams made songs such as 'Cold Sweat' sound like a series of carefully co-ordinated electric shocks and surges. Ultimately, funk lent to black music a much harder, tougher, rougher edge than soul did.

As was the case with reggae, there was a global response to this latest sound, with many groups on the African continent embracing Brown's vocabulary and blending it with local rhythmic traditions to produce joyously complex dance music, a process that was given momentum by artists such as Cameroon saxophonist Manu Dibango. His hugely influential worldwide hit 'Soul Makossa' had shown that this trans-continental exchange of energy could yield commercial success as well as artistic bounty. Funk went international. This was a follow-up to the earlier embrace of R&B and soul in West and Central Africa. The 'Soul to Soul'[1] revue had taken Ike & Tina Turner, Les McCann & Eddie Harris, Wilson Pickett and others to Black Star Square in Accra, Ghana in 1971, and three years later James Brown appeared in Kinshasa, Zaire.

There was also a considerable movement of musicians between the 'Motherland' and Europe, as a result of Africa's changing socio-political conditions, including armed conflict. For instance, during the mid-1960s, the thriving highlife scene in British cities such as Manchester had been stymied by the outbreak of the Biafran Civil war in Nigeria, because several players had returned home to take up arms for different sides in a religiously, ethnically charged, post-colonial struggle that led to high casualties through famine as well as combat. But the war came to an end in 1970 and there was also an oil boom as the output of crude oil expanded and huge revenues started to flood in. As a result, major investment bolstered the Lagos arm of corporations such as EMI, which thought nothing of dispatching Lagos staff to the legendary Abbey Road studios in London to observe the Beatles making a masterpiece, or financing a number of recording sessions in London for maverick Nigerians such as saxophonist Fela Kuti. He had moved away from the high-life music he'd played in the 1960s and was now filtering funk into symphonic, horn-laden works that would eventually transcend known genres and become an entity of its very own, Afrobeat.

Fela's *London Scene*, which was recorded at Abbey Road, displays an important stage in the evolution towards Afrobeat; it shows the skill with which Kuti was able to capture something of James Brown's brazen, barbed aggression and create a distinctively Nigerian idiom, aided by Tony Allen's agile drumming. Some songs swooned with sensuality while others, bristling with anger, were fearlessly confrontational, spitting out diatribes in pidgin and Yoruba against corrupt neocolonial elites, as well as the toxic legacy of colonialism. It was a bravery that Fela paid for with state harassment and severe beatings, as well as the death of his mother.

Britain's continuing role as a hub of the international music industry drew many other players from across Africa. Some groups migrated from Africa to London on the back of success in their country of origin and endorsements from the BBC World Service, which ran competitions to find the best local groups that could then be heard globally. There was no lack of talent to discover. For example, a significant Nigerian band was The Funkees, the spelling of whose name made a clear statement of their embrace of the latest African American dance music and their intent to customise it. Led by the excellent percussionist, Sonny Akpan, they started out in the city of Aba, attracting faithful audiences at local clubs when, following the end of the Biafran war, nightlife became possible again. The band featured two guitarists (Harry Mosco and Jake Solio) whose gritty rhythms locked in effectively with dense layers of percussion and organ. Their buoyant, very danceable sound struck a chord with Africans based in London when the group relocated there in the early 1970s.

Other Nigerians, who either relocated to the UK or recorded here, included Blo who, like Fela, collaborated with Cream drummer Ginger Baker, and Super Combo. From Kenya, came Matata who had formed in the 1960s in Nairobi, where they established themselves at a club called Brilliant, before heading to London in the early 1970s. They landed a deal with President, the label which had enjoyed major success with The Equals, and cut two fine albums, *Air Fiesta* and *Independence*, which had a bustling, bongo-heavy sound that was a near perfect union of James Brown and Manu Dibango. Monster groove tracks such as 'Wanna Do My Thing' were outstanding.

If Africa had gone funky, Caribbean musicians in Britain were not left behind. Vocalist-guitarist Bobby Tench and drummer Godfrey McClean, both of Trinidadian heritage, went on to launch the much-loved London combo Gonzalez, before Tench opted to leave and join superstar guitarist Jeff Beck. Gonzalez had something of a revolving door of players – including saxophonist Mick Eve, guitarist Robert Ahwai, percussionist

Lennox Langton, bassist DeLisle Harper and vocalist George Chandler – though the changing line-up still managed to gel on songs that drew together funk, jazz and Afro-Cuban rhythms and gave space for players to stretch out and improvise.

That attitude reflected what had been an important part of the London scene for many years – the jam session. At venues in Soho such as Bag O'Nails and Flamingo, many players had taken part in impromptu sessions when blues, rock and jazz musicians congregated, and when funk started to make an impact, Black and multi-racial bands essayed the style at venues such as the Speakeasy, the Pheasantry and the Cricketers among others. One of the most important focal points was the first floor of Ronnie Scott's jazz club, simply known as Upstairs at Ronnie's. It became an invaluable thoroughfare for singers, guitarists, bassists, keyboardists and horn players for whom performance there was the means to advance musically and find partnership with others that could then possibly translate to the studio. This was an informal incubator; many unnamed funk combos played there.

Gonzalez cut 'Funky Frith Street' as an oblique acknowledgment of such a nurturing environment. Just over a minute and a half long, the tune was an obvious insider reference to Ronnie's club. With its crackling guitar, strutting bass and honking saxophone, the piece gave a snapshot of the scene that had fostered the growth of Gonzalez and other British bands. The beat was straight out of the playbook of the JBs, James Brown's revered backing group, which had also notched up several hits of its own and exerted an immense influence around the world.

In the midst of all this fine music, an important question beckoned: could there be a homegrown British funk that broke free of the vocabulary of its US progenitors? For all their undeniable excellence, Gonzalez and many of their peers remained largely moulded on an American template. By contrast, London-based African ensembles exploring funk such as Matata achieved an immediate and tangible difference, which was their decision not to sing in English on all their material (indeed Matata meant 'trouble' in Swahili), their songs were more oriented to Africa than the UK. There was also a band whose members were from the West Indies and who would create a peerless Black British songbook.

Bra Gonna Work It Out
Cymande was the band that produced a strain of British funk that ingeniously blended not just African American and African Caribbean musical elements but also the spiritualities of the time, including Rastafarianism, which stamped a strong identity on their work. This was a group that drew on the core principles of jazz and soul but also used calypso rhythms on much of their material and, most importantly, managed to knit them

together so as to make something that expressed the complexity of their lived experience and creative dynamism as post-colonial migrants in the UK. They were unique.

Between the early and mid-1970s, the band made three albums that are high water marks in Black British, indeed British music: *Cymande*, *Second Time Around* and *Promised Heights*. The wealth of superbly written songs on these recordings, as well as the consistently high standard of performance, have more than stood the test of time. This was a pan-Caribbean ensemble that had members from Jamaica, Guyana and St. Vincent, though they became indelibly associated with south London where they settled. Also notable was the fact that the band had a wide range of age-related experience. The youngest, such as drummer Sam Kelly, had come to England as a seven-year-old, while the elders, like percussionist Ray King, was 23 when he arrived. Members of the band saw this blend of youth and maturity and the co-existence of individuals at different stages of development as essential building block for their music. 'Even though we were all Black and from the Caribbean,' noted lead vocalist Joey Dee, 'we all left the Caribbean with different experiences and that gave us a good concept. We were just the right combination of people to deliver it.'[3]

The formation of the band was haphazard. Guitarist Patrick Patterson, bassist Steve Scipio and saxophonist Michael 'Bami' Rose were in another outfit and found themselves stranded one night when the drummer couldn't make a gig at the Oval House, Kennington. Sam Kelly, who lived nearby and was on their radar, received a call to step in, and everything clicked, even though Kelly recalls that the music was 'quite complicated'. That may well have been because the wider backstory of the players crossed stylistic lines – Patterson, Scipio and Rose had been members of the band led by legendary Nigerian percussionist-bandleader Ginger Johnson and a jazz-rock combo, Meter. Patterson had also played with reggae favourites, The Rudies, so there was a broad vocabulary to draw on. Members of the group also took a keen interest in the cutting edge of Black music in America. That meant serious listening to Miles Davis's groundbreaking experiments with electric sounds, as well as to the politically charged, mystical musings of multi-reed player Rahsaan Roland Kirk. One of his great signature tunes, the ironic, deeply provocative 'Volunteered Slavery' was a song Cymande covered in its live shows. Wisely, the band took a patient, organic approach to its craft and they brought cohesion to the disparate elements they drew on with endless days of jamming in a basement in Brixton. Then gigs started to come, and a buzz about the group reached the loose community of followers of soul-funk combos in London. When they were heard rehearsing in a club in Soho by the producer John Schroeder (who had enjoyed major success with the instrumental easy-listening group, Sounds Orchestral, as well as Helen Shapiro), he was immediately taken by their sound. 'I found myself caught up in an atmosphere of electric excitement,' he recalls. 'My brain pummelled with music and rhythms which had an incessant infectiousness.'[4] His ear was drawn to 'the drums and bass... those two guys had an incredible thing between them, they just felt each other. Sam Kelly the drummer played with a lovely rhythmic feel and Steve Scipio, the bassist, fitted in the groove.[5] Schroeder offered to produce the band's debut album.

Cymande was licensed and distributed in by America by Janus, a subsidiary of the iconic Chicago label, Chess, which had released music by blues, R&B and soul icons such as Bo Diddley, Etta James and Ramsey Lewis. Cymande's lead single, 'The Message', from their first album made the Billboard charts, piquing enough interest for the group to tour America as a support act to star vocalist, Al Green. The woozy, wavering guitar riff at the heart of the track had a charm that found favour with African American audiences and earned the band the honour of appearing at the iconic Apollo Theater in Harlem. In almost fairytale fashion, the Black British debutants found themselves with a minor hit that put them in the company of several major names. 'The Message' had the distinction of being the only British song to feature on *Superbad*, a compilation of American artists released by budget label K-Tel that capitalised on the soul-funk market and licensed Marvin Gaye, Curtis Mayfield and Stevie Wonder.

That auspicious start to Cymande's life as recording artists did not lead to sustained commercial success, and their return to Britain after the stint in America was a sobering one. Sales of subsequent albums were modest and gigs were restricted to small or mid-size venues that were a far cry from what they had experienced in the USA.

Everything about the band distinguished them from the bulk of their peers, laying bare a creative identity that was exciting and confusing for the way it straddled borders. Here were a bunch of West Indian musicians in South London who created a synthesis of funk, jazz and Caribbean folk music that was hard to categorize. It was a crown of achievement but also a millstone around the group's neck. Cymande didn't really fit anywhere. They can be filed under soul-funk, but their aesthetic also had an undeniable pronounced 'island' flavour, a rootsy sensibility that related to their lives prior to moving to Britain. Yet reggae they were not.

Ultimately Cymande made a kind of modern Black British music that might be termed Progressive Caribbean, insofar as the songs – based on strong rhythms, rich melodies and enticing vocal choruses – could also develop into intricate arrangements that defied the conventions of pop, at least the fare deemed suitable for radio play. Cymande had their own thing. Given their producer John Schroeder's background in the lighter, classically inflected end of pop, it is notable that the music was in no way sanitised or softened. Perhaps he brought a certain clarity to Cymande because the scoring of the horn section may have been a touch tighter, yet the essence of the group sound was very much intact, primarily because of the band's distinctive instrumentation. Cymande had three saxophones: one tenor, Peter Serreo, and two altos, Michael 'Bami' Rose (who also doubled on flute) and Derek Gibbs, who doubled on soprano – and no brass whatsoever. The absence of trumpets and trombones meant that there was often less brightness in the timbres, so the reeds came across as beautifully airy, particularly when they entered the upper register. The sound was sensual. Equally significant was the fact that the group did not have a pianist and this created more space in the overall landscape of the music, which was well anchored by a super solid unit of drums, bass and guitar. When the congas, bongos, cowbells, shakers and other percussion launched a barrage of polyrhythms, the groove was redolent of West Indian and African processional traditions. All the hand-drums were ancestral.

One could describe Cymande's music as bonafide street funk in the sense there was no excess gloss or polish. Yet for all that, many of their compositions had great attention to detail. One of the seminal pieces in the Cymande songbook, 'Bra', makes this abundantly clear. It is a finely honed gem. Taken at a leisurely mid-tempo, the piece opens with a stately, dignified horn motif that soars over a tightly marshalled funk backbeat, with a guitar scraping away in the background before fading out altogether on the first verse, so the music gains an unexpected additional clarity. Drums and bass lock into a punchy central syncopation, but it is really the percussion that moves centre stage, bubbling away in a kind of rousing implied double time, injecting a vigour into the movement of the song and contrasting with vocals that are relaxed rather than emphatic. The music intensifies on the chorus, announcing, 'But it's alright we can still go on' as the bass now rolls forward, and the guitar returns to give more grit and gristle to the track. A delicately mapped alto saxophone solo, full of subtle light and shade, is heard before the second verse and chorus. Next comes the breakdown. Horns, guitar and vocals all drop out and the band reduces to its core axis of drums and bass. The bass jumps through an octave with all the fierce intent of a boxer landing an uppercut, before it skips back down to its root note, heartily punching a fourth on the way, and in the eight beats it takes for the movement to unfold, the essence of funk as a form of studious ambush, irresistible propulsion and relentless attack is calmly distilled. Super tight, super tough, super bad.

Then a quite magical thing happens as the line starts to repeat. We hear a high, crisp metallic ping that suggests a cowbell, but there is too much cut-through, too much of a piercing quality in the tone for that to be the case, and as the sound becomes more prominent, one guesses that this is a 'brake drum', or hubcap of an old car, such as was used in some of the earliest ensembles to march through the streets of Trinidad at Carnival. In any case, the joyously skipping patterns impart a prominent calypso flavour, while a bass drum pumps out a steady 4/4 beat underneath. Here, the whole geo-cultural identity of this part of the arrangement stretches between Black America, Africa and the West Indies, as if Cymande had somehow managed to morph into a composite of funk group, sabar troupe and steel band. Yet they created all this in a south London basement.

Part of 'Bra''s appeal lies the fact that the percussion does not play the same riffs, but flits between short and long phrases, bringing improvised variation to bear upon the steady metronomic drive of the bass drum, creating a delicious tension between the upper register line that is loose and fluctuating, and a low one that is bolted right down. It is one of the great passages of polyrhythmic interplay of modern Black music and prefigures new genres that would not materialise until some two or so decades after 'Bra' was recorded. With the benefit of hindsight, we can hear stirrings of the house revolution of the later 1980s, when producers were looking for the perfect beat to sample and manipulate into electronic dance music that would capture the imagination of the latest generation of clubbers. That was precisely what Vaughan Mason, leader of the studio project Raze achieved when he sampled 'Bra' to create 'Jack the Groove', which was a massive hit on both sides of the Atlantic in 1986.

Cymande's relevance for the future did not stop there. Another one of its irresistible compositions, 'The Message', built on a perambulating pentatonic bassline and soothing vocal melodies, provided the breakbeat for McSolaar's 1991 hit 'Bouge De La', which stands as a foundational track in the history of French hip-hop, helping to cement the art of 'crate digging' and sampling as a global phenomenon. Several other American rap groups such as The Fugees, De La Soul and EPMD all followed suit and raided Cymande's catalogue. The band helped to build the future from their past.

Wings of a Dove
On top of their skills as purveyors of superior grooves, Cymande also showed considerable ambition on extended works such as 'Dove', a ten-minute piece with a deeply haunting refrain, guitar improvisations and sparkling eastern-style flute motifs, which leaned much more towards jazz than funk. The symbolism of the title was part of the visual, cultural and spiritual identity of the band. The sleeve of the album *Cymande* featured a painting by bassist Steve Scipio that depicted a dove perched on the head of a Rastaman, its wings spreading out around his eyes to fringe his face with the most curious, white-feathered locks. Many traditions were tied together in this quite striking image. As Scipio explained:

Cymande is part of an old West Indian nursery rhyme, where there was a phrase in the nursery rhyme that used to be 'band cymande', and we did toy with naming ourselves 'band cymande' but we thought that was too long. It was a nursery rhyme about a dove and a pigeon and at the end of the day the dove came out the winner, so that's how we chose the dove as the symbol of peace and love.[6]

Vocalist Joey Dee had another take on the matter that reflected the frequent sound-play of West Indian nation language, and how a single written word could reflect patterns of speech, particularly one with a distinct rhythmic character. 'The name came about by "see dem man deh", which is total creole, so when you played around with it you got Cymande.'[7]

While these insights show how strongly the band was rooted in the culture of Caribbean folk, perhaps even more important were the reflections of Rastafarianism practiced by percussionist Pablo Gonsales. These became one of the defining elements of the band's identity. In fact, Cymande knew small groups of Rastafarians scattered around south London who gave them direct knowledge of the Jamaican-born belief system and influenced the group's use of Nyabinghi drums and rhythms that acted as a potent accompaniment to the gatherings to give praise to 'Jah'.

This led Cymande into new territory. The combination of a vocabulary that was becoming associated with Bob Marley, Burning Spear and others in the roots reggae movement, and the beguiling hybrid of funky basslines, jazz chops and heavily-layered, Rastafarian percussion made songs such as 'Zion I' unique. As much they might claim African American 'art music' as a source of inspiration, and had reprised Rahsaan Roland Kirk, the band took the important decision to record only original material. They also placed Rastafarianism at the heart of much of their lyrical content, which is why, referring to the Nyabinghi drum, they coined 'Nyah rock' to define their aesthetic as something entirely of their own making.

This struck a chord with British reggae bands who had the same spiritual leanings. As Dennis Bovell, leader of Matumbi, recalls, Cymande was deadly serious about their identity. Their drumming, their replacement of colonial-era standard English with Rasta idioms such as 'I man dread' and 'I man beard', and their engagement with current popular music technology – pedals and effects – made Cymande something that could not be heard elsewhere. Dennis Bovell stated that '(Percussionist) Pablo Gonsales influenced Matumbi a lot in Rastafarian culture. Every performance was accompanied by a kind of prayer to Jah, with the drums in true African roots style, mixed in with Nyabinghi, the repeating drums, the tribal sound and a very African way of singing. This was what was different about their sound… and they had loud guitars with wah wahs!'[8]

With the bass right in the foreground of the mix on many tunes, it is not surprising that Cymande's sound struck a chord with West Indian artists and audiences who shared the same references as Bovell. In many ways, Cymande's contribution to the evolution of Black music in Britain can be summarised by the synthesis described above, which was by no means in keeping with the stratifications of the record business at that time.

Trawl at random through the Cymande songbook, from 'Bra' to 'Zion I' to 'Rickshaw', 'Fug', 'Bird' or 'Crawshay', and what you hear is a band that had found a personal vocabulary borne of many elements. This created a core sound with a number of sub-strands: instrumentals, vocal numbers, funk tracks, soul laments, Caribbean folk tunes and spoken word passages that lent the music a strong sense of ritual. There was the socially conscious sound of 'Brothers on the Slide' in which a clipped, tense rhythm proved the backdrop for a warning to Black people not to become stereotypes who end up 'wrecking your folks' name'. This was one of the few Cymande tracks to betray an American influence, specifically that of Curtis Mayfield. On the other hand, the group was resoundingly 'island' on compositions such as 'Pon De Dungle', 'Breezeman' and 'Sheshamani.' The sound of Chicago this was not. All this placed them in an uncommon position on the cultural map in the early 1970s Britain. Black communities, especially West Indians, had always enjoyed a range of African American and African Caribbean music as well as pop that came from both sides of the Atlantic, but the impact of reggae and sound system culture meant that there was an intriguing relationship developing between it and various genres such as jazz, soul and funk.

There were differences. If Jamaican artists had freely covered the songs of Mayfield, Stevie Wonder and Booker T & the MGs and others, sound system operators were more selective when it came to deciding if the original versions of any of the above could actually be played alongside the latest reggae tunes that were finding favour. There was a degree of border control, so to speak. A soul-funk band that actually made it across the lines had achieved no meant feat, and, as Dennis Bovell recalls, the most memorable boundary-crosser was Cymande. '"The Message".... that was one of the non-reggae tunes that crossed over into sound system world.'[9]

One size doesn't fit all
This endorsement was not matched by revenue from record sales. So, a steady income had to come from gigging, and this meant the unglamorous labour of loading band and equipment into a Dormobile van and heading from one venue to the next, which could be anything from pubs committed to live music such as The Hope & Anchor in north London, to the college circuit. For Cymande and their peers such as Gonzalez, who also had horn and rhythm sections as well as vocalists, band size was the problem.

Roger Saint Pierre, journalist for the magazine *Blues & Soul*, which documented the era, makes this practical point about the financial pressures faced by groups:

> The nature of funk in those days tended to be six to eight to ten piece bands. It was very hard for them to get paying work because you only had relatively small venues and the kind of money they would pay, once you start spreading it eight or nine ways, there's not a living wage. And that was the real trouble... the London funk scene, there was plenty of music going on, plenty of people around but a lot of them never ever got to gig... They'd be just rehearsing or making records or whatever... But there just weren't the venues that were the right size, because the bands weren't big enough [i.e commercially successful] to fill the huge theatres. On the other hand, they were too big for the little clubs. We've always had that lack of a mid-way venue in London that holds 800 to 1200 people where a band that isn't known nationally can fill the place.[10]

Inevitably the economics of keeping a large combo together took its toll, along with the demands of producing high quality material and finding a consensus among different personalities. Cymande did not make it past the early 1980s, but there were other exponents of soul-funk who recorded with varying degrees of success.

For example, F.B.I., started by singer Root Jackson (see Chapter 1) was a very accomplished combo that lived up to the meaning of its acronym – Funky Bands Incorporated. A nine piece with a rhythm and horn section, fronted by the excellent twin-lead vocals of Jackson and Collette (Bonnie) Wilkinson, a woman with a powerful delivery, they honed their richly detailed sound through three years of doing gigs throughout country. F.B.I. also backed visiting American singers who did not travel with their own musicians, such as Atlantic records icon Percy Sledge, in a way that paralleled the first wave of British reggae artists who accompanied visiting Jamaicans. Such 'pick up' bands had to be competent enough to learn material very quickly, which was also a vital step on the road of progress. In the case of F.B.I., their stock rose sufficiently for them to gain support slots to American soul stars such as Kool & The Gang and UK blues rock legend, Alvin Lee. It was Lee who came across F.B.I. when they made an appearance on a popular kids TV show, *Magpie*, and gave them the chance to record at his own Hook End Manor studio near Reading. The eponymous album *F.B.I.*, cut in the mid-1970s, was a very strong 8-track set with a high standard of writing and arranging, mostly from Jackson, though there was one cover, an accomplished take on Stevie Wonder's 'Keep on Running'. The quality of the engineering also stands out and this is no surprise because the man behind the desk was Chris Kimsey, who went on to produce the Rolling Stones and Jimmy Cliff. There is a particular weightiness in the drums and bass and crisp snap in the horns that provide an excellent dynamic background for the vocals.

F.B.I. were eclectic. Their work had echoes of U.S. pacesetters Fatback and Kool, above all through the jazz leanings of the horns, as can be heard on the slinky strains of 'Bad Deal'. They were also capable of quite majestic numbers like 'Talking About Love', with its delicate shifts of harmony and an atmosphere of deep yearning set to a rippling mid-tempo Latin beat. Most interesting of all was 'The Time is Right to Leave the City', a song which combined potent brass with a skipping calypso rhythm that was a reminder of Jackson's Carriacou heritage. It shows that the band's aesthetic could shift at will, that they were skilled enough to sustain what Jackson called 'the American vibe' while pivoting to other cultural spaces. The bursts of percussion, the hefty barrage of cowbells and woodblocks could convincingly evoke the rich musical traditions of Havana or Nassau as well as New York.

But despite the beauty of their music and their popularity as a live group, F.B.I, a multi-racial band with a female vocalist who was not black, sometimes found itself on the receiving end of racism and sexism, as can be seen in an infamous review of a gig the band did at Dingwalls. Bonnie Wilkinson is described as 'a white girl singer who may not be the best looker but has quite an impressive voice with good range and power.'[11] It is difficult not to wince at the cruelty of the putdown. Was the only positive element of the mention because Wilkinson performed what was not seen as a natural role for white girls? The crassness grates.

Ironically, one thing that stands out in the history of early 1970s British soul-funk was the presence of white solo singers and bands, from around the country, who made excellent Black music. For example, Kokomo comprised Liverpool-born vocalists Frank Collins and Dyan Birch as well as Hertfordshire singer Tony O'Malley, all of whom had been in the close harmony band, Arrival. They made polished, smartly arranged soul, often with a marked inclination towards jazz. Joe Cocker was the Sheffield-born singer who had debuted in the blues, but his gruff, gravelly tone was well suited to hard funk backbeats, as he proved on a pounding mid-tempo song such as 'Woman to Woman', which, as was the case with Cymande, has since become a treasured item for hip-hop acts in the 1990s to sample, such as Ultra Magnetic MCs and EPMD. Carole Grimes was another fine singer-songwriter who moved stealthily between soul, blues, jazz and funk.

But most commercially successful of all was the Average White Band who, hailing from Dundee, carried a name cased in irony and self-deprecation. The group had a well-drilled horn section, two strong lead vocalists in Alan Gorrie and Hamish Stuart and, above all, an ability to write a good tune, such as the instrumental 'Pick Up the Pieces' (clearly influenced by James Brown's band the JBs), which became a million seller in 1974.

They also enjoyed the patronage of the legendary American producer, Arif Mardin, who signed them to the prestigious Atlantic label and matched the consistently high standard of material the band wrote with the input of several grade-A American jazz musicians, such as percussionist Ralph McDonald and saxophonists David 'Fathead' Newman and Michael Brecker, who all did sessions with AWB. Throughout the 1970s, the band grew in stature through collaborations with US soul singer Ben. E King and created a body of work that, like previous examples, has been extensively sampled by hip-hop producers over the past few decades.

Still active to this day, AWB are a British soul-funk band that has stood the test of time, particularly through their ability to renew personnel in the wake of the tragic death of original members such as Robbie McIntosh. Their longevity is a counterpoint to the transience noted elsewhere, though breakups were often followed by the formation of new combos featuring players who were drawn from the ruins of other ensembles. Notable here was Gonzalez, who begat Olympic Runners, a group helmed by producer Mike Vernon and bolstered by the presence of excellent players such as Delisle Harper. Olympic Runners made very palatable soul music in the early 1970s before fading out by the middle of the decade. They were convincing in their adaptation of American templates, and they also showed just how far out on a limb the likes of Cymande had gone by opting to bring such a conspicuous West Indian element into their aesthetic. Indeed, it was the artistic excellence of Olympic Runners, Gonzalez, AWB, F.B.I, Kokomo and several others, that highlighted how Cymande transcended the genre, by proclaiming an Afro-centric spirituality at the heart of its music.

This anecdote from drummer Sam Kelly about a Cymande concert in Whitley Bay near Newcastle in the northeast of England makes it clear they could still be an alien entity for some listeners. 'It was one of those gigs where it was about as far away from London as you could get. They had the bingo and you had to stop playing halfway through. We thought we were gonna die. But it went down a storm. They said…"direct from South Africa" we have this band! If they'd said we were from Brixton, I don't know if it would have gone down so well. They said we were from South Africa… It was one of the best gigs we ever did! We thought it was funny when we were actually introduced. The guy came out with the mike… We're gonna have the bingo… but now directly on stage (I won't do the accent) we have…. Cyanide!'[12]

So here was the reality of life on the road for the most original Black British band of the early 1970s. Their name was toxified, so to speak, in the most unlikely of contexts. Yet the corruption of Cymande to Cyanide is nonetheless strangely, charmingly fortuitous if we think of the quaint consonance that Cyanide has with 'Zion I'.

And nothing could be more humorously fitting than an evening in which a game is played to calls of 'Garden Gate, Harry Tate, One Fat Lady', while music is provided by a group inspired by West Indian nursery rhymes of doves and pigeons, as well as the righteous prophesies of Jah Rastafari.

Notes

1. *Soul to Soul* was issued by Atlantic in 1971 and also features Roberta Flack, the Staple Singers, and Voices of East Harlem.
2. Not to be confused with the American run featuring Gloria Jones.
3. Featured on *Promised Heights: The Story of Cymande*, a radio documentary broadcast on BBC London Live, 30/12/2001 presented by Kevin Le Gendre and produced by Ollie Chase and Ray Paul.
4. Sleeve notes of *Cymande* (Janus) 1972, also reissued on the Sequel record label in 1999.
5. Featured on *Promised Heights: The Story of Cymande*.
6. Ibid.
7. Ibid.
8. Ibid.
9. Ibid.
10. Ibid.
11. Part of the 1970s newspaper cuttings featured on the inner sleeve of the 1992 reissue of F.B.I (*Kongo Dance*).
12. Featured on *Promised Heights: The Story of Cymande*.

8 THE ELEPHANT IS NOT IN THE ROOM (IT'S IN THE SKY)

The combination and the fusions came because we are Africans and we knew the rhythms and the music of Africa, and because we have travelled overseas and listened to a lot of music like jazz, blues, rock. So, ok, if this is the case, these are all our experiences, we will cook it and put it one pot.
— Teddy Osei, founder of Osibisa

That voodoo that you do
Britain may not have had the Jim Crow laws and segregation of the USA, but it's worth looking at black representation in popular culture before claiming any moral high ground. Discriminatory language and attitudes that could be heard and observed in the playground, the sports arena and the shop floor were reflected and reinforced on prime-time television without any sensitivity to the feelings of the 'other '. Racist insults, put-downs and destructive myths were all there in the scripts.

Millions of viewers could tune in to hear the hapless white working-class homeowner, Eddie Booth, blithely call the Trinidadian next door a 'nig nog' in *Love Thy Neighbour*,[1] the 1972 sitcom that dramatised race relations in post-war Britain at a time when immigration had become a toxic part of the political agenda. The fact that the white main character was shown to be an obtuse fool did not erode the implication that a racially mixed street was a problem, and if there was an appeal to the absurdity of some white attitudes in the show's plotlines, this did not disguise the fact that they depended on racist tropes of great ancestry, none more so than voodoo performed naked on an English common.

As if by black magic, that same theme, the 'strange, heathen' religion of Africa, was at the heart of one of the biggest films of 1973, *Live and Let Die*, which became the latest instalment of the James Bond franchise and grossed $161 million at the box office. The movie had a well-crafted score featuring original songs by Paul McCartney, George Martin and the Olympia Brass Band, whose performance of the music of funeral parades shows the deep African Creole elements of New Orleans musical culture. But this is offset by gross racial stereotypes of exotic and terrifying supernatural 'savage rituals', including human sacrifice. Unsurprisingly only her majesty's heroic and unflappably suave secret service can rescue victims from the lethal strike of a cutlass.

Culturally speaking, the movie was a double-edged sword. A clear attempt to cash in on the blaxploitation genre of *Shaft* and *Superfly*, *Live and Let Die* had a number of hip soul references in addition to the unforgettable Mr Big/Kananga, a thoroughly convincing villain played by Yaphet Kotto, who makes Roger Moore's 007 look uncomfortably am dram. Even more ironic is the fact that the Trinidadian actor who was cast in the role of the pantomime evil high priest, Baron Samedi, Geoffrey Holder, had done a huge amount to promote Caribbean and steel pan culture in America, as his brother Boscoe had in the UK. It is sad to see him reduced to such buffoonery.

Balanced and empowering depictions on screen of Black culture were still hard to come by, and, as in many of the films discussed in the previous volume, the role of Black music was frequently the only redeeming feature. Even in a British film directed by an African American, the same can be said. Sidney Poitier's directorial debut, *A Warm December* was set in London and featured West Indian and African actors – Esther Anderson, Earl Cameron and Johnny Sekka – playing African dignitaries in what is a doomed love story with a sub-plot concerning the prevalence of sickle cell disease in Black communities. The result is engaging but lightweight. If the film says little of significance about the lived realities of Black Britain, it does give a glimpse of how musical culture was changing. In a scene in a packed club, the sounds are provided by a lively five piece group called Zubaba. Clad in dashikis, patterned waistcoats, headbands, sunglasses and medallions, the ensemble resonates with the Afrocentricity that had been sweeping black Diasporan culture and politics in the age of Black Power and the Black cultural assault on Western aesthetic conventions.

Surrounded by other revellers, Poitier and Anderson throw themselves into the dance circle formed at the front of the stage and pull out their slickest moves as the band builds up a head of steam, tracked by tight camera angles and close-ups. If the moment is intended to place a spotlight on a Black social gathering in 1973, then no greater symbol of a new behavioural code can be seen than when one of the smiling brothers in attendance gives a double 'high five' as the musicians start to cook. Playing electric guitar, Hammond organ, bass, drums and congas, the band has a strong foundation in blues, riffing on what is essentially two chords, with a sharp focus on the 'one', lots of percussion well to the fore, creating energetic currents amid the steady rhythmic stream. Zubaba was Western pop embracing Africa. But there is an intriguing truth about the band. They were actually the West Indian combo, Symarip, discussed in Chapter 4, the anointed rulers of the sub-genre of skinhead reggae, who had chalked up hits such as 'Skinhead Moonstomp'. Here they were making music that took them to 'the motherland', with 'hand drums' as the primary vehicle for the journey in sound.

Africa, Centre of the World…in London Town
It was not as if percussionists had not been heard in many successful British jazz, soul and funk bands prior to this moment. African musicians who commanded the complex vocabulary of hand drums had long exerted a fascination on musicians and audiences in Britain. In the 1950s and 1960s, the percussionist Frank Holder worked with the John Dankworth Orchestra, while Neemoi 'Speedy' Acquaye gigged with Georgie Fame and Rocky Dijon with the Rolling Stones. Hand drums were, as noted in the previous chapter, vital in the music of Cymande.

In African music, the intricate layering of rhythmic lines that kept rotating, so as to suggest an eternal circle, broke with the western pop convention of short pieces built on verse and chorus. One talented and influential artist who exposed British audiences to this tradition was Mustapha Tettey Addy. He was discovered by Mike Steyn, a Cape Town-born producer who founded the independent label, Tangent. He recorded comedians, such as the provocatively named Blaster Bates, and avant-garde jazz, such as the Spontaneous Music Ensemble, a 'super group' that featured drummer John Stevens, trumpeter Kenny Wheeler and saxophonist Trevor Watts, the latter of whom went on to work extensively with African musicians in the 1980s and beyond.

Descended from a long line of musicians in the Ga tradition of Ghana, Tettey Addy was a child prodigy who rose to the rank of 'Dadefoiakye' or master drummer. This was how Steyn presented him on his 1972 debut album, *Master Drummer from Ghana*, in which Addy gave a demonstration of the rhythms that had been handed down to him by his revered elders. Each of the ten pieces highlighted a specific concept.

While the jabbing accents used in a 12-beat cycle caught the ear on a piece such as 'Ewe Atsimivu', there was also the mesmeric sound of Ga gongs, which were used in pairs, one being high pitched and the other low, a principle that was also applied to the tuning of Ashanti Ntumpani, often used at funerals or festive social occasions. Metrically and timbrally, there was a change of tack from one track to the next, making the point that in Africa the very term drum needs qualification – namely which drum to use and for what purpose. The second album Addy cut in 1973, *Kpanlogo Party*[2] saw him lead the group, Oboade, in which he was joined by four other drummers – his brothers Yacub, Oboe and Ismaila Oboe Addy as well as Thomas Annan, all of whom were able to convey the energy of kpanlogo, a dance rhythm which suggested 'an atmosphere of people having a fine time'. Its charm and gaiety made it a worthy rival to high-life, which was hugely popular throughout West Africa.

Kpanlogo was also mixed with another beat called Age, and the results were songs that were irresistibly boisterous and humorous, with no compromise on high standards of performance. A compelling document of the richness of Ghanaian musical culture, Addy's tracks were recorded in concert at the Africa Centre in Covent Garden in central London. The venue had been founded in 1961 by Margaret Feeny (1917-2012), an intellectual and future Liberal Democrat politician who was the General Secretary of the Catholic Institute for International Relations. It became a hub for both expatriates from the Motherland and those with an abiding interest in African culture, a meeting place for students, thinkers, artists and entrepreneurs who sought to create a degree of solidarity and share common values as the former British colonies turned into independent states that sought to define a new place for themselves in a post-imperial world. The centre's cultural activities in this period included a film season, *Africa at the Pictures*, as well as debates and concerts, and by the mid-70s it was staging plays such as *The Trial of Dedan Kimathi* by the Kenyan author Ngugi wa Thiong'o as well as gigs by Tettey Addy and other musicians.

The *Kpanlogo Party* album and live performances helped to consolidate and expand audiences for African music in Britain. At the Africa Centre, the vision can be seen as inherently political insofar as it promoted a wide range of music from across the continent, rather than from just one territory. This was certainly the case when the promoter and DJ, Wala Danga, founded the Limpopo club there every Friday or Saturday night. With the creation of an African kitchen on the ground floor serving pepper soup, the sense that patrons were either experiencing home away from home or engaging in new cultural immersion was complete. Whilst no other space was as iconic as The Africa Centre, there were a number of smaller venues up and down the country that also staged performances by musicians from Africa and the West Indies. All this was part of a growing awareness of Africa in the consciousness of people of African heritage around the world. No longer Negro, they called themselves Black or in some cases African, a significant shift in attitude amongst former 'coloured colonials' who were largely taught that the 'Motherland' was synonymous with all that was not civilised.

Heard of Elephants
This political adoption of an African identity had a clear parallel in musical modernisation. African artists, who were as open-minded as their European counterparts, embraced the dominant strands of pop, acquired western instruments such as the electric guitar, bass and drum kit and began to invigorate local traditional rhythms. The previous chapter noted such bands as The Funkees and Matata, from Nigeria and Kenya respectively, whose music was generally perceived as Afro-funk, though Afro-rock was the term

that came to have more currency. In fact, there was no strict dividing line between the two: Afro-funk bands could rock out and Afro-rock groups could be funky. Ultimately, these terms were vague, for they didn't state where in Africa the particular artists were from, but the buzz words, so important for marketing, nonetheless signalled an African engagement with the contemporary, fast changing sounds of the Black Diaspora.

Chief among the incumbents was Akido (with members from Ghana, Nigeria, Jamaica and London) who blended a powerful backbeat, crunching guitars, vocals and clattering percussion, and Assagai, who included brilliant South African jazzers, trumpeter Mongezi Feza, saxophonist Dudu Pukwana and drummer Louis Moholo-Moholo (discussed in Chapter 5), along with Nigerian bassist-guitarist, Fred Coker. In both groups, the addition of percussion (shakers, cabassa, bells, bongos and congas) on top of the usual drum kit created a notable density as well as polyrhythmic richness.

Listen to Akido's 'Psychedelic Baby' and Assagai's 'Telephone Girl' and what stands out is the scratchiness, the sweatiness, if not the dirtiness of the sound. Where 1950s Afro-pop forms such as hi-life had a sheen, a lushness of timbre, here there is a rough edge, above all from the guitars, which are given wailing reverberations by way of a wah-wah pedal on generally bulked-up chords – the kind of heavy ensemble sound that could satisfy audiences tuned in to the surges of volume favoured by the Stones and Led Zeppelin.

Assagai were signed to Vertigo, a subsidiary of the major label Phillips, which had enjoyed success with new rock bands such as Black Sabbath. This gives an idea of the potential breadth of Assagai's market appeal as the latest incarnation of Black music that could interest white rock kids as well as Black listeners. But although the band had enough pull to make an appearance on *Top of the Pops*, they proved a short-lived affair, as did Akido, who recorded just one album. The group that really bucked the trend was Osibisa. They went on to become one of the most successful Black acts of the 1970s, selling albums in large numbers and creating a worldwide fanbase that led to bookings alongside some of the biggest names in rock, pop and soul, as well as headline shows at venues such as London's Royal Festival Hall. As live performers they were outstanding. They had a very busy diary in their heyday. For instance, on a tour of Germany they were on the same stage in Frankfurt as Uriah Heep and Jeff Beck, while in America they played alongside Funkadelic and Mandrill in Philadelphia. On another occasion, they were on the same bill as B.B King, Al Green and the Staple Singers. As noted in Chapter 7, the pioneering pan-Caribbean group, Cymande, had also gigged with Green, but Osibisa consolidated such opportunities to achieve a degree of crossover success that eluded many of their predecessors. In 1972, they played the Summer

Festival at Crystal Palace Bowl and were second only to Arlo Guthrie in the running order, above Roxy Music, then one the great success stories of the glamrock scene.

Just a year before they achieved that billing, Osibisa were still one of dozens of bands doing the college circuit, and if on paper a show at Reading University with Rory Gallagher seemed inconsequential at the time, it is now a badge of credibility for those who had the good sense to be there. Gigs such as these were the making of an international act.

'We became a unique, all black band,' said founder Teddy Osei.[4] There was indeed an indefinable quality to Osibisa, in no small measure because of its range of influences and diverse personnel, for as much as the band became the definitive embodiment of Afro-rock, it was a truly Black British or diasporan ensemble insofar as it comprised Ghanaians Osei, drummer Sol Amarfio and trumpeter Mac Tontoh, as well as West Indians, guitarist-vocalist Wendell Richardson (Antigua), bassist Spartacus R (Grenada), and keyboardist Robert Bailey (Trinidad). Empire's many children had come together.

These were skilled players with strong personalities who had a welter of life experience before they formed the band, none more so than Osei, the son of a gold and brassmith. Hailing from Kumasi in the Ashanti region of Ghana, he had learned talking drums and bamboo flute while attending a missionary school as a child, before studying architecture and working briefly as a buildings inspector. However, he realised that music was his true vocation when he happened upon a slew of instruments inherited from a local Salvation Army band. After trying out strings and horns, Osei decided to start his own group, initially playing drums before turning to saxophone, learning riffs from the records of swing legends Duke Ellington and Count Basie, in the absence of formal tuition.

Hi-life, the popular music of the day in West Africa, was the staple vocabulary of Osei's first bands, The Blue Jewels and The Comets, with whom he toured Ghana and Nigeria in the late 1950s, steadily building their reputation with a string of hit singles which showed a solid command of the style that was filling dancehalls far and wide. Britain, though, was the inevitable destination for Osei's career development and he came to London in 1962 to study music and drama. Like many of his peers, he had to turn to menial work to support himself, finding a job as a dishwasher at the Grosvenor House Hotel in Park Lane, a none too glamorous position but one that had also been held by Kwame Nkrumah, Ghana's first president when the country threw off Britain's colonial yoke that year.

The dramatic course of events that followed provides a vivid illustration of the turbulence against which the lives of many budding African artists unfolded, subject to the geo-political convulsions of the post-independence world. The Ghana government gave Osei a scholarship a few years after his arrival in the UK, but this was withdrawn in 1966 after Nkrumah was deposed in a CIA-backed coup that had grim echoes of the CIA's involvement in the assassination of Patrice Lumumba in the Congo some years earlier.

Osei's life took more unexpected turns. After unsuccessful attempts to find work as an actor, he threw himself into music full time, forming a band that played soul and hi-life with former members of The Comets, his brother, trumpeter Mac Tontoh, and drummer Sol Amarfio, who had been in London since 1961. The group they formed, Cat's Paw, was offered a two-month residency at a hotel-restaurant in Tunisia, and it was there that a creative penny dropped, as Osei made clear in an interview with journalist Robin Denselow. 'Being back on African soil after so many years meant that more African ideas and songs started coming into the music.' The result was a rebooted combo, now named Osibisa, that took off on their return to London. The band thus had a truly global backstory: born in West Africa, incubated in North Africa and fully matured in Britain. 'We were all living in north London, Finsbury Park and we started rehearsing. Somehow Wendell [Richardson] dropped into the rehearsal and liked it and he came back the next day. Robert Bailey (brought by Wendell) also came in and listened and liked it, and then Spartacus',[5] Osei recalled when asked to explain how the core of the band formed.

Mostly it was through their shared interest in African American genres, rather than links between the kinds of popular music of their respective homelands that they found common ground, though, as Richardson stated in 2019: 'Generally, the music of hi life is not much different to calypso really. But I didn't play calypso and Robert didn't play calypso… We were nourished in jazz, we liked jazz, soul, blues. I was doing a lot of blues at one point.'[6]

Osei also confirmed a similar set of references when asked about the nature of what they created. 'The combination and the fusions came because we are Africans and we knew the rhythms and the music of Africa and because we have travelled overseas and listened to a lot of music like jazz, blues, rock. So, okay, if this is the case, these are all our experiences, we will cook it and put it one pot. That's how you have Osibisa.'

This open-mindedness defied any reductive parochialism that uninformed commentators might have assigned to a band from Ghana, and Osibisa proved a serious rival to any act in pop. The four albums cut between 1971 and 1973, *Osibisa*, *Woyaya*, *Heads* and the soundtrack of the blaxploitation movie *Superfly TNT*, which strengthened their foothold in America, were remarkable for the consistent quality of the material.

True to the eclecticism that inspired him, Osei led Osibisa as a band that moved seamlessly through different moods, atmospheres and sonic settings, while retaining artistic coherence. They produced high energy rhythms in which the drums beefed up the low end – the toms being pounded so as to produce a layer of additional bass, while the concise, skittish brass drew on the vocabulary of Stax soul to lend further drive, as was the case on the startling 'Music for Gong Gong'. This piece simply catapulted into life. Built on a sprightly, yearning horn motif, and needling guitar, the song has a buoyant, irresistibly danceable beat. Additional nuance is provided by Robert Bailey's Hammond organ, which wraps the haunting brass in lengthy sustained notes, before moving into feverish syncopation that captures some of the hot soul sauce of the great Booker T & The MGs. The temperature rises further in the break, where chattering percussion – a clack of wood blocks, hiss of shakers and rumble of congas – builds a thrilling bridge between Ghanaian rhythmic intricacy and the breakdowns of American funk – except that Osibisa used more drums than James Brown and made more noise than Mustapha Tettey Addy.

That is why 'Gong Gong'[7] remains so important as an idea as well as a song. It made an organic language by combining tradition and modernity; placing the unique timbres of 'old' African instruments within a context of new technology without any adulteration of the former. Amid the barrage of electric sounds created by Osei and his ensemble, the principles that underpinned the Ga culture were still discernible, above all in the wide dynamic range created by the elements of percussion, so that if listeners paid attention, they could hear the differences between the various low and high-pitched drums – symbolic embodiments of male and female energy – that brought sophistication to songs.

Furthermore, Osibisa did something that a lot of their English peers either would not or could not, as the writer Richard Williams pointed out, taking a swipe at the cults that had grown up around the self-indulgence of some soloists who had precious little showmanship. 'They took audiences that had grown used to sitting on the floor and marvelling at superfast lead guitarists, grabbed them by the scruff of the neck and made them dance.' Keeping still was not an option.

Osei confirmed how different Osibisa were. 'At that time, rock musicians would just come on the stage and play with no additional energy to put into the music. But we came on and brought a whole life of sound, a whole life of ideas, a whole life of meaning to the stage. That's what got everybody interested, Osibisa came along with their exploding sounds, with their rhythms, with their excitement, to get people up and make them feel good.'

Footage of the band in their prime bears this out. With a dress sense that was both uber-hip and unabashedly rootsy – which meant colourful dashikis, headbands and very often bare chests – the musicians bounced around as they played, providing a visual cue for the audience to follow suit. The party on stage was an irresistible open invitation for one off stage. There were also rousing, stirring chants as well as lead vocals, which brought a strong pop sensibility to the music along with its heritage of everything from hi-life to blues, R&B and a soulful, gospelised strain of jazz.

Osibisa's cover of 'Spirits Up Above', one of the most emotionally charged compositions in the repertoire of the legendary American multi-reed player, Rahsaan Roland Kirk, underlined another important part of the band's artistic identity: its commitment to more sensitive, introspective ballads as well as dance tunes. The enchanting 'Woyaya' had a strong church flavour that may have been an unconscious throwback to Osei's earliest musical experiences at a Christian missionary school. Perhaps the final element that made Osibisa so appealing was the band's use of meters that were not constrained by the ubiquitous 4/4 of the majority of western pop. Some songs were in 6/8 or 12/8, others in 9/4, and 7/4, and there could be a seamless movement between several time signatures in one piece. This struck a parallel with jazz and progressive rock acts such as Return to Forever, Yes and King Crimson, whose fans may well have appreciated this common denominator. Conversely, there were African listeners who related to western bands for this very reason, even though 'prog', often derided in areas of the UK music press, is not readily associated with Black audiences. Peter Adjaye, aka AJ Kwame, founder of Afri-Kokoa one of the key club nights in London the 2000s, grew up in Accra in the 1970s and recalls the fervour that greeted groups like Yes.

'We liked them because of the sophistication in the way the songs were written and the beat changed. You don't think of Africans getting into progressive rock because of the image, but we did because of what we could hear the musicians doing with time and pulse.'[8]

Furthermore, Yes and Osibisa shared the same graphic designer when it came to their imaginative album sleeves. Roger Dean's drawings of the 'Flying Elephants' – who were made to hover in midair as if they had somehow been lifted off the ground by some supernatural force – are now part of a canon of admired pop artwork.

Yet if the band – who sustained success throughout the 1970s with hit singles such as 'Sunshine Day', a joyous melody set to a slinky groove that struck a loose parallel with Latin-rock superstars Santana – came to embody African music that was palatable to western ears, then a sense of motherland identity always remained in their songs. This was not least because the band retained a linguistic duality. While English speaking audiences could understand and sing the words of 'Think About the People', 'Move On' or 'Fire', they had to work harder on the correct pronunciation of 'Ayiko Bia', 'Adwoa' and 'Woyaya'. This was some five decades after Paul Robeson sat down at the School of Oriental and African Studies to thumb the pages of books on Ga and Twi so that he could embrace what Empire once called the 'barbarous dialects' of the dark continent. Osibisa's multilingualism was empowering, though many broadcasters failed to say the name of the band properly. The Anglicised adulteration put the accents in the wrong place to produce the phonetic mangle of Oh See Bee Sah, whereas the correct rendering was Ossi Bissa, in a clipped, staccato rhythm that was delivered with a lot more punch.

While musical fashions inevitably changed, as we shall see in later chapters, Osibisa survived well into the 2000s and beyond, despite numerous changes of personnel. Innovators of Black music in Britain during the 1970s, their place in history is assured. The appearance of tracks like 'Music for Gong Gong' on modern-day playlists attests to the band's originality and ongoing relevance to millennial audiences.

Lastly, Osibisa's success was a considerable source of pride for West Africans in the UK at a time when the dominant strands of Black British music were Jamaican and African-American. The fact that a band led by Ghanaians, with Caribbeans as colleagues, sounded so aptly modern and exerted an influence on pop is not to be overlooked. They knew Ga rhythms but also went far beyond them. In the early 1970s, there were far fewer West Africans than Caribbeans in British society, so Osibisa brought their culture into the spotlight. Families from Ghana positively glowed anytime the band made *Top of the Pops*.

The Other Third World
Generally speaking, the sub-text of Afro-rock is that Black musicians were invigorating non-Western traditions by way of Western modernity, bolting together old and new, or rather making the former contemporary For the most part, keyboards, electric guitar and bass lie at the centre of the argument, insofar as they provide the power surge, literally and figuratively, to take groups versed in Ga drumming, dancing and singing into packed stadiums, and it is hard to conceive of Osibisa without Robert Bailey, Wendell Richardson and Spartcus R, who brought such force, finesse, and backbone to the band.

Even so, African percussion, with its rhythmic and metric complexity and extended textural palette, should not be reduced to an ancillary position in this reading of events. The conga, in the hands of a skilled practitioner, provided an entirely new musical vocabulary and opened doors to Western artists just as the guitar did for their non-Western counterparts. Ginger Baker, who achieved superstar status with Cream, had become as smitten with African grooves as he was with jazz, and regularly sat at the feet of Nigerian percussion legend Ginger Johnson before striking up an enduring friendship with Fela Kuti, with whom he would also record. There was much to learn from artists born in ex colonies.

Hence the important adjunct to the story of African players absorbing rock is that of English players absorbing African rhythms, mostly through the presence of West African hand-drummers in Britain in the early 1970s. There was what could be called the 'high five': Remi Kabaka, Gaspar Lawal (Nigeria), Reebop Kwaku Bah, Neemoi 'Speedy' Acquaye, Rocky Dzidzornu aka Dijon (Ghana). Their collective credits are too numerous to list, but they include work with legendary folk-rockers Nick Drake and John Martyn, Paul McCartney and the Rolling Stones. Kabaka and co were among the most sought-after percussionists in early 1970s rock because of their command of a wide range of instruments that included the expressive talking drum as well as their ability to fit into varied musical settings where they sometimes had to take an assertive lead rather than just providing tasteful accompaniment to heavy guitars.

Two excellent groups benefited in particular from their input. Ginger Baker's Airforce was an ambitious band launched by the former Cream drummer that had an evolving line-up that featured Kabaka, Kwaku, Acquaye, Lawal and Dzizornu alongside many leading figures from British rock and jazz (Ric Grech, Phil Seamen).[9] Then there was the imaginative pop act, Traffic, which featured Reebop Kwaku Bah on albums such as *Welcome to the Canteen* and *The Low Spark of High Heeled Boys*. Steve Winwood, co-founder of Traffic, had already signalled his intent to move in a non-Western direction in the late 1960s when he was still part of the Spencer Davis band. The overtly African flavour of 'I'm A Man' indicated that complex polyrhythms were part of a possible new direction for the band, so the eventual arrival of Kwaku Bah further down the line made perfect sense, especially when you hear how brilliantly he performed on the albums noted above. Also impressive was his work on *Short Cut Draw Blood*, an excellent solo album that was made by another Traffic member, Jim Capaldi, a gifted drummer and songwriter.

Even more interesting was Third World (a quite distinct group from the Jamaican reggae band of the same name), which again teamed Winwood and Kabaka with percussionist-saxophonist-flautist Abdul Lasisi Amao, one of the early members of Osibisa. The one album the trio recorded in 1973, *Aiye Keta*, was a superb entwinement of bracing African rhythms, articulate, expressive solos and at times fiendishly funky riffs, as if classic soul soundtracks such as *Uptight*, *Blow Up* or *Shaft* had magically soaked up the energy of Lagos or Accra and then been transplanted to London.

Kabaka, under the name Afrocult Foundation, would go on to score a film a few years later. *Black Goddess* (*Deusa Negra*)[10] was extraordinary music with a strong jazz and ancestral African slant that accompanied a daringly subversive Ola Balogun story of slavery and the practice of African religion in Brazil.

As for Reebop Kwaku Bah, his career had a truly transcontinental itinerary. Having made his way to New York to work with American pianist Randy Weston, before heading to England, he also had his own projects. He made two excellent solo albums, *Reebop* and *Anthony Reebop Kwaku*

Bah. Both sets were skilful, personal takes on jazz-inclined Afro-rock, with the second featuring the talented Swedish guitarist, Janne Schaffer. Such recordings were significant because they enabled Bah, Kabaka and others to upgrade from their previous sideman status and show that they could thrive centre stage. Not short of charisma or exuberance, they took to the spotlight as easily as the guitarists and singers that rock and pop audiences were used to seeing as the all-important front men, who were most frequently white.

Devil's Best Tunes
What makes the early 1970s such a fascinating and complex period in the history of Black music in Britain is the fact that there are numerous exceptions to rules, or general truths. Fluid boundaries between genres produced bands that were difficult to market, and perhaps understand. If Afro-rock is a largely accepted term, then there was also what could be described as Rock-Afro, as in rock made by Africans and West Indians who were happy to 'plug in' and crank out a heavy sound at high volume. We could call it Black British Rock.

The exponents are obscure but definitely worthy of attention. And some are related to Osibisa. Prior to joining that iconic outfit, Antiguan guitarist Wendell Richardson was in an interesting if short lived group, The Sundae Times, which featured his compatriot, bassist Calvin 'Fuzzy' Samuels and Dominican drummer Conrad Isidore. They released a handful of singles and one album *Us Coloured Kids*, an explicit reference to their ethnic minority status, which was produced by Eddy Grant of The Equals. Based in north London, the members of The Sundae Times had played with Jamaican legends, The Skatalites, and American soul singer, Edwin Starr but their core musical values were electric blues, jazz, rock and pop, which shaped pleasingly melodic songs such as 'Jack Boy'. Richardson was a decent singer and the lean but tough sound of the three-piece outfit came across well in the studio. If The Sundae Times showed the versatility of West Indian musicians, then Batti Mamzelle was a case of outright subversion. Their producer was the Trinidadian keyboardist Robert Bailey, another Osibisa alumnus, and the eight-piece combo featured his very talented brother Richard on drums as well as Winston Delandro on guitar. While the name Batti Mamzelle means 'crazy lady' in old Trinidadian French creole – the whole concept of the group was to modernise West Indian musical tradition.

'It was a rock band incorporating Trinidadian steel pans.' The resulting sound was original, at times forceful, at times sensual, but above all it made the point that West Indian musicians in Britain could claim post-Beatles pop as their own, just as they did calypso, ska, reggae and soul. *I See the Light*, the one album the group recorded in 1973, is something of a lost classic that has a number of well written tunes, above all the title track, excellent lead vocals by Jimmy Chambers and the skilfully marshalled pan section of Miguel Barrads, Russel Valdez and Ralph Richardson.

Another outfit that confirmed the ability of West Indian musicians in Britain to make left-field moves was The Gass. Initially employed as the stage band for the successful musical *Catch My Soul*, discussed in Chapter 6, the band had very gifted players in guitarist-vocalist Bobby Tench, drummer Godfrey McClean, bassist Delisle Harper and organist-pianist Derek Austin. They wrote captivating songs that had deep roots in the the emotional immediacy of blues and R&B, but branched out into the misty intrigue of psychedelia and a nascent jazz-rock, as some of the arrangements on the group's sole recording, *Juju*, show. These do not lack structural ambition or thought-provoking lyrical content, as exemplified by songs such as 'Cool Me Down', a fantastically frenzied soulful boogie.

Lastly there was Demon Fuzz – arguably one of the best band names of the time with its strong anti-establishment message, using one of the popular critical synonyms for the police – who developed a sound that fitted somewhere into a Santana-Osibisa continuum, yet had the individuality to set it apart from both. Demon Fuzz's debut album *Afreaka* was a provocative work that engaged with the psychedelic rock era. The album had a spaced-out, hallucinatory atmosphere, jangles of congas, explosions of raucous guitar, wailing trombone and saxophone, tumbling modal grooves and lyrics that vaguely joined the mystical to the ecological, complete with a praise song to the planet, a hymn to Mother earth. The music resonated with flower power and *Hair*-like pacifism. Demon Fuzz had spent time in Morocco and on some pieces there is also an intriguing quasi-Arabic flavour in the repeated riffing, a parallel with groups like the Beatles and the Stones who had also looked outside Europe and America for inspiration. The group's members embarked on changes of direction that were as exciting as daring. Many artists had moved freely between R&B, reggae and soul, but few made as great a change as the Trinidadian guitarist, Winston Raphael Joseph, who had a backstory as both a ska and a steelpan player. In the year before Demon Fuzz was born, he co-founded the Ebony Steel Band, an ensemble that would dominate Notting Hill carnival's annual panorama competition for the best part of a decade. Here was the kind of versatility that epitomised not just the extent of African-Caribbean talent in the Britain but its mercurial, shape-shifting nature, its restless daring, unpredictable ways.

Stylistically, Demon Fuzz's music was as close to progressive rock as it was to any style of Afro-rock. The openness of the musicians, their willingness to allow different genres to intermingle, their spirit of experimentation, the looseness of some of the arrangements and the tightness of the playing, worked together to produce music that is hard to pigeonhole.

Their songs made the point that there was no clear dividing line between the many versions of Black music and rock pop in early 1970s Britain. This was most apparent in their most politically charged song, 'Remember Biafra', a heartfelt lament for the Nigerian civil war that had a heavy reggae vibe, with stinging percussion, skulking horns and a commanding spoken-word performance that bemoaned 'the death of a nation, the murder of a people, a race in suffocation.' Although a relative footnote in the history of Black music in Britain, Demon Fuzz's music became highly sought after in the 1990s and after, in a loose parallel to the rebirth Cymande underwent when producers and crate-diggers heard audio gold in their original and sadly neglected recordings. Such stories of belated appreciation are sadly an integral part of music industry folklore, and those who await reappraisal are too numerous to mention.

All the bands mentioned in this chapter, from Zubaba and Osibisa, to Batti Mamzelle and The Gass and Demon Fuzz, represent many incarnations of Black music in Britain that are different yet loosely connected. All drew on blues, rock, jazz, soul and African and Caribbean rhythms, to varying degrees, to create their own original songbooks that have endured and continue to inspire audiences with the sense of possibility and unpredictability that made their work vital. Here were musicians that came from Africa and the Caribbean who contributed immeasurably to the evolving musical culture of Britain by blending what they had with what they found. The result was Black music that outdid mainstream pop with its energy and power as well as the intricacy of its rhythmic content.

A key influence on many of these groups was Jimi Hendrix, the African-American visionary who had shown that the blues could stretch and morph into music that was both rock and something far beyond it. His untimely death in 1970 left a huge void in pop, yet his recordings acted as a playbook for any prospective artists who wanted to make original music. His friendship with West Indians such as Eddy Grant and Bobby Tench is often overlooked, as if to imply that Hendrix was only down with 'the white boys' and had little contact with or relevance to Black Britain. It was not so.

As the next chapter will describe, there was a Black singer, greatly inspired by the legendary American, who was about to smash the British charts who didn't play reggae or Afro-rock, who did rock his own way, making a number of revealing references to his own lived experience.

And he wasn't from London. In fact, he wasn't from England.

Notes

1. *Love Thy Neighbour* ran for eight series on ITV from 1972 to 1976.
2. *Kpanlogo Party* was issued by Tangent in 1973.
3. There was also Africa Day launched by the Organisation of African Unity (OAU) in 1963.
4. Interview with Teddy Osei, *Talking Africa*, 2015 (Blackrook Media).
5. Ibid.
6. *Arise News*, 2019.
7. See Luisito Quintero's excellent cover of *Music for Gong Gong* (Vega, 2007).
8. Interview at the V&A, London, 2016.
9. A sprawling cast of players including the ubiquitous, very talented Steve Winwood.
10. *Deusa Negra* was reissued by Soundway in 2011.

9 THE OTHER DUBLINER

> It was the first time I'd heard Philip called a nigger, so I attacked the girl, and the nun attacked me.
> – Philomena Lynott, mother of vocalist-bassist Philip Lynott.

Hook, line and sinker
In the early 1970s, most new bands embarked on the road to success by being the support to an established act. The unknown warmed up for the known and enjoyed the bonus of a larger audience than they could expect to draw on their then slim reputation. Touring with seasoned 'pros' could also be a learning experience. Conversely, doing a short set for a crowd that had not come to see you had its downsides, especially if the headliner was Slade, a four-piece from Wolverhampton that had confected a boisterous, brash, glittery glam rock that emphatically 'let the good times roll'. Loud, louche and fun they were one of the biggest names of the day, and the string of dates that a young Irish band had secured with Slade was in danger of being cut short because they were going down so badly, they were close to an early return home. The novices from Dublin were Thin Lizzy and their vocalist-bassist, Philip Lynott, faced with what would have been a devastating setback, had to step up and be a real leader. He had to come of age as performer there and then. Guitarist Eric Bell explains what happened after the band was told to do something to stop boring the rows of fans who voted with their lungs, mercilessly chanting 'We Want Slade!': 'The next night I looked over at him… every now and again he [Philip] would throw this shape, he'd be out front with the bass for about four seconds then he'd go [strikes a dramatic pose] and he'd go back to being shy Philip. About three minutes later he would do another one, which lasted about five seconds. Then he'd go back to being shy Philip. He started very gradually checking the audience out and feeling more at home with them and realising this. I did this pose, and nobody threw anything at me.'[1]

This is a priceless reminder of the central place of self-confidence, swagger and showmanship in rock, and in the story of the man who was famed for radiating energy under the glare of the stage lights. The gig was an important moment in Philip Lynott's life; he had almost broken down in tears when he was read the riot act; he underwent a startling transformation. The man who laid down the law to him and his bandmates was

Chas Chandler, the manager of Slade who had made his name as the man who discovered Jimi Hendrix, the performer who was one of Lynott's inspirations and would remain a kind of guiding spirit throughout his life. There were undeniable similarities between the two. Both contained a behavioural duality that saw extravert and introvert, uninhibited performer and understated onlooker, co-exist and intermingle, to create unique, complex individuals. Both resolved their inner differences in a magnetic charisma on stage. Lynott was once slated to play Hendrix in a biopic that never came to fruition.

From that make-or-break moment on the Slade tour, Thin Lizzy went on to become one of the biggest rock bands of the 1970s and early 80s, basking in the glow of elite, globetrotting stadium tours and thousands of devotees who came to worship at their altar. Several top ten albums and singles, the most well-known of which, 'The Boys Are Back in Town', became a soundtrack to generations of town-trashing stag nights, and broke the group in America. Lynott made it and had no shame in enjoying the trappings of success. As he said in an interview with Gay Byrne on RTE's The Late Late Show in 1981: 'I was tired of hearing rock & roll stars saying how sorry they were for themselves and how they disliked fame and how they were bothered.'

The interview also revealed Lynott's view that the benefit of marriage was the obligation to be faithful to one woman, a none too subtle nod to a famed and well-indulged sexual appetite that was one element in a marathon of unrestrained revelry. 'I was famous and thought, great, the women are after me. People wanna buy me free drinks. I really went for it, hook, line and sinker.' Lynott was candid about his lifestyle choices. As the archetypal rock star, he embodied an unabashed masculinity and heightened sexuality, right down to the tight leathers, piratical silver earring and bass held out as a penis extension. The hunger to succeed that Bell describes in those early days can be seen etched on his face in the hours of footage of Thin Lizzy in their pomp – the time when the crunching power chords of guitarists Brian Robertson, Gary Moore and Scott Gorham provided the electric sparks that flashed over the solid ground created by Brian Downey's drums and Lynott's bass. On stage and in life they went at it hard.

Lynott's musical ability should not be overshadowed by the snazz of his stage presence, complete with 'shapes' aplenty. Listen closely to any number of Lizzy tracks and his playing is anything but perfunctory. He has a heavy, well-controlled tone, good intonation, effective use of long and short phrases that bring strong melodic and rhythmic qualities to a song. When he opted for muscular, repeated lines, he imbued songs with the propulsive and relentlessly aggressive drive that defined hard rock, and though hard rock and its related ritual praxis of 'head banging' became the stomping ground of an almost exclusively white, largely male audience, it did not, in the hands of Lynott, as was also the case with Hendrix, entirely lose its musical blackness. As much as 'The Boys are Back in Town' and other big Lizzy tunes may define the band as exponents of something quite different to soul music, there was often funk amidst the blast of noise. This is an important point to make because the concise history of modern popular music states that rock wholly seceded from R&B in the late 1960s. But the R&B fundamentals of swing and syncopated rhythms were never entirely squeezed out of new forms of pop in which the guitar rather than horns was the dominant voice. Thin Lizzy, for all their investment in a new 'hard' sound, did not forfeit the kind of pentatonic licks and 'chicken scratch' chords that had made Black audiences bust a move. 'Johnny the Fox Meets Jimmy the Weed', 'Bad Reputation', 'Ray Gun' and 'Call the Police' are all smart examples of how to put crashing beats and breaks under a catchy verse and chorus. Hendrix's 'Little Miss Lover' was an obvious stepping stone in creating a rhythmic drive that should have hip-hop producers running to their samplers without delay, and, like Hendrix, Lynott understood how soulful a tune could be when he dropped the tempo. The gorgeous 'The Friendly Ranger at Clontarf Castle' and the languorous 'Slow Blues', both of which move at medium pace, are wonderfully airy pieces of rock with an understated but resonant funkiness.

The latter composition features on an early album *Vagabonds of the Western World*, which is a fine set of songs that shows Lizzy to be right at the crossroads of soul and rock, particularly on the brilliant 'The Hero and the Madman', where Eric Bell, a talented guitarist who was able to fulfil the brief of a power trio with his vivid extended soloing, creates a hail of wah wah flickers that provide a tremulous backdrop for Lynott's voice. With its smorgasbord of references to mythical warriors on steeds, the lost city of Mars and tormented stage actors, the song indulges in the most fanciful notions of human misadventure, yet the dot-dash nature of the lyric absolutely works because the lamenting tone of the lead singer is enhanced by a teasing, tangoish slant in Lynott's slinky basslines.

As Bell and many others attest, Lynott was not initially confident in his own vocal ability – yet again a parallel with Hendrix – and at one point stopped singing altogether to undergo a tonsil operation. Playing bass and singing at the same time is not an easy task because it requires the player to execute a line, which may comprise several notes rather than a few chords, to keep locked in with the drums, and to focus on the vocal pitching of a melodic figure different from the bass riff, which is probably why there are fewer vocalist-bassists than there are vocalist-rhythm guitarists. Lynott managed to master both skills and deploy them well in Thin Lizzy songs.

For a start, Lynott had a compelling voice. He grew up immersed in the blues and R&B, from Muddy Waters and John Lee Hooker to Hendrix and Van Morrison, key influences for musicians all over Britain in the 1960s. The explosive shouts and screams, the lustful gasps and exhortations, the surges and sighs, the roar and rasp were all there in Lynott's performance, but he also had a particularly beguiling timbre that was grainy and low. It was highly effective when he pushed into fortissimo yet could also suggest tenderness if not vulnerability. He took to ballads very well, and the delicate acoustic strains of 'Saga of the Ageing Orphan', 'Chatting Today' and 'Dublin' reveal a gifted storyteller who was able to convey pathos and melancholy in a reflective, confessional mode.

Thin Lizzy's first three albums, *Thin Lizzy*, *Shades of a Blue Orphanage* and *Vagabonds of the Western World*[2] are important entries in the canon of early 1970s British rock, primarily because they retain a strong blues flavour and also blend in several elements of the band's Irish heritage.

Sisters of No Mercy
Pain and trauma were part of Lynott's backstory, and this shaped his worldview and artistry both directly and indirectly. He came of age at a time when Ireland's black population was very small, mostly the byproducts of the country's long history of Catholic missionary work throughout the British Empire. There were as few as 1,100 students from African nations, mostly Zambia, in early 1950s Ireland.

Lynott's mother, Philomena, left Ireland to find work in Birmingham where she met his father, an Guyanese serviceman, who had to defend her from taunts of 'nigger lover' at the end of the evening where they first met and she accepted his invitation to dance. Worse was to come when she fell pregnant and gave birth at a Midlands hospital after an unsuccessful attempt at an abortion by way of a gin cocktail. She was given an unforgettably rude awakening of what was in store.

'When I got there and the nurses realized I didn't have a ring on my finger, I was a tramp, a hussy, the nurses treated me like dirt,' she recalled. 'The moment Philip's head entered the world they all ran for cameras; they'd never seen anything like it because he was born with a thick head of curly hair. The next day the matron came up to me and said your landlord and landlady came up to see you, but we showed her your baby and they've walked out, and they've packed your stuff and they've dumped you here with us.'[3]

As was the norm in post-war Britain, unmarried mothers were often sent away to special 'homes', an ironic term for places that oppressed their residents in emotional and often physical ways, particularly when the shame of illegitimacy became the scandal of a birth that crossed the colour line. As Philomena reported of her time at one of these austere church-run refuges, 'I was the only one with a black baby and the girls battered me... I heard the girls saying (about me) that this is the mother of the nigger. It was the first time I'd heard Philip called a nigger, so I attacked the girl, and the nun attacked me.'[4] Inevitably for the time, there was also pressure placed on Philomena to give her baby up for adoption.

It is difficult to imagine the psychological trauma the young mother must have faced with her baby whose presence made it difficult to secure accommodation. They had to leave Birmingham for Moss Side in Manchester, where the poverty Philomena endured was so extreme she sustained herself and her child with stew boiled down from bones thrown out for dogs by local butchers. Circumstances became desperate and it was decided that Philip would be sent to his grandmother in Ireland so that he could be raised in a more stable environment. Philomena said, 'It was heart rending to leave him. I would go home to Ireland and Mammy had still never told the neighbours that he was mine. She told them all Philip belongs to a friend of Phyllis's; his mother has died and I'm looking after him for his daddy.'[5]

Denial thus followed rejection, and it is not surprising that Philip Lynott became the archetypal hard man from Crumlin in Dublin as a realistic means of survival. As group member Eric Bell noted, 'He had a pretty hard time in school because he stood out completely. He was the slag or the little black boy.'[6] There was support from one of Lynott's male relatives, a forthright uncle who visited the establishments Philip attended to confront his nephew's tormentors before he and Philip proceeded to 'get stuck in' to gain sufficient respect to avoid future confrontation.

Growing up as one of the few people of colour in Ireland in the 1960s was hard enough, but the absence of his mother and father must have been particularly difficult to bear. The consensus is that the problems posed by Lynott's minority status contributed to strengthening his determination to succeed in life, though the sense of emptiness or desire to know more about his own history would not have been easy to negate. According to a former band mate, one of the few times when Lynott let his tough exterior soften and shed tears was after his uncle died. There are no reports of any contact between Lynott and his father, though, as his mother recalled, 'He used to ask me questions and I always told him that his father was a fine man.' Little is known about Cecil Parris, except that Philomena said, 'He never denied being his father and that it was just a case of... we didn't get married. That's all there was to it. And he did want to marry me and take care of you. But life didn't go that way. I just feel there was something in me that was my way of saying well thank you for my lovely son.'[7]

Little black boy with the brown skin
Lynott and his mother (who ended up running a successful hotel in Man-

chester) remained close, but it was in Dublin that he discovered music by spinning through the record collection of one of his uncles. Lynott's first group was a covers band called The Black Eagles, but he went on to play with a string of other groups that included Orphanage, Kama Sutra and Skid Row, whose founder Brook Brush Shields sacked him because of problems with his voice, though he gave him bass lessons to assuage a guilty conscience. Then Lynott took control of his own destiny when he formed Thin Lizzy with drummer Brian Downey and guitarist Eric Bell, who had played with Van Morrison. Both were part of the generation of young Irish men who pledged allegiance to the crackle of electric music rather than the acoustic flutter of folk, or what they saw as the cobwebbed tradition of 'show bands', all suits, ties and crooners who performed easy-listening music for chaste dancing couples. In their early years, Thin Lizzy suffered the indignity of having to follow these groups doing 'Strangers in The Night' and 'Danny Boy' and being ridiculed by audiences when they hit their power chords and shook the amps. As Bell noted, 'Ireland was behind England, musically.'

The name Thin Lizzy referred to a character, Tin Lizzie, from *The Dandy*, sister publication of *Beano*, the magazine Eric Clapton was seen holding on the sleeve of the John Mayall album *Blues Breakers*. In choosing the name, the young Irishmen signalled their allegiance to the English guitar heroes of the day, so it was ironic that Lizzy's breakthrough hit, 'Whisky in the Jar', which climbed to number 6 in the UK singles chart in 1973, was an Irish folk song that, as Bell tells it, the band played simply to pass the time during a rehearsal which was yielding little creative energy. There was no intention to include the piece in their repertoire. They had better things to offer. But the melody appealed to their manager, an Englishman, who told them to commit it to tape. So, the Irish rockers struck gold by playing the kind of Irish traditional music they had seen as crass in their youth. It became meal ticket and millstone. There is footage of Lynott, on stage at Lizzy's commercial peak, being heckled for the hit and tetchily snapping back. 'Not whisky in the fucking jar!'

Perhaps Lynott was also responding to the fact that 'Whisky in the Jar' was originally the B-side of a single, and the original A-side, before it was 'flipped', was a composition that could not have been more personal to him. 'Black Boys on the Corner'[8] was one of his first major reflections on his life as a person of colour in a world that thinks he doesn't belong.

Given the fact that Africans or West Indians were rarely seen in Ireland during Lynott's formative years, it is revealing that he has opted to use the plural rather than singular for the subject. Possibly he is imagining a solidarity and safety in numbers that he did not enjoy and yearned for. The piece begins with a burst of defiance: 'One of the black boys said/I need none of your pity.' Underneath these words is a stark, snarling, guitar figure, a staple funk-rock riff. If there are power chords driving the beat, the idea of self-empowerment fuels the lyric, in spare, tight clauses that suggest Lynott's desire to exert control over his existence. When he says 'Take a tip, take no back lip', he could be issuing a pep talk to either himself or any other Black boy on the corner. In the chorus Lynott makes it clear that he will not accept any limited definition thrust upon him:

> I'm a little black boy and I don't know my place, I'm just a little black boy,
> I just threw my ace, I'm a little black boy, recognise my face.

Thereafter comes the break down and the rumble of congas (which briefly appeared in the intro, giving a vague Latin-funk quality to the song) is heard again before Eric Bell launches into a well-paced solo, in which he bends and elongates notes to up the emotional ante and echo the metaphorical raised middle finger of the words. The rhythm takes on a more fluid swinging momentum (a reminder that rock & roll has boogie woogie in its DNA) and then Lynott spits out his next set of ideas with even more belligerence.

> One of the black boys said
> I'm giving a warning
> People been putting me down
> I'm giving a yawning

It is impossible to tell exactly how much lived experience has been applied to a performance, but Lynott's call to arms has a credible emotional charge. The racist taunts to which he was subjected in his childhood, and memories of an uncle who was ready to let his hands do the talking in his nephew's support, lend credence to the idea of Lynott as an outsider-fighter, which resonated with the warrior figures of Celtic myth that he was known to have enjoyed reading about as a child. Behind the image of the rockstar-bad boy there was a singer with more personal things to say, in songs such as 'Saga of the Ageing Orphan', with its bleak opening focus on a separation between father and son, and the admission that there is no greater fear than that of growing old on one's own. 'The Boys are Back in Town', the 1976 hit that made Lizzy a big pop name has eclipsed the less well-known 'Black Boys on the Corner', yet together the two songs are revealing signposts in the life of Philip Lynott.

Big noise in the Big Smoke
It was not long before the Black Dubliner became a Black Londoner. He and the other members of Thin Lizzy moved south to further their careers. Little is known about his engagement with the African and West

Indian communities of the capital, though he was one of the many artists who gravitated to the creative hub that was the Iroko club, founded by the legendary Nigerian drummer Ginger Johnson, where Lynott would have met Caribbean funkers as well as Black rockers and jazzers drawn into the orbit of this charismatic master drummer.

Whatever the nature of his contact with Black London, Lynott wrote another song about race that is arguably more personal than 'Black Boys on the Corner'. Again, it has largely slipped through the cracks of recognition because it was the B-side of the single 'Rosalie'. The song has a title that defined Lynott and the times in which he lived: 'Half-Caste.' Offensive in its proximity to 'half breed', the term reflected the woeful inadequacy of the language of race in a post-war Britain where paranoia over a mongrel population had induced a big fear in small minds. The product of a 'mixed marriage' was not yet referred to as 'mixed race', and Lynott's decision to confront his status as a bi-racial individual may well have been triggered by a heightened awareness not just of the capital's racial divide but also of the complexity of its racial politics where shadism as well as outright racism were widespread, and where Black Power militancy sometimes included prejudice against people of mixed race. Lynott frames the song from his own perspective and against the standpoint of others he encounters. He explains events, and also cleverly leaves them open to interpretation, though he is very precise in the statements he makes. He starts in 'the coloured section' of town and makes it clear what people think of him.

> I got a girl in Brixton town,
> Her daddy don't like me hanging round.
> The boy ain't black, the boy is brown.

We can assume the disapproving father of Lynott's lover is Black to make sense of his rejection of a mixed race boy, a 'half-caste', somebody who is not Black. In the second verse, the location changes to the other side of the tracks, Richmond in West London, known for its largely affluent population, handsome residences and savannah-like park, and here the presumably white father of Lynott's girlfriend subjects the suitor to an altogether more blunt form of antipathy:

> I got a girl up near Richmond way
> Her daddy don't like me to lead the girl astray.
> The brown is born to serve, you say

In keeping with other Lynott pieces 'Half-Caste' has a spare, economic literary style. Its vocabulary is plain, the observations direct, the emotional charge strong. Both the Black and white worlds are against the brown, the heartbreaking reality of the mixed-race individual who finds no place in either ethnic group. Just like Saffronia in Nina Simone's 'Four Women' (Between two worlds I do belong), Lynott seems in no man's land, but he signs off the verses with the boldest of retorts. At the end of the first verse he sings: Don't they know it's a half-caste town? At the end of the second he sings: 'Don't they know it's a different day?' There is a defiant movement from outsider to warrior and rebel who has a multi-cultural vision. This is Lynott's redemption song.

Significantly, though the connection is rarely seen, the Black Irishman brought Jamaica directly into his range of styles on 'Half-Caste' for the piece is indeed reggae not rock. Specifically, the song's languid bassline and clacking rimshots on the drums recall Bob Marley's 'Stir It Up'. There is also a current of additional percussion, possibly cowbells or wood blocks, that constantly ripples around the central beat to bring a soft, swaying calypso flavour to the rhythm, thus creating a sonic levity that contrasts with the gravity of the subject matter. This is a serious statement in a gentle dance.

Compositions like 'Half Caste' are a testament to the versatility of Lynott and Thin Lizzy and the complexity of his relationship with Black culture. The execution of the song is also far too accomplished for it to be passed off as pastiche, suggesting that Lynott took more than a passing interest in what Marley was doing musically and what he stood for politically. Both were mixed race. Marley was abandoned by a white father and Lynott by a black one. Both had struggles. Both knew poverty. Both achieved success.

Interestingly, 'Half-Caste' was featured on no album. It was a hidden track, which suggests that such politically charged material may have been deemed at odds with Thin Lizzy's image as hedonistic rockers. Had their label decided that it could not sell Lynott as the bad boy with a social conscience, a lyricist willing to match his celebration of a walk on the wild side with an unsentimental look at the minefield of race relations? For the most part, the Black rock star with the white wife, Caroline Crowther, daughter of TV personality Leslie Crowther, was not seen as somebody who was down with the struggle, in touch with Black Britain. But Lynott's post-Lizzy album *Solo in Soho* debunks that assumption with a song that suggests he thought that, for all his material success, he was not fully enfranchised. 'Ode to a Black Man' is the most overtly political piece Lynott ever wrote. Set to a barrelling blues-rock rhythm, punctuated by spirited harmonica solos by Huey Lewis, a star in his own right who enjoyed a close friendship with the singer, the piece connects key chapters in the history of Black America and Africa via Lynott's personal experiences. The song has an extraordinary opening in which Lynott admonishes one of the great figures of post-war Black music, Stevie Wonder, for one of his most experimental works, *Journey Through the Secret Life of Plants*, a beguiling naturalistic fantasia with lots of off-kilter songs and strange sound effects that Lynott 'doesn't wanna hear'. He then embarks upon unconditional praise for Civil Rights icons, Dr. Martin Luther King Jnr and Muhammad Ali, men whom Wonder had also celebrated in his work.

Thereafter Lynott expands the whole political context of the song to align African American and Caribbean musicians, exponents of blues and reggae, as well as the New Orleans piano legend Professor Longhair, with African anti-colonial leaders, arriving at the 'three Rs': Robert Johnson, Robert Marley, Robert Mugabe (who at the time could be seen as the freedom fighter, not the dictator he later became). The focus on African liberation is continued with references to another hall of fame that can be heard just as the song starts to fade out – Joshua Nkomo, Jomo Kenyatta and Haile Selassie. Lynott still has time for more political provocation.

> If you see Malcolm tell him I'm vexed, vexed
> If you see Jimi... Jimi Hendrix
> If you see my brothers tell them it's clear
> I been living on the wrong side but now I hear
> I been living on the wrong side but now I hear.

A real Dubliner
Given the relative segregation of rock, reggae and soul listeners in the late 1970s and early 1980s, it is possible that this rallying cry was not heard by Black listeners, and that some who did hear it may have kissed their teeth that such an exhortation was coming from a man who was far removed from their world of daily police harassment and sub-standard housing. I would argue that the very fact that Lynott chose to address his blackness in such a direct way, when his social status offered him partial though not total immunity from racism, was in itself an act of courage. Put simply, he did not need to make a statement. It seems clear that despite his acceptance by the world of celebrity, Lynott retained a sharp enough eye to see through its superficiality and know that he was still a minority. Indeed, he was actually making an overt step towards Black music post-Lizzy when he formed a group that could not have been more redolent of African American culture – Phil Lynott & The Soul Band – that featured two black Britons, guitarist Gus Isidore and bassist Jerome Rinsom.

Artists invariably leave questions hanging when they die young, and Lynott's death in 1986 at the age of just 36 after a struggle with drug and alcohol addictions invited speculation on his future musical direction. It is possible that he was about to embark on a path leading towards contemporary R&B and dance music, leaning towards a more electronic sound. He did sessions with producer Paul Hardcastle[9] and expressed frustration over what he thought was the homogenisation of guitar-based music.

Phil Lynott's loss was keenly felt. Amid the outpourings of grief from both a devoted fanbase and fellow musicians and the haunting images of his widow and two young daughters at his funeral, the idea of the celebrated rocker as an enduring enigma is impossible to discard, given the nature of his being, his multiple identities. Yet his sense of self could also be abundantly, incontrovertibly clear. From the clips of him correcting American interviewers who called him British, to the poignant songs such as 'Eire', Phil Lynott was very much an Irishman or rather a Dubliner, as he told Gay Byrne on The Late Late Show in 1981 when discussing how he felt about having to spend time outside the city.

'When I moved away, I thought, well, I must come home because I really suffer from homesickness. If I don't get back to Dublin not so much Ireland, Dublin. I'm a real Dubliner. If I don't get back to Dublin within three months, I really start to suffer from homesickness.'

With such a profession of faith it is tempting to think that Lynott's Irishness eclipsed his blackness, that he was an Irishman who was black before he was a Black man who was Irish. Yet when fielding enquiries about the order of importance of nationality and ethnicity, he had no hesitation in saying which element would hang heavier in the balance.

'Does it concern you whether you're first Irish or first black?' Lynott was gingerly asked by the television presenter, Sue Cook in 1981. 'No, I'm an Irishman,' he said. 'The black-white question is a load of… bull.' However, in the very same interview on Nationwide, a teatime programme not known for profound political discussion, Lynott went in the other direction. 'I draw on that Irish heritage and my father was black, and I'm black. For me it's a norm. For everybody else it's a little funny. Hard luck on everybody else.' The exchange barely lasts a few minutes, but it gives one of the most revealing insights into how Philip Lynott thought and what he had to contend with in his life – the burden of being a minority within a minority, and the status of being doubly colonised, a black man from a Gaelic island that had been brutally oppressed by the English. Here was a brown-skinned, mega Afro'd, half-Guyanese Dubliner vying for chart supremacy at roughly the same time as Elvis Costello was using the term 'white nigger' in the lyric of his song 'Oliver's Army' to denote what the British military called Irish Catholics.

How did Lynott negotiate the inability of people to get their heads around the notion of a black Irishman and an Irishman who is black? How did he deal with English people who hated both Blacks and Irish and Irish people who hated Blacks? One senses that he did not so much embrace both his personae as allow them to evolve in line with his own sense of self, free of the need to choose, which is tantamount to real and courageous fulfilment.

There is an uncompromising, hard edge to Lynott's lyrics that make it clear that he did not entertain any easy sentimentality in his search for the words to translate thought and feeling. He had sparks of lucid truth. Against the absolute love of his Dublin heartland there is the reality of its limitations. On the gorgeous paean, 'Dublin', he reaches a peak of illumination when he ponders: 'How can I leave the town?/That brings me down/ That has no jobs/That's blessed by god.' James Joyce would have seconded that sentiment. In that moment Lynott becomes the spokesman for several generations of his white compatriots, his own mother included, who faced the daunting necessity of emigration, as had his own West Indian father.

Lynott found his pot of gold by way of music, enjoying the irony of colonising England with an Irish folk song, but anytime we hear that electrified and electrifying rendition of 'Whisky in the Jar' the question of who we see and what they represent confronts us as surely as the pistol and rapier pointed at Captain Farrell while his money he was counting. If Lynott subscribed to the dream of a colour-blind life, away from the 'black-white thing' discussed in one interview, he was also either sufficiently honest or unguarded to eschew it in another. On RTE's *The Late Late Show* he chose to frame his greatest role model in unapologetically racial terms. 'Jimi Hendrix as an artist was very deep and very involved. He was one of my heroes; he showed to me that a black fella could be the front of a band and be completely respected for what he did.'

Though a proud Irish patriot, or rather Dubliner, Lynott knew that a person of colour was at an inherent disadvantage in the entertainment world, and that the transformation of an ethnic minority artist into a global icon empowers those who follow. Black and Irish and Irish and Black, Lynott was not willing to compromise either of the two defining elements of his identity. That self-realisation was heroic. Whether that was acknowledged to its full extent is another matter, for the prevailing image of the wild rock star seems to have largely overshadowed that of a thoughtful individual acutely aware of divides in the society in which he lived. It is ironic that only after Lynott released 'Out in the Fields', an anti-war song which paired him, a Southern Irishman, with Gary Moore, a Northern Irishman, did some interviewers begin to take him for a socially conscious writer, as if his previous statements on his ethnicity apparently counted for very little.

On the TV show, *Music Box*, he was told that he was finally being political. Lynott was not impressed. 'What do you mean at last? I've been saying things all me bleedin' life!'[10] The messages were loud and clear in the songs.

The only thing anybody needed to do was listen.

As Lynott was reaching the end of his life in the mid-1980s, another supremely gifted Irish 'black fella' of mixed race rose to prominence in the world of sport. Paul McGrath became one of the greatest players to wear the red of Manchester United and the green of Ireland. Much later in his life, McGrath revealed the extent to which his childhood had been traumatic because of abandonment when his parents' relationship collapsed, the severity of a long period of total psychological breakdown in the midst of his football career, and of his dependence on alcohol that led to the erratic behaviour that destroyed his personal relationships and led to several suicide attempts. McGrath's story is another testimony to the many stresses and strains that framed Philip Lynott's early death and the way extraordinary talents can arise in the midst of much personal pain. Lynott, the real Dubliner, the Black Dubliner, the other Dubliner, made artistic statements that have proved to be timeless, his lionisation evident in the life-sized statue that stands tall in Harry Street, his bass like a four stringed Excalibur to be wielded in every battle song. He marvelled at Celtic myths in his youth and went on to become one of Ireland's true legends.

Notes
1. *Outlawed: Thin Lizzy and The Real Phil Lynott* (dir. Sonia Anderson, 2006).
2. Thin Lizzy, *Shades of a Blue Orphanage* and *Vagabonds of the Western World* (Decca, 1971-73).
3. *Outlawed: Thin Lizzy and The Real Phil Lynott* (dir. Sonia Anderson, 2006).
4. Ibid.
5. Ibid.
6. Ibid.
7. *The Rocker*. RTE documentary 1995.
8. 'Black Boys on the Corner' is not featured on any Thin Lizzy albums, which invites speculation about whether it was deemed too political for a predominantly white fanbase.
9. Producer and keyboard player Paul Hardcastle enjoyed success in the 1980s as a member first of a soul band, Direct Drive, and after with the duo, First Light.
10. Music Box 1985 youtube Maxoom 2 Sep, 2006.

10 THE SPOOK WHO SANG ON THE FLOOR

I don't want no honky in my family. You dig?
— 'Brother Louie' by Hot Chocolate

What kind of ting dat? I don't want no honky in my family. You dig? So just let him go because I man don't please.
— 'Brother Louie' by Matumbi

Front Loaded
Twenty-four years after the arrival of the Empire Windrush, it was increasingly obvious that Black and Asian people had put down roots in the United Kingdom. They were here to stay. Evident, too, was the fact that even as British society was becoming more diverse, there was a virulent minority bitterly opposed to those changes. Shamelessly trading in the xenophobia that has always been part of English culture, organisations such as the Anglo-Rhodesian Society, the Racial Preservation Society and the League of Empire Loyalists (who had Conservative MPs as members) were part of the old school. They were joined by a populist and racist organisation of the streets, the National Front, whose membership doubled between October 1972 and July 1973 in some 32 branches up and down the country. One rallying cry of the NF was a response to the arrival of some 27,000 Asian refugees from Uganda, forced out by Idi Amin's dictatorship, a hostility inflamed by photographs in the right-wing popular press of plane loads of sari wearers disembarking at British airports.

To reinforce the Powellite message of repatriation, the NF encouraged the open targeting of Black people, all assumed to be immigrants, either in their homes or in the street. 'Nigger and Paki bashing' became alarmingly common. Overt racism was a regular part of the response of sections of football crowds to the emergence of a new generation of Black players such as Clyde Best and George Berry, following in the footsteps of Walter Tull and Albert Johanneson,[1] and the NF was particularly active in recruiting amongst the "hooligan" end of supporters. The sight of a union jack flag stitched on to team banners came to signify a thuggish brand of terrace-based racism, and 'Keep Britain White' graffiti was seen up and down the land. That this was an attempt, frequently violent, to hold back other more positive developments in British society is clear when one considers the parallel emergence of multi-racial bands in territories where the lines between R&B, soul and rock were freely being crossed. This had been happening since the late 1960s, and, as discussed in previous chapters, there is no shortage of examples to cite, such as The Foundations, The Equals, Blue Mink, The Gass, Gonzalez, F.B.I, and Olympic Runners.

Another Black and white act that became hugely successful in the 1970s and early 80s, building a large body of work that secured an international fanbase, was Hot Chocolate. This group was formed in south London at the tailend of the 1960s by Jamaican singer, Errol Brown, Trinidadian bassist Tony Wilson, English drummer Jim King and guitarist Franklyn De Allie and Grenadian percussionist Patrick Olive. Their debut single had been a reggae take on The Beatles 'Give Peace A Chance', but their main focus was an accessible, radio-friendly hybrid of pop and soul, with which they enjoyed many hit singles, well-received albums and worldwide tours which made them a household name. It became impossible not to have heard such effortlessly catchy hits as 'Every 1's A Winner' and 'You Sexy Thing', or to have seen Brown's distinctively shaven head on *Top of the Pops*.

Oh Brother, what colour art thou?
Although best known for such erotic escapism, Hot Chocolate struck a serious tone in its 1974 commercial breakthrough, 'Brother Louie'. The song depicted the consequences of an inter-racial relationship, a subject that had been integral to the wave of 1950s films that included *Pool of London*, *Sapphire* and *Flame in the Streets* in Britain[2] and *Guess Who's Coming To Dinner* in the USA in 1967. But if Black and white people could make music together, love across the colour line, because of the prejudices it laid bare, was much more contentious. Peaking at number 6 in the UK singles charts in 1974, the 'Brother Louie' of the song's title is whiter than white and he falls for a woman who is black as the night, descriptions that had a quasi-*Othello* dramatic undercurrent.

Cast against a soulful yet restrained rhythm, punctuated by slivers of electric piano and a guitar, picked with enough sensitivity to make it sound like a weeping mandolin, the lyrics of 'Brother Louie' make extensive use of colloquialisms and the kind of exaggerated tropes that reveal the extent to which long-held ideas about racial difference have permeated language.

>   Danger, danger when you taste brown sugar.

As might be expected, Brown argues for tolerance and equality, and as in Thin Lizzy's 'Half-caste', discussed in the previous chapter, the singer details the censure to which the couple are subjected by the girl's Black family and the boy's white one, making the point that the ill-fated lovers cannot escape the alarm and rejection of each set of parents, both of whom take a dim of view of colour-blind liberalism. A scandal is in the offing. What would the neighbours say?

The band increases the dramatic charge of the arrangement by opting for spoken interludes, with both Black and white father's laying down the law, again using the racially divisive slang of the day. Whites are honkies and Blacks are spooks, (a term more prevalent in America and arguably softer in emotional impact than British insults such as wog).

> I don't want no honky in my family, you dig
> I don't want no spook in my family, get it.

The second line, delivered in a crisp RP, was voiced by the British blues legend, Alexis Korner, who had worked with Hot Chocolate's producer, Mickie Most, in the band C.C.S. (See Chapter 5), while the first line, which crackled with West Indian inflections, was possibly done by Brown. In any case, these voices made it clear that this was Britain, and that the protagonists were part of a fast-evolving, post-colonial world. The song acquired an even greater cultural impetus when it was covered by three American artists; the rock band, Stories, who topped the Billboard Hot 100 with their version, just six months after the release of the original; jazz vibraphonist Roy Ayers, who played it as an instrumental, and the psychedelic soul group, The Undisputed Truth, whose producer, Norman Whitfield, rehoused the fine melody in a grandiose architecture of swirling strings and slashing wah-wah guitars. Hot Chocolate had made Black music in Britain that succeeded in America. One could say the same of the Beatles and The Rolling Stones, but Hot Chocolate were a multi-racial soul combo rather than a white rock or pop band and they had foregrounded the Caribbean element of their identity in the spoken word interlude on 'Brother Louie'. None of the American artists who covered the song could pull off a credible West Indian accent or reposition such a specific stylistic element in their interpretations. By accident or design, the Black Brits had a degree of inimitability. The only group that could match them for Black colloquialism was the British reggae band, Matumbi, discussed in Chapter 4, whose beautifully sensual version of 'Brother Louie' saw the group's leader Dennis Bovell break out-into patois that was noticeably 'roots'.

> What kind of ting, dat? I don't want no honky in my family. You dig? So just let him go because I man don't please. You got it? Right.

The use of the term 'I man' signalled the pervasive linguistic influence of Rastafarianism, whilst Matumbi's decision to reprise Hot Chocolate said much about the ongoing the engagement of reggae with soul. This reflected a strong awareness of prevailing trends among West Indian audiences. As Bovell told me in 2022:

> The idea of doing a reggae version of 'Brother Louie' was not for release but to make dubplates to sell to the sound systems... Because the sound systems were eating up cover versions, so we did that so we could make some quick food money. ... But when we went to Trojan, our record label, to play them all our other serious songs we'd written ourselves, they didn't much care for the song we'd written about Enoch Powell's speech 'Go Back Home', but they liked the cover of Hot Chocolate. Where they thought 'Go Back Home' was too political, what was more political than 'Brother Louie'? ... So we got our politics across.[3]

Furthermore, Matumbi's take on 'Brother Louie' brought a conspicuous British entry to the canon of reggae artists who put their own slant on early 1970s socially-conscious soul music from Black America, with key examples being Ken Boothe's 'Is It Because I'm Black', Bob Marley's 'People Get Ready' and Tinga Stewart's 'Why Can't We Live Together?'[4]

'Brother Louie' was not Hot Chocolate's only piece of social comment. Above all there was the 'The Street', a thought-provoking song about the realities of urban living, well served by Errol Brown's distinctively nasal voice, which was actually hard to place culturally and tonally. He was not an ersatz American or a straight up West Indian, but something undefined, though he still had to endure the juvenile racist slights of the BBC presenter Dave Lee Travis, who dubbed Brown 'the walking, singing Malteser'.

Hot Chocolate could be funky on occasion but they were not in the street funk mould of bands such as Cymande, Gonzalez and F.B.I. Generally speaking, Brown and co had a more polished sound and significantly less jazz content, with very few solos taken in their studio output. They proved the ability of Black British artists to make accessible, radio-friendly iterations of soul that had mass market potential, particularly if the lyrical content leaned towards affairs of the heart rather than focusing too heavily on politics. Hot Chocolate created a body of work with a consistently high standard of writing, as evidenced on successful albums such as *Cicero Park*, *Hot Chocolate* and *Man To Man*.[5] In fact, the South Londoners had regular single hits every year between 1974 and 1986 and, following the break up of the original band, Brown performed as a solo artist until around 2002; he died of liver cancer in 2015. Hot Chocolate reformed in 1992 and still perform around the world today. They reached new audiences by way of their inclusion on the soundtrack of the British box office smash film, *The Full Monty* in 1997.

As an addendum to the notable passage of 'Brother Louie' across the Atlantic, it's worth mentioning other UK soul exports of the time which were taken up by US artists. The peerless Harlem vocal group, The Main Ingredient, enjoyed success with a beautifully understated, lithe piece of funk, 'Happiness Is Just Around the Bend', which was penned by the talented London jazz organist-vocalist, Brian Augur, who led a fine multi-racial band called Oblivion Express. Two years later a lesser known but nonetheless intriguing American act, Love Child's Afro Cuban Blues Band, made a more surprising move. A group of top American session players under the aegis of producer Michael Zager, they cut a lushly orchestrated version of 'Black Skin Blue Eyed Boys', the lyrically provocative take on racial politics that Eddy Grant had written for The Equals back in the late 1960s. Black America was clearly listening to Black Britain. Tunes found new homes. Melodies went back and forth across the Atlantic. Musical exchange took place.

Our sensational friends in the north
One common route to a record deal was the talent show, which in its most common manifestation could involve a dozen or more aspirants trooping one after the other onto the stage of a British working man's club and either disarming their audience with a good tune or a sweet voice or being shot down by a heckle or two.

In the mid-1970s, mainstream radio and television got wind of this potentially drama-fuelled format and covered the bluntly titled Pub Entertainer of the Year. This was one of the first steps on the road to success taken by four young Black men called Sweet Sensation. Their extravagantly cut outfits suggested they were a new take on legendary vocal ensembles such as The O'Jays, The Temptations, or The Jackson Five, yet rather than hailing from Philadelphia or Detroit they were straight out of Manchester. Mostly all born in Jamaica in the early 1950s, they had come to Britain as boys and had grown up in the Moss Side area, which had a lively jazz and hi-life scene centred around legendary venues such as The Nile and Reno. Delroy Alexander Drummond, Junior Daye, Marcel King and St. Clair Palmer had voices that harmonised with sufficient skill for them to garner a local following and be shortlisted for national events that would subsequently break them to a far bigger audience. After PEOTY they appeared on ITV's *New Faces*, an altogether snazzier affair on which one of the judges was Leslie Crowther, father of Caroline, wife of Philip Lynott. This proved a turning point in Sweet Sensation's career because another of the judges was the orchestral composer and producer, Tony Hatch, who was impressed by their performance, and brokered a deal for them with Pye, the record label created by a manufacturer of television sets that expanded into the pop market in the 1960s. It had an eclectic roster that included trad jazz band leader, Chris Barber, rock pacesetters, The Kinks and trippy folkster, Donovan. Perhaps, most significantly, Pye had signed multi-racial soul combo The Foundations in the late 1960s and may well have thought Sweet Sensation were capable of emulating their success.

Although the band's debut single, 'Snow Fire', was a flop, the follow up 'Sad Sweet Dreamer', released in October 1974, went on to top the UK singles chart and also reach number 14 on the Billboard Hot 100. In January of the following year, another single, 'Purely By Coincidence', peaked at number 11 in Britain, though it made little impact across the Atlantic. An eponymous album followed, but Sweet Sensation were unable to consolidate that initial burst of success. Throughout the decade, the group continued gigging and drifted further into the middle ground of pop-cabaret, the corollary of which was participation in the Song for Europe contest which, in essence, took them back to their talent show origins. From so much once going right, things ended up going wrong.

It is easy to understand why they made the breakthrough in the first place. 'Sad Sweet Dreamer' was an overtly sentimental melody swathed in the kind of lush strings and whispered harmonies that come over well on daytime radio. Lead vocalist, Marcel King, had a boyishly appealing, pretty voice and wholesome cuteness, which most probably had the label banking on the tailwinds of the Michael Jackson mania blowing over the Atlantic. However, Sweet Sensation's appointed songwriter, a man called Des Parton, was unable to pump out ten or more gold standard tracks to fill an LP that had wide appeal, and when the group did get to grips with a lively tune such as 'Mr Cool', whose funky strut is a world away from the mellow sashay of 'Sad Sweet Dreamer', they sounded frustratingly constrained, almost neutered against the bump and grind in the groove. This begs the question of artistic control and development. How much say did 'the boys' have? If you look at footage of Sweet Sensation in their prime at the Hardrock, Stretford, Manchester, there is no denying their talent. One has to wonder what they could have achieved had they been nurtured by producers and writers with a greater understanding of soul's direction of travel in the 1970s, of how to retain a balance between musical ambition and commercial appeal, and perhaps most importantly of all, how to retain a sense of artistic integrity.

Another batch of four
Another band that began in much the same way as Sweet Sensation but had much greater and lasting success was a group from Liverpool who appeared on Opportunity Knocks, the X-Factor of its day. The Real Thing (as they later became) had the vocal ability, quality of repertoire, stage presence and professionalism that enabled them to make a major breakthrough as Black British artists in a music industry still largely stuck in a Black American paradigm. When they topped the charts with 'You to Me Are Everything' they added to the canon of unabashedly emotive love songs that became staples of the wedding reception. Four young Black lads from Merseyside entered the national psyche as a result. They hailed from Toxteth, an area to the south of Liverpool known for its poverty and

high concentration of families of African and West Indian origin. They upheld a heritage of Black scouse talent which included players such as guitarist Zancs Logie and singer Derry Wilkie,[6] and bands who rose to prominence in the early and mid-1960s, the most accomplished being The Chants, a doo wop group comprising five vocalists, that included Eddie Amoo, of Ghanaian-Irish heritage and his brother Chris; both became part of The Real Thing.

The group, as yet unnamed, secured a deal to be managed by London-based Tony Hall,[7] an A&R executive who had signed Jamaican jazz musicians such as Dizzy Reece to the Tempo label in the 1950s and actively promoted their cause in America. When Hall heard The Real Thing audition, he made an astute choice of a name for them. While driving though Piccadilly circus he spotted a neon-lit advert for Coca Cola whose strapline struck him as the kind of catchy three-note calling card that could work for the new act. The Real Thing was a drink that became a band.

They released singles such as 'Vicious Circle', 'Plastic Man' and 'Daddy Dear' to little fanfare before their 'big break'. Hall was smart enough to hear in 'You to Me Are Everything' (written by Kenny Gold and Mickey Dene) a melody that had hit stamped all over it and was a perfect fit for his new charges. The track climbed to number one in the singles chart as the mercury rose relentlessly during the famous heatwave of 1976. It is tempting to dismiss the song as lightweight fare, but its longevity points to something more. Its lavish melody and lustrous hooks exert immediate appeal, especially the opening piano motif, which tingles over four bars with minimal harmonic variation. The vocal phrases glide over smartly mapped chords while the hyperbolic sentiment of 'I would take the stars out of the sky for you', is made credible by the momentum of Chris Amoo's low, commanding voice, his grainy, slightly raspy tone being seductive rather than simpering. Above all, the arrangement has the sumptuous orchestration that puts it in the slipstream of the epoch-defining work of soul legends such as Isaac Hayes, Gene Page and Barry White.

While inspired by America but made in Britain, 'You to Me Are Everything' was important insofar as it proved that a Black British group could have mass appeal. The Real Thing were the first ever Black Britons to top the charts. Not Black artists who had come to the UK, but ones who were born here. This is not a distinction to be taken lightly. They did something that had not been done before. The success of their other singles, 'Can't Be Without You' and 'You'll Never Know What You're Missing' consolidated The Real Thing as bonafide pop stars who spoke in broad scouse accents in radio and television interviews, embodying Black Liverpool, a community that was not on the radar of many in the UK in the mid-1970s. Afro'd, attractive, athletic and able to work the dungarees sans T-shirt look like no others, Amoo and co. also climbed another rung on the ladder of mainstream pop power as sex symbols. They were wanted by women, many white, and no doubt regarded with a certain amount of envy by other men, many also white. This pin-up status brought them further into the world of celebrity, from prime-time pop shows with teenage girls ogling them, to a Thames Television Special in honour of Muhammad Ali, which produced an interesting show of transatlantic brotherhood. As Eddie Amoo recalls, 'After the show we were all in the Green Room and all these people were throwing themselves all over him, he just made a beeline for us... He made a point of walking right through all these people and came over to us and stood talking, laughing and joking with us for about fifteen minutes. In terms of star status we were nothing compared to some of the people in that room. I was so proud. The guy was so clever, so fast.'[8]

Disco Days
As if by chance, another scouser crossed Ali's path, another boxer who was known for his accurate hands as well as nimble footwork. John Conteh was the Liverpudlian who won WBC, British, European and Commonwealth titles. His combination of elegance, power and speed made him the kind of role model for which young Britons of African and West Indian heritage were searching, at a time of under-representation in the media. Here was a hero who would give Black kids from Birmingham, London, Liverpool, Leeds and Manchester something to shout about.

Conteh was also drawn into pop culture, an advantage for somebody with a relatively short career such as boxing. His appearance on the sleeve of Paul McCartney's 1973 album *Band on the Run* alongside the likes of Clement Freud, Christopher Lee, James Coburn and Kenny Lynch underlined his household name status, which was given further credence a year later when he was chosen as the subject of *This is Your Life*. This prime-time TV show was predicated on the idea that the career and professional achievements of a 'personality' were sufficiently notable that the viewers would be interested in their backstory. The personality was supposed to be surprised by the unexpected appearance of presenter Eammon Andrews and 'the big red book' which contained the pictures and press cuttings that charted the celebrity's childhood, youth and adulthood.

Conteh also had small screen roles. He was in *Man at the Top*, a thought-provoking drama on the evils of Big Pharma which allows the sterility of African women as collateral damage in its pursuit of profit, and he was also in the ludicrous soft porn fantasia, *The Stud*,[9] in which he has mercifully brief cameo while the rest of the cast had roles better forgotten. While the movie banked heavily on the appeal of steamy sexual encounters and gratuitous flashes of flesh, the central premise of the film was an attempt to capitalise on one of the key cultural phenomena of the time:

disco. *The Stud* was a trashy British hitch on the American bandwagon that was *Saturday Night Fever*, which brought to mainstream audiences a scene that had gay, Black and Latino roots through the prism of a straight white hero.

The emergence of disco in the early 1970s is a prime example of the synergy between a genre of music and a place of social interaction – the discotheque, a space where people come to dance, flirt and have fun, specifically to records spun by a DJ, just as they had done at West Indian sound system dances or blues parties. In other words a whole lot of rebranding was going on. Discotheque, which means record library in French, became a buzz word that had club owners up and down the country scrambling for a piece of the action, which is why, amid the wealth of venues that adopted the new craze, from working class haunts such as Crazy Daizy in Sheffield to the exclusive Tramps in London, disco's most important venues were the pub rooms, wedding receptions, company dos or school halls, mostly employing a guy with a mobile disco kit. The immediate democracy of disco was part of its power. And the Best Disco in Town could be found in any city.

Inevitably, there is confusion about what actually constitutes the genre because the term encompasses a range of music played in places where people came to loosen their limbs, as much as it does a specific compositional template. There is a marked difference between the lush orchestrations of Van McCoy, People's Choice and Gloria Gaynor, the pummelling electronic rhythms Giorgio Moroder made for Donna Summer and the alarmingly inane thud of Baccara or La Belle Epoque. Chic on the other hand, a group with firsthand experience of the disco of all discos, Studio 54 in New York, had soul, funk and jazz chops that made their work anything but disposable. Disco may have been reduced to the musical formula of a heavy 4/4 kick drum, crisp upper register rhythm guitars, frantic strings and bland lyrics, but many of its exponents, Chic above all, went far beyond any such limitations.

The soundtrack of *The Stud* was notable for its transatlantic nature, including the very soulful harmony vocal group, Odyssey, as well as the funky Rose Royce, whose 'Car Wash' had already featured as the title track of another movie, a sign of shameless cashing in if ever there was one. From the UK there were glam rockers Roxy Music and pop stars 10cc, as well as soulsters Hot Chocolate and Linda Lewis. The Real Thing, who actually appeared in the movie, performed the quite dire number 'Let's Go Disco', an ill-advised attempt to jump on the bandwagon. Thankfully, the scousers would make music of which they could be proud in the coming years.

Across the Water – Again
Whilst the subject of this and previous chapters is the documentation of homegrown Black British talent, arrivals from across the Atlantic still made an impact. In the lineage of African American servicemen (Jimi Hendrix, Geno Washington, Herbie Goins to name but some), was a G.I from Dayton, Ohio, Johnnie Wilder, who formed the group, Heatwave, which became a major chapter in the story of British soul as it took in the influences of 'disco' in the mid-1970s.

Heatwave was born of Wilder's desire to make it as an artist rather than pursue a long-term career in the military. He started singing in clubs when he was stationed in Germany and after relocating to London he met Lincolnshire-born keyboardist-pianist, Rod Temperton, and the group they formed became an international ensemble with players of several nationalities – American guitarist Eric Johns, Swiss bassist Mario Mantese and Czech drummer Ernest 'Bilbo' Berger. Last but not least came another singer, Wilder's brother, Keith, who fleshed out the vocal harmonies, and, like his sibling, was a fabulous performer.

The group signed to the UK label GTO, which was distributed by Epic in America, and made its debut album *Too Hot to Handle* in 1976. While Heatwave's sharply drilled rhythm section was a major part of the soul-funk combo's appeal, the stack of synthesizers, which lent a multi-hued backdrop to expressive lead and backing vocals, was also a key asset. Perhaps most significant in the success of the group was Temperton's contribution. His formative years had been spent playing in dance bands in his native Lincolnshire – he was born in Cleethorpes in 1949 and, like many of the post-war generation discovered R&B and rock by listening to Radio Luxembourg. He was a master songwriter who could match pumping basslines and backbeats with finely wrought melodic lines that would shift through key changes or middle eights, so as to create an engaging narrative arc. The unabashed celebration of nights out at the hallowed disco was the theme of the band's breakout single, 'Boogie Nights', which peaked at number two in the UK charts and in the American Billboard Hot 100. It was an irresistible piece of dance music deeply rooted in the Black pop tradition of a driving groove supplemented by a wide variety of vocal and instrumental hooks, above all Temperton's glossy keyboard lines.

Temperton's melodic sophistication was matched by the vocal range supplied by the Wilder brothers. Many of the songs made much of the alternation of Keith's smoky baritone and Johnny's wispy falsetto, in the rich lineage of doo-wop and harmony singing that ran from The Chords and The Platters to The Persuasions and The Temptations. Yet some of the best Heatwave tunes were much more than dance music. Along with the enticing rhythms came wily key changes, a wide dynamic range, skilful breakdowns and lengthy codas that had an emotional and narrative depth that rounded out the sense of physical release triggered by the beat of a song such as 'The Groove Line'. Heatwave's complex orchestrations were done by John Cameron, whose classical and jazz education had made C.C.S. such an interesting take on blues-rock back in the early 1970s. Added to this artful approach to disco was Heatwave's irrepressible black sass and swagger. This was encoded in their language. Tropes like 'lay-it-on-me', 'beat your booty' and 'ooh-wa ooh-wa' did not come from Temperton's childhood in Cleethorpes, nor did the title of 'Ain't No Half Steppin', which is an ages-old African American colloquialism for the need for honest dealing and straight talking rather than any 'jivin'. In other words, the Wilder brothers evidently taught Temperton something of their own vernacular, giving him a slice of life of Dayton, Ohio as they knew it. Enjoying success into the early 1980s, Heatwave were an important entry in the history of transatlantic Black music, because they were able to offset commercial appeal with artistic integrity, escaping from the more facile end of the disco sub-genre with which they were largely associated. The Wilder brothers were also outstanding dancers. And, of course, they were meant to scale the heights of stardom with gifted piano man from Cleethorpes.

More transatlantic soul
While Heatwave, Hot Chocolate and The Real Thing were racking up large record sales, other Black British bands, more or less within the soul genre, plied their trade with less chart success. There was Clancy, a relatively unknown outfit, who were a notable example of 'serious session talent' drawn from a number of fields, who came together to form a multi-racial band that was sufficiently accomplished to land a deal with the major label, Warner. Anchoring the rhythm section were the gifted Jamaican drummer, Barry Ford, a man who had distinguished himself in reggae combos, and the Nigerian percussionist, Gaspar Lawal, whose extensive list of credits included stints with Ginger Baker among others. Colin Bass was, appropriately enough, on bass, Dave Skinner on keys and Dave Vasco (lead) and Ernie Graham (rhythm) played guitar. They had all worked in rock and soul bands before coming together.

Although Clancy were short lived, the two albums they recorded between 1975 and 1976, *Seriously Speaking* and *Every Day* are worthwhile documents of both an electric and eclectic musical vocabulary that reflects Britain as a meeting place for English and post-colonial artists with open minds. Their blend of state-of-the-art synthesizers and flying congas pushed them into vaguely similar terrain to leading exponents of jazz-fusion and progressive rock who favoured long solos. Yet Clancy also kept faith with the format of verse and chorus and for the most part wrote very good songs, embellished by high standards of performance. They veered tantalisingly between soul and rock without ever fully landing in either genre. Their practice of having several members of the band contribute compositions brought considerable variety to their repertoire.

Moon was another group with a somewhat similar outlook, though the blues and funk quotient were higher on *Too Close for Comfort* and *Turning the Tides*, two albums that reflected the bridge built between songwriters who had an ear for strong melody and musicians wedded to improvisation and richly layered arrangements. With an impressive rhythm section, lead and rhythm guitars and two reeds – alto (Doug Bainbridge) and tenor saxophonists (Nicky Payn), the band was enhanced by the presence of a gifted lead vocalist, Noel McCalla, born in London of West Indian heritage but raised in Coventry. They were aided by having New Yorker Stewart Levine as producer of their first album; he had collaborated with artists as disparate as Hugh Masekela, jazz-fusion supergroup, The Crusaders and Motown writer-singer, Lamont Dozier.

Last but not least was Hummingbird, a group that was originally all British but became transatlantic when it was joined by a member of Love Childs Afro Cuban Blues Band (mentioned above), who can legitimately lay claim to being one of the greatest funk-soul drummers of all time – Bernard 'Pretty' Purdie. Revered for his work with Aretha Franklin and James Brown, Purdie replaced Conrad Isidore after the recording of Hummingbird's eponymous debut album and appeared on the follow-ups *We Can't Go on Meeting Like This* and *Diamond Nights*. The nucleus of the group comprised three players who had been part of Jeff Beck's band – English keyboardist Max Middleton and two Trinidadians, bassist Clive Chaman and guitarist-vocalist Bobby Tench, discussed in Chapter 8, later joined by guitarist Robert Ahwai. There were contributions by vocalists Madeline Bell and Linda Lewis, but Hummingbird was essentially anchored around Tench. His rugged, rasping tone and fiery guitar playing together spoke of a command of the blues and R&B, and gave him exactly the right sort of presence to lead a group as he had done with The Gass. There were other intriguing influences that flowed into this new venture. Middleton's work on electric piano often had the bubbling syncopation and harmonic sophistication trademarked by Herbie Hancock, while Purdie and Chaman made for a quite formidable drums and bass axis that was able to turn with subtlety and power, as it did on a stellar, string-laden version of 'You Can't Hide Love', a gorgeously plaintive theme that had also been performed by a number of artists, including Earth, Wind & Fire.

Sadly, Hummingbird did not endure. It became yet another one of the groups that broke up after making just a few albums and gigging regularly, which was not at all uncommon in the 1970s. There were countless bands that were formed, entered the studio, played a string of live dates and then bit the dust pretty soon afterwards. That high turnover said several things about the reality of the music industry at this time. Not least of the challenges was competition from groups on the live circuit. Of the British contenders, Heatwave were standouts, with their superlative rhythm section as well as frontmen who had such joyous stagecraft that a song could culminate in the bass player climbing on to the singer's shoulders and swaying in perfect time to an intricately mapped rhythm. The majority of rock groups simply could not make that kind of showstopper move.[10]

Yet nobody matched the American giants Earth, Wind & Fire with their highly theatrical, if not magical live show, in which band members levitated like Aladdin's genie with a jet-heeled groove. They remained unsurpassed as entertainers as well as artists, and the British public could not get enough of them. When they appeared at Bingley Hall, Stafford in the mid-1970s, those who were quick off the mark and bought front row seats were offered up to ten times their price by fans who were not content with the vantage point of the middle rows. Only seeing was believing.

Notes

1. South African born Albert Johanneson played for Leeds United in the 1960s.
2. All covered in *Don't Stop the Carnival* (Peepal Tree, 2018).
3. Interview with the author, February, 2022.
4. Several of these tracks feature on *Darker Than Blue: Soul From Jamdown 1973-80* (Blood & Fire, 2001), compiled by author-curator-label owner Steve Barrow.
5. The Hot Chocolate's songbook has several gems, notably 'Emma', 'Call The Police' and 'Heaven Is in the Back Seat of My Cadillac.'
6. Derry Wilkie was the legendary Liverpudlian R&B singer from the 1950s.
7. Tony Hall was also an announcer at the famed Flamingo jazz club in London.
8. Louis Julienne, 1 from 8, featured on HYPERLINK "http://www.louisojulienne.co.uk/" \h wwww HYPERLINK "http://www.louisojulienne.co.uk/" \h.louisojulienne.co.uk
9. *The Stud* (dir. Quentin Masters, 1978) grossed $20 worldwide.
10. *Musikladen*, 19 Nov 2018.

11 OPEN TO PERSUASION

How do you market a black person who is singing what you would term as white music? I'm singing things that are not necessarily rooted in blues and jazz and funk and soul. As a black woman I should be singing purely gospel or blues or some kind of Delta sound or Motown sound. That's what I should be doing as a black person. That's not what I was doing and they had to work out, ok this isn't a black person doing this, how do we sell that to the public?
— Joan Armatrading

If you're black in the States even though they throw bricks at you and you sit at the back of the bus you're American. In England you're not English, which is very weird. If you're born in Manchester you're Manchester. You don't have to be black to play black music and you don't have to be white to play white music.
— Labi Siffre

Aggressive Instruments
Disco era Black popular music, embodied by previously discussed groups such as Heatwave and Hot Chocolate was, for the most part, packaged with a certain glamour and glitz. The artwork of albums released by these bands usually favoured elaborate designs, eye-catching, bright colours and overstated fashion or photography that conveyed sex appeal. So, nothing could have been more anomalous than the sleeve of Joan Armatrading's eponymous 1976 album. The singer's abundant Afro is fading into a black background and the focus is on the Ovation acoustic guitar held at her waist, the wooden body bathed in an orange haze so as to blur its curved shape, while the tuning peg at the end of the neck catches a single shaft of light that makes it a lone star against a dark sky. The portrait has real gravitas. The photograph was taken by Clive Arrowsmith, the man who had shot Paul McCartney's *Band on the Run* sleeve. It deserves a place in the pop imagery hall of fame on artistic merit alone, but its point lies in the statement it makes about the tools of Armatrading's trade. Six and 12-string guitars, instruments for the most part associated with the world of folksinger and singer-songwriters, came to define her artistry, because she did much more than strum a few chords to frame a voice that had a power that was often unassuming but nonetheless as arresting as that record cover.

In short, Joan Armatrading played as well as she sang and wrote. Listen carefully to the skill of her chording, the fine glistening of arpeggios and the heavier crash of her bass notes, fingers hard on the fretboard so as to shore up the low range of her harmonies, and you'll hear a musician who has a command of her instrument that enabled her to add crucial detail to any verse and chorus she sang. Watch any of the many hours of concert footage available on the Internet and you'll witness a wide range of techniques, from ultra precise 'palm muting' to an eye-of-the needle attack with a plectrum that brings fleeting countermelodies and coiling resolutions into the slipstream of her voice. You'll soon understand that when she accompanies herself on guitar, the instrument is not at all subservient to the singer.

'The big guitar rock gods don't scare me,' said Armatrading, before making a candid statement on the gender divide in pop. 'There are good female guitarists, but the instrument is dominated by men, and I can see why. It's a very aggressive instrument. When I play the acoustic, I tend to hit really hard, and when you get to the electric it's a loud, aggressive, strutting thing, which is men.'[1] And she was once told that certain techniques were too difficult, even for men.

By the time *Joan Armatrading* was released, she had already made two other albums, *Back to the Night* and *Whatever's for Us*, which together marked the arrival of a significant new talent in contemporary music, British or otherwise, whose performance standards and artistic integrity were undeniably high. Armatrading had found her vocation at a very early stage of her life and was fully determined to pursue it.

> Songwriting is in my blood. I'm at my happiest when I'm writing. I started to write songs at the age of 14. Before that I used to write limericks, funny short stories and jokes. My mother bought a piano for the front room because she thought it was a great piece of furniture. As soon as the piano arrived in the house, that's when I started to write songs. I'm self-taught on the piano and guitar. I got my first guitar when I saw it in a pawnshop costing £3 and asked my mother if I could have it. She said she had no money but if they would swap it for two old prams then I could have it. I still have that guitar. The neck is wide and as young girl my hands would have been smaller than they are now. I actually don't know how I was able to play that guitar I guess it must have been determination.[2]

This musical desire was framed by a family backstory that broadens perceptions of not just who Black Britons of West Indian origin were, but exactly where they came from. Jamaica was firmly anchored in British consciousness when it came to the image of the archetypal 'coloured immigrant', but settlers also hailed from the lesser-known territories with populations below 50,000, such as Carriacou, Montserrat and St. Kitts, whose capital Basseterre was the birthplace of Armatrading and her parents.

Circumstances were modest. Her father was a carpenter and mother a housewife. In keeping with many other Caribbean families who had limited work and childcare options, they moved to the Brookfields area of Birmingham with their eldest boys, while Joan, one of six siblings, was sent to Antigua to live with her grandmother, only making the crossing to England when she was seven years old. The experience of 'staggered arrivals' in Britain was a phenomenon that produced a wide range of responses among the later arrivals in a family: from feelings of abandoned loneliness to a strong spirit of independence or can-do adaptabilty.

As Joan recounted, the acquisition of a piano and guitar in the family home set her on a creative road as a teenager. She sang hits such as Simon & Garfunkel's 'The Sound of Silence', at her brother's request during an amateur night at Birmingham University, and also performed songs she wrote at local clubs with school friends. But before she entered the music industry, Joan, who had great a love of comedy in her childhood, worked in the female ghetto of the typing pool. She played guitar in her tea breaks. It must have been obvious where her interests lay. She got the sack. This was followed by an opportunity much more suited to her destiny – an offer to join the cast of the British production of *Hair*, the 'American tribal love rock musical' that also featured African American vocalist Marsha Hunt (see Chapter 6). With her Afro puffing out to her shoulders, Armatrading more than looked the part, and while she stopped short of shedding any clothes for the role, the experience was empowering. More importantly, Armatrading struck up a friendship with fellow actor, Pam Nestor, and in between rehearsals they started working on material together, with the latter putting lyrics to the former's melodies, though the roles were also occasionally reversed. Both were equally interested in playing and writing, melody and lyrics. They formed a prolific team.

Living In the City
In the early 1970s, the duo amassed the best part of 100 songs before they were advised to take their work to the publisher, Essex Music, which had T-Rex on its books. They were signed on the spot and assigned a producer, Gus Dudgeon, known for his work with Elton John, who agreed to mid-wife the recording of 14 pieces that became the album *Whatever's for Us*,[3] credited to Armatrading as a solo artist, though it was essentially a collaboration between her and Nestor. The results were excellent. Tracks such as 'Visionary Mountains', 'All the King's Gardens' and 'Mean Old Man' showed that the duo had a chemistry that yielded beautifully wrought melodies as well as sharply observed lyrics on the vagaries of human nature. The songs solely credited to Joan stood out for a lucidity that

was often couched in narrative simplicity. Right words, right sound, right feeling.

Armatrading moved to London in order to build her career, an experience quite probably explored in 'City Girl', arguably the highlight of *Whatever's For Us*, where she evokes the feelings of a new arrival:

> You came into town with your big ideas
> You'll find out that life is just not that way
> There's such a lot of big fish in the sea

Personal though the lyric may be, it is also a vivid summary of the West Indian immigrant experience. For town read Britain and for City Girl read the daughter of a family from a small island, such as St. Kitts, and you have a scenario that resonates for people of colour in Britain, both pre- and post-Windrush. The word 'big' tells a true story, that of ex-colonials who have been weaned on the idea of the 'mother country' as the place where everything is big. And being a 'big shot' in the Caribbean has a particular meaning that does not carry over to the metropolis. Dreams can be dashed. Competition is stiff. That is the reality check Armatrading sings about in her reference to 'big fish in the sea'. It is a candid admission that her career path will be anything but straightforward, one that relates to the thousands of migrants from the Caribbean who had to swim with the great white shark of racism and classism as they negotiate life in post-war Britain. She is astutely distilling a personal but universal disappointment.

Stylistically, *Whatever's for Us* drew on a range of idioms moulded by Armatrading's melodic and lyrical sensibilities, which meant that the material shuttled organically between folk, blues, soul, and rock, with every track having a specific sound-world marked by the threads of percussion, harmonium, sitar or French horns that were woven around the core structure of richly voiced acoustic guitar chords. Armatrading's voice is by turns discreet and commanding, her tone often caught between mid and low range, only rising to an ecstatic high when the moment really demands it. There is no showboating. It's all focus.

Although *Whatever's for Us* was critically acclaimed, it sold poorly. Regardless, Armatrading continued her impressive musical development throughout the 1970s with a string of fine albums including *Back to the Night*, *Show Some Emotion* and *To the Limit*. As a composer-singer-player, she built a body of work that stands as a major achievement in modern British music, with songs that provide moments of emotional solace as well as songs that tell society about itself.

Her greatest works are bona fide anthems. Several stand out. 'Tall in the Saddle' is a gorgeous but spiky ballad about an egotistical lover heading for a fall, which has a brilliant electric guitar solo and a shift to a higher tempo that dramatically galvanises the piece beyond what was suggested in its initial bars. 'No Love for Free' is a showcase for the low, grainy beauty of Armatrading's voice against a backdrop of acoustic guitar played with highly effective dynamics and variety of attack, while 'Cool Blue Stole My Heart' has a rolling rhythm anchored by teasing slides of double bass and emboldened by flurries of piano and organ. 'Love and Affection', arguably Joan Armatrading's signature, is a heart-stoppingly beautiful ballad that has one of the greatest openings in the history of pop composition. Over the gentlest ripples of acoustic guitar that have the majesty of a baroque harpsichord, the singer intones the unforgettable line: "I am not in love but I'm open to persuasion", and the blend of ornate sound and resigned honesty, an insight that so accurately describes real life, can reduce any sensitive adult to tears. She has told the stories of millions in just ten words. As the song progresses, Armatrading maintains the emotional heat in consciously plain language, that fits with myriad chord changes. She subverts the standard verse-chorus model and opts for short, punchy improvisations with a deliciously loose, almost casual shot of repetition – 'I could really move, really move, I could really dance, really dance, really dance, really dance, I could really move, really move, really move, really move' – and this gives the song an emphatic power. From out of nowhere, rhythm becomes a primal force in the arrangement. An initially wistful mood suddenly lifts and bursts into a state of euphoria. But it dissolves back into the lush harmonic waters of the song as Armatrading makes more soaring melodic statements that eventually lead to the emotional release of Jimmy Jewell's brief but potent alto saxophone solo and a swell of low-register backing vocals that have a hint of a South African township choir. This is a very complex composition that achieves the enviable feat of flowing seamlessly through its cycles of intricacy without presenting itself as a piece of grandiose musical architecture. There are so many shifting moods and textures in the four minutes twenty seconds of its existence that it feels like a miniature symphony in the way that some of Stevie Wonder's best work does. Call it an art song for hearts and minds.

Not quite gelling
Over time, Armatrading created a discography that maintained such high creative standards that practically every one of her compositions has some notable quality. Her fourth album release, *Show Some Emotion*, confirmed her excellent musicianship and melodic gifts as well as an effective creative relationship built with an established producer, Glyn Johns, who was highly rated for his work with the Rolling Stones and Led Zeppelin.

Listen to the broad range of Armatrading's songs and it is worth returning to the debate of where she fits on the cultural exchequer. A close inspection of the credits of her recorded output reveals that she has collaborated with talented players from a variety of backgrounds. Percussionist Gaspar Lawal was an essential name in Afro-rock; guitarist Andy Summers, years before he hit pop gold with The Police, had a strong jazz sensibility; while double bassist Ron Matthewson was a noted British jazz musician who recorded with American legends such as Joe Henderson and Bill Evans. Armatrading surrounded herself with players who could perform advanced rather than basic musical tasks – a necessary requirement given the sophistication of her writing. For the most part, the songs sound as if they were conceived without any specific genre in mind, and this openness means that all kinds of resonances, whether folk, rock, blues, or soul, emerge rather than appear as rigidly predetermined elements. In short, Armatrading appeared to be making her own genre from a wide range of genres.

Yet the question of how to market her remained thorny, to the extent that her label, A&M, seemingly exasperated by her lack of major success, took the extraordinary step of taking out an advert in the music press that read like a political manifesto, or rather an appeal to a hostage taker on the FM wave band who had kidnapped our Joan because of her anomalous status:

> You might not have heard her music because radio doesn't know what to do with her. She does not fit into any preconceived format. It's a shame that Joan is too talented to fit. Walk under the ladder. We will give you a free Best of Ep. It's time to free Joan Armatrading!
> She's not a black act, she's not a white act, she is a class act

The cussed issue of record genre categorisation, a bugbear of countless ethnic minority musicians who feel they do not have the same artistic license as their white counterparts, was certainly not something that Armatrading or her management was able to dismiss. Because of the guiding principle of marketing by way of comparison to established models, she was an absolute conundrum. There was no point in billing her as the new Aretha or the next Nina when she clearly was not – or a 'funky Joni' or 'female Jimi' for that matter. With the greatest of ironies, the originality of Joan Armatrading was a liability. She herself was more than aware of the deep-lying, historically rooted racialisation of the music industry that had, right from the days of Race records back in the 1920s, confined black artists to specific genres and consumers rather than afford them the option to play any music, or rather make music that straddled stylistic borders.

How Armatrading was perceived in cultural terms is not clear-cut despite her notable artistic achievements. As a musician who stands right at the crossroads of many genres she has never exclusively been an exponent of Black music. The chord changes and rhythms that define the foundational vocabulary of blues and gospel are not present in many of her compositions. This is very much her prerogative. But one can also argue that the mere fact her writing is so difficult to pin down stylistically stands very much in a Black tradition that has long blurred the lines between the blues, folk, gospel and pop. This is something encapsulated by artists such as Leadbelly, Odetta, Richie Havens, Terry Callier and Phoebe Snow. Armatrading could be seen as part of this lineage, or at least as an individual who found creative freedom within it. Then again, she sometimes strikes a parallel with the work of Janis Ian and Joni Mitchell, hugely talented white North American women adept at deconstructing affairs of the heart by way of winsome melodies and gilded harmonies that provided solace to a post-Woodstock world. Armatrading's material was created in a Black British, post Windrush world, but the common denominator with Ian and Mitchell is artistic excellence

The truth was that she was throwing a disturbing pebble into the murky waters of a music industry in which the colour of one's skin can open or close doors of opportunity, determine access to markets and audiences, and, perhaps most maddeningly of all, lead to perceptions and appraisals according to what an artist is supposed to be doing rather than what they are doing. Armatrading's complexion is dark. She had an abundant Afro. She was destined to be seen as an R&B diva, or a gospel super sister, but that was not where she was coming from. Perhaps Armatrading's importance lies in the way she makes us question our understanding of or rather presumptions about socio-cultural boundaries and ethnic essentialism. She wasn't a dyed-in-the-wool soul, jazz, funk or reggae artist. She was exercising her right as a composer who has the gift of translating melody into an emotional current powerful enough to affect listeners of many constituencies. Armatrading knew the deal as she asked:

> How do you market a black person who is singing what you would term as white music? I'm singing contemporary stuff, I'm singing the kind of thing, not imitating that, but the kind of thing Joni Mitchell and James Taylor and all those guys are singing. I'm singing things that are not necessarily rooted in blues and jazz and funk and soul. As a black woman, I should be singing purely gospel or blues or some kind of Delta sound or Motown sound. That's what I should be doing as a black person. That's not what I was doing and they had to work out, ok this isn't a black person doing this, how do we sell that to the public? We're looking at something but we should be hearing something else. We're hearing something that isn't quite... it's not quite gelling.[4]

Luckily for the cause of good music, Joan Armatrading carried on being Joan Armatrading – and she did have to resist advice to change her name. She did not fit into neat and tidy spaces. The maverick has not faded to this day as she continues to make music on her own terms, right down to composing symphonies. But she was not the only Black artist doing excellent work and not being seen as standard Black.

Saying Things that You Would Never Say in Conversation.
Labi Siffre was another significant figure in British music in the mid-1970s who also crossed boundaries, landing in spaces that caused confusion for audiences, defying the expectations that attended Black singer-songwriters. His ability to make music that straddled folk, pop and soul was not the only hurdle he had to clear. Appearances were also deceptive. Siffre was savvy enough to realise that even before he'd played a note of music, judgments were being made about his image, or rather the lack of it, in the sense of glamour and glitz. Footage of a self-effacing, almost diffident young man in a tank top, perched on a stool, holding an acoustic guitar (something that might well be called 'The Armatrading syndrome' for UK artists of colour), carried a particular stereotype, about which Siffre did not hold back his feelings when he was interviewed for BBC's *Sounding Out* in 1972. He knew exactly what was going on.

> A lot of people of course see a gentleman from the hotter part of the Commonwealth walk on the stage… Good heavens he's not wearing a gold lamé suit! Good heavens he hasn't said 'hi y'all' or evening! Where is his 95-piece backing group and the go-go girls, and they don't believe it until… they go away not believing, he's putting me on, man.[5]

The use of the term Commonwealth positions Siffre squarely: being the son of a Nigerian father and Bajan-Belgian mother puts him within the realm of post-colonial history to which he opposes the razzle dazzle synonymous with African American R&B and soul traditions, with the big production right down to orchestra and dancers. He knows that he is viewed through a prism which is not relevant to who he is. His authenticity becomes an apparent lack of authenticity, or even a failure for not delivering on the preset criteria. Singers have to be believed, or they fulfil beliefs projected onto them.

But dressed 'properly black' or not, Siffre proved the real deal when it came to crafting an appealing melody and thoughtful lyric. The string of excellent albums he made in the first half of the decade – *Labi Siffre*; *The Singer and The Song*; *Crying, Laughing, Loving, Lying*; *For the Children*; *Happy, Remember My Song* – is the sign of a disciplined artist who was true to his own demanding work ethic, namely that if you start a song then you should be able to finish what it promises. Containing over seventy compositions, those six albums recorded in just five years combine quality and quantity. Siffre wrote impressively distilled pieces, sometimes no more than a few minutes, sometimes coming in just under six, that wove additional layers onto a melodic backbone that often had an irresistibly catchiness, sometimes with a sprinkle of blues, sometimes without. He changed at will.

His biggest commercial success summarises that ability. Released as a single in 1971, 'It Must Be Love' peaked at 14 in the charts and became a favourite in the singer's repertoire as well as a romance staple for successive generations of listeners. The rhythmic-harmonic foundation of the song is a lightly strummed acoustic guitar line, whose high resonance implies the hearty swing of a 1920s banjo player, providing a trail of brightness to which Siffre brings simple but penetrating illuminations on what unfolds in a relationship. He homes in on moments of truth expressed in language that is anything but florid, from 'I never thought I'd miss you half as much as I do' to 'I know that it's you that I need to take the blues away'. The verse gives way to a gently rising pre-chorus, given more body by the arrival of discreet flutes before Siffre attacks the chorus in earnest, bolstered by the puff, swirl and swell of heavier woodwinds that dramatise his emotional state, for the beauty of the lyric is not just a declaration of love for another but the awakening to it. The song is really about honestly acknowledging what is in one's own heart.

Yet if the plain directness of the lyrics served the song so well, Siffre still questions the very function of language, or rather its potential redundancy within the field of human communication: How can it be that we can say so much without words? the song asks. Indeed, so much of Siffre's motivation and achievement as a lyricist is the recognition of the fumbling inadequacy of language in affairs of the heart. Maybe a great love song is essentially an articulation by inarticulate beings. When he was questioned about how to find the right words for a song, Siffre's response was thought provoking:

> I'm not at all poetic... Poetry is not one of my strong points at all. I always believe that poets should write poetry and lyricists should write songs. There are things that you can say in a song that you would be too embarrassed to say in conversation. In a song you can say it and it sounds correct. And also it's a cowardly way of saying things that you would never say in conversation.

My Name Is...
True as that assertion may be, it also points to the possibility that instrumental music is the solution to that conundrum. And, like Joan Armatrading, Labi Siffre plays to a very high standard. By accident or design, the guitar solo, a slowly winding staircase of notes that runs over 16 bars, but feels longer for its relaxed pacing, adds meaning to the story of 'It Must Be Love'. Indeed, Siffre's early aspiration was to be a jazz soloist: 'I decided to be the next Wes Montgomery,' he said, referring to one of the founding fathers of modern jazz guitar. That desire to follow in the footsteps of a great improviser perhaps explains how Siffre ended up as part

of the house band at Annie's in London, a club run by the esteemed Scottish jazz singer, Annie Ross, of the vocalese trio Lambert, Hendricks & Ross. Prior to the gig at Annie's, Siffre, who was born in Hammersmith, West London and educated at a monastery school in Ealing, also gained a knowledge of music theory at the renowned Eric Gilder School in Soho. After doing a number of day jobs in Britain that included being a taxi driver, he had a stint with various soul bands in Cannes in the south of France, before he came back to the UK and started a solo career in 1970.

Though known for the success of 'It Must Be Love', whose gentle momentum exerted an appeal on easy-listening programmers, Siffre had plenty of African American DNA in his songwriting bloodstream. He recalls making a start in music by standing in front of the fireplace miming to Little Richard and Fats Domino, and also wanting to be 'the next Jimmy Reed.' Thereafter, the target was Joe Williams, whose lordly baritone graced many recordings by Count Basie. Siffre also found that his voice was at one point becoming 'a strange mixture of Mel Tormé and Billie Holiday', two legends who rank high in the pantheon of jazz vocalists. Listen to each in turn and try and imagine a synthesis, and what Siffre argues is not so fanciful. His own timbre has a beguiling blend of weightiness and airiness, a materiality and ethereality that allow him to pack a real punch on some phrases and then waft and hover over others, which works well for the wide stylistic range of his songbook.

There are lots of Labi Siffres. To one set of ears he can pass for one of the most accomplished of the post-Simon & Garfunkel tunesmiths, a man who can craft a bejewelled audio short story in 'Bless the Telephone', but also imply the orchestral grandeur and lush harmony of a classic Bacharach song on his anthem, 'Nothing in the World Like Love'. Yet if, as Joan Armatrading stated of her own material, Siffre is not always rooted in blues, jazz, funk and soul, these foundational elements of Black music can still be heard throughout his work, and nowhere is this more apparent than in *Remember My Song*, recorded in 1975. With an orchestra, electric rhythm section and a sleeve design that showed the artist wearing a tuxedo a la Harold Melvin, sitting with a carafe of red wine in a well-appointed dining room, this album could be seen as the moment when EMI, the major label to which Siffre had signed following his earlier releases on Pye, made an unabashed play for the sophisticated soul market previously cornered by the Americans. Regardless of any deliberate nods in that direction, Siffre's writing hit new peaks of excellence, revealing that he could be, to quote Nina Simone, another wilful genre chameleon, funkier than a mosquito's tweeter.

'Sadie and the Devil' was the kind of crackling country blues that Simone herself might have been happy to cover, whilst 'The Vulture' had the vigorous, backbeat-led, mid-tempo groove that the pop end of disco had largely sanitised rather than invigorated, dulling the cutting edge of funk rather than sharpening it. Here the guitar, bass and strings slashed away with the kind of intensity that had made R&B such an irresistible force for post-war British kids in the days when crooners walked the earth. Even more impactful was 'I Got The', which showed how to induce drama into music by way of ambitious scoring. The arrangement by Big Jim Sullivan, a noted producer and session guitarist for stars such as David Bowie, taps right into the soundtrack vocabulary patented by such as Quincy Jones and Lalo Schifrin in the heyday of car chase and crime caper music. A tapestry of swish strings, by turns alluring and unsettling, threads around a central bassline that is stupendously funky in its use of space between octave leaps and chromatic runs, teasing the ear at a relaxed bpm rather than a frantic one. If the introduction to the piece provides an object lesson in how to gradually layer and criss-cross the different elements of the band, then the verse and chorus see Siffre declare that he has the blues, though his emotional load will soon be lightened when he gets to his lover. The piece goes through two choruses, with the singer becoming more hotly impassioned on the second, before it cools and embarks on a key change mapped by a heavy thud of bass against a solid snap of snare. The effect is so startling it is easy to overlook the fact that bassist Dave Peacock (one half of the cockney pub song duo Chas & Dave who enjoyed chart success in the 1980s), is just playing groups of two terse eighth notes that land on the pulse like boulders on hard, dry earth. The tight grip on the activity makes the point that funk can really scale the heights of expression when players do less rather than more. Siffre supports the bass notes with squelchy electric piano chords that sneak upwards before long trails of strings and fleeting brass countermelodies fill out the score. In the coda, the band speeds up to a ritzy Saturday night show-time finale, and there is a spike of humour here, which might well remind us that Siffre once said that he preferred the comic strip Peanuts to the Bible. One of the songs he cut at the start of his career, 'Rocking Chair', also showed his roots in R&B, but 'I Got The' was on a different level entirely, and for the breakdown alone it has a special place in musical history. As was the case with Cymande's 'Bra', Joe Cocker's 'Woman to Woman' and Average White Band's 'Schoolboy Crush', it became one of the great British breakbeats, a tune that caught the ear of producers and helped to launch the career of superstar American rapper Eminem[6] in the late 1990s.

Not to See the Artist
If you take a cursory scan at Siffre's composition titles, the word that comes up several times is one of the simplest and most meaningful in the lexicon of music: song. It really is a kind of mission statement that can lead to the most direct, literal reflection of where a piece is created, as

in the enticing 'Hotel Song', or there can be a more direct, emotionally charged plea for acknowledgement, as in 'Remember My Song'. Siffre has been candid about the need for craft, and the intriguing relationship between vocal and instrumental sounds.

> If you start a song, if you're any good at all, you should be able to finish it. I find the music the easiest and the words second, but one of the hardest things of all for me is subject. If I'm close to it, there's a lot of mathematics in writing songs. You get a word at the end of a line and there are only so many words that will fit or scan, and you just have to hope that one of those words will lead you on to something that means what you want to say. I'd like to write a song in which there was no rhyme whatsoever, for example just take a conversation, record a conversation and then put it to music.[7]

That thought-provoking statement could make for a worthwhile exercise at any contemporary popular music academy, though in fact jazz musicians have long been transcribing speech and shaping improvisations around it, but it is an important reminder of Siffre's considerable work ethic. Such is the clarity of his purpose, it is tempting to suppose that the socio-cultural and political issues that weighed on artists of colour in the pop world of the mid-1970s were of little interest to him. There is no direct treatment of race in his lyrics, yet in the same interview his plea for a kind of neutrality – colour-blindness may be too strong a term – suggests that he was all too aware of exactly how race shaped perceptions of music.

> I would like the audience not to know who I was and not to see me... in completely all forms of music in fact... not to know the artist, not to see the artist, not to know who wrote the song or the piece. But just to hear the music completely devoid of anything and evaluate the music on its merits. I don't believe in giving the audience what it wants anyway, I believe in giving the audience my best and making them like it.[8]

Siffre was also disarmingly frank about African American and Black British identities, and the related question of who should play what. 'If you're black in the States, even though they throw bricks at you and you sit at the back of the bus, you're American. In England you're not English, which is very weird,' he said. Yet he holds the view that ethnicity does not determine one's command of genre, 'If you're born in Manchester, you're Manchester. You don't have to be black to play black music and you don't have to be white to play white music.'[9]

Given the fact that just a few years prior to these comments, journalists and musicians thought nothing of calling Chris Farlowe a 'white Negro', because he managed to sing soul without being a 'brother', Siffre's assertion that the world of sound should not be prescribed by racial boundaries was a breath of fresh air, but who was willing to listen to him was a moot point. The ideal of a music industry free of the prejudices that blighted civil society was one of the biggest of pipe dreams for an artist, of course, and the hard edge of Siffre's honesty was welcome for the way that he nailed the myth of race as a determinant of genre.

Also on his mind was the question of content as well as form. What was an individual singing about? Were they saying something? Were they representing their community? Were they taking a stand? Siffre had no qualms on the issue. He simply went his own way. 'I'm what you'd call an unhealthy agnostic I'm not a protest singer.'[10] The same holds for Armatrading. She excelled at what could be called love songs with intelligence and insight.

Both artists have a large LGBTQ fanbase, and though there are no explicit references to sexuality in their work, 'It Must Be Love' and 'Love and Affection' are truly universal songs that are as applicable to gay as to straight romances. And though Siffre never attempted to hide his sexuality, there was little discussion, respectful or otherwise, to it in the music press in the 1970s and 1980. Whether this silence reflected a respect for privacy or an unwillingness to see gay and lesbian identities as contributing to the breadth and depth of Black music is open to question. One can only guess if either artist, in a different era, might have explored more publicly their 'double minority' status of black and queer. Armatrading married her long-term partner Maggie Butler in 2012, but has made no public statements about her private life, which is her inalienable right. Yet it was perhaps those very qualities in her personal life that led her to make powerful social comment in a song such as 'Barefoot and Pregnant', one of the great feminist anthems of the 1970s. Even, then, in an interview she gave to *Spare Rib* magazine, Armatrading gives a carefully nuanced explanation of her motivations: 'I'm not sitting down and saying it's ok, I'm writing specifically for feminism or specifically for a black person or specifically for a woman... As a woman who is mindful of women being treated fairly and properly then of course I'm involved in that.'[11]

Adult Window Shopping

Joan Armatrading may well have been intrigued by 'Red Light Ladies'. Issued in 1972, the song made an interesting social comment. It cast a non-judgmental eye over scantily clad sex workers on display in the vice area of Amsterdam. Compared to 'Love For Sale', Cole Porter's incisive 1930 summary of the 'world's oldest profession', the lyrics were notably darker. The women were passive playthings.

> Red Light ladies, where did your love go?
> Sitting in your windows like dolls,

Waiting to be sold.
Lay, ladies, lay.

Linda Lewis, who worked with Armatrading, wrote these words and accompanying bluesy music. She was a vital addition to the stock of 'homegrown' Black British talent who emerged in the late 1960s. In fact, she was part of a lineage of singers born in the UK who had either African or Caribbean heritage that included 1950s icons Shirley Bassey, Cleo Laine and Elaine Delmar, and her music had great artistic integrity, with the bulk of her output centring on affairs of the heart rather than political issues.

Hailing from West Ham, east London, Lewis, whose mother was Guyanese and father Jamaican, attended, firstly, stage school and then a convent school where she was encouraged to write poetry. She made a brief foray into the world of film, with a non-speaking part in *A Taste of Honey*, a classic 'kitchen sink' drama that tackled the subjects of class, race, the generation gap, homosexuality and illegitimacy. On a decidedly lighter note, Lewis was one of the thousands of fans seen screaming at the Beatles in *A Hard Day's Night*.

Lewis soon had the chance to sing rather shout hysterically. She joined a ska group, the Q Set but it was an impromptu appearance in a Southend club with the backing band of blues legend John Lee Hooker that launched her music career in earnest. Hooker introduced Lewis to producer-A&R, Ian Samwell, who signed her to Polydor. In 1967 her single 'You Turned My Bitter into Sweet' was released with little commercial success, though it did find favour on the Northern soul scene. Lewis subsequently worked with US expat soul singer Herbie Goins, and with his Jamaican guitarist, Junior Kerr, she formed White Rabbit, a band influenced by west coast rockers, Jefferson Airplane. Lewis then went on to replace American vocalist Marsha Hunt in soul-rock combo, The Ferris Wheel, with whom she toured Europe extensively.

Lewis jammed with various artists at the inaugural Glastonbury festival in 1970, headlined by The Kinks, and for which tickets cost £1, and came with the added bonus of free farm's milk as well as a 'lightshow, diorama, films, freaks and funny things.' More importantly, she made a sufficient reputation for herself to work as a first-call backing vocalist, and did sessions with British rock and pop royalty, from David Bowie and Elton John to Marc Bolan and Cat Stevens. In 1971, Lewis made her first album, *Say No More...* which showed that she was capable of skillfully treading a middle path between soul, folk, rock and pop, and during the 1970s she made no fewer than seven solo albums.

A self-taught guitarist and pianist, Lewis knew how to interpret a melody with all the nuance and attention to detail that defines the best singers, and whether she was opening her heart on a tender love song, such as 'Lullabye', or imploring listeners to loosen up and dance on the charmingly mellow funk of 'Rock A Doodle Do', which peaked at number 15 in the 1973 UK singles chart, her performances were consistent and credible.

Depths Not Shallows
As a vocalist, Lewis had an impressive technique. Her five-octave range allowed her to glide seamlessly into the upper register with an assurance that eluded many of her peers, and on much of her material her phrasing was captivatingly ethereal, as if she had drifted into a dream state to reveal her deepest feelings. There could also be a slender, almost fragile finesse in her voice that was Billie Holiday-esque.

However, she was always much more than a singer. Like Joan Armatrading and Labi Siffre, Linda Lewis was an excellent composer. She had a gift for original melodies and well-crafted lyrics that enabled her to tell stories that had wit as well as emotional charge. She either wrote or co-wrote practically all the songs on accomplished albums such as *Say No More…* and *Fathoms Deep*, but it is *Lark*, recorded in 1972, that represents the creative peak of Lewis's work.

An important entry in the canon of British music of the decade, the 13-track masterpiece was entirely penned by Lewis and jointly produced by herself and guitarist Jim Cregan. The quality of the material is outstanding. Every composition has a thematic richness that is enhanced by Lewis's technique and emotional investment, but it is above all the choices made in terms of instrumentation and arrangement that show the artist to her best advantage.

There is an airy quality in the music. There is space. There is openness. Many of the songs, even the ones in which Lewis has a gusty, punchy delivery, conspire to float and hover like feathers that won't touch the ground, even though they are anchored by a firm underlying beat. Lewis is on rather similar territory to that of Laura Nyro, Terry Callier, and Richie Havens, who all bridged the gap between the tradition of folk blues and the modernity of soul, jazz and pop to varying degrees. A common denominator between these artists, apart from the poetic slant in the their lyrics, is the use of a small, strong but supple rhythm section, and that choice also proves to be of importance on *Lark*. The core sound is really acoustic guitar, bass and percussion, and this relatively sparse, limpid setting serves the material very well.

Gerry Conway plays drums on two tracks, 'Reach for the Truth' and 'Old Smokey', but on the other 11 pieces it is either he or Emile Latimer who features on percussion. Instead of a hefty kick, snare and cymbals, it is a pair of congas that provide the main groove, creating a fluidity that enhances the more sensitive, delicate turns of Lewis's voice, which nonetheless hits peaks of volume and has passing rhythmic flurries. 'Waterbaby', inspired by folk icon Cat Stevens, who also happens to be a Cancer, is a highlight. The changes in tempo and shifts from dark to bright chords match the wide spectrum of colours in Lewis's voice, which is framed by sensual streaks of electric piano and propulsive, bluesy soloing by guitarist Jim Cregan. Tailed by these incisively wiry, finger-picky improvisations, Lewis varies her pitch in both understated and emphatic fashion, especially on a memorably impassioned coda where her repeated plea of 'keep on flowing' brings the arrangement to a rousingly funky climax as the congas bubble away beneath her.

Elsewhere on *Lark,* the artful use of instruments that are less commonly heard in pop, above all vibraphone and marimba, embellishes the tonal palette of the music without being too obtrusive. On 'Been My Best' a moment of magic occurs when Lewis's hummed line is doubled by Poli Palmer's flute, so that it feels as if the singer's breath is blending into the whisper of a late summer breeze, vividly adding to the intimacy of the song and reinforcing the impression that the performance is unfolding in a rural rather than urban space. It's easy to imagine the golden melody ringing out at Glastonbury.

Nudge Nudge Wink Wink...
If the fine singing and exemplary playing on *Lark* can draw comparisons between Lewis and legendary North Americans who worked at the crossroads of soul, folk, jazz and pop, such as Laura Nyro, Minnie Riperton, and Phoebe Snow, there were nonetheless clear cultural differences that could be discerned. Lewis did not hide her identity. The final track of *Lark* was a short piece called 'Little Indians', which, rather than being a studio recording, was taken from a live set in which Lewis addressed the audience in a very clear *London* accent. And if the sound of her speaking voice flagged up her origins, then there were lyrics she had written that had salient references to a childhood spent in Britain.

Say No More... could well be a cheeky nod to comedy upstarts Monty Python's eyebrow-raising double entendre 'nudge nudge wink wink... say no more', while a more direct statement on Lewis's life experience comes in the shape of 'Hampstead Way'. The song evokes the artist commune in Hampstead, north London in which she once lived, where fellow residents included Robert Wyatt, drummer-singer of the legendary progressive rock band, Soft Machine. To accompany these local cultural signposts there is also the use of specific British colloquialisms in some of Lewis's songs that mark her out as an artist engaged in an interesting transatlantic exchange of ideas and modes of speech. She thought nothing of slipping the endearing Cockney expression 'Bless 'em all' into the outro of 'Moles', and as soulful as she is on 'Play Around', Lewis draws on a frothy informal vocabulary that is decidedly more Canning town than California.

> Another night at the disco
> I'm dressed up to the nines
> Looking tasty, feeling wasted
> Spending lolly with a friend of mine.

The colloquial verve of our side of the Atlantic thus surfaces in Lewis's African American-based music, and although she did not make this cross-cultural blending a recurrent feature of her songbook, the lyrics of 'Play Around' show that she wouldn't deny a working-class London vernacular, her undeniable birthright as a proud Eastender.

And yet for all her talent, Lewis still had to endure the same struggle as countless women, Black and white, in a male-dominated music industry that sought to impose control over her career and force her to sing the kind of songs that prioritised mass appeal at the expense of creativity. For example, Lewis's cover of 'It's in His Kiss', originally recorded by Betty Everett in 1964, may have given the British singer her biggest success in 1975, but the arrangement and production were a blatant, regrettably bland attempt to ride the disco wave of the era. Lewis, whose natural artistic centre of gravity was that of a singer-songwriter strumming an acoustic guitar, casually dressed in denim, clashed with producers who wanted to mould her into a sparkly soul glamour queen against her wishes, and, looking back, she admitted great discomfort at her lack of agency: 'I really hated that period when I went disco diva. I got very disillusioned and got tired of being treated like a puppet.'[12]

This chimed with the experience of other black women singers, notably P.P. Arnold, discussed in Chapter 6. Indeed, the essential questions of setting a career direction, choosing a repertoire and working with a producer with whom an artist could collaborate on an equal footing, rather than be blindly beholden to, have bedevilled artists with 'double minority' status, namely being non-white and non-male, for decades.

There is a long history of unhealthy power dynamics in the music industry that has often seen publishers, record labels, agents and managers view artists as nothing more than cash cows, or as Nina Simone was once described, racehorses, who are there to do the bidding of their handlers rather than create any worthwhile art on their own terms.

Arnold was not given the chance to record her own songs, but Lewis and Joan Armatrading made a huge step forward for female artists of all ethnicities because they brought their fine original melodies and lyrics to the fore and created songbooks that have stood the test of time. Armatrading has an interesting take on why Black women resisted second-class citizen status, showing that they had the fortitude to stand their ground. 'Men in the business said you've got to sing pretty because you're made that way as a woman. Black women don't sing pretty because they haven't been brainwashed into being weak. They have to be strong and just get on with it.'[13]

Notes

1. *Joan Armatrading: Me, Myself, I* (Dir. Poppy Edwards).
2. Ibid.
3. *Whatever's For Us* (A&M, 1972).
4. *Joan Armatrading: Me, Myself, I* (Dir. Poppy Edwards).
5. *Sounding Out* BBC, 21 Feb, 1972 (BBC Archive).
6. Eminem, *My Name Is Eminem* samples Labi Siffre's 'I Got The'.
7. *Sounding Out* BBC, 21 Feb, 1972 (BBC Archive).
8. Ibid.
9. Ibid.
10. Ibid.
11. *Joan Armatrading: Me, Myself, I* (Dir. Poppy Edwards).
12. *The Guardian* obituary, Peter Mason, 7/5/23.
13. *Joan Armatrading: Me, Myself, I* (Dir. Poppy Edwards).

12 THE REVOLUTION WILL NOT BE CAPITALIZED

> It was an image of Babylon. What we aspired to but where we are, running away from that which you're running into. It was an idea to bring the aspirations and the challenges to those aspirations all in one place but in an image that was really easy to decipher. The palm tree? We'd never seen a palm tree, but we'd definitely seen mashed up Beetles, the poor man's car, the urban landscape…a concrete jungle.
> — Mykaell Riley, Steel Pulse on the sleeve of the album *Handsworth Revolution*

Pressure Drop
'Being strong and just getting on with it', to paraphrase Joan Armatrading, was an aphorism that surely resonated with Black people in Britain in the mid-1970s, not just a woman trying to make it in the music industry. The struggle of ethnic minorities for social justice had finally resulted in legislation that at least acknowledged there was an issue when the Race Relations Act of 1976, or rather the latest version of legislation from 1965 and 1968 passed through parliament. In theory, the act offered safeguards to ensure that people of colour could assert their rights in the fields of employment, education and the provision of goods and services. In addition, a new body, the Commission for Racial Equality was founded to monitor the act and raise awareness of the existence of racial discrimination and the injustices that flowed from it.

What Black people in Britain themselves felt and their pessimism about whether state institutions would bring any redress was expressed in the film *Pressure*, made by the Trinidadian photographer and filmmaker Horace Ové, who had worked in Rome as an actor and had been strongly influenced by Italian neorealist cinema. When he moved back to London in the early 1970s he became part of a Black British artistic community that sought to articulate views about its place in British society and refusal to accept second-class status.

The film, finished around 1973/4, was not released officially until 1976. The delay at the instruction of the movie's own funder, the British Film Institute, tells you all you need to know about the work's uncompromising direction, the BFI's anxiety about its government funding, and the lack of agency of Black artists seeking to have an independent voice heard. The scenes depicting police brutality against peaceful activists, which resonated with the Mangrove restaurant affair, alarmed the funders. The same fate had befallen the television play *Fear of Strangers*, starring Earl Cameron, for the same reason in 1964. The police beat up folks who were black. That information had to be kept out of the public domain. As Ové later reflected: 'This film can't be shown here because it was dealing with the real world. At the time nobody was willing to expose themselves.'[1]

Ové had been turned down by a number of production companies before the BFI agreed to fund it. He was breaking new ground in telling truthful stories about the racism of the police and employers. But *Pressure* was also a film that addressed divisions within Black British communities and the West Indian household, portraying the deep alienation of a son who did not come from the islands. He is at odds with his elders as well as with wider society. '*Pressure* was based on the reality, on what was going on in the country at the time,' Ové said. 'The kind of problems black people were having with racism, the kind of problems the younger British kids, black kids growing up here, and their problems.'[2] There were different registers in the narrative, with the scenes of the youth wandering carefree in Brixton market marking a sharp contrast to tense encounters with the police and employers.

From today's standpoint, *Pressure* perhaps has much more to say about race as seen from a male perspective than from the position of Black women. Its strength lies in its characterisation, particularly of the dominant figure of Tony as a teenager, who is intelligent and heading towards a political awakening, finding himself on a socio-cultural battleground that has skirmishes on anything from food – he mispronounces pattie as paté, prefers fish and chips to avocados – to job interviews in which it is presumed he has newly arrived in England even though he was born in London. His mother's assertion that his English education means that 'nothing should stop you' is shown to be a hollow illusion.

Hence the film's theme song, credited to Wonder Boy and the Sisters, with lyrics penned by Ové, decries 'mental pressure, physical pressure, parental pressure.' That unholy trinity was framing the lives of the new generation of Black Britons, who saw their home as here in Britain while they were still perceived as outsiders from over there, in the West Indies, and suffering the indignity of being told to 'get back to your own country.'

Roughly contemporary to *Pressure,* was *Step Forward Youth*, a documentary made by Menelik Shabazz in 1977, which focuses on Black London teenagers of Caribbean heritage. It has a series of remarkable first-hand accounts of that new generation's marginalisation in British society. One astute interviewee, talking about classroom racism, said: 'British means white to me.' She is also seen finding solace in a sound system dance, realising that her peers, like the fictional characters in *Pressure*, were being anglicised by way of daily norms, such as diet. She also argues that reggae has come to play a key role of cultural preservation. The music is like an umbilical cord to the homeland she doesn't know.

> It's the only thing left. We're born here, never having been to Jamaica, the custom of eating West Indian food is slowly leaving... having to eat school dinners because our parents are out all day. West Indian food is gone. What else is there left? There's just music. And where is all the music coming from? Jamaica. It just has to be reggae.[3]

Black music in Britain thus became a bridge between Black people inside and outside of Britain, across history and geography, and a link in an increasingly complex socio-political chain.

Exodus in Ladbroke Grove
Reggae rhythms provided the soundtrack to *Pressure*, and the arrival of another new crop of artists dovetailed with the release of the film. Indeed, the musician who led an important Black British band of the time could have featured in one of the film's scenes in Portobello market, as a character or an extra. After all, he was an actor and that was his stamping ground. Television viewers with sharp eyes might have remembered him from the BBC 1 children's adventure series, *Here Come the Double Deckers* and the arthouse drama *Leo the Last* as well as *Diamonds Are Forever*. Brinsley Forde, born in Islington to Guyanese parents but raised in west London recalled: 'I was learning about Rasta and it was difficult for me; there were no parts for young black actors at that time. And I kind of had to make a decision: what do I do? And I decided with music. I could go to the studio, I could record so I leant towards music and later on I formed Aswad, so it was perfect.' His immersion in the world of Trojan ska and then reggae in his formative years, as well as his love for the guitar, had drawn him inexorably towards that decision. It helped that one of his good friends at school had a sound system and Forde himself, briefly in his teenage years, had his own sound system, appropriately named Youth. He knew that world well, having soaked up the energy of master operators such as Coxsone, Duke Vin and the lesser-known Nick Burton (in Cricklewood).

As a player, Forde cut his teeth with older West Indian artists in London such as the Jamaican-born singer Junior English, who had a major success in the mid-1970s with the single 'In Loving You', but Forde's ambition to strike out on his own was realised when he formed Aswad. The band's original line-up comprised himself, bassist George Oban, guitarist Donald Griffiths, keyboardist Courtney Hemmings and drummer Angus Gaye. These youngsters, who had been in other outfits, had the precious opportunity of being allowed to rehearse in the garage of Forde's parents, which, echoing the testimony of Dennis Bovell earlier in the book, gave them a safe haven from casual persecution by the police. In Shabazz's documentary, *Step Forward Youth*, Gaye was recorded speaking about being punched by a police officer after being arrested for no reason, and more to the point, realising that he was powerless to hold the assailant accountable.

If the music of Jamaica was the source of inspiration, then Rastafarianism, with its embrace of Afro-centricity, was crucial to Aswad's genesis and evolution. Hence Forde was dubbed Chaka B as an onomatopoeic reference to the crisp, cutting sound of the rhythm guitar, while Gaye became Drummie Zeb for obvious reasons, Oban became Ras Oban and Hemmings, Khaki. Most meaningful of all was the band's choice of name:

> I found it in a book of African names. I was looking for a word that would be very easy to say for European people but had a meaning to it. And Aswad meant black in Arabic, so we were telling our story from a black perspective. We were young black kids growing up in England.[4]

Landing a deal with Island, Aswad recorded an excellent eponymous debut album in 1976 that was followed by *Hulet* three years later. Both were important chronicles of Forde's generation's frustration and defiance. This was emphatically expressed in the patois of songs such as 'I a Rebel Soul' while the central image of 'Concrete Slaveship' had a clear resonance with Bob Marley's 'Concrete Jungle'. But the piece that perhaps most vividly defines Aswad was 'Can't Stand the Pressure', a title that echoed Horace Ove's film and Toots and the Maytal's great 1968 song, 'Pressure Drop'. The chorus expressed the condition of Forde and his peers as one of desperation – 'Oh, oh can't stand the pressure/Oh oh can't bear the pain'. Faced with such bleak circumstances, the response was one of self-empowerment. With the biblical inflections prevalent in Rastafarian reggae, Aswad implored the bredrin to gird their loins and dare to be seen and heard rather than cower in fear.

> Why standeth in the shadows
> Muted by your cry?

Other songs such as 'Judgment Day' carried a spirit of resistance, defining Forde and co as a band born of Rastafarianism's militancy. Musically, Aswad were very much in line with the sound of classic 'roots reggae'; their tempos were leisurely rather than frantic, the central axis of drums and bass impressively solid; the guitars curt and crisp in their chords; the keyboards discreet yet effective in harmonic colouring, while Forde's lead vocal sounds unabashedly Caribbean. And if countless hours spent listening to Jamaican music in their formative years had served Aswad well, then further education came by way of the chance they had to back one of the great singer-philosophers in the Rasta movement at the time, Winston Rodney, aka Burning Spear, when he appeared in London in 1977. The resulting live album shows that Black British musicians could play to a sufficiently high standard to accompany vocalists of the calibre of Rodney. The concert took place at the Rainbow Theatre in Finsbury Park, north London, the venue that saw Bob Marley take another step towards stardom following his previous triumphant appearance at the Lyceum. Working with Jamaican artists such as Burning Spear gave Aswad a direct link to reggae at a key point in its development, and further invaluable experiences came unexpectedly, as Forde recalled:

> I was working at a greengrocer in Neasden, and Peter Tosh walked by! The Wailers were staying around the corner. I was a big fan of the Wailers. I think I must have had seven cuts of one of the Wailers' tracks. So, I was a big fan, so I went around there (where the band was housed... And in the end I took my guitar and amps and stuff round to the house, and we used to jam. Family (Aston Barrett, the revered bass man of the band) wanted me to play bass, so a lot of my early musical (education) came from that.[5]

A Band Reborn
The opportunists who cash in on Marley stories are legion; if all claimants are to be believed, there would be a stadium full of journalists who kicked a football with him. By contrast, the close engagement of Forde and his peers with Marley and his group, can be seen in the proof of genuine cultural exchange. The Island Records studio, at 8-10 Basing Street, Notting Hill, was where the sessions for Marley's *Catch A Fire*, *Burnin'* and *Exodus* took place. At the time, Marley was living on the first floor of this building. Dennis Bovell, founder of Matumbi as well as the operator of a sound system called Sufferer Hi Fi, remembers how a kind of informal focus group or trial listenership was formed when Marley and members of the Wailers felt that the material they were working on was ready to be shared with others. 'On Friday night, he would come into our club, hear the sound system,' Bovell told me in 2022, recalling the residency he had at the Metro in Ladbroke Grove. 'Because he loved the way the sound system was heavy, Family Man (Barrett) would cut me a couple of dubplates that I could play, so that Bob could sit upstairs and look at the audience and see how the audience was dancing to the songs.'[6] Testing out tunes on the dance floor to gauge whether they would fly or die had long been a pragmatic approach to making music intended for recording, particularly at a point when there was intense competition among post-war Jamaican artists. Bovell was in the highly privileged position of being among the first to hear freshly-minted mixes of anthems such as 'Exodus', and this

12: THE REVOLUTION WILL NOT BE CAPITALIZED

would have had his conviction in the identity of Matumbi well and truly reinforced. The 'movement of Jah people', the 'back to Africa' Garveyism and the rejection of a colonial worldview defined the Marley classic, but Bovell had already taken Matumbi down that road, primarily because of the influence of the strong Rastafarian strain in Cymande (see Chapter 7). 'Matumbi means reborn in Yoruba,' Bovell explained:

> There was a book called *Mister Johnson* by the novelist Joyce Cary. It's about the British occupation of Nigeria and the characters are Sergeant Gollup who is English and Mr Johnson is his clerk. In the story Gollup has a very beautiful black woman as his girlfriend and her name is Matumbi. I thought this was a beautiful word and thought that when we formed the band that was gonna be the name. That was at a time when people were desperately seeking their Africanness, so to have an African word as our title and then completed by dressing in African robes that was what Matumbi was all about. We were reclaiming our African heritage.

Ironically, Cary's novel was criticised by the Nigerian novelist, Chinua Achebe, for its cultural clichés, yet the text nonetheless inspired Afro-centricity in Britain. Matumbi put forward a clear non-western lexicon in other ways. Just as Aswad had done, bandmembers adopted Rasta-style names: Drummer Bunny Donaldson was Jah Bunny, bassist Eaton Blake was Jah Blake and Bovell himself was Blackbeard.

As noted in Chapter 4, Matumbi had enjoyed the invaluable experience of backing Jamaican singers such as Pat Kelly and if their superb cover of Hot Chocolate's 'Brother Louie' was a breakout song for them, the originals they wrote were no less impressive. 'Wipe Them Out' and 'Go Back Home' were powerful critiques of far-right politics, while their debut album *Seven Seals* included other outstanding pieces, such as 'Guide Us Jah', 'Hypocrite' and 'All Over this World (Money)', that showed what a great command Matumbi had of the roots reggae idiom. Matumbi were also particularly interesting from a musical point of view because of Bovell's wide-ranging interests. Although he was wholly committed to reggae, his love of R&B and soul permeated the arrangements in direct and indirect ways. There was a shot of US funk in some of the songs – most explicitly expressed on a take of Kool & The Gang's 'Funky Stuff', which was renamed 'Reggae Stuff' – and an ingenuity in the backbeat that paid respect to Memphis legends Booker T & The MGs. Perhaps, though, it was Matumbi's gift for memorable melodies that stood out, such as 'Empire Road', a gorgeous tribute to the West Indian community, complete with references to the foodstuffs imported from Jamaica and Guyana, which the band wrote for *Empire Road*, the groundbreaking TV sitcom about a Black British family in Birmingham.

Midlands Runnings
Written by Michael Abbensetts, *Empire Road*, which ran between 1978-79, featured memorable individual characters, such as the patriarchal landlord figure played by Norman Beaton, touched on profound cultural shifts within the Caribbean community, above all the embrace of Rastafarianism by youngsters, and was also very much a portrait of a place: Birmingham in the Midlands, whose Black population numbered around 8,000 and had roots that reached back to pre-Windrush migrants who had been employed in munitions factories during the second world war. By the 1970s this was a community focused on the Handsworth district of the city, home of the reggae band, Steel Pulse.

Whilst the Caribbean community in Birmingham was not the largest in the UK, according to Steel Pulse's percussionist, Mykaell Riley, it had a distinctiveness and vitality. 'It was so Jamaican, outside of anywhere in the UK. We had been crowned capital of the Jamaican community in the UK because per square mile we had more Jamaicans crowded into a small space, which was Handsworth,' he told me in 2022. 'That created its own sub-culture where it was as Caribbean as you could get outside of Jamaica, minus the sun, minus the sea. People from London referred to going to 'country' when they were heading to Birmingham because they were going to crash and collide into an unexpected Jamaicanness – attitudes, way of talking, which was pretty close to Jamaica. It felt very black.'[7]

Guitarist-vocalist David Hinds, guitarist Basil Gabbidon, his brother, drummer Colin and bassist Ronald McQueen, were also part of Steel Pulse's early line-up, which changed over the years. Weaned on ska, rocksteady and reggae, the band, whose inspired name implied beats with industrial strength, or the flow of life with a hard riddim, started to record in the mid-1970s, releasing singles, the third of which 'Bun Dem' was produced by Dennis Bovell in his guise as Blackbeard. They continued to steadily develop over the next few years, and were signed to Chris Blackwell's Island records in 1978, becoming label mates with Aswad. Steel Pulse toured with Bob Marley in July of that year, which led to the band engaging with Rastafarianism. But Riley is keen to point out that there was no sweeping universal conversion, or mass ascent to holy mount Zion, but rather a variety of responses that reflected the existence of a range of worldviews and personalities. There was no consensus.

'That mix existed within the band, because everyone didn't become Rasta,' he says. 'I wasn't interested. I couldn't bridge the approach which says the state owes us and we're not gonna work for Babylon. That was too simple. There was another group that was activist, another passive; it was just a complex mix of ideas. Coming back from the Marley tour I'd say at least half the band had bible in hand, reading the Old Testament. But everybody was not moving at the same pace.'

As the disparaging comments about 'dem Rasta-fa-Ryans' in *Empire Road* made clear, there was a fair dose of contempt among older West Indians for the belief system of Marley and co, but Riley points out that identities at the time were complex. One should avoid oversimplifications of what exactly constituted a Black British sense of self:

> In Birmingham we had more varieties of Rasta than anywhere else in the UK because of this hardcore, tightly-knit community of people from Jamaica, cheek by jowl to people of Jamaican parentage born in the UK and that created its own friction and interpretations... At one end you've got: 'We need to become Rasta because that's a pathway to becoming ourselves' and then, at the same time, you've got 'Hold on we're not Jamaican and we're not African.' The Caribbean community in the UK split between 'Am I more British than Jamaican, if so which way am I travelling?' Travelling towards Africa is not something I can make sense of as I'm still trying to make sense of this Jamaican British thing. The other section says 'I'm British... that's it. One of the agendas was there's something about this band that is not authentic Jamaican, but it is authentic in what it's attempting to represent, a British response to Jamaican music and we wanna capture that but we still want something Jamaican in the production space.[8]

Steel Pulse established itself as a different kind of reggae act in a conceptual setting that was about place, which was neither London nor Kingston but Handsworth, Birmingham, and a complexity of identity that encompassed different ways of being Black and of Jamaican heritage in Britain. Their music was not simply and exclusively 'roots', because they were actively coming to terms with the fact that they were caught between the birthplace of their parents and the environment in which they grew up. Their fine debut album made where they were abundantly clear. If the name Steel Pulse had gravity, then *Handsworth Revolution* had gravitas. Again, the combination of words in summoning both place and intention, signalled the band's sense of self-empowerment at a time when their community was both marginalised and stigmatised. The music was a call to arms.

The sleeve featured a striking illustration by Andrew Aloof, based on an initial idea by David Hinds, himself a talented artist. It suggested a blend of urban decay and what would then have been referred to as Third World poverty. In the background were two decrepit tower blocks, leaning visibly from neglect, symbolising the reality of life in a big city for immigrants, while the foreground had a Black family standing next to a Volkswagen Beetle, a car of choice among West Indians, flanked by green foliage, palm trees and the crumbling masonry of an outhouse. The tableau was a strange meshing of British slum and Jamaican shanty town, the collision of two parallel locations in a surreal, provocative piece of psycho-geography.

'It was an image of Babylon,' says Riley of the artwork for the album. 'What we aspired to but where we are, running away from that which you're running into. It was an idea to bring the aspirations and the challenges to those aspirations all in one place but in an image that was really ease to decipher. The palm tree? We'd never seen a palm tree, but we'd definitely seen mashed up Beetles, the poor man's car, the urban landscape.... concrete jungle.'[9]

In the distance the name Steel Pulse was etched into an expanse of craggy hills, a place of sanctuary in Rastafarian ideology and more broadly in diasporic slave narratives. This vivid graphic design set the tone for the songs on *Handsworth Revolution*. Uncompromising, unfiltered, unambiguous, the material was the work of young Black British men who were wont to speak their minds on what they saw as an alarming situation on their doorstep, which also related to oppression on a wider scale. The album was a comprehensive enumeration of the iniquities suffered by people of colour in a variety of places. Hence the brilliant opening line of the title track, the first piece on the album, which has an ancestral, proverbial richness, a kind of folk wisdom deeply rooted in Caribbean mores. It was an imaginative way of advocating unity and solidarity.

> I say that people of Handsworth know that one hand wash the other.
> So let's join hands my brethren.

There follows a string of aphorisms that identify and denounce the exploitative western world as Babylon, the den of iniquity with its assorted evils, from phoney laws to poor wages for hard labour, thinly veiled euphemisms for the lived reality of persecution by the police and lack of opportunity in employment. The solace offered to sufferers is the presence of Jah, the Rastafarian personification of the deity who gives guidance to those who seek alternatives to Judeo-Christianity. And while Steel Pulse speak of revolution in Handsworth, they connect this to the harrowing persecution of those in the African Motherland who are also under the heel of a monstrous power:

> Only Babylon prospers/And humble suffer/They're our brothers in
> South Africa/ One black represent all, all over the world.

Tellingly, as they were recording *Handsworth Revolution* in 1977, the African Caribbean Self-Help Organisation (ACSHO) staged Birmingham's first African Liberation Day in solidarity with African nations and the wider Black Diaspora. This brought together one of the biggest gatherings of people of colour in Britain at that time, though the event was largely ignored by the mainstream national press.

Elsewhere Steel Pulse celebrated the joy of music in 'Sound Check' (If anything should mash up me head/Play the music me can't dead') while 'Macka Splaff' eulogised the kind of stick that was hand-rolled rather than one made of wood, with which mistrustful church-going West Indian parents might beat children who had strayed onto the path of Rasta.

While Steel Pulse identified themselves as representatives of Handsworth, their songs also reflect an interest in wide-ranging subjects, historical and contemporary, that take the listener far beyond this locality. They engage with Black America and the extreme racism faced by African Americans in 'Ku Klux Klan', the text of which sees the band call for a violent response to the scores of lynchings, rapes and maimings perpetrated by that infamous white Supremacist faction. Years later, Mykaell Riley recalled the censorious reaction of the BBC to the song, no doubt exacerbated by the band's appearance in the ghostly pointed hoods of the notorious hate group:

> Radio One had already taken umbrage with us because 'Ku Klux Klan' would have been a hit single... but they just decided to ban it. They didn't wanna make it big news by (officially) banning it because that's promoting it, so they were just not gonna play it as it would create civil unrest in the UK. We were working against the tide... I made the costumes. I sorted out all the original costumes from the 'dead man's shop' we used to call it, the local charity shop. How can we tell a story as a band and individually, and also support the lyrical narrative? With 'Ku Klux Klan' it's a bit of a no brainer, the challenge was getting the band to wear it. Wha' ya go with da dodgy piece of cloth? Imagine the impact though.[10]

At the time, singer-guitarist David Hinds was reading black revolutionary literature from Caribbean writers such as Walter Rodney and Marcus Garvey and by African American Black Power icons such as Angela Davis and George Jackson. From them, he was drawn to investigate history, and this produced another startling composition, 'Soldiers', which he wrote after seeing *Soldier Blue*, a key 'revisionist western' of 1970 that dramatised the 1864 Sand Creek massacre in which American cavalry butchered Cheyenne and Arapaho villagers, many of whom were women and children.

'I imagined that scenario in relation to us as Africans being slaughtered like the Ethiopian invasion and the invasion of the Zulus by the British. We just flipped the script and interpreted it to how we are seeing ourselves being treated,' he told me. Setting such an emotive subject to music is by no means an easy task, but 'Soldiers' is arguably a composition and arrangement that shows Steel Pulse's creative maturity and intelligence. They took what might be called a standard roots reggae template and enhanced it with nuance to serve the song's narrative. It is built on a familiar medium tempo in which the beat rocks back and forth on the incisive syncopations of organ and guitar while intermittent short rolls of high-pitched percussion are used to punctuate the vocal phrases. The lyrics talk of bloodletting in graphic terms, but the ambiance created by the rhythm section is one of relative tranquillity rather than violence, though there is an intriguing horn line, a baritone or bass saxophone that blasts a long groaning note into the air, lending weight to the finely threaded groove. That is joined by a contrasting guitar sound, played very sparingly by Basil Gabbidon. Against the steadiness of the underlying beat, he improvises a series of balmy riffs, often with a bluesy bending of notes that pierce the surrounding rustle. His tone is beautiful, glistening and bright, recalling the lustrous flamenco motifs in the intro to 'Prediction', though here his performance is all about restraint rather than flourish. At the halfway point of the song, that needle-like tone becomes an almost religious sound when it is cast against a birdsong effect, a gentle twittering, possibly done on a synthesizer, that shifts the whole atmosphere towards a feeling of sanctuary, as if a natural mystic was indeed blowing through the air. Then the beat stops dead and, under a spectral trail of reverb, Hinds implores: 'Give I back I witch doctor/Give I back I black ruler.'

The lyric chants down the violence perpetrated in the name of Empire and in the coda there is a brief exchange of hard-strummed guitar chords and a tumble of percussion before the disappearance of the band leaves only a deeply haunting echo of Hinds's voice. The requiem is over.

The more you listen to the performance, the more you appreciate the sensitivity of the guitar licks, which play the role of a mourner whose tears and wails fall like cleansing rain onto the blood-soaked land. 'Soldiers' is a pivotal track because it consolidates reggae as a form of social commentary which sets great store by beauty, by a seductive finesse in the textural palette, in contrast to the confrontational and arresting nature of the lyric. The music has great exactness – such as in the way Gabbidon's weeping guitar stays on exactly the right side of sentiment rather than becoming sentimental. That artistry is also striking in Hinds' voice on the title track of *Handsworth Revolution*. When he sings 'Equality' he turns the prosaic into the poetic by way of languorously curling melodic inflections. That single word stretches into the music and it summarises Steel Pulse as a creative as well as political force. The band supported Bob Marley & The Wailers on a major European tour in 1978, a defining moment in their development. It was clear that Marley appreciated the fact that they were his admirers not his imitators.

Shot in the Dark
By this point in the later 1970s, reggae albums were being featured in the pages of the rock press as well as in specialist Black music magazines. This was no doubt happening in the slipstream of Marley crossing over to the mainstream and capturing the imagination of white audiences who had

either followed the evolution of Jamaican music through previous incarnations of ska and rocksteady or who were coming to it afresh. The growing diversity of audiences for reggae would have been more than ironic to Hinds and co because they had suffered a certain amount of rejection by fellow West Indians in the early stage of Steel Pulse's career. Many promoters preferred DJs/sound systems to bands because they were cheaper and did not require substantial technical resources in order to set up. Some selectors were happier to play reggae versions of popular soul hits rather than endorse bands with original material, but most challenging was the fact that, as Britons, Steel Pulse were sometimes seen as not authentic, not the real thing, second class. As Hinds said:

> Because we were a British black reggae band there was a stigma, a negative stigma in the community where because you're from Britain the reggae music that you're producing was not good enough compared to that in Jamaica. So when we actually got nationally known it was not based on what we were doing in the black community.

Indeed, it was predominantly white bands who played the new strain of rock known as punk, snarling and snapping against polite society, who started to give support slots to Steel Pulse. When they opened for The Stranglers and The Clash in mainstream venues, they significantly enlarged their audience. Of even greater significance was their involvement in Rock Against Racism (RAR), a landmark moment in British cultural and political history that sought to use the power of music to stem the growing tide of racism, not least among A-list musicians such as David Bowie, who turned bizarre apologist for Adolf Hitler, and Eric Clapton, who, having enjoyed success with a cover of Bob Marley's 'I Shot The Sheriff', declared support for Enoch Powell and raged against wogs and coons at a gig in Birmingham in 1976. To this day, he has issued no public apology for these abominations.

Rock Against Racism came about when a group of activists headed by Red Saunders, who had done street theatre in a company called Agit Prop and campaigned for majority rule in Zimbabwe and South Africa, denounced the superstar guitarist in a letter to NME, which was met by widespread support. RAR co-operated closely with the Anti-Nazi League and other organisations set up to counter the National Front. This pushback against the far right led to events such as 'the battle of Lewisham' in August 1977, in which neo-nazis clashed violently with a loose alliance of anti-racists and trade unionists. To take the fight further, Saunders and associates hit upon the idea of staging concerts as a rallying point for those who believed in racial equality. Saunders saw the possibility of connecting popular music to the labour movement. 'Obviously we'd tapped into some progressive thing that the Left didn't realise, the reason was culture… to mobilise as many people as possible around musical events with a multi-racial bill,' he explained:

> We thought we're gonna have an anti-fascist carnival in the heart of NF territory Victoria Park, where NF was getting 26% of the vote. That's when I was shitting myself. These were dangerous times. If you were an NF street fighter and you heard about a RAR gig you were gonna go and smash it up, tear down the posters and intimidate people. These were volunteers, this wasn't Amnesty International with people being paid thousands of pounds a year. These weren't just gigs at carnival; there were leaflets handed out too. There was important discussion. You ended up having bands that would never normally play together to audiences that at that time would never get together. So, people got united through music and someone who only normally listened to rock or pop suddenly went, 'Oh that's reggae I kind of like that.' So the line-ups ranged from punk such as The Clash to rock & pop groups like the Tom Robinson Band right through to reggae acts like Steel Pulse. RAR showed that ordinary people can fight for a better world.[11]

For Mykaell Riley of Steel Pulse, RAR had a particular resonance because they were already accustomed to white audiences through their relationship with punk bands, not to mention the fact that the Clapton incident took place in Birmingham. 'Of all things, this occurs in our neck of the woods!' he stated emphatically. 'Our stance becomes really important. It's a stance we already had, but to hear 'Blacks and Asians get out of the country' after he'd just covered 'I Shot The Sheriff'… this was the manifestation of Babylon. We didn't even use the word cultural appropriation, he just teef everything we created. That was the legacy of the colonial system. That played into what we were about and gave us a credibility you just couldn't purchase. If we weren't the real deal then, in the eyes of the press and the media, we became the real deal. This is a British response to a British racist in music, this is a black British response to this statement made in Birmingham by a band from Birmingham.'[12]

Way Out West
Another of the key reggae bands who took part in RAR was a formidable outfit from Southall called Misty in Roots. Though they had a far lower profile than Aswad, Matumbi and Steel Pulse, they were probably as influential and revered because of the excellence of their musical output as well as their integrity and strong ethics. First and foremost, they were committed to artistic freedom and retaining control over their work. They launched their own label, People Unite, to release their recordings and those by other reggae acts such as Zabandis and Rudo Nathalie Xavier, as well as by the punk band, The Ruts, whose adoption of Jamaican

vernacular on songs such as 'Babylon's Burning' and 'Jah War' reflected what appeared to be a genuine identification with the condition of young Black Britons.

Misty's nucleus was bassist Tony Henry, drummer Julien Peters, keyboardist Vernon Hunt, guitarists Chesley Sampson and Delbert Mackay, and vocalist Walford 'Poco' Tyson, with his brother Delvin and Dennis Augustin on harmonies. They were championed by BBC Radio One DJ, John Peel, whose embrace of reggae was a significant step forward from the days when Jamaican artists made records about the lack of airplay they received from the corporation. Peel's show also invited bands to play live and these sessions could raise a band's stock if they performed well. Misty did superb sets between 1979 and 1982 that were as good a calling card as any group could have hoped to give to touring agents. The quality of the songs, couched in 'roots' language, from 'True Rasta Man' to 'Live Up Jah Life to 'Africa', was matched by the instrumental brilliance of the band.

Although Misty did issue well-received studio albums such as *Wise and Foolish*, the stage was where the group came alive, and they made one of the best live albums of the period in any genre, *Live at the Counter-Eurovision* in 1979. Held at the Cirque Royal in Brussels, the event stood as an alternative to the glossy continental talent show remembered as the launching pad for Abba and the ducking stool for dozens of forgettable artists. The concert's political sub-text was a collaboration between Pour Le Socialisme and CAFIT – Collectif D'Animation Pour La Formation Et L'Information Des Travailleurs, two agencies which supported workers' rights. When Misty in Roots took to the stage at an event, they were standing on a platform of blue-collar resistance rather than bureaucratic empowerment, and this context lent further credibility to the band as genuine outsiders in the music industry who espoused left-wing ideals as well as Rastafarian faith. Perhaps more than any of their peers, the Southall brothers were walking the walk, or skanking the skank, making it clear that under the barrage of their drums and bass, their revolution would not be swallowed up by capitalism.

And what a mighty noise the band made. *Live at the Counter-Eurovision* has enormous muscle in its rhythmic foundation. The picked notes of the guitar often come across as so low as to be a second bassline, while sustained organ chords glow and growl over the beat in the manner of the Jamaican Hammond maestro, Jackie Mittoo, providing blasts of heat that waft in and around the impassioned three-part vocals. The contribution of the Tyson brothers and Vernon Hunt is crucial insofar as they often move in unison to create another layer of thickness in the ensemble sound, as well as sometimes, in contrast, leaving substantial amounts of space. They mesh conversational spoken word passages and melodic phrasing, the highpoint of which is the thrilling 'Judas Iscariote', a song where the lyrics are part delivered as ex-tempo conversation before the hook 'Do you remember?' lends a curt implication of swing to the rhythm. Here, the organ also comes to the foreground in huge block chords that drift around the passionate vocal. The band's advanced musicianship, with Vernon Hunt's work on keyboards really quite outstanding, make it clear that Misty took their craft very seriously and brought fresh imagination to the roots reggae idiom.

Furthermore, one of the key moments on the Peel sessions showed their ability to throw quite delicious curveballs. 'True Rasta Man' has a sensual sway that spells out the path of righteousness for disciples of Jah, but its briefest of introductions contrasts effectively with the rest of the arrangement. A decidedly loud pummel on the snare is matched by cracking guitar licks set to a raggedy beat that would have been familiar to jazz audiences. It is Dave Brubeck's 'Take Five', a hit in 1959. The quotation lasts for barely a few measures before 'True Rasta Man' starts in earnest, but the charming quirk is effectively theatrical, the music appearing to go down one road and then veering off to another. It is also a reminder of the close engagement of West Indian artists with American jazz that reaches right back to the embrace of pioneers from Armstrong to Ellington to Parker. As Steel Pulse's David Hinds also reported: 'We were checking out groups… the jazz-fusion groups like The Crusaders for what they were doing with chords.'

Misty in Roots continued to record excellent music in the 1980s, with the album *Wise and Foolish* a highlight, and despite the loss of bandmembers in tragic circumstances (Delvin Tyson drowned), the band has endured and continues to perform regularly to this day. Like Steel Pulse, Matumbi and Aswad, they have their place as pioneers of British roots reggae. And there were other quality acts in the mid-1970s who should be mentioned. From Wolverhampton came Capital Letters, whose album *Headline News* has more than stood the test of time. From Manchester came X-O-Dus, who, like Steel Pulse, had early material produced by Dennis Bovell, and from London came the excellent Black Slate who enjoyed chart success with singles such as the irresistibly catchy 'Amigo'. The sense of a reggae community was to be found in small but meaningful gestures, such as Steel Pulse coming to Aswad's aid at a Birmingham gig when a broken bass bin derailed their soundcheck, or Brinsley Forde of Aswad showing David Hinds around Island records when the latter were on the verge of signing a deal, or Dennis Bovell taking Brinsley to the *Top of the Pops* studio. They had to stand together. They were all living inna Babylon.

Notes

1. Horace Ové, Galeforce Television March 4, 2010.
2. Ibid.
3. Shabazz's body of work also included the important *Burning An Illusion*.
4. All City Taxi Talk Show, Brinsley Forde.
5. Ibid.
6. Interview with the author, February 2022.
7. Interview with the author May 2022.
8. Ibid.
9. Ibid.
10. Ibid.
11. Ibid.
12. Ibid.

13 CHILDREN OF THE GHETTO

> We lived in Stanhope Street. It was the main street in Toxteth where all my family lived, off Stanhope Street. Stanhope Street was the hub and all the streets off it, like Tennyson Street, is where my friends, cousins, grandmother lived. We just wanted to show it as it was. When we took that photo I lived about one minute away from there. All them people in the photographs we knew, people we grew up with. It was the community.
> — Chris Amoo of The Real Thing on the artwork of *4 From 8*

Not gonna get off lightly
As noted in Chapter 12, *Empire Road* was an important moment in British television history because it held up a mirror to West Indian migrants in Birmingham in the mid-1970s, a time when intergenerational change and conflict started to bite hard. To some parents, their England educated kids were getting ruder than rude. In a short but memorable scene that highlighted Norman Beaton's superlative gifts as a comic, his character, the patriarch, Everton Bennett, has just returned from a trip with his wife Hortense (Corinne Skinner Carter) to their native Guyana. They sit down with her brother Walter (Joseph Marcell, later known for his part in *Fresh Prince of Bel Air*) for a welcoming cup of tea but because of his pronounced stammer, Walter manages to shower Everton with spittle before he has the chance to sip his brew. With the kind of majestically contemptuous gesture that was one of Beaton's talents – his demeanour is pained and his delivery exudes a purringly soft, nonchalant superiority – he wipes his cheek and tells Hortense, 'Your brother's practicing to be a punk rocker!' That sharp quip is met by a gormless chuckle and the conversation quickly dries up, but the exchange reflects the indignation older Black Britons felt towards such teenage upstarts – even though they were no match for the rude boys of Jamaica – who contented themselves with putting safety pins through their ears, sniffing glue, and 'gobbing' at one another as if it was a ritual of bonding. Imagine what the scene would have been like had Marcus Bennett, Everton's son, stomped into the kitchen wearing bondage trousers, a ripped T-shirt, studded leather jacket and a dog collar.

'Shame and Scandal' would have been calypso revival number one.

Despite parental disapproval, there was engagement between Black youth and white punks, though each had their distinctive styles. It is a subject that can be seen from several different angles. The person who appears to have been a noteworthy bridge was the South London fashion pacesetter and DJ Don Letts[1] who brought significant reggae records to the attention of members of the Sex Pistols and The Clash, who had already been drawn to ska in their formative years. The nights Letts spent spinning the latest Jamaican music at London clubs such as the Roxy provided an important gateway for white suburban kids into Black music, and that interest was most explicitly symbolised by the decision of The Clash to cover Junior Murvin's seminal 'Police And Thieves', a parallel to the relationship between Misty in Roots and The Ruts, discussed in the previous chapter. Matumbi maestro, Dennis Bovell, produced The Slits, and there was Bob Marley's 'Punky Reggae Party', as another emblematic link between the two worlds.

Shared marginalisation from mainstream society may suggest a natural affinity between Mohawks and Dreads, but some commentators who observed Black music in Britain at the time offer a dismissive view. The open violence at punk gigs compared to the trance-like ambiance of reggae gatherings, not to mention the highly problematic shock tactics of young white girls wearing Nazi swastikas was a cultural difference, and there were polarised artistic outlooks. Lack of technical ability was a badge of honour in punk culture whereas it was the opposite in reggae, where playing out of time and key was simply not an option given the high standards among fellow musicians and the demands for excellence by audiences. The Clash may have covered 'Police And Thieves' but that didn't mean it could be played at a sound system dance. The divide was more than musical. As Mikey Massive argued: 'The objectives of the two lifestyles had absolutely nothing in common.' He was a Rastafarian and reggae journalist who wrote for rock (*NME*) and Black music titles (*Black Echoes*) in the 1970s. 'Rastafari are children of Africa seeking a return to the homeland of our Ankhcestors, whether by way of a liberation of the continent's political system through the dismantlement of neo-colonialism which would lead to a mass migration (Repatriation) of diasporan Afrikans, whereas punk seems to be simply a nihilistic rejection of the (Babylon) system without a coherent strategy to maintain the industrialisation their practices rely upon or effect the social justice they claim to espouse.'[3]

Of course, though for a time Rastafarianism seemed synonymous with reggae, not all mid-1970s Jamaican reggae was informed by Rasta ideology and there were various definitions of Rastafarianism, with some believers claiming to be more orthodox than others, holding different views about separation from other races and from Black ('baldhead') non-Rastafarians. The Earthmen in Birmingham, who donned sandals in winter and were vegan before the word was invented, quickly took umbrage with any lesser idea of what Rasta could be. Mykaell Riley of Steel Pulse recalls their stance and how it differed from other brethren who were also in the

Midlands. 'There was no bridge between them and punk... no, no! This is what was interesting to me. But you also had what I'd call the liberal Rastas, and their message was love, so I can't in all good faith say I only love black people. This mix of approaches to Rasta was also very real.'[4]

Yet if there were possibilities of kinship between Rastas and punks, the behavioural differences were stark as Steel Pulse found out when they supported groups such as The Stranglers and The Clash. 'The punks adopted us as an alternative punk band not as a reggae band,' says Riley. 'It was weird because they wanted to do all the things they would do when attending a punk gig with us, spit at you, chuck beer, jump on stage and fight. And we fought back, literally. We made it clear where we were from... and not that we condone violence, but if you think you're gonna come and do what you do to band X, you're not gonna get off lightly. We can deal with any kind of punk audience. We're coming out of Handsworth. Fighting a few white folk? That's no big deal. We were doing that every day on the street. We weren't afraid to tell them upfront at the beginning of the gig... I'd be saying if you spit at us we'll spit back, if you jump on stage we'll kick the shit out of you.'[5] Looking back on the period Riley uses one word repeatedly: confusion.

Punk was a fleeting phenomenon and its short lifecycle coincided with the important initiatives of Rock Against Racism as well as the explosion of disco which, by extension, could easily ignite both racism and homophobia because of its core Black and gay fanbase. This led to paradoxes, the greatest of which was that some among the white community simply didn't know whether they were bigoted or not. Listening to Black music and insulting if not assaulting Black people had deep roots, reaching back to the well-to-do, polite society patrons who applauded African American syncopated orchestras in the 19th century, but would happily crack jokes about 'low niggers' and deny the use of the front door of a hotel to Black musicians. In the 20th century there were some skinheads who stomped to reggae and happily stomped on Black people's heads.

Steel Pulse had very mixed audiences, including hardcore National Front fans who cheered wildly in the venue and then sold fascist literature outside, as well as heavy metal fans and punks. There were, as Riley recalls, from gigging in Birmingham and the north, a minority of Black people who crossed some of these lines and became punks of colour, complete with the safety pins, studded leather jackets and raised middle fingers to the state. The elders of Empire Road would not have been impressed.

Identity parade
In this subset, the most notable was a Black woman, Poly Styrene. Founder of the group X-Ray Spex, she was one of the most memorable products of the punk scene both for her individuality and her ethnicity. Born

Marianne Joan Elliott-Said in Bromley to a Scottish-Irish mother and a Somali docker father, she was brought up in the mono-racial environment of Hastings, Kent. As a child she showed artistic inclinations but had an unstable early life and left home as a teenager, hitching around Britain to attend music festivals. After seeing The Sex Pistols perform in Hastings, she was inspired to lead a band of her own, though prior to that she took a stab at making reggae and released an unremarkable single, 'Silly Billy', in 1976 under her real name Mari Elliott.

Poly Styrene grabbed attention with X-Ray Spex, though. Alongside drums, bass and guitar, the band featured saxophone, an uncommon instrument in punk, that immediately made the band stand out. In fact, the relationship between the horn and voice proved very effective. Poly had a prickly delivery that blended well with the braying sax, stoking up an urgent belligerence on much of the material. The band's debut single, 'Oh Bondage Up Yours', was banned by the BBC, no doubt alarmed by such a confrontational title, while the subsequent 45s, 'The Day the World Turned Day Glo' and 'Germ Free Adolescents' made the lower end of the charts. That last song was the title track of the 1978 debut album that made it clear that Poly Styrene was a fiercely original writer who had a strong melodic sense and the ability to produce thought-provoking lyrics with political substance.

'Germ Free Adolescents' is a wonderful mid-tempo piece with a subtle slant in its rhythm that could have accommodated an offbeat 'chaka' reggae guitar, and a patter of rimshots on the drums. It was perhaps the nearest to a punk-reggae union in her work. For the most part, the X-Ray Spex sound was spikier in tone and timbre than anything connected to reggae, and had an underlying barrelling aggression that framed Poly's voice in an appropriate way. Both the music and lyrics stand head and shoulders above most of her peers in punk. Among recurrent themes are the dangers of consumerism and the duplicity of advertising that she sees on television and the high streets of Britain that are gripped in a frenzy of destructive materialism. Tracks such as 'Warrior In Woolworths' and 'Plastic Bag' are astute comments on the way that shops have become consumer traps while 'Identity' is a forthright interrogation of the place of the individual within a controlling capitalist system.

> Do you see yourself on the TV screen? Do you see yourself in a magazine?
> When you see yourself does it make you scream?

In the last verse, the text takes an alarmingly darker turn with a reference to smashing a mirror and slashing wrists, a projection of a troubled state of mind that questions the perils of fame as well as the curse of petulant behaviour. The lyrics were blunt and profound. The world of celebrity is depicted as a machine that will drive victims to distraction and Poly Styrene seems prophetic when one considers the impact of social media in the 2000s, the cult of likes and shares. The cry of the song, thrust into life by the singer's high, abrasive tone, is as confrontational as it is urgently existential: Identity is the crisis, can't you see?

The rhetorical power of the line lies in its universality. Who does it not apply to? Punks fighting the establishment, Rastas fighting Babylon, women fighting misogyny, consumers fighting consumerism, an individual fighting herself. It later emerged that Poly Styrene suffered from a bi-polar disorder which lent a personal dimension to her words, but perhaps one hears, too, the situation of a bi-racial woman with an absent Black father with whom, as far as can be seen, she had no relationship. There is no explicit mention of a such a situation, but when the daughter of a Somali man and Scottish-Irish woman asks whether you see yourself when you look in the mirror, it is hard not to surmise that she is talking personally as someone who, for all her strength of character, is vulnerable precisely because of the ambiguity of who she is, or the confusion her existence sows in the minds of others.

Before X-Ray Spex, there had been notable examples of Black women working with or fronting British bands, such as P.P. Arnold with the Small Faces and Madeleine Bell with Blue Mink, as discussed previous chapters, but they are not usually seen in the same context as Poly because they were working in R&B, rock, pop and soul. Punk was not perceived as Black music, so Poly, with no gospelised scream or sequinned gowns, existed as a grand subversive, breaking with all assumptions about what a Black woman performer should sound and look like.

Because punk was seen as oppositional to mainstream rock, one hesitates to link Poly to Philip Lynott, but the similarities are nonetheless obvious. Both were of mixed race. Both had Black fathers they did not know. Both were talented. Both had a real sense of individuality. Both were rebels, though Lynott was never afforded the kudos of 'cool' awarded to Poly by those in the rock press hitched to the punk bandwagon. She became an object of fascination because of her singular fashion sense, her eye for the design and artwork of her albums and her undeniable charisma. There was very little enquiry from the music press into her blackness, though. It is not clear whether that was her decision or that of the journalists who engaged with her.

Despite the snooks that she cocked at prevailing expectations of female beauty – she wore braces on her teeth, manly military tunics and peaked caps – Poly was still subjected to the kind of objectification and misogyny that reflected the disturbing gender dynamics in pop. At the end of a filmed gig there is a stage invasion by an all-male audience, several of whom openly grope the singer and demand 'Give us a kiss!' like wet-behind-the-ears teens on a first date. It is a sexual assault to the extent that Poly has to be rescued by roadies and bandmates. The scene is horrific. What was her identity at that point? Artist or a piece of ass.

For all the lucidity and prescience of her songs that took a stand against consumerism and materialism, slapping down the Saturday shopping high street experience for the hollow gratification of any 'Warrior in Woolworths', Poly's gender still prevented a full appreciation of her talents. She may have been lauded for her intelligence and originality, but it is hard to escape the view, even without that ghastly scene described above, that she was often reduced to the role of strangely cute 'half-caste', with no feminist leverage or proper girl power, as if these elements of her being were dispensable within the male-led propulsion of punk towards outrage at all costs. She would remain a mystery as X-Ray Spex were gone in a flash, after Poly's mental health seriously declined.

Joy and pain
As punk set off moral panics in the mainstream press, the daily task of supporting a family or indeed oneself, sustaining a career or securing a first job after leaving school or college continued to exercise the minds of both Black and white people. Improved social security was one of the achievements of the postwar Attlee Labour government, but by the mid-1970s the situation of citizens forced to live on unemployment or sickness benefits was anything but rosy. The weekly trip to the D.H.S.S – Department of Health and Social Security, later shortened to D.S.S as if health had become an unaffordable luxury – to be grilled about what actions you had taken to find work, turned into a depressing ritual for long queues of downtrodden people crammed into drab, unprepossessing offices in the hope of getting their giro cheque before deciding how best to make it last for a long seven days, after which the drudgery would start again.

Inevitably, a colloquial term was coined for unemployment benefit –an archaic word revived for the purpose. Dole had its origins in the 13th century as a derivation of the phrasal verb 'dole out' as in to make a charitable donation to the destitute and underprivileged, and the D word became synonymous with social failure as well as economic hardship, entailing an undeniable stigma for those who were obliged to rely on it.

No song was more powerful on the subject than 'Living on the Dole' by the Cimarons, the British reggae band that had first achieved success in the early 1970s and, like Matumbi and Aswad, been called to back Jamaican artists in the UK. The track detailed the despair of the unemployed and the breakdown of industrial relations in Britain. The infamous 'winter of discontent' of 1978, during which trade unions and a Labour government faced off over pay-levels, led to the grimly ironic headlines such as 'Crisis, what crisis?' and the view that the country was in deep freeze in every imaginable way, as inflation and a spell of bitterly cold weather started to bite into people's sense of wellbeing. 'Living on the Dole' was sucking the life out of those unfortunate enough to be consigned to the scrapheap.

The song had another lease of life when it featured on the soundtrack of a landmark in Black British cinema, *Black Joy*. This film starred the ubiquitous Norman Beaton, Floella Benjamin, and Oscar James, who, like Beaton featured in *Pressure*. It depicted West Indian life in London at the time, from scenes of vinyl-hungry punters eager to snap up the latest hot tunes in a record shop, to ravers loosening their limbs at the iconic Cue club. The film is a historical document of a time when an all-Black British cast on the silver screen was a rarity. In terms of tone, mood and narrative it could not be further from *Pressure*, with *Black Joy* light-heartedly foregrounding a series of jocular characters, like con artist Dave King (Beaton) and the naïve but endearing Ben (Trevor Thomas). There is no violence in the narrative, though it connects to the Jamaican film *The Harder They Come* by portraying the arrival of a country boy to the city. Ben travels from Guyana to London, where he is quickly fleeced, before learning to hold his own and hustle a hustler, without straying into gun-toting, outlaw, folk hero territory. There are moments of sharp realism, such as the racial discrimination Ben experiences when he's looking for work – another similarity to *Pressure*. After finally finding a job as a dustman, Ben is told by white colleagues that 'his lot' don't need to walk the streets as they can swing from the tree tops – standard workplace and playground 'banter' at the time.

North Western Numbers
Black Joy had a transatlantic soundtrack that featured African Americans – Aretha Franklin, Billy Paul, Harold Melvin & The Blue Notes – and several black Britons – the Cimarons, Linda Lewis and The Real Thing. The Cimarons were the sole outlet for any socially conscious lyrics in the film. Junior Murvin's 'Police and Thieves' features briefly in one scene but it was not part of the commercially available soundtrack. This fuelled the narrative that the main genre of Black protest music was reggae and not soul, helped by the fact that the soul songs on *Black Joy* – Franklin's 'I Say A Little Prayer'; Paul's 'Me And Mrs Jones', Melvin's 'Don't Leave Me This Way' and The Real Thing's 'Lightning Strikes Again' and 'Dance With Me' – dealt with affairs of the heart – or hedonism.

Detractors of the Liverpool group, discussed in Chapter 10, might have sneered, tired of the ubiquitous sound of 'You to Me Are Everything', the big hit of the summer of 1976, yet The Real Thing were in the midst of a radical change of artistic direction when their music appeared on *Black Joy*. Their second album *4 From 8*, issued in 1977, marked a departure from their eponymous debut, both in terms of visual presentation and content. Out was the studio shot of the band showing four Black men in prime physical condition. In was a dramatic depiction of an urban wasteland, probably a surprise to a loyal fanbase expecting another set of love songs encased in lush arrangements. The sleeve was full of dark rather than blue skies. A wall of unevenly laid bricks was cut away like a surreal stage on which stood a wonky mishmash of buildings in a collage that suggested what Curtis Mayfield called 'the other side of town'. The band stood under the sign 'Upper Stanhope Street', and a stray dog in the foreground reinforced the vibe of a city in decline.

This was home. As vocalist Chris Amoo explains, he, his brother Eddie, Dave Smith and Ray Lake, were in historically Black Liverpool, and the many Polaroid snaps on the inside cover were of their people.

> We lived in Stanhope Street. It was the main street in Toxteth where all my family lived, off Stanhope Street. Stanhope Street was the hub and all the streets off it, like Tennyson Street, is where my friends, cousins, grandmother lived. We just wanted to show it as was. When we took that photo, I lived about one minute away from there. All them people in the photographs we knew, people we grew up with. It was the community… all the photos… that's exactly what it was.'[6]

Visually, this was a journey to the African-Caribbean heartlands of Merseyside, or Liverpool 8, from where the 4 brothers came, which made the title of *4 from 8* a code that was easy to crack. Musically, this was the band's finest hour, the moment when they fulfilled the talent that had brought them to the attention of their manager, Tony Hall, several years before. It gave them the chance to record a set of their own songs that dealt with social issues rather than stick with the romantic fare provided by other writers. There was also a desire to have the band taken seriously by making the jump from a singles act to an album outfit, capable of sustaining the interest of listeners over 8 to 10 tracks that formed a coherent whole. Gone was the handful of big hits, that would be advertised on the front sleeve, with some additional 'filler' to justify the price tag of a longplayer. *4 From 8* was a statement of maturity for The Real Thing.

Boys To Men
Because they had enjoyed runaway success with what could be called a relatively light if not softer iteration of soul music, some might have assumed that the formative influences of the band were groups such as The Temptations and The O'Jays. While this was true, Amoo reveals that they were also immersed in the harder Afro-Latin funk of Mandrill and War, and the radical Black Power politics of The Last Poets, a group who helped to shape the birth of hip-hop in the 1980s. Also on their radar were the crown princes of socially conscious Black popular music, Marvin Gaye and Curtis Mayfield.

> We were listening to all these bands coming out of America singing about where they come from. It just came natural to us (to say) we've got our own heritage here and we want people to hear where we come from. The reason we did *4 from 8* is we thought now that the public's here, let's show them what we're all about. It was naïve for us to think that. The reason Tony Hall took on The Real Thing was because of what we were writing at the time, the political songs. He couldn't wait to get off, (to get away from) 'You To Me Are Everything'. He wanted people to hear that we were capable of writing and that we had a more serious side, we had our own way of writing. *4 from 8* was our way of trying to let people know what The Real Thing were seriously about.

Indeed, Eddie Amoo, Chris' older brother and noted songwriter had been well on the way to message music in his formative years and had been able to play his composition on racial identity, 'A Man Without a Face', to his hero Curtis Mayfield, when he met him in London. The legendary Chicagoan said that the lyric was too heavy. This, coming from a man responsible for some of the great protest songs of the 1970s, was arguably the ultimate endorsement of the political substance of The Real Thing. Perhaps Mayfield's comment led the group to greater nuance. While earlier songs such as 'Vicious Circle' took aim at the establishment and immoral lawmakers in general, *4 from 8* presented a slice of life in 'L8' (standard form of i-d for all locals). They were dealing with a city in which a football idol, Tommy Smith, the indomitable 'Anfield Iron', had thrown the shameful epithet, 'white nigger', at Toxteth-born Howard Gale, one of the first black players to make an impact for the Reds, and where an unofficial colour bar still existed in venues in the centre of town. The sense of racial divide was inescapable, and this had led to the evolution of Toxteth as a self-contained zone that had to craft a world of its own in the face of exclusion and marginalisation. As Amoo explained:

> Places like The Jacaranda and The Blue Angel (where black music was played)… they were in the city centre and at one point in time they weren't open to black people, you didn't go in them clubs… There was no way that black people could go there. We had our own clubs like The Embassy… they were huge houses which had one sort of floor done out with all the equipment and that's where all the black people used to go for the American, Jamaican and African music.'[7]

Stanley House became another community centre at the heart of Toxteth social life. As Amoo added:

> Stanley House was also a very important place in Liverpool because they used to pull in all the black people from Birmingham, London or Manchester. Once a month they'd have this huge dance and they'd come in

coachloads and that's when all the West Indian music was getting played, reggae was all that was getting played. In places like The Embassy, it was a real mix, heavy reggae along with funk, whatever was current for black music. And all the Americans used to come from the bases only to them clubs; they didn't venture into the city centre. Stanley House was right in the heart of Toxteth, It was everything, it was the youth club, the social club, and it was the rehearsal room, it was the community.

Conveying this reality through words and music was one of the missions of *4 from 8*, and while the album was not devoid of love songs, such as 'Love is Such a Wonderful Thing' and 'Down to the Way You Feel', it was 'Plastic Man' that signalled a more philosophical side of the band's lyrical content. The three track 'Liverpool 8 Medley' presented the Amoos as storytellers relaying their experience of growing up in a place that always got a bad press.

> Listen to the music
> Hear about a place
> People call the shady side of town
> Listen to the rhythm and you're gonna trace
> Angry feelings going round and round.

Their response was self-assertion; this was a place 'with things to say', and their direct, plain language gelled powerfully with the vocabulary of funk – scratchy rhythm guitar, sturdy, jumpy bass and a pinging cowbell pattern that gave the song an Afro-Latin flavour that would fill dance floors.

The second piece in the medley, 'Children of the Ghetto' was marked by a notable drop in tempo. A bed of airy strings, long notes sustained like mist in midwinter, glistening keyboards and a precisely picked guitar, created the poise of a soul anthem shaped by harmonic sophistication and attention to detail. In texture, the arrangement had finesse, suggesting a degree of reverie or contemplation. Yet in the midst of this tranquillity, a strong rhythmic energy created by a series of tight rolls on the snare drum introduces a vaguely militaristic feel, as if a summons to action was being launched, just as the first verse rings out. Underneath all the silk there is stone. Amid a crack in the beauty lies austerity.

The voice of Ray Lake rings out. His falsetto soars over the pulse of the music with sumptuous clarity and tenderness, an invocation that captures the imagination from the very first couplet:

> Children of the ghetto runnin' wild and free
> In a concrete jungle filled with misery

While this sets the tone for the whole piece, the thoughtful lyric fans out to address major areas in the L8 experience. First, there is the hostile media that pursues a sensationalist narrative around the lives of young Black people – 'always in the news' – which demands the resolve to survive the heavy emotional toll this takes: 'Toughness is the motto/ Bitter are their views'. With those four words of the second line, The Real Thing tap into a deep well of language developed over the years by artists of colour speaking out on the debilitating effects of second-class citizenship. There is the notable precedent in Nina Simone's 'Four Women' which contains the searing line 'I'm awfully bitter these days.' Bitter. A sense of having no value in society, of being not so much the other as the non-existent. Bitter. A feeling of invisibility. Bitter. A draught of shame if the white woman who falls in love with you is denounced as a 'nigger lover', or a revered sportsman says he wouldn't want his daughter to bring home a 'coon'. Bitter. The adjective is a sledgehammer summary of what it means to be Black in a world that denies your humanity and the possibility of self-fulfilment. Bitter are the blues. Bitter are the views. Lake sings that last line softly, with a kind of focused resignation. The delicacy of his timbre and the relative lack of volume increases the power of the statement. A scream is more destructive when it is held in, not let out. The shaft of light that gives hope to this sombre tableau is solidarity: 'Deep inside the ghetto there's a unity/that cancels out the sorrow and the misery'. As those words fill the air, one might look at the pictures of Toxteth residents on the inner sleeve of *4 from 8*, from the lads huddled around the pool table, to the elders who stand straight and proud.

The strength of the lyric and the structural subtleties and contrasts of 'Children of the Ghetto' make the song a landmark in British music, Black or otherwise. It has a minor tonality in which voice, strings and rhythm section conspire to ebb and flow between shadow and light, while a low count of beats per minute sees all those elements hover and amble rather than stride forward, even though the drums maintain a strong pulse, a trail of energy tucked under the meditative calm. That hint of funk, the possibility of bluesy physical release, materialises quite dramatically on the key change over which Lake sings 'there's no inspiration to brighten up the day', pushing his voice to breaking point, threatening to crack that gilded falsetto on the fourth syllable of the lengthy third word, expressing rather than suppressing his pain, revealing a tortured youth in the body of a grown man. Bigotry can scramble both boyhood and manhood.

Yet the redemptive power of the song, its call to unity, is vividly conveyed in the framing of the resonant lead voice in a pattern of call and response. Lake intones 'Children of the ghetto' and the ensembles harmonises on the graceful descending line 'keep your head' before marking a pause for the uplifting resolution 'to the sky'. The other decisive movement in the song is a jolt into a higher tempo around the 3-minute mark that introduces a double-time cymbal beat, vaulting bassline and a finely calibrated piano solo from Pete Nelson. The musicianship evident here reminds us that the players with whom the Real Thing worked, such as drummer Nigel Martinez, guitarist Vic Linton and string arrangers Nick Harrison, who scored 'Children of the Ghetto' and Paul Buckmaster, noted for his collaborations with Miles Davis, were skilled in the complex vocabulary of jazz. This Amoo confirmed emphatically: 'Well, that's exactly what it was supposed to be. We were very influenced by jazz, that's what we were listening to, I was very, very aware of Miles Davis.'[8]

'Children of the Ghetto' was the highpoint of the 'Liverpool 8 Medley', which closed with the irresistibly upbeat 'Stanhope Street', the song dedicated to Toxteth's central thoroughfare. But as much as 'Children of the Ghetto' was the jewel in their creative crown, the composition proved to be problematic because it signalled an incongruity with the band's previous work, or rather the piece clashed with perceptions of the four young men from Toxteth who had made good against the odds. Although *4 from 8* was intended to announce The Real Thing as accomplished and independent artists who had something to say, there was no doubt in Amoo's mind about the commercial potential of 'Children of the Ghetto' because it combined meaningful social commentary with a beautiful melody. But their label Pye did not see it that way, much to Amoo's chagrin. 'I could never understand why we were not allowed to release it as a single,' he lamented years later. The decision still rankles.

More seriously, the album barely disturbed the lower reaches of the British and international charts, and The Real Thing found themselves in the invidious position of not being able to reach listeners who might have related to their new work, because they were defined in the mainstream as inoffensive purveyors of a safe, inoffensive pop-soul hybrid.

'We were caught between two things. All the hip funkers would not go out and buy Real Thing songs because it wasn't 'cool', but 'Children of the Ghetto' and 'Liverpool 8' were too heavy for your 'You to Me Are Everything' guys.'[9] If ever there was a case of a band being a prisoner of its past, The Real Thing was the textbook example. Initially, they had the support of the rock press, but in the mid-1970s the tide turned decisively towards punk, which was deemed 'in' and away from soul or progressive rock, whch were not. Amoo recalls how journalists, who had once travelled to Toxteth to attend The Real Thing's gig, changed their tune:

> They used to come and see our shows, even at Stanley House. Before we had the hit, our show was full of songs similar to and of the same depth as 'Children of the Ghetto'. I'll always remember we did an interview with a guy called Chris White from *Melody Maker*. We went over to his house once and we got chatting; he was a serious writer. The day we released 'You to Me are Everything' the label organised a big press thing for us and Chris came and he said, 'I'm made up for you guys but you

know from now on you're gonna have to forget the heavier things.' He was right. That's when they stopped seriously covering us. They had to cover us because we were in the charts but it was a different type of coverage. *NME, Sounds, Melody Maker* used to really be into the band What they couldn't stand was 'You to Me…'[10]

The effects of this predicament were far reaching, certainly when one considers that the blanket exclusion kept the instructive reality tales of Stanhope Street off the national agenda. But also important is the fact that the political exhortations of The Real Thing came to resonate with the thinking of other Black British artists who were not seen as protest singers or rabble rousers intent on sticking it to the establishment. The grand exponent of the sophisticated love song, Joan Armatrading, released a quite astounding track, 'How Cruel', that evoked the trials and tribulations of people of colour in language that was hard, spare and impactful, in the no frills depiction of the practice of 'nigger bashing' as well as discrimination in general and the widespread phenomenon of white flight. And there was also the question of racial authenticity to contend with:

> Some people want to see my blood gush out
> And others want to watch while I cry.
> I heard somebody once say I was way too black.
> And someone answers that she's not black enough for me.
> I bite my tongue and it bites me back.
> I bought a house and the neighbours moved.
> I had a dog but it was stolen.

Brilliantly layered, the stanza ranks among the best social commentary of the mid 1970s, but it is interesting that 'How Cruel', is presented as no more a defining moment in Armatrading's career than 'Children of the Ghetto' is in The Real Thing's, possibly because the perception of her as a tender analyst of the emotions holds such sway.

While Armatrading was speaking her piece, a voice from the past (which had never gone away), Eddy Grant, also popped up with an album, *Message Man*. This reminded the world that his militancy had not dimmed since the days when he wrote 'Police on My Back' for his first group The Equals. Blending reggae, soul, and calypso rhythms, the album included a number of songs whose titles were explicit about the subject matter they dealt with: 'Race Hate', 'Hello Africa' and 'Soweto.'

Between them Grant, Armatrading and The Real Thing made significant contributions to the canon of Black music in Britain that plugged into the urgent representation of the lived experience of African Caribbean communities. The statements made by these artists stand up today as notable chronicles of the mid-1970s, though they are often missing from the retrospective assessments of the cultural-political activities of the period, which tend to foreground artists discussed in the previous chapter such as Steel Pulse, Matumbi, Aswad and Misty in Roots. The common denominator between these three bands was a close alignment with the Rock Against Racism (RAR) movement, with its cross-genre festivals. This raises the question of that movement's representation of Black music at the time, namely whether or not the campaign could have had a broader scope if it had aligned soul and pop alongside reggae and punk.

RAR founder Red Saunders was refreshingly frank on the fact that some of the omissions were ill advised, taking place amid pressures to draw large audiences and count on the significant draw of certain artists. He said, 'I think you're absolutely right. This is where the kind of naivety came in. How far you compromise is a big thing. You may compromise a bit because if you've got a really good soul band, or that night you got the word that Elvis Costello can only do that weekend, you're probably gonna choose Elvis Costello because you think that will get more people in. I suppose in a sense [being] slightly obsessed with the culture of the time because it was bottom up, and also because when you're running a big political campaign you've got to choose your strategy. Would we have had Eddy Grant, The Real Thing and Joan Armatrading if we had our time again? Yes, but that's too easy to say. Yes. I thought Eddy was fantastic… all of them were. We did what we did, we have to live with that and we have to live with the cock-ups as well.'[11] Like most political initiatives, RAR was anything but comprehensively harmonious and cohesive, and as one might have surmised, the behind the scenes running of the movement was marked by 'arguments, confusions, contradictions' as well as the triumph of mobilising thousands of people against the National Front. Dealing with sharp-elbowed managers intent on gaining top billing and extended stage time for their artists was one challenge, as was the need to stay true to the ideal of being 'against the giant rock star syndrome', not to mention the racist bile spewed by Eric Clapton. But if there were discussions with big names who would have appeared ideal on paper – John Lennon, Bob Marley, Paul McCartney – which came to nothing, then there were also revealing moments in which defenders of the cause found themselves in uncomfortable proximity to the very targets of their action. Jimmy Pursey of Sham 69 had members of the British Movement in his own road crew, the Clash's notoriously fractious manager Bernie Rhodes derided the anti-Nazi league as 'anti-pencil sharpeners', and one of the giant rock stars about whom RAR was very wary had ideas that were way beyond 'off message'. 'We had a weird back and forth with Pete Townshend,' says Saunders. 'He supported the Southall Kids Are Innocent gigs we did at the Rainbow theatre to raise money for Misty in Roots' People Unite Co-Op, which had been smashed up by the police. Pete Townshend was brilliant... he came and donated all his stuff. Then suddenly in the middle of it all somebody said to me "Oh, Townshend said he can bring... Eric Clapton!" Of course, they were mates.'[12]

It is clear that Rock Against Racism was fighting racism at the heart of rock as much as it was using rock to fight racism. RAR's immense achievement as a grass roots, ground-up initiative that had a transformative effect on British society is now set in stone. But it also throws into sharp relief the complex nature of racial dynamics within the field in which it operated, as well as the oversimplifications about genres of Black music. The framing of reggae as 'rebel music', and therefore relevant to RAR was accurate, but it did not follow that soul offered *only* shallow escapism and was therefore irrelevant to RAR. Saunders did point out that soul was programmed at certain gigs but the bands in question, like Jabba and Limousine, had a relatively low profile and could not alter the prevailing misconception.

Images are powerful. Clichés die hard. The fragmentation, sectarianism and judgmental thinking in pop culture stopped people listening to 'Children of the Ghetto' because it fell on the wrong side of the threshold of cool, whereas reggae did not. Yet reggae and soul overlapped in their demand for high musical standards as well as the use of key words with a common ideological thrust. Marvin Gaye urged the world to 'save the children.' Bob Marley stated 'children get your culture.' Aswad hailed 'African children' and Steel Pulse entreated the bredren to 'make way for our children and their children.' As for The Real Thing, they sang for and as the children of the ghetto. Black people up and down the county from Birmingham and Bristol to Manchester and London, as well as Liverpool, could relate, but the band did more than lament life in material deprivation. They also identified the struggle within, the severe trials of the ghetto of the mind.

Notes

1. See Don Letts' *Culture Clash*, SAF, 2007.
2. The Ruts.
3. Interview with the author, February 2022.
4. Interview with the author, May 2022.
5. Ibid.
6. Interview with the author May 2022.
7. Ibid.
8. Ibid.
9. Ibid.
10. Ibid.
11. Ibid.
12. Ibid.

14 BLOOD 'N' FIRE

Dem frame up George Lindo up in Bradford town
but the Bradford blacks dem a rally round
– Linton Kwesi Johnson

Lions and Tigers
A funeral procession edges forward, flanked by a brass band playing the kind of languorous melodies, with swelling and floating notes from the trombones and trumpets, that conjure up the history of New Orleans. Soulfulness blows across the solemnity. But the journey to the final resting place is far from the sweltering sunshine of Louisiana. Behind the mourners there are low-rise flats, while the streets are lined with Ford Cortinas whose red paint somehow contrives to be another shade of grey in a tableau that seems to have been bleached of colour, despite the efforts of the steady-steppin' horn players of The Adamant Ensemble[1] to bring a touch of brightness to the occasion. The footage is of an event that took place in Butetown, Cardiff, Wales, in spring 1978, the dignified parade in honour of a local hero, Victor Parker, a 68-year-old guitarist of Barbadian heritage who had been the cornerstone of Cardiff's jazz scene for twenty-five years. Like several of his peers born at the turn of the 20th century, he had ventured to London several times in the interwar period, but unlike the Deniz brothers, Frank and Joe, who became members of big bands and small groups in London during a period commonly referred to as 'black British swing', Parker returned to Cardiff and had a long residency at the Quebec hotel in Crichton Street in the city centre.

A recording made in 1976, a few years before his passing and issued in 2022, is an invaluable document of Parker's work, showing why he won so many hearts and minds. The repertoire is packed with show tunes and standards, from 'Cheek to Cheek', 'C'est Si Bon' to 'Solitude' – songs associated with Ella Fitzgerald, Louis Armstrong and Duke Ellington. Parker generated a solid, tasteful swing on strummed chords that drove the rhythm in concert with the discreet but effective drumming of Jed Williams, while a young English trumpeter, Chris Hodgkins, laid down a number of eloquent solos on this lively beat. The group is energised and engaging.

Parker was not a grandstanding artist but the measured, effective nature of his performance emphasises the value of a reined-in rhythm player as the equal of a more showy improviser. On one of the highlights of the set, a reprise of 'Undecided', Parker pares the sunny arrangement right down to short, pithy lines and leaves a huge amount space for 'breaks', in which uninhibited audience members chant the tune's well-known lyrics. That joyously participatory moment is perhaps an apt reminder that jazz evolved from accessible, popular structures in the 1900s to the far more complex aesthetics of bebop in the 1940s, and that if Parker could not be heralded as a 'modern' icon, he was keeping alive the 'root strata' of Black music, which would still serve many forward thinkers.

Parker knew a bunch of classic tunes, but first and foremost he comes across as committed to the jam session, when players come together to embark on a creative journey for which there is no pre-programmed destination. The guitarist was, despite his lack of national renown, part of a select group of Butetown's Black residents who achieved much in the fields of entertainment and sport. There were the singers, Patti Flynn, another local jazz legend, and Shirley Bassey,[2] who went global with her performance of 'Goldfinger', and also the legendary rugby player Billy Boston,[3] whose heritage, like Bassey's, was West African. Working class heroes they may have been, but there is no escaping the truth that ethnic minorities in Butetown had the bleakest of prospects, as the commentary on Parker's funeral spells out:

'For Cardiff's 6,000 or so coloured community who are not stars, life holds a little less promise. 25% of the youngsters are unemployed, 83% of the families have no car, 40% are members of single-parent families – that's four times the national average and more than half the families are in receipt of free school meals.'

Butetown was long Cardiff's most deprived area, a ghetto of people of colour for more than a hundred years, even though the city was prone to pat itself on the back for the excellence of its race relations: 'We've never had any trouble here. We're all one big happy family!' Yet this does not stand up to the historical facts stated in the voice-over: 'Cardiff was the scene 60 years ago of some of Britain's worst race riots and many Butetown folk believe the root cause of their deprivation is plain old-fashioned prejudice.'

The brass band has faded by that point in the clip and the statement above casts something of a shadow over the whole event being filmed. The united front between Black and white around a single artist cannot deflect attention away from the daily struggles of Butetown residents of African and West Indian descent. One of the most striking images of the day is that of a charismatic pallbearer, whose heavy beard and mid-length dreadlocks attest to the spread of the messages of Bob Marley, Burning Spear, Matumbi and Steel Pulse far beyond the higher profile 'Black ghettos' of London, Birmingham and Liverpool.

Seeing a 'Tiger Bay Rasta' in the mid-1970s underlines the evolution and complexity of Black British society at this time, as there are plenty of 'baldhead' men next to him. But the point is both that the Black presence outside the capital of England was substantial and that older forms of Black cultural activity persist alongside what took new and radical guises. When a chief immigration officer recommended the establishment of concentration camps for Black males in Butetown in 1919 because he thought the presence of colonial seamen was undesirable, he could not have envisaged a time when a white brass band would lead a procession in honour of a local West Indian musician. Black British radicals, though, were aware of that past, and of a present which also made life for ethnic minorities one of trial and tribulation.

LKJ is the Mvp
Throughout Britain, the threat of incarceration to Black people was most visibly signified in the infamous 'sus laws' that gave the police the power to stop and search, harass, intimidate, arrest and ultimately physically abuse people of colour. This was a national problem.

On the 15th of February 1978, George Lindo, a black textile worker living in Bradford, Yorkshire was framed for the robbery of a betting shop by the police and jailed for 11 months. He always protested his innocence, and it was later found that he had been found guilty on the basis of testimony by a discredited officer who had also given false evidence in other investigations. Lindo's case was a gross miscarriage of justice, compounded by the fact that the deputy Chief Constable in the case directed that this information about the false evidence be withheld from Lindo's defence counsel. On the 8th June, 1979 the conviction was quashed.

Perhaps the most chilling aspect of the Lindo affair was the behaviour of rank-and-file police and the clinical nature of the cover-ups undertaken by senior officers. This grimly echoed the tragedy of David Oluwale, a homeless Nigerian who had been hounded to death by members of the Leeds constabulary in 1968. The difference between the fates suffered by these two Black men was that, at the time, Oluwale had no champions, no activists in significant numbers, but Lindo did. Protests were organised locally by the Bradford Black Collective, which had already taken measures to defend the West Indian community from police brutality. In the late 1970s, the Black and Asian population of Bradford numbered around 13%, predominantly South Asian, the majority of whom lived in wards in the south of the city.

Footage of the protests that took place over George Lindo's arrest makes it more than clear that feelings were running high. During one of the demonstrations outside Bradford's now demolished Tyrls police station, there is a young man Black man with a striped hat and a megaphone addressing the throng of pickets that numbered some 300 in a call and response protest. His name is Linton Kwesi Johnson. He makes a case for Lindo's innocence, chanting 'Him is a working man, him nuh carry no dagger, him is not no robber,' and with each line the assembled crowd hollers the name of the accused, with the exchange culminating in the leader's urgent, uncompromising demands: 'Dem have to let him go! Dem have to free him now!'

The creolised language in this transcription puts Jamaican culture at the heart of the address, but what is also significant is the strong rhythmic drive that underpins all of Johnson's statements. The words are set to a pulse. The rich timbre of his voice, the motion and resonance of each word is given power by its careful relationship with time; the syllables are mapped over the seconds to create a sense of cadence, that magical rise, fall, swerve and sway that makes speech dynamic rather than static. Johnson's delivery created music without musicians.

The chant for Lindo was a potent marriage of art and activism, of culture as a weapon, such as it had been for the Black Panthers in the USA, and its British outgrowth, of which Johnson had been a member. His creative development was closely tied to the political awakening he experienced as a young man who arrived in Brixton, south London from his native Jamaica at the age of 11, attended secondary school in nearby Tulse Hill, where he was steered away from his primary ambition to become an accountant and advised to enlist in the army – Johnson's first-hand experience of the systemic prejudice that faced West Indians in British society. He joined the Race Today Collective, discussed in Chapter 4, and was involved in other landmark organisations such as the Caribbean Artists Movement, founded in 1966 and whose activities included readings and discussions, mostly at the Keskadee centre and in members' homes. When LKJ joined in 1971, CAM was coming to the end of its life as a Caribbean-focused writers organisation and was engaging with more community-oriented activities at the West Indian student centre in Earls Court. This involvement took him on a quest to discover Black and Caribbean literature and led to a life-long relationship with the Trinidadian publisher and activist John LaRose, who, with his English partner, Sarah White, founded New Beacon Books, as a publishing house and a bookshop. These outlets were pivotal to Johnson's personal development.

> It all began with me going to New Beacon which was in John and Sarah White's front room in Finsbury Park in north London before they had the shop and trying to get books by black authors because we'd started a literary group in the Black Panther movement. Then there was Andrew Salkey, he was John's very close friend, he introduced me to Andrew and they both became my mentors.[4]

Salkey, author of several novels, introduced Johnson to Jessica and Eric Huntley, the Guyanese activists who founded Bogle L'Ouverture Press, which published Johnson's debut poetry collection, *Dread, Beat An Blood*.

The Lady… She Haffi Go

That landmark work, which chronicled the realities of being Black in Britain in the 1970s, was birthed as Johnson was soaking up important influences from a variety of sources, pioneering writers and theorists as well as innovative 'mike men', or 'Dee-Jays', who would improvise passages of spoken word over rhythms with a linguistic and metric verve that paralleled American poets and 'personality jocks'. He reported:

> Basically, what I was doing I was writing for the page and the stage at the same time. It was all a part of, I guess, ideas promoted by people like Kamau Brathwaite about the importance of orality in Caribbean literature. I was influenced not just by the poems I read in books but by the music of the reggae 'Dee-Jays'… like U-Roy, Prince Jazzbo and Big Youth, who was my favourite of those guys. And the early Jamaican 'talkin' tunes.' I was attracted to the spoken word set against music.[5]

At early gigs Johnson recited verse over prerecorded backing tracks that were played on a Revox tape machine before moving on to work with a group of Rastafarian drummers in Brixton who were called Rasta Love:

> I thought, wouldn't it be great to bring out my poetry to music; surely that's how to reach a much wider audience, because people would be more inclined to listen to a record, buy a record. The audience for poetry weren't exactly buying books in their hundreds and thousands. I thought music was the way forward. My music was reggae of course, and I was just basically trying a thing. Of course, when I used to recite on my own without the drummers, people used to say to me that those poems sound musical, it sounds like reggae you know. So I just tried a thing and lo and behold it resulted in a career in reggae music.[6]

It was Dennis Bovell, leader of roots favourites Matumbi, who arranged the 1978 recording of *Dread Beat An Blood*, which was credited to Poet and the Roots, but essentially set Johnson's texts to drums, percussion, bass, guitar and keyboards. The album was a vital document from both a socio-political and a musical point of view because it captured key moments in Black British history and cast them against a sophisticated sonic backdrop hinted at in Johnson's early, unaccompanied performances. Now his words in defence of West Indians persecuted by the police rang out to a much wider audience, enhanced by the chatter of rimshots and the bullish surge of the low end. On the back of the album was a picture of Johnson holding a megaphone flanked by two stern-faced constables outside Bradford's Tyrls Police Station, where he had read poetry for George Lindo. The piece, 'It Dread Inna Inglan', started with a recording of Johnson using the loudhailer in call and response with the crowd at this event, before the band came in, transforming the song into a masterpiece of musical poetry. The opening rhyme was a condensed, unforgettable chronicle.

> Dem frame up George Lindo up in Bradford town
> but the Bradford blacks dem a rally round.

To detail that sequence of events vividly, Johnson delivers a quasi-pentameter couplet, creating tension between the 11 syllables of the first line and the 10 of the second, the careful craftsmanship of the text aiding its political reach. As noted in Chapter 13, there are seminal Black British songs that are identified with a particular locality, such as Stanhope Street in Liverpool, or Handsworth in Birmingham, validating areas of the United Kingdom that were stigmatised as 'coloured ghettos' but now had to be seen as places where music and culture blossomed. Johnson, the Black Londoner, here hails the mobilisation of black Northerners. 'Dem Bradford blacks dem nuh tek it nuh more.' The provinces are brought into a conversation on Black social progress that had been conducted for the most part in the metropolis. The very title Johnson chose for the tale of George Lindo, 'It Dread Inna Inglan' purposefully connects the local to the national. As Johnson explained, the making of networks had been going on for some time:

> That's right, the Race Today Collective was part of what we call 'the Alliance'. We worked together with the Black Parents Movement, which was founded by Teena Sylvester and Roxy Harris and several others, and we had connections up and down the country, with people like Gus John in Manchester, the Bradford Black Collective, a group of activists – African Caribbeans and people from Africa – who took their inspiration from the Race Today Collective. We had these connections.[7]

This vital history is included on the album notes for *Dread Beat an Blood*. 'Man Free', the piece written to mark the release of journalist Darcus Howe from jail, had a number of acronymic references that were clarified in the credits. B.P.M. was the Black Parents Movement, B.S., Black Students Movement and R.T.C. the Race Today Collective. C.D.C was the Carnival Development Committee, in which Howe had been heavily involved since the late 1950s, to ensure carnival retained its autonomy as it came under increasing pressure from the establishment to exist in a confined space such as a park rather than on the streets.

The friction between the police and Britain's Black population was amplified in Margaret Thatcher's infamous statement in 1978, made in the run up to the general election, which still resonates to this day: 'People are really rather afraid that this country might be rather swamped by people with a different culture. If there's any fear that it might be swamped, people are going to react and be rather hostile to those coming in, so if you want good race relations you've got to allay people's fears on numbers. That's one thing that's driving some people to the National Front but at least they're talking about some of the problems.' News items on national television helped lay bare the fault lines. In a vox pop, white passersby were emboldened to say: "She's perfectly right." There was no holding back.

Black members of the Wolverhampton Anti-racialism Committee condemned Mrs Thatcher's remarks as 'very much racist', and others concurred, arguing that they legitimised extremists: 'She is making the National Front more respectable.' As for L.K. Johnson's appraisal of the Iron lady he was unequivocal about what she was doing and what needed to be done in order to stop her doing it anymore:

> Maggi Thatcher on di go
> Wid a racist show
> But she haffi go

Johnson called for a Black united front that crossed cultural, ethnic and generational lines, between migrants and their children – 'African, Asian, West Indian and black British' – arguing that because they were 'here to stay inna Inglan', these constituencies needed to pull together. What galvanised his message was the combustible and hypnotic character of the music Johnson made with Dennis Bovell, with the blending of the former's voice and the latter's basslines over an insistent beat. This would come to be termed 'dub poetry', connecting poetry to dub as an instrumental genre of reggae in which the intricacies of the mix and the startling shadow play of reverb and delay created a highly influential new lexicon of sound. Other Jamaican artists such as Jean 'Binta' Breeze, who also made albums with Bovell, became associated with 'dub poetry', though Johnson found the term limiting: 'I prefer to call it reggae poetry'.

Johnson emerged as one of the key articulators of what the Black British community experienced in the second half of the 1970s and early 1980s; he chronicled the marginalisation and persecution of Black immigrants and their offspring in a revolutionary artistic form, to which his primary target audience of young Black people could relate. The rich musicality of the work made it accessible to those who would not have considered themselves as having any interest in poetry.

As some of his peers were doing in the Caribbean, he used Jamaican vernacular, though it was not yet an accepted part of the British poetry scene – in the same way that reggae had been excluded by British popular music programmes, which looked down on it as a lesser form in a lesser language.

By setting his recited reality tales to surging bass patterns, Johnson built a bridge between pop culture and radical political thinking that invites comparison, not so much sonically as conceptually, with African American spoken word artists such as The Last Poets, Gil Scott-Heron, Jayne Cortez and Nikki Giovanni, all of whom performed their poetry to a wide range of Black music, particularly jazz.

As his second album, *Forces of Victory*, showed, Johnson's work continued to develop a skilful synergy of music and words, which, as the title suggests, expressed a confidence in the capacity of 'the people united' to take the struggle for social justice to their oppressors. There are tracks where Johnson recites unapologetically the need for militant action, such as 'Fite Dem Back' and the possibility of taking control of one's own destiny, such as 'Independent Intavenshan'. But he also recognises the seriousness of the challenge facing the youth of today ('It Noh Funny'). These songs reflected the state of mind of the 'rebel generation', Johnson's peers, who had to contend with the harsh rejection and open hostility of Thatcherite society.

Johnson gave them solace in times of strife by reporting on events in an almost verité style: 'I was walking down the road the other day when I hear a little yootman say.' Whether this individual faces the ignominy of homelessness, the drudgery of a dole queue or the perilous lure of petty crime is perhaps not as important as the fact that the poet is seeing them, and that he recognises, as 'Want Fi Goh Rave' makes clear, that they have come of age. They have a right to life's needs: socialising, and enjoying time away from the slog of daily life. In a narrowly defined context of politicised art, that sentiment might be frowned upon but, as the song argues, it is precisely because of the soul-destroying circumstances of many young Black Britons that the desire to find some kind of release and pleasure actually has political significance.

Another kind of rock
The role reggae played as a vehicle for protest was a defining part of its appeal, particularly in the slipstream of Rock Against Racism (RAR), whose events presented British exponents of reggae as activist performers. Affairs of the heart were not considered their primary subject matter, though it is worth remembering that Bob Marley felt free to lay bare his deepest emotions, whether through the plea to a lover that he didn't want to wait in vain, or in the erotic overture of 'Turn your lights down low'. Even so, certain zealous Rastafarians admonished him for being too 'soft' on albums like *Kaya*, recorded in London in 1977.

In general, at this time, reggae had a warrior subtext. The subsidiary founded by Virgin records to enter the market for reggae was called The Front Line, an evocation of the black enclaves up and down the country; its photographic leitmotiv was a hand gripping a length of barbed wire and dripping blood as a result. Trenchtown may have been in Jamaica but the idea of taking 'a small axe' to Babylon transferred readily to British soil.

Inevitably, another path had to open up to accommodate a strain of reggae that provided a space for lyrics that broached the subject of relationships, of attraction, longing, heartache and joy, the ebb and flow of feelings in the universal life-cycle of coupling and breaking up.

Between the mid- and late-1970s an important sub-genre was born in the UK that fulfilled that need. Lovers rock became the soundtrack for a generation of Black Britons who sought a romantic form of reggae that would facilitate the mating rituals and feats of seduction that took place at dances or blues parties, where the uncompromising urgency of Rasta message music was not the ideal soundtrack for such moments of intimacy. Even so, as the breadth of Marley's song writing shows, the notion of love, whether human or divine, could have a political dimension insofar as it consolidates the humanity of the oppressed. For the 'Tuff gong' there was no contradiction between Rastafarianism in its rebel guise, where Babylon falls by way of blood and fire, and Zion as the path of love, as in 'Could You Be Loved?' and 'Is This Love?', both sublime laments,

The very phrase, Lovers Rock, has an intended duality in its grammar: both as an imperative and a statement. Many recall that they heard DJs command 'Lovers... rock', understanding that the word 'rock' carried powerful connotations of both physical and emotional release. The term also connected to other earlier incarnations of Jamaican music such as 'rocksteady' and the contemporary militant strain of 'rockers', the rhythm-led style of the masterful 'riddim twins' the drum and bass heroes, Sly Dunbar and Robbie Shakespeare.

There were, of course, commercial imperatives. Record buyers wanted new rhythms and new sounds, and Jamaican music had proved abundantly that it could mutate at will and produce a wide array of sub-genres, including ska, rocksteady, reggae, and dub. And as Dennis Bovell, the prolific producer who was one of the chief architects of lover's rock, points out, there was a very specific participant audience for the new genre. He had started playing softer, romantic tunes at his Sufferers Hi-Fi sound system dances, which attracted conspicuously larger numbers of women, and, consequently, more men, interested in meeting the women. Bovell would draw further inspiration from a song by a legendary Jamaican melodica player and composer:

> Augustus Pablo had a song called 'Lovers Rock', and I thought it was a great title. So we felt we're gonna have this music called lovers rock. It's gonna be music for dancing to, call it smooch reggae if you like, some-

thing where couples can get hold of someone when you turn the lights out. It was purely a sexual thing; we wanted to be at one with the women. Coming from that Augustus Pablo song, 'Lovers Rock', I decided that lovers rock were two words that went together well, to be this new hybrid of London-based reggae that was a couple dancing style. It wasn't hard, it was all about love and it was rocking as well... lovers rock.[8]

Soon after, Dennis Harris, owner of a record shop in Brockley, south London, who branched into making music in his own right, actually used Lovers Rock as the name of a label he founded in 1977, and in the years that followed it became a key sub-genre in the history of reggae music, marking the moment when an idiom born in Britain achieved global recognition and subsequently impacted on Jamaican music.

As is the case with many chapters in musical history, there was a significant pre-history to the birth of the new. Two years prior to Dennis Harris going into production, vocalist Louisa Mark recorded 'Caught You in a Lie', after renowned sound system operator Lloydie Coxsone asked Bovell to produce a single for him. This track struck a chord with the reggae fraternity and was followed by several others that also broadly dealt with the vagaries of relationships, the key artists being Marie Pierre, Susan Cadogan and Jean Adebambo. In the space of a few years lover's rock became a space for female artists with voices that had the richness of timbre and emotional depth to give credence to the subject matter in question.

'It has to be a love song and it's mainly female vocalists,' Bovell makes clear:

> At the time when I started having female vocalists on a wide scale in my productions, women weren't really involved in reggae that heavily, unless they were backing vocalists providing the harmonies for a male singer. It's true to say that there was and still is Marcia Griffiths from I-Threes and Rita Marley and Judy Mowatt, and they were great singers but they were still relegated to second division when Bob Marley was singing because it was like a man's world. Girls were shoved to the side, in the background. I thought, well Aretha Franklin is the queen of soul why haven't we got a queen of reggae?[9]

Black and Proud

The new strain of royal Black female vocalists at the forefront of lovers rock stood out for many reasons. Louisa Mark and others were still teenagers, with little recording experience, and the freshness of their voices shaped the identity of the genre. There were also discreet but notable structural changes in the melodic shape of songs in comparison to classic roots reggae, as John Kpiaye recalls. He was a member of one of Britain's first ever reggae bands, The Cats, and a fine session guitarist and producer. Speaking of Louisa Mark's anthemic 'Caught You in a Lie', he said:

Her voice was so distinctively young, but she had a kind of presence about her, a conviction. I remember going to dances and you'd hear it all the time; it didn't sound like anything coming from Jamaica. It's a slow record and the 'rub a dub' dance was just starting so it was perfect for that... In comparison, the female singers in Jamaica at that time, like Marcia Griffiths, they were big women They weren't young girls. They sounded like grown women whereas 'Caught You in a Lie' that was by a young girl. Rhythmically it was different, the bass was nothing like in Jamaica... the feel of the thing changed and a lot of the time the bass is playing very melodically and not just repeating the same two bar sequence. The arrangement had a sophistication but also a subtlety going on.

It was after hearing that record that Brown Sugar started to want to sing. It was such a massive influence. Had that not come along, the whole lovers rock thing may well not have happened.[10]

Brown Sugar was a London vocal trio, consisting of Caron Wheeler, Carol Simms and Pauline Catlin. The girls had an average age of fifteen and were still diligently practising harmonies in the school playground when, in 1977, Kpiaye wrote and asked them to sing 'I'm in Love with a Dreadlocks', which was a kind of answer tune to 'Curly Locks' by the Jamaican vocalist Junior Byles. As those two titles suggests there was a focus on the Rastafarian, as a proud wearer of hair untouched by European combs, and Brown Sugar's profession of love for a Rasta was matched by political songs on the eponymous album the group recorded, such as 'Black Pride' and 'Dreaming of Zion', alongside lover's rock songs.

Kpiaye recalls that the girls were keenly aware of the struggles faced by the black community in Britain and were on the same wavelength as him insofar as neither had an interest in doing love songs that used the standard trope of 'baby, I can't live without you.' He gives short shrift to the idea of there being another sub-genre called 'conscious lovers', as his interaction with Brown Sugar and their peers made it clear that there was really no such distinction. An unforced, organic intermingling of 'roots' and 'lovers' occurred because of the simultaneity and contiguity of the genres:

> At the time lovers happened, you also had this explosion of roots bands Aswad, Matumbi, Steel Pulse, Misty in Roots. You'd do a session, the producer might have two artists... one doing 'lovers', one doing 'roots', so it didn't seem to me to be unusual to mix the two because at the time when I was doing lovers I was in my late 20s, so I was politically aware of what was happening socially in Britain, with all the racism and what have you. I mean I read Malcolm X, Eldridge Cleaver and Angela Davis. So it didn't feel strange to make a song you could dance to, rub a dub to but still listen to the lyrics. I think Brown Sugar continued to write stuff in a similar vein.[11]

They were the pre-eminent vocal harmony combo in lovers rock, but the genre had many excellent solo female singers, including established Jamaicans such as Yvonne Sterling and Doreen Shaffer, who had been recording since the early 1970s, or newer arrivals such as Paula Clarke and T.T Ross, a white English vocalist who enjoyed success with 'Last Date' and a cover of John Lennon's utopian paean 'Imagine'.

This shift of attention away from the male singer was important for the obvious reason of offering a wider range of perceptions of reggae but also because it provided an alternative to the image of Jamaican-influenced British music as the preserve of the male group, that trusty five or six piece unit that stood as a kind of microcosm of the ghettoised community. As mentioned in the previous chapter, Matumbi, Aswad, Steel Pulse, Misty In Roots, Cimarons and Black Slate came to define the British reggae scene, and they embodied the 'band of brothers' ideal, in which collective energy is the equal to any charismatic frontman.

Lovers rock put not just a woman, but an individual centre stage, and certainly, with a name such as Adebambo, there is a clear sense of an African Caribbean heritage that underpins the singular rather than plural voice stamped on a recording. Even so, just as was the case in the bulk of American soul and British pop, the assembly line of the music, from composition to production, arranging, playing and engineering of the material, remained very much in the hands of men. While there was a certain amount of recalibration of the gender balance of reggae, the division of labour and consequently the power dynamics that framed it, pointed out how long the road was towards true equality. In lovers rock, the presence of a star woman standing in front of a mike highlighted the absence of a woman leaning at studio's mixing desk, or hunched down over a piano or wrapping their fingers around a bass guitar.

Vivian Clark, who was raised in Ladbroke Grove, west London, to Jamaican parents, became part of the roots scene as a member of the Brimstone, a combo that did have a woman in its rhythm section, the keyboard player, Angela Francis, and recorded a classic lovers single 'Come and Take Me'. Clark has an interesting, personal take on the subject, as she explained in a north London café in 2022:

> The women were trying to deal with family responsibilities, and still are. We were prominent in the home, making sure that children went to school, looking after others. Women had to make sure everything was working. It's not that women could not get more involved in the music side... I think they could but a lot of the time they chose to make family a priority and did not have time for much else. I mean at one point I cut short my first job abroad in Germany to come home and look after my mother who wasn't well. And we were more interested in singing than in being behind the desk. It felt great that the women – they had something

to really connect with audiences, the songs… They felt warm, you could relate to the situations they were singing about at the time. For me, it was an eye opener and inspiring because you had all these beautiful young voices who could sing from the heart. It was about a British female presence. But you have to realise the impact of a Louisa Mark in our music… I mean you couldn't go anywhere without hearing her. They pushed British reggae to another level. It wasn't just about Jamaica. I really do praise the women, the British talent because they just stepped up.[12]

Questions of gender aside, lovers rock, by the end of the 1970s, had produced an outstanding canon of songs that were part of the soundtrack to Black British social life. The following tunes are nothing more than a sprinkling of the cornucopia: Audrey Hall's 'Heart of Stone'; June Powell's 'Please Mr. Please'; Pam Hall's 'Perfidia'; Jennifer Day's 'Together'; Betty Padget's 'My Eyes Adored You' and Cynthia Shloss's 'Sad Movies.'

Labels such as Trojan and Attack started to record the genre in addition to the singles released by Dennis Harris' Lovers Rock label and male singers also performed in the new style, highlighting a longstanding tradition of the 'sweet voice' that had a sensitivity and finesse that was not at all incompatible with a sense of virility. Leading the pack were Pat Kelly, Delroy Wilson, Freddie McGregor, John Holt, Barry Biggs and above all the peerless Gregory Isaacs, whose moniker, 'the cool ruler' was entirely appropriate for a man whose tenor was misty and ethereal yet so commanding it seemed to float out of a speaker box and drift right through any assembled mass of people, who, to quote Linton Kwesi Johnson, want fi goh rave. In keeping with John Kpiaye's comment about points of intersection between lovers and roots, Isaacs was equally compelling whether he sang a lament such as 'Night Nurse', pining for his paramour, or an anthem in defiance of an oppressive establishment, 'Easy, Take It Easy (Babylon Too Rough).'

Got it covered
Regardless of the conscious tunes of Brown Sugar, lovers' rock crystallised as a genre in which a first person narrative investigated the emotional spectrum that comes with a relationship, from the highest highs to the lowest lows, which in many lyrics was distilled in the fate of waiting. That blessed phone call could take a whole side of vinyl.

London-based producers and players also continued to embrace African-American music just as Jamaican musicians had drawn on jazz and R&B to create their own kind of boogie and then ska. Hence the influence of lushly orchestrated mid-1970s soul music, epitomised by the music from labels like Philly International, with its unabashed sentimentality, came into play, yielding rich material for new interpretations. And as with reggae versions of earlier soul, some of the best lovers versions were so good that the original was eclipsed by the cover, a key example being Sugar Minott's heavenly 'Good Thing Going', such a masterpiece in its own right it was almost universally forgotten that the first artist to record the tune was a young man called Michael Jackson.

One could also point to Elizabeth Archer's version of Roberta Flack's 'Feel Like Making Love', which, like Minott's remake, has the virtue of injecting a kind of 'lively up' energy into the arrangement that contrasts with the sensitivity of the vocal. But perhaps of all the pieces in this Black America-Black Britain creative continuum that had the greatest significance, it was the version of 'Lovin' You', originally made by the Chicagoan vocalist, Minnie Riperton (a huge hit on both sides of the Atlantic), which was covered by the singer who became one of the great 'Queens' of lovers rock: Janet Kay.

Born in Willesden, north London, to Jamaican parents, Kay had no formal musical training as a child but took an interest in singing from an early age, tuning into TV shows like *Tonight at The London Palladium*. Her entry into the world of recording is instructive because it underlines the informality with which careers were being made in reggae, including its continued embrace of youth. She had just left school and was invited by a friend to attend a rehearsal by roots champions Aswad at Harrow Road, west London.

> I'd never really sung properly on a live mike other than in a makeshift studio that we had at school, so I went in, and I was uh, uh, uh [sings wordlessly]. Anyway Tony Gad (keyboardist for Aswad), he overheard me, and he was good friends with Alton Ellis, the Jamaican reggae legend And they lived on the same road as Alton, who was not only a singer he was a producer as well. He was looking for a female artist to do a cover version of 'Lovin' You.' So, Tony said to him, well I might have found the girl for you. I heard this girl sing in the rehearsal room, she's got quite a high voice, she might be able to do that song.[13]

'Lovin' You' provided a launchpad for Kay – once Ellis secured the approval of her elders and betters. 'I said to my parents can I go to the studio? They said no, we don't know this man (Alton Ellis). I kept pleading for about a week and in the end, they said right, you need to tell him to come to the house and ask your dad's permission. So, Alton came to the house, and they had their conversation'. Kay was able to start her career in earnest when 'Lovin' You' showed her range. After that, 'Silly Games', a 1979 collaboration with producer Dennis Bovell, broke her to a mainstream audience as the song reached number 2 in the UK singles chart and landed her appearances on *Top of the Pops*. This was while she was still working as a temp, a sign that the supposed glamour of the music industry could not mask a lack of financial reward at its fringes. There was no payment for the track, which was recorded in a small studio in Chalk Farm, north London, where the artist endured the indignity of having to sit on the floor in between takes. Luxury items such as chairs were not yet an option.

Despite the Spartan nature of the surroundings in which it was made, 'Silly Games' was a highpoint in Black music in Britain. It had a sophistication that moved beyond the two or three chord model that had been prevalent in reggae. The harmonic pathway of the song moved between major and minor keys to bring a distinct emotional shift as Kay expresses the forthright desire for her lover to be clear in his intentions to her. The melody slips adroitly through doubt and hope before Kay hits the searing high note that dramatically ratchets up the tension that has been slowly building, framed by the vivid colours of electric piano and synthesizer. Both were used to create gently caressing, sultry, piping sounds that were a perfect backdrop for the delicacy of Kay's voice.

Synthesizers played a significant role on the breakthrough lover's rock anthem, 'Caught You in a Lie' by Louisa Mark, and the genre was partly defined by their presence. Bovell's key collaborator, guitarist-composer-producer John Kpiaye, pointed out how the latest technology made a sizeable impact on the sessions at Gooseberry Studio, where many classic tunes were laid down. As he recalled:

> It was one of the first studios to have a little keyboard to use. It could have been monophonic but then double tracked to build up layers. I mean the early synths were hired in and a programmer came along to create the required sounds because you couldn't save any of the patches that had been used on previous tracks. So it was all done on the hop really. I think on 'Caught You in a Lie' there were lots of overdubbed tracks to produce polyphonic sound. And the other instrument used on a lot of stuff was the Solina, a string synthesizer.[14]

Essential as the rainbow of textures offered by keyboards was to the vocabulary of lover's rock, the rhythm section remained, as is the case in all Jamaican music, a basis for the sonic architecture. One of the great conceptual feats of the genre was the use of contrast between instruments. If you listen to the dub version of 'Silly Games', what stands out is the killer beat provided by Drummie Zeb, which has a stark, almost abrupt syncopation that sends a sizzling tremor of energy right through the track. So as much as the keys sway you gently, the drums rock you forcefully. There is a clever hardness-softness dynamic at play.

Another track cut a few years earlier has a similar ingenuity. A nonchalant melody skims over the most explosive, depth-charge rhythm created by a snare drum from which notes are pummelled out at a tempo and decibel level that is distinctly higher than that of all the sounds that hover around it. Once again, tough rub-a-dubs with tender, and the textural range and subtleties of arrangement in lovers rock come masterfully to the fore, as the instrumentation and voice provide a wide range of vibrations, from the silky and slender threads of the electric keyboards to the spikes and shards of the drum kit. The blend is artful.

The track described here, 'Thinking of You', was made by one of the greatest and perhaps most overlooked singers in the genre, the late Candy Mckenzie. Raised in Kilburn, north London to Guyanese parents, she worked with British roots heroes Aswad, did sessions with Bob Marley and rocksteady legend Alton Ellis, and recorded the first songs under her own name with dub legend Lee 'Scratch' Perry in 1977. She continued to make consistently excellent music throughout the decade and into the next. The sister of the highly respected reggae guitarist, Bunny McKenzie, she also wrote under her own name and created a body of work not confined to a single genre. In fact, Candy McKenzie upheld the lovers rock-soul continuum by lending her nuanced, crystalline tone to a number of R&B/dance styled songs, and she also recorded one of the essential cover versions of the 1980s, a superb synth-led take on 'Remind Me', an anthem by the great American jazz pianist-vocalist Patrice Rushen.

It is important to recognise that versatility. There has been a long line of 'queens of lovers rock' such as Janet Kay, Carroll Thompson (who, like McKenzie, was a very gifted writer as well as singer and wrote enchanting tunes such as 'What Colour?' and 'Hopelessly in Love'), Sandra Cross and Sylvia Tella. These artists were all sufficiently open-minded and talented to branch out into other idioms. For example, Tella, born in Manchester to Nigerian parents, debuted in a band that backed German disco sensation Boney M in the mid-1970s and went on to collaborate with pop-soul combo, The Blow Monkeys, before recording a string of singles with the premier British reggae production team, Mafia & Fluxy, throughout the 1990s. In 2000 she made a dazzling appearance on 'Electric Lady', a collaboration with Neon Phusion, which matched her potent voice with programmed beats.

No less interesting was the crossover of lovers rock and the wider world of acting, both on stage and screen. Janet Kay and Victor Romero-Evans, who became a hugely popular figure on the lovers scene, both worked with the Black British film director Menelik Shabazz and appeared in 1980's *Mama Dragon*, an adventurous reggae-rock musical written by Farrukh Dhondy for Britain's Black Theatre Co-operative. The compositions were excellent and ranged from the gorgeously misty lovers rock of 'Talking to a Stranger', to the heavier roots numbers such as 'Urban Insurrection', 'A Dreadness', 'Herbie Get Time' and 'In Brixton'. These tunes addressed the socio-political realities of growing up as the 'second generation' in England, and resonated with *Babylon*, Franco Rosso's seminal film about Black British youth and sound system culture which was made in the same year. Romero Evans also appeared in that movie and the soundtrack was written by Dennis Bovell, who as noted above, was one of the architects of lovers rock. In other words, the prime movers of Black music in Britain were spreading their wings in a number of different directions. They made songs for the rub-a-dub moments at a blues dance, and they also created the rhythms that fuelled shocking scenes of young dreadlocks running for their lives as unmarked police cars bore down on them. This was a movie. But it was also a daily reality.

Notes

1. Victor Parker's funeral is on youtube.
2. Between 1958-2020, Shirley Bassey put out 34 studio albums, 7 live albums and 26 compilations.
3. Billy Boston (1934-) was a professional rugby league player, who played mainly for Wigan and for Great Britain. He was regarded as one of rugby's greatest ever players.
4. Interview with the author, May 2022.
5. Ibid.
6. Ibid.
7. Ibid.
8. Red Bull Music Academy, 2017.
9. Ibid.
10. Interview with the author, August 2022.
11. Ibid.
12. Interview with the author, October 2022.
13. Janet Kay music, 'One Track Minds', 25 September 2017.
14. Interview with the author, October 2022.

15 WHY CAN'T WE LIV TOGEVVER?

> If people from here go on holiday, they go to the Caribbean, but if they want to get rid of you they call you a West Indian.
> — Kenny Wellington, trumpet, 'funk-jazz' combo, Light of the World.

Grove in the Groove
Rapid change has defined black music throughout the African Diaspora since the late 19th century. It's not so much that there has been a proliferation of genres, but more that any one style becomes a kind of mothership from which spin numerous satellites carrying new ideas that extend and enrich its fundamental vocabulary. The arrival of lovers rock attested to the richness of reggae as a parent of many rhythmic children, as well as the coming of age of second-generation West Indians in Britain.

For every sound of now there was a sound of then. In the late 1970s, the songs that formed the soundtrack to the lives of the Windrush arrivals of the late 1940s could not have seemed more passé, outdated, irrelevant and, to a large extent, unwanted. Calypso, epitomised by legends such as Lord Kitchener, appeared to have run its course, and the very idea of sharply suited, trilby-wearing masters of wordplay holding their own against either a roots rebel hailing Zion and chanting down Babylon, or a queen asking her man to stop playing silly games, was hardly the order of the day.

But Trinidadian popular music had itself embraced change. Rather than suddenly shuffling into silence, calypso, which had been a notable source of inspiration to African American jazz artists such as Sonny Rollins, did not close its ears to current events in Black music, Stateside. Soul became a fresh conceptual power source for calypso, and the connection between the two genres sparked into something called soul-calypso, abbreviated to the far sassier name of soca. Here was something that was fresh.

The Mighty Sparrow, who had performed in the UK many times throughout the 1960s, was one of the most high profile old school calypsonians who embraced the new school, while talented producer-bandleaders such as Ed Watson made music that retained calypso's percussive DNA but stirred heavy bass, glossy synthesizer sounds and surging horn lines into its bloodstream to create a dance music that responded to the demand of audiences for something that was modern rather than traditional.

Soca duly delivered a release of energy and an outpouring of joy to which there was no limit.

In Britain, the artist who most reflected these dynamic transformations was Eddy Grant. His ecumenical approach to writing since his debut with The Equals in the late 1960s had produced numerous songs that sat tantalisingly between soul, pop, rock, ska and calypso, sometimes suggesting a strange proto-soca, as in 'Black Skin Blue Eyed Boys'. His recordings under his own name were no less eclectic, and albums such as *Message Man* and *Born Ya!*, which marked the return of The Equals, reflect that variety. The latter album contained the monumental groove of 'Funky Like a Train', which had a starkly clipped, daringly staccato backbeat and delicately picked guitar, making the music simultaneously heavy and light. Then there was the mesmerising 'Walking on Sunshine', a track which was one of the most original marriages of West Indian and African-American rhythmic sensibilities of the era, a seamless blend of funky clavinet licks and ricochets of percussion that were the heart and soul of a carnival band. The many singles Grant released with the Coach House Rhythm Section, the session players of his Coach House Studio in north London, were also similarly imaginative in the way they brought different genres and sub-genres into the same creative space to create something that was impossible to categorise. An anthem such as 'Time Warp'[1] epitomised the capital of England as a melting pot that not only made music across cultural borders but built bridges between eras. The textural richness of the arrangement, foaming and squelching away to the sound of lengthy, dreamy synthesizer chords, lifts the listener right onto a futuristic plane where machines rule the earth yet the central pulse is still a clanging percussive beat, which evokes the ringing cowbell patterns that were present in calypso and soca. Grant's music carried them both, and boldly declared that the Chicago house music of the future had antecedents in the Caribbean.

Taking it to the streets
Another artist who had far less commercial success but nonetheless made an important contribution to this musical hybridisation was Roy Alton. He was from Dominica, a linguistically intriguing West Indian island and former British colony located between the French departments of Martinique and Guadeloupe, and whose inhabitants speak French-inflected creole as well as English. With a population of only 70,000, Dominica has unsurprisingly far fewer expatriates in Britain, than those who came from Jamaica, Trinidad or Barbados. Alton started singing at the age of 12 before settling in England in the early 1970s where he launched his career in earnest, collaborating with Sonny Roberts, a Jamaican producer who founded the UK's first black-owned recording studio and also

released music on his Planetone and Orbitone labels. Between the mid and late 1970s, Alton issued five albums that showcased his strong vocals on well-written songs, reflecting an interest in a range of music from across the Caribbean, including reggae, calypso and soca, as well as African American idioms such as funk, and Afrobeat from Nigeria.

A topic that regularly crops in his repertoire is carnival; *Mas in the Grove* references Ladbroke Grove and Notting Hill Gate as prime thoroughfares for the annual procession of steel bands and costumed revellers. The artwork that accompanied Alton's records is a visual representation of the event, and Alton's eclecticism and emphasis on racial harmony married with carnival is the defining feature the sleeve of one of his best works, *Carnival in Ladbroke Grove*.[2]

The cover has a montage of pictures showing both black and white revellers as well as women masqueraders at the head of the road march. In a surreal touch, there are drinking mugs superimposed above them, arranged to say 'milk + barley = ovaltine', which would resonate with generations of children who were weaned on that British hot drink that was exported to the Caribbean in the form of Milo. More topical is the sight of two policemen to the left of the ravers, one of whom has a heavy, carpet-pile moustache that might have landed him a gig with Disco superstars, Village People. But the sight of law enforcement officers on the sleeve of an album entitled *Carnival in Ladbroke Grove* would have had other meanings than that of carnival fraternisation. Strained relations between the police and Black community was a major theme in British social history in the 1970s, and Carnival became a high profile arena in which simmering tensions inevitably boiled over.

Since its inception in 1959, carnival had grown exponentially, far outperforming initial projections of what was a local event to garner a reputation as a joyous day out that attracted crowds of up to 150,00 by the mid-1970s. The Black population of Notting Hill still had to endure substandard accommodation as well as regularly hostile interactions with police who had framed the area through the prism of the Mangrove 9 affair and suspected that there were militant tendencies that needed to be rooted out. The police and the law-and-order establishment did not want to see large numbers of West Indians out in public. Containment in a park was suggested. As Darcus Howe, one of the historic 'Mangrove 9', said: 'It was clear they wanted the carnival off the streets… the police, the home office, newspapers. I used to sleep, eat and drink this stuff. I was known as a public figure. People stopped me in the street… Darcus are we having the carnival? Marley's hymns of freedom were everywhere. We were saying we're not putting up with this no more… We said no! We're not going… this is not a game.'[3]

Things came to a head in 1976 when police numbers were increased twentyfold over the previous year. 1,400 officers were deployed for the two-day event in August and the ranks of 'Babylon' were so massed that Howe, upon arriving from Brixton, shuddered in disbelief and later mused on this being 'a police carnival'. Indeed, the discreet presence of former years, encapsulated in the image of the pair of officers on Alton's *Mas in Ladbroke Grove*, was replaced by an imposing quasi-militarisation of white-shirted constables with black epaulettes and silver-badged helmets mixing with the purple fabrics and gold bent-wires of the bands. Footage of the event shows officers watching stony-faced as the procession unfolded, but there were more telling instances of institutional racism laid bare elsewhere. When the white journalist Robert Elms asked the police to allow him through the cordon they had formed, one of them sneered: 'Why do you want to join all the niggers?'[4]

Heavy-handed policing and intimidation tipped the event into pitched battles, which resulted in Howe and his family having to barricade themselves in the Mangrove restaurant as truncheons smashed windows. The sight of squad cars slamming into reverse under a hail of stones and bottles was one of the most emblematic images of black youth waging war inna Babylon. They were 'downpressing' the agents of evil by sheer strength of numbers and unfiltered anger.

In 19th century Trinidad, there had seen similar outbreaks of violence when the colonial authorities tried to ban carnival, and now its transplanted form in London saw history repeat itself. Carnival became an opportunity for Black British-born children to assert themselves. The free poster that accompanied Linton Kwesi Johnson's album *Forces of Victory*[5] was a still of the Race Today Renegades and Glissando Steel Band on the march through Notting Hill. And who was lurking just behind them? A policeman in uniform. Babylon too rough, for sure.

Way Out West
The resistance displayed by West Indian youth was proof, if any was needed, to a racist Home Office that black teenagers were inclined to violent disorder. Hence Stop and Search (Sus), an implementation of an 1824 Vagrancy Act that gave the police the power to detain anybody deemed to be loitering with intent to commit an offence, revived since the 1960s, was now applied even more viciously. This targeting of young Black kids elicited responses in rhythm. Linton Kwesi Johnson's 'Sonny's Lettah' was his classic anti-Sus poem, and he was not alone in naming the enemy. There was also a song, called 'Dole Age', made by a fine group called Talisman who hailed from Bristol. The sleeve of their record featured a lone dread tailed by an officer with a dog on a lead, exactly the kind of disheartening tableau that epitomised Babylon to the core. Talisman were one of several reggae artists who came to prominence in the West Country city in

the late 1970s and early 1980s, reflecting Bob Marley's influence all over Britain. There were also groups such as The Radicals and Restriction, but the band that made the biggest impact was Black Roots, primarily because it had very high standards of musicianship and also because it made a point of acknowledging and celebrating its locality. While Steel Pulse talked of a 'Handsworth Revolution', Black Roots invited the world to skank to the 'Bristol Rock'.

It was an eight-piece with a powerful rhythm section, led by Jamaican-born musicians, lead guitarist Cordell Francis and vocalists Errol Brown and Delroy O'Gilvie. Black Roots toured extensively in the UK and Europe, where they won over audiences with a well-wrought sound that made much of the tumbling nyabinghi drums played by percussionist Kondwani Ngozi. Although the band gained a following as a live act, its fanbase widened considerably when it recorded a number of sessions for the BBC Radio One show presented by John Peel, an avowed fan, who was as a champion of reggae at the Corporation. His endorsement helped to consolidate the national status of Black Roots. The band also wrote the theme tune of the BBC tv series *The Front Line*, which at the height of the Sus laws, told the story of two half brothers of Caribbean heritage, one a policeman and the other a Rastafarian.

As residents of St Paul's, the area of Bristol that had been the hub of the Black community since the end of the Second World war, Black Roots made regular appearances at the local carnival, an event that, like those of London and Leeds, had a history that reached back to the 1960s. While this annual open air gathering served as a rallying point for Caribbean culture, a local venue, The Bamboo Club, became pivotal in the growth of Black social life. Located in Portland Square, it first opened its doors in 1966 and its founder, a local white entrepreneur, Tony Bullimore, who was married to a Jamaican nurse, Lalel, knew that there was a pressing need for a 'safe space' for Black people in a city whose colour bar had given rise to the famous bus boycott a few years prior. Bullimore recalled:

> We're finding that our members are bringing friends here and they feel quite proud of the fact that the club is done out the same as an English club and that people can come in here, friends of West Indians can come in here and enjoy themselves and it takes away this inferiority complex that we haven't got anywhere to take our English friends. Now they can take them here.[6]

Equally important was the fact that the club became part of the national touring circuit for leading reggae and soul acts throughout the 1970s, with the likes of Jimmy Cliff, Desmond Dekker, John Holt, Derrick Morgan, Percy Sledge and Ben E. King being among the artists who appeared, in addition to a number of sound systems from the city and outside it. The venue was a favourite among many visiting artists as Dennis Bovell, who gigged there with Matumbi, told me in 2022:

> It was on two floors, a ground floor and basement. In the basement there was a bar with a TV screen and camera hooked up to it so you could see the act upstairs. In the 1970s that was a first in the UK back then. The Bamboo was the rave place.[7]

Clubs with live music and good sound systems can be transformative because they show aspiring musicians and selectors what can be achieved in performance, as well as providing audiences with the chance to hear music that speaks of their lived experience. As part of their 1973 Catch a Fire tour, Bob Marley & The Wailers' performed at The Bamboo, and the concert has acquired legendary status for its impact. Tragically, the club burned down in December 1977, taking with it the 5,000 piece record collection that had been amassed during its tenure. Venues in Bristol that tried to fill the breach were The Studio, on the Redland campus of Bristol Polytechnic and Dockland Settlement, a youth centre where St Paul's residents could hear local bands and socialise, enjoying a game of table tennis or five-a-side football. This was the venue where one could hear singer Joshua Moses, another key part of the Bristol reggae scene. He had a flexible vocal delivery, at times sensitive and understated, at times emphatic and commanding, which was well served by the Full Force and Power band.

Born in Jamaica but resident in Britain since the age of 12, Moses occasionally cut lovers' rock leaning material such as 'Pretty Girl', a beautiful song whose melody was reminiscent of the R&B classic 'Cupid' made famous by Sam Cooke, but his forte was heavy roots material in which he professed Rastafarian faith and resistance to Babylon. Tracks such as 'House of Dread', 'The Suffering', 'Rise Up' and 'Jah Time Has Come' were further examples of the quality of UK reggae in which performance, lyric and musical backing were strong. Above all, Moses and his combo showed that appealing melodies could be made more effective when they were infused with the haunting, otherworldly sound effects provided by echo and the fading out and in of different instruments that were an integral part of the vocabulary of dub.

Debuting in 1978, Moses was a stalwart of the Bristol scene throughout subsequent decades, even though he had long periods of silence. Along with others such as Sharon Benjamin ('Mr. Guy'), he was an important solo singer who had enough talent to enjoy national not just local recognition, but, sadly, none of the bands discussed here were ever signed to major labels, so the cornucopia of talent in St. Paul's remained largely unknown outside the area. Although bands issued recordings on their own labels, these did not have the level of distribution or promotion to reach larger audiences. Yet tracks such as Talisman's 'Run Come Girl', with its lithely insistent, spiky beat, compares favourably to the work of London bands such as Aswad and Matumbi. Dennis Bovell produced 'Africa is Our Land', Joshua Moses's debut single and one can only speculate how different his career might have been had that relationship developed further.

Climate Change
By the late 1970s, Bovell's talent as an engineer-producer had been recognised by artists outside reggae and one Bristol band with whom he made a whole album was The Pop Group. They were inspired by the raucous energy of punk but intent on offsetting the structural limitations of that genre with the input of funk and avant-garde jazz. Vocalist Mark Stewart sang banshee-frenzied anti-capitalist lyrics while a rhythm section led by pianist-guitarist Gareth Saeger made an agitated, off-kilter barrage of noise that was given additional dub-wise resonances by Bovell on their excellent debut album *Y*. There were effective passages of shadow play, alternations of dark and light timbres, stark shifts of frequency and skilled expansions and contractions of notes so that phrases drifted in and out of earshot to create a symphony of omission as well as transmission. Along with all the anger came provocative artistry.

More creativity came from Gareth Sager, a Scot who had moved to Bristol in the mid 1970s to be part of the jazz scene, when he launched another band, Rip, Rig & Panic. For anybody interested in the history of jazz, the name was familiar as the title of one of the legendary Rahsaan Roland Kirk's finest albums. This blind, multi-reed virtuoso, who often played several horns at once, was also a fine composer, and his spirit of adventure, sense of daring and danger inspired RRP. Sager was joined by drummer Bruce Smith, pianist Mark Springer, bassist Sean Oliver and two vocalists, Oliver's sister Andrea and Neneh Cherry, a Swede who was also the stepdaughter of the innovative African American jazz trumpeter-composer, Don Cherry, who also later performed with the band.

Musically and lyrically, RRP stood out as one of the most outlandishly interesting propositions in British music of the early 1980s through their cohesive blend of European art references (their record sleeves reproduced classic images by Picasso and Cocteau) and words that had a cussed, unapologetic subversiveness that conspired to say much about the unremitting austerity of what the reggae massive called the 'Dole Age'. If titles such as 'Knee Deep in Shit', 'Change Your Life', 'Totally Naked (Without Lock or Key)' or 'Tax Sex' didn't tell you that a life under a Tory government was bleak – because a levy on carnal relations was not so fanciful given the impending horror of the poll tax – then there was a slew of other songs that took a hammer to morally contemptible governments dragging the world to destruction. 'Beware Our Leaders Love the Smell of Napalm', 'Liars Shape Up or Ship Out' and above all 'Another Tampon Up the Arse of Humanity' displayed the same sharp lyrical edge as a number of politically engaged American bands. RRP were not the Dead Kennedys with horns instead of guitars, but they had an outlook and perspective that aligned. The noisy, tetchy, angry energy of the words that Cherry and Oliver spat out did not preclude a marked dance sensibility in RRP's music, arguably more so than The Pop Group had offered.

On three albums, *God*, *I Am Cold* and *Attitude*, RRP pulled off the feat of creating a rhythmic foundation that on several occasions had the skipping airiness of big band music, even though it was played by a small combo. Their songbook also contained tracks with a decidedly upbeat, joyous, playful brightness that offered a contrast to their more confrontational sounds, such as 'You're My Kind of Climate', which bounced along to choruses of shimmering brass and reeds that had a ramshackle charm. As for the superb 'Storm the Reality Asylum', its skulking bluesiness reflected the band's deep immersion in Black music. At the heart of the piece was the kind of lively, limb-loosening shuffle that had served countless blues and R&B artists for decades. The band carried undercurrents of history with them but also managed to swim in a tide of their own, partly because Cherry and Oliver did not have classic African-American soul voices, partly because there was a conspicuous lo-fi roughness around the edges in the engineering and production that set them apart from mainstream Black music in the US where the sheen supplied by well-appointed studios was prevalent. RRP's loose, wrangling pulse, as well as its explosive energy and subversive lyrics made for an inspired blend of pop, funk and avant-garde sensibilities, an expression of open minds and fearless views. They and the music that came out of Bristol in this period point to an environment that warrants further study in terms of the city's divisions between conservative elites and an explosive radicalism, tensions rooted in the city's involvement in the transatlantic slave trade, embodied in the figure of Edward Colston, and zones of urban settlement marked along the fault lines of race and class. Among RRP's peers, two bands stand out. Glaxo Babies, with songs that blended the hard groove of James Brown, the volcanic eruptions of 'free' brass players, and the messy, scrappy, abrasive character of punk, produced the classic album *Nine Months to the Disco*, while Maximum Joy, who had members from the former combo (saxophonist Tony Wrafter) and The Pop Group (bassist Dan Catsis) also made songs that moved coherently between bright, snappy rhythms and dark dub infusions. Their producer was Adrian Sherwood, who would go on to become a major figure in British reggae in the 1990s with his important On-U Sound label.

Booty Call

The Bristol groups had shown that a British response to Black American music could produce something that was pleasingly hard to categorise, and it is worth pointing out that idioms that had grown from the blues permeated other areas of rock in the UK, and were being heard by millions of listeners, who did not necessarily identify the material in those terms. This was possibly because marketing departments understood the deep tribalism that underpinned the music press and readers. For some, disco, soul and funk were dirty words.

The most obvious example was the music of Ian Dury & The Blockheads. With a repertoire full of wit, and performances boasting impressive musicianship, this multi-racial band, led by the charismatic, watchable white singer Ian Dury, who had an on-stage bravura that belied the effects of contracting polio in his childhood, was seen as the leading light of pub rock or new wave, though several of their best songs were clearly shaped by Caribbean and Black American influences. 'Inbetweenies' was slinky, jazzy piano-led soul; 'What a Waste' sultry, moody reggae, and 'Hit Me With Your Rhythm Stick' a strange concoction of funk, rock, reggae and jazz-fusion centred around a pummelling, pile-driver bassline and an instrumental break in which two saxophones were played simultaneously in the manner of Rahsaan Roland Kirk, source of inspiration for Rip, Rig & Panic. What deflected attention away from these facts was Dury's cockneyish accent, the one thing that seemed antithetical to Black music in the 1970s. But listen carefully to some of the lyrics and he ventures very far from norf Lundun. After all, what does he invite us to do on 'Inbetweenies'? *Shake your booty*. Your ass will be free when your mind knows that Black talk is where it's at. The hokey cokey is out tonight, mama. To convey the vividly sexualised notion of dance, Harrow-born Dury uses a timeless trope born of the African American experience, the effect of which is all the more conspicuous as it is articulated by an artist who is so roundly, charmingly Anglo-Saxon. Dury and his writing partner, the talented pianist Chaz Jankel, clearly understood that the language of R&B and soul had its place in their aesthetic, and this engagement with African Americana is yet more explicit on the excellent solo albums Jankel would later record.

The defining aspect of Dury's songbook was a fascinating blend of an emphatically English tone, local Kilburn references, undeniably funky backbeats and well-measured jazz chops. Black music, white singing. There was thus a clear distinction between Dury's sound and that of the popular British soul bands that were roughly contemporary in the late 1970s. Hot Chocolate, Heatwave and The Real Thing had singers who were largely modelled on the classic gospel-blues inflections of legends such as Ray Charles, Stevie Wonder and Curtis Mayfield, all of whom had influenced UK artists since the mid-1960s. Whether or not they spoke with a metropolitan or regional accent when they were offstage, it was unthinkable that Black artists born in Britain would bring the tones of the East End or Merseyside to a song where they implored their audiences to 'Get on down'. The orthodoxy of singing R&B American style prevailed, until Londoners of Caribbean heritage dared to break it in 1979.

Hustler's Convention
Light of the World were possibly the first Black artists to commit a Cockney twang to tape on the song 'Liv Togevver', whose subtitle 'Greater London Funkathon' was a riff on the Greater London Marathon. It was an assertion of their right not to be defined by the American accents of their musical heroes. The piece starts with a pub scene, with orders being placed for 'a triple scotch' instead of a 'lite an' bittah' before the sharp rebuttal in a Sid James style accent of 'leave orrf... whach' ya take me forr?', because, as all regular drinkers know, spirits will always cost more than draught beer. LOTW were staking a strong claim to Britishness, sounding as English as Ian Dury. And they simply did not care. 'Absolutely yes!' says the band's trumpeter, Kenny Wellington. 'This is who we are, and we're not gonna hide from it ... we were who we were. I don't know why a lot of bands didn't do this. From the day that we walked on stage, we sang in our London accents.'[8]

In a racist society in which many still rejected the very idea of a Black Englishman, Light of the World were not going to be sent back to Jamaica; home was in east London, and this conscious, courageously 'authentic' manifestation of their status was a logical updating of the multi-cultural pop made by The Equals back in the 1960s. LOTW were 'cockney blacks' talkin' cockney talk. 'Liv Togevver' was not just an Anglicisation of Black music drawn from African American sources, but an expression of Black Britishness in music that did not have any cultural or political filters. The rest of the band's material had classically soulful, identifiably Black vocals but that intro and its choruses were an audacious declaration, or rather it was real people reflecting real lives.

'Liv Togevver' was featured on Light of the World's eponymous debut album, a record issued after the singles 'Swingin' and 'Midnight Groovin' had helped to establish the band as an important new name in UK soul. This was just a few years after another London combo, Hi-Tension, had alerted the music industry to the groundswell of new young Black talent and it was revealing that their second hit, 'The British Hustle', was a statement of identity, a recognition that they were from here rather than over there, even though the title was a response to one of the ever changing dances of Black America. The hustle had rocked New York before it arrived in London.

Hi-Tension, like Light of the World, were part of a generation of British-born Black children who had chosen to play African American derived music, and that said something important about the broader listening habits of the Black British community, namely that the rich songbooks of Detroit and Memphis had their place alongside those of Kingston. The diverse record collections of their parents, who had a taste for R&B, jazz and country & western as well as ska and rocksteady, made that clear.

Inevitably, there were Britons of West Indian heritage who started to play soul, and London-based groups such as 70 Proof, Kandidate, Hudson People and Hot Waxx were among the notable names on the scene. Reggae was not the only form of popular music that inspired Black teenagers, even during the years when Bob Marley was in the ascendant. Indeed, it was Island, the label that broke Marley to the world, that signed Hi-Tension, a group that enjoyed chart success in 1978 with its eponymous debut single. An eight-piece from Willesden in north west London, Hi-Tension grew out of Hot Waxx, whose nucleus had two sets of brothers, the McCleans, guitarist Paul and saxophonist Patrick, and the Josephs, keyboardist-vocalist David and bassist Ken. There was also the vocalist Phil Fearon (who went on to form another group called Galaxy). These youngsters were all inspired by leading American soul-funk ensembles, such as Earth, Wind & Fire, Brass Construction, and Kool & The Gang.

Hi-Tension's rhythm section was augmented by a four-piece horn section, and developed a sound that revealed the multi-faceted nature of British soul. The US foundation was clear enough in the crackly 'chicken scratch' guitar style, bumpy, driving, bass lines, short vocal riffs and the roaring brass typified by Kool & The Gang. While these features made 'Hi-Tension' appealing, the prominence given to Jeffrey Guishard's outstanding percussion, above all his work on timbales, brought a marked Latin and Caribbean flavour to their music, which also permeated swish mid-tempo songs such as 'There's a Reason'. Their debut album was produced by a highly experienced musician who had lived through another important chapter in the history of Black music in Britain a few years before, namely Afro-rock. He was Kofi Ayivor from Osibisa.

Hi-Tension picked up a head of steam when they made it to *Top of the Pops*, but this interest from national television was not sustained. Members of the band later spoke revealingly about how they were received by the show's producer:

> In the changing rooms this guy came up to us and goes you guys are very lucky. You guys are really lucky to be here because normally... were not gonna let no others in. You're very, very lucky.

To be young, gifted, Black and British, and allowed to grace mainstream television, reflected the extent of institutional racism in British media. Hot Chocolate and The Real Thing had broken through a few years earlier, but pop was still a fickle world where the majority of gate-keepers remained white.

Worlds Collide
Access to mainstream broadcasters, and approval from the powerful rock press was an issue for young Black soul artists as well as lack of distribution and promotion. There was the age-old barrier of approved models and blueprints. Hi-Tension's music hinged as much on unison vocals and chants, as it did lead vocals, so they did not fit the template of a group with a recognised front man as a focal point for audiences. They were an ensemble rather than leader plus subordinates. The band was really a kind of collective, an anomaly compared to other UK artists who made it to prime time TV shows.

The fact that Hi-Tension went through numerous personnel changes and did not follow its eponymous debut album within a year of its release only magnified the sense of their being a novelty in a world where the attitude of record company managers to longevity, continuity and vision was often brutally linked to fashion and sales. Whilst some did think in terms of life beyond a second or third recording, others clearly did not.

Light of the World's experience was not dissimilar. They made their breakthrough with the single 'Swingin'' in 1979, and found themselves in a situation that mirrored that of Hi- Tension just a year before. There was not a sufficient number of copies of the record pressed to meet demand; after an appearance on *Top of the Pops* raised their profile, they quickly sold out the meagre stock. Nobody expected that level of success. Fortunately, the band was championed by two A&R men at Ensign records, Nigel Grainge and Chris Hill, a highly influential DJ on the soul scene, and the youngsters seemed to have made their way. But when Light of the World's young trumpeter, Kenny Wellington, discussed career prospects with industry insiders, there was no great expectation that life on the road or in studios would last. 'We were told "you'll have a couple of years of this, lads."'[9]

We were sitting in a pub that borders Victoria Park in east London and Wellington, a sprightly 60-ish year-old with long dreadlocks, African print jacket and engaging, genial demeanour, had every reason to feel happy with his lot, given that he lives nearby, has regular work and feels that he got something right in the way he has raised his children. He told me that when he was a teenager learning the trumpet, after initially playing guitar, his primary motivation was to emulate his heroes Kool & The Gang and play iconic venues such as the Hammersmith Odeon or the Rainbow. He and various school friends, all of whom were of Caribbean heritage, embarked upon their grand adventure with those goals in mind. It was

Kool's 'Light of Worlds' that inspired the name, but seeing the Jackson Five on television was another inspiration. LOTW included saxophonist David 'Baps' Baptiste, guitarist Neville 'Breeze' McKreith, drummer Junior King and a prodigious bass guitarist, Paul 'Tubbs' Williams. He was just 13 years old. A significant growth in the music available to hear broadened their tastes. Pirate radio, particularly stations such as JFM, Horizon and Solar kept them up to date with soul, funk and jazz fusion while US import albums and singles could be found at vinyl emporiums such as Bluebird, Record Shack and Contempo. The arrival in the mid-1970s of the magazines *Black Echoes* and *Blues & Soul*, with reviews and interviews, also provided further vital information about what to listen to.

LOTW was part of a loose, wider aggregation of players, which included bassist Camelle Hinds, drummer Errol Kennedy and keyboardist Lipson Francis. Several ensembles, starting with the short-lived T.F.B (Typical Funky Band), Central Line and Imagination emerged from this hub along with a dance group called Torso. Wellington added, 'There was a thriving community of performing arts people in east London. We used to rehearse at the place in Clapton, and then there were players who came from Stoke Newington and Stamford Hill.'[10] The homegrown soul-funk scene was signalled by the arrival of several other bands, mostly from the capital, such as Freeez, Second Image, UK Players, Atmosfear and Savanna, while from the environs of the Isle of Wight came Level 42, whose keyboardist-vocalist Mike Lindup was the son of the Belizean-British actress, songwriter and singer Nadia Cattouse. Perhaps the most important point that Wellington made as we sat with a cold lager on a hot June day was that there was a degree of serendipity and informality in the way that Light of the World and their peers evolved.

Record shops have traditionally been places for networking as well as sales, and it was an outlet in Seven Sisters in north London called Sheridan that played this role because it also had a rehearsal space. There, Wellington met other musicians such as trombonist Nat Augustin, who had wandered into the store and heard a jam taking place. For Augustin, playing music was more of a pastime than a profession because he had a steady job as a postman, but even more significant was the presence of Jean-Paul 'Bluey' Maunick, who worked in the shop. He played guitar and began to broaden the musical references of the group. He had extensive knowledge of American artists who were marketed as jazz-fusion, a catch-all term that included anybody from Weather Report and the Brecker Brothers to Ronnie Laws and Grover Washington Jnr.

The other American band that inspired LOTW was The Crusaders, whose *Chain Reaction* album brought a bluesy as well as greasy southern fried quality (they hailed from Texas) to their excellent improvisations on instrumental originals and versions of popular soul and funk hits.

And while Light of the World and co were influenced by electric jazz in the early 1970s, they were not disconnected from the acoustic 'tradition'. The band, as much as it made dance music, also learned from some of the highly accomplished British soloists who were part of the post-bop and avant-garde scene. Wellington took lessons from trumpeter Dick Pearce, who had worked with a range of legendary artists, including Dudu Pukwana, Michael Garrick and Keith Tippett, but there was another important educational platform available to him. He explained:

> In south London they have a real tradition of acoustic jazz and that stems from Goldsmiths College. That was a meeting place, and lots of us would go down and jam together, go to a place like Howard Riley's workshop and Kathy Stobart's big band. A lot of guys didn't think oh, because we were doing dance music and were young we didn't need to learn. We didn't come straight from the streets.[11]

This is one of the most revealing 'hidden facts' about the genesis of Light of the World that Wellington was generous enough to share. The bulk of historical accounts of British jazz do not highlight the engagement of young Black players, making apparently 'light', groove-based music, with older white players doing the 'heavy' stuff, which had a greater degree of abstraction. If formal tuition from a jazz musician of Riley's stature significantly aided Wellington, then it's worth noting that they maintained links decades after being in a practice room together, when Riley appeared on recordings of his former pupil's solo work.

Sacked by Soca
Taking lessons at institutions such as Goldsmiths and the London College of Music may have given a proto-LOTW the kind of solid grounding that was crucial to their growth as musicians, but other elements of their formative years were testing to say the least. Some of their early gigs laid bare the segmented nature of Black music in Britain at the time, when a soul-funk band booked to a venue which demanded a different genre of music could fall foul of a hostile audience or promoter who took a dislike to the kind of beat they were playing. At the legendary Cue Club in Paddington, west London, the pioneering sound system operator, Count Suckle, actually ran his fingers across his throat to tell LOTW it was time to stop playing because they weren't going down too well among reggae heads, while a gig at a venue catering specifically for the latest Trinidadian music turned out to be even more disheartening, to the extent that the band had to resort to the kind of drastic action that would make it into a Spinal Tap script. Wellington recalled:

> We went to a soca dance to play, we thought yeah, they're gonna love

us, we'll take 'em by surprise. We started playing and everybody stopped dancing and started shaking their firsts at us! 'We don't want this music! We want soca!' Two numbers and we were off the stage! Yeah, we took all the hard knocks. At the time we had a percussionist Norman Walker and when that venue… refused to pay us, Norman leapt over the counter, actually took the cashbox and went outside, took our fee, then threw the cashbox back into the club. It wasn't all plain sailing. We'd done all the dives, with the big thick sticky carpets and all. We didn't just emerge overnight.[12]

Funky Flying Squad
If there is a humorous undertone to that story, then the rejoinder to it is that the working conditions endured by the band could lead to tragedy. It is easy to forget that groups had to take real risks to be able to fulfil their precious bookings. That meant long trips up and down the motorways, usually in a cramped van rather than a luxury touring bus, in all weathers. Disaster struck when LOTW's vehicle was hit by a juggernaut as they were heading to London after a gig in Glasgow. They were driving in a blizzard. Percussionist Chris Etienne was killed in the crash. 'We were in disarray for a little while,' says Wellington solemnly.

They regrouped. Jean-Paul Maunick made a substantial contribution to the band as a writer but gigged less, while drummer Everton McCalla, keyboardist Pete Hinds, and Mancunian percussionist Gee Bello became significant new additions, giving LOTW a new impetus that served a second album, 1980's *Round Trip*, very well. It was made with a bigger budget and produced by Wayne Henderson, trombonist and member of The Crusaders, one of LOTW's sources of inspiration. Of all the songs featured on the album, 'London Town', with its references to Regents Park and Trafalgar Square was the clearest indication of 'home ground' and a 'second generation' identity that expresses harmony rather than discord – 'I'm in love with what I see/The streets of London always appeal to me.' Indeed, Wellington and co were seen then as emblematic exponents of what was termed 'Brit funk' or jazz-funk by journalists, even though this was not used by the band members themselves, who had their own signifier. 'We called it funk-jazz,' says Wellington. 'Not jazz-funk or Brit funk.'[13]

That was not an insignificant distinction. The fact that LOTW foregrounded funk rather than jazz reflects a nuanced understanding of Black music history, namely the principal role served by funk as a popular music that nonetheless had very high standards of performance and a fair amount of syncopation and improvisation. Questions of terminology aside, the music was marketed to clubs. Compilation albums such as *The Best of British Jazz-Funk* that featured LOTW and their peers, Central Line and Freeez, contained the subtitle: 'Over One Hour of Continuous Dance Music.' The songs were released in extended mixes to fill nighclub floors.

In this context, it made sense for LOTW to play at high tempo. Their tunes, especially their singles, created waves of energy through upper register guitar lines, hard strummed to create a timbral brightness in the music that was enhanced by the weight and brawn of the brass and reeds, adding to the impact of the rhythm section. A big sound, a sense of orchestral power delivered at pace, was a crucial part of the LOTW *modus operandi*. 'We'd done quite a few gigs before recording and we recorded at the tempo we used to play them at live,' says Wellington. 'Lots of bands record and then just play faster on stage, which gives the music a different feel, really.'[14] Indeed, the ten-minute epic, 'Time', challenged dancers to keep up when they took to the floor. Nothing could have provided a greater contrast with the relaxed, leisurely lean of roots reggae or lovers rock, and although LOTW's funk-jazz was not expressly a reaction against that idiom, it could be argued retrospectively that it was important because it showed the pluralism of Black music in Britain at the time. If the Jamaican strain of music was slow and the African American was fast, LOTW was intent on presenting a version of their lives that was rooted in daily experience. This led to artistic and cultural references that could be transparent to some and opaque to others, depending on where they had grown up and what access they had to mainstream culture, above all the kind of thing that celebrated swaggering bad behaviour. The band made that clear on 'Liv Togevver', their ode to cockney funk. The spooky descending chord sequence in the intro was actually an adaptation of the theme tune of *The Sweeney*, one of the most popular shows on British television in the mid-1970s, which portrayed the criminal investigations of the 'flying squad', tough inner-city detectives that Wellington and co all avidly watched, fascinated, as a whole generation of impressionable boys were, by the grimy circus of fast cars, violence and profanities. This was ironic because another important LOTW song broached the issue of police harassment. 'The Boys in Blue' was based on fact not fiction. 'We were just doing songs of our experience but the relevance of that tune still holds today,' said Wellington. 'Had we fallen foul of sus? Absolutely, on quite a few occasions. They were like, why are you standing here? Right, we're gonna take you down the station.'[15]

That was the fate that Black men, whatever their musical allegiance, had to face in the early 1980s. Regardless of the appearances on television, the magazine covers and the shows around the country, artists of colour had the stark reality of second-class citizenship to contend with. An old press shot of Wellington and the band shows them standing next to a Ford Cortina, with one of the boys sprawled on the roof of the car, as the rest display the beaming smiles of young men in their prime, living the dream. But how dangerous was it (and still is) to be found driving while Black? As LOTW sang, the police thought you had a 'special look.'

Away from the glamour of the stage or nightclub, there was risk whenever they were in a public space, behind the wheel of a car or even on an underground train. Wellington was acutely aware of what it has meant to be an ethnic minority, to have people question his place in society, to know that there is still an uphill battle for acceptance that is closely tied to the hypocrisy of the way colonial history was and still is being processed. 'If people from here go on holiday, they go to the Caribbean, but if they want to get rid of you, they call you a West Indian,' he says. 'Well, who do you think you are? It's a question (we asked in songs). Are you connected to your identity, or do you let people tell you who you are?'[16]

Notes

1. Coach House Rhythm Section, 'Nobody's Got Time/Time Warp', (Ice) 1977.
2. Roy Alton, 'Carnival in Ladbroke Grove' (Tackle, 1976).
3. *Daisypumpkin 23*, BBC documentary, Summer of 1976.
4. Ibid.
5. Linton Kwesi Johnson, *Forces of Victory* (Island, 1979).
6. BBC Bristol archives.
7. Interview with the author, February 2022.
8. Interview with the author, June 2022.
9. Ibid.
10. Ibid.
11. Ibid.
12. Ibid.
13. Ibid.
14. Ibid.
15. Ibid.
16. Ibid.

16 LEVEL VIBES

He wasn't keen on Sam, he'd just call me African!
– Sam Jones on Bob Marley

Return of Rudy
Light of the World may well have asked who you were, but in 1981 the question was where you were, or at least what was going through your mind when all the trouble in the world came knocking on your front door. It was a watershed year in the history of Black Britain. A string of events highlighted both the pressures and persecution to which people of colour were subjected, as well as their capacity for resistance, their commitment to voice dissent, and the power they wielded to make themselves heard.

The New Cross massacre in January 1981 saw a fire at a house party claim the lives of 13 young Black people, leading to anger at the indifferent response of the authorities, ready to pass the tragedy off as an accident rather than arson, and to the mobilization of 20,000 people in the Black People's Day of Action in March of that year. The following month, Operation Swamp 81 was launched, to step up the already widespread application of the SUS laws. The fearsome Special Patrol Group (SPG) stopped and searched over 900 people in Brixton alone. Walking while Black was really not advised. The systematic surveillance of West Indian youth on the street was compounded by arrest and detention on the most spurious grounds. It was just as Light of the World warned: the boys in blue are watching you. The popular BBC 1 comedy show, *Not the Nine O'Clock News*, lampooned police brutality with its 'PC Savage' sketch, in which a constable is reprimanded for victimising a 'coloured gentleman' for possession of 'curly black hair and thick lips', an exchange which ends with the bigot being transferred to the SPG. But this was no laughing matter. Many in uniform did think and act like that, with impunity.

Something had to give. The combination of persistent police harassment, chronic unemployment, poor housing and disenfranchisement led to a series of civil disturbances in Black communities around the country in the spring and summer. Black people were now heard loud and clear. As on earlier occasions, the clashes were often sparked by a single incident, an arrest, an instance of brutality, a raid on a café such as the Mangrove in 1971 or at the Carnival of 1976. Such moments of self-assertion were written large in the consciousness of African Caribbean communities. High profile outbreaks of violence, referred to as riots by the authorities and acts of resistance by the civilians who took part in them, occurred not only in Brixton, London but also in St. Paul's, Bristol and Toxteth in Liverpool, Moss Side in Manchester, and the Meadows in Nottingham. Trouble also broke out in Bradford in Yorkshire and High Wycombe in Buckinghamshire. Cities with multi-racial communities and histories of immigration were bound together by the same recurrent pattern of discrimination in education, employment and policing, and this war inna Babylon could not be indefinitely tolerated. The government had been warned in the songs of the late 1970s, years before the showdown, but took no notice. As Merseyside soul champions, The Real Thing, stated on 'Children of the Ghetto', 'bitter are the views'. Resentment finally boiled over. Images of young black men – mostly but not exclusively, as whites were also involved – taking to the streets and fighting pitched battles with officers whose eager truncheons could and did lead to deaths during protests, as the case of Blair Peach[1] attested, made for predictably sensationalist headlines in the right wing gutter press. 'To Think This Is England' hollered *The Sun*, in a dramatic hyperbole that barely concealed the notion that national identity was under attack as projectiles rained down on the riot shields ready to protect the security forces of a former imperial power that had once ruled half the world. *The Daily Express* spoke of 'mob violence going nationwide' after the 'flare up' in Brixton, an explosive turn of phrase that was intended to throw more fuel on the raging ideological fire started by talk of the country being swamped by immigrants.

In stark contrast, *Time Out* magazine, London's essential cultural guide, turned the spotlight on police tactics and featured a highly revealing quote from the Met's spokesman: 'We control the streets of London and that's all there is to it.' With its nod to the Sus laws, the statement went to the heart of a key issue in civil society, namely the extent to which a public space belonged to all members of the public.

Shocking middle England, confronted with newspaper images of truncheons on skulls, dreadlocked or baldheaded, may have been manna from heaven to editors who believed that a picture was worth a thousand slurs, but there were words a plenty from Lord Scarman who, in his report in the aftermath of the Brixton disturbances, concluded that 'urgent action' was needed in order to stop racial disadvantage becoming 'an endemic, ineradicable disease.' Since it took another decade for the McPherson report to conclude that the police were 'institutionally racist', it is clear that Scarman's warning was not heard. Scarman's report was also limited by its focus on Brixton. The dire straits of Liverpool, both for its Black population and white majority, subjected to the infamous 'managed decline' of Thatcher's economic policy, never received the same attention. People were suffering in Bristol, Manchester, Leeds and Nottingham, cities that had all exploded.

But if Scarman was London-centric, developments in Black music were not. Indeed, keeping track of everything at once posed a challenge. Steel Pulse had put the Birmingham reggae scene on the map in the mid-1970s, and by the early 1980s, the nearby town of Coventry drew national attention for its music. Like its neighbour, Coventry was multi-racial, but less immediately equated with the history of West Indian immigration to Britain. In the early 1990s, the city had a Black population of less than 5,000, much smaller than the size of the South Asian community of predominantly Indian heritage.

While there was a club scene, as one might expect, created by Black people in Coventry that centred around venues such as the Railway Club and later the Spon Street West Indian Centre, there was also a significant creative multi-racial hub that formed around Lanchester Polytechnic. One of its art students was Jerry Dammers, a keyboard player who had embraced several of the major strands of African American, American and Caribbean culture, turning him into successively a mod, a hippie and a skinhead, the consequence of which was a deep dive into R&B, jazz, psychedelia, folk rock and reggae. A love of Jamaican music led Dammers to start writing songs that were shaped by the older genre of ska, epitomised by such as Prince Buster (Cecil Campbell, 1938-2016), and to later form a band, The Specials, as well as an independent record label, 2-Tone, which became a major story in British popular music during the Thatcher years. A coterie of other groups, namely The Selecter, also from Coventry, The Beat, from Birmingham, and The Bodysnatchers and Madness, both from London, were all associated with what was dubbed the 'ska revival'.

The distinctive visual symbols that represented 2-Tone – a mohair suited figure with shades and a pork pie hat – was an explicit acknowledgment of the 'rude boy' style that had defined early 1960s Jamaican music, where the emphasis was on sharp threads, with trousers cut high above the ankle and pencil ties to that conferred a kind of kempt, ordered stylisation.

Hearing tracks such as 'Gangsters' by The Specials and 'Three-Minute Hero' by The Selecter in the early 1980s was a revelation for the reason that knowledge of ska (for those of us whose elders, such as mine, hailing from Trinidad, had not weaned us on that specific strand of musical history), was not widely available. Hearing the imitations of Prince Buster's 'chekeh chekeh' vocal rhythms was new. Hearing a higher tempo than the one Bob Marley had used in reggae was fresh. Hearing a comical reference to Prince Buster's Judge Dread was hip, especially as it spawned Judge Roughneck, a character played by Specials vocalist Neville Staples.

The Specials would emerge as a dynamic spearhead of a multi-cultural movement based on the fact that the pre-reggae heritage of Jamaican music was strong enough to be used as a platform for new British pop whose substance took it beyond facile nostalgia or pastiche. There was an element of irreverence and emotional release in 2-Tone that endeared it to young audiences drawn to the raucous nature of gigs in which fans could end up skanking wildly next to their heroes on stage, while its spirit of independence, encapsulated by the fact that Dammers had launched the 2-Tone label himself, made it part of a historical lineage of smart and independent self-starters found in African American R&B and soul as well as Jamaican reggae and British punk.

While 2-Tone became one of the great features of UK pop in the early 1980s, and stood on an inclusive 'black and white unite' premise, it is important to acknowledge that the movement also met with censure from some in the reggae fraternity who objected to the fact that The Specials and co were, stylistically speaking, looking back rather than forward, an understandable argument for those who were aware of the wider history of Jamaican music. Because 2-Tone bands had grabbed the ear of the mainstream media and stormed the charts, British roots reggae groups now found themselves marginalised, and many sound system dances did not countenace 2-Tone songs. The influential magazine *Black Music* broached the complexity of the situation in a cover story on the label under the headline: Rip Off? Revival? Revolution?

Boom and bust
Regardless, Dammers proved himself capable of writing songs that depicted the angst and frustration of youth as well as the stagnating, humdrum nature of mainstream British culture. On the one hand, there was the superbly witty 'What I Like About You Most Is Your Girlfriend', on the other, there was the more disturbing 'Stereotypes', a song about a vacuous existence that leads to delusional thinking and self-destructive behaviour, resulting in early death. The song contains one of the most unforgettable lines in 1980s pop: 'He's just a stereotype/he drinks his age in pints' – a rhyme that is a vague ally to Prince's impish 'Act your age/not your shoe size' ('Kiss').

For anyone who listened closely to what Dammers was doing, it was clear that he was not confined to a simple rehash of ska, even though the joyful covers of classic tunes like 'Message to You Rudy' and 'Enjoy Yourself' were winning The Specials a nationwide audience. There was work of more gravitas, more heaviness on the cards. It arrived in the shape of 'Ghost Town'. Few songs capture the desolation of the Thatcher years more powerfully and convincingly. Set to a spare dub reggae backdrop that sizzles with tension, the song's arrangement showcases the interest Dammers had in jazz, muzak and Eastern-Arabic music as well as all things Jamaican. The inspired decision to foreground the melody with a haunting flute theme shifted the psycho-geography of the piece, which suggested that a circle of vibrations had magically formed between Kingston, Coventry and Cairo. The sight of the band taking a lonely nighttime drive through a grim, soulless east London in the video of the song was chilling, because the deserted streets evoked a city either still cowed by the Blitz (which had destroyed the centre of Coventry) or futuristic images of nuclear war.

Hearing 'Ghost Town' as a teenager was revelatory because it struck a deft balance between art and entertainment, engaging form and political content, lyrics that meant something and sounds that moved us literally and figuratively. We danced to it at my local youth club in the Medway towns in Kent, an area hit particularly hard by the closure of the dockyard in Chatham and where spiralling unemployment debilitated and embittered entire families. Drinking one's age in pints became a way of trying to sterilise pain, not a stereotype. In our first spark of consciousness we knew that this was a song about real sadness, an indictment of the hard times that were evident all around us.

The sight of a skeleton hunched over a piano on the picture sleeve of the single chimed with the doleful sound of trombonist Rico Rodriguez and trumpeter Eddie 'Tan Tan' Thornton, both legendary Jamaican musicians and session players in British pop. These two revered elder statesmen blew their brass in a relaxed but gripping *danse macabre*, their delivery as steadfast as the journey through dystopia. The big, bulbous timbre of Rico's trombone was like an ominous dark cloud that obscured the slow fading light of Paul Heskell's flute, creating a tonal range that consolidated the disturbing landscape of the song's A-section. Astutely weaving in and out of earshot was Dammers' warbly, watery keyboard, a discreet, ethereal presence that was jolted off its beat by the bright fairground rocking of the contrasting B-section, which was full of irony and snarky mockery, as if an amusement park had been taken over by smiley ghouls intent on making mischief and spoiling teenage kicks. 'Ghost Town' was hazily mysterious, icily seductive and deeply affecting. It was the plight of millions distilled into several minutes of angst-ridden rhythm that wound down to a sinister whistle of wind. And the lyrics were no less important for their denunciation of the dire consequences of Thatcherite economic policy as well as the linguistic and cultural complexity that framed them. The voice of Neville Staples was unmistakably Black, shaped by clear Jamaican inflections – 'Why must de yoot fight against themselves?/Government leaving de yoot on the shelf' – but the white lead singer, Terry Hall, also intoned creole when he reminisced about pre-Tory good times – 'inna de boom town'. As if anthropologists with any acumen didn't already know it, mainstream British youth was talking African Caribbean just as it had African American for decades. Immigrant tongues as well as sounds held sway. The nation was in organic cultural flux.

'Ghost Town' reached number one in the UK singles chart in the summer of 1981. Issued just a few months after the civil disturbances that were an indictment of a cruelly dysfunctional government, this modern pop masterpiece perfectly captured the mood of the country. With cruel irony, The Specials were on the verge of disbanding, as the creative peak of 'Ghost Town' had caused unbearable tensions and irreconcilable differences among the group's members, but the runaway commercial success of the song was nonetheless an endorsement of the enduring appeal of Jamaican music and its potential to reach large audiences when given such an original slant by artists of imagination.

Dammers had proved himself to be a thinker, motivator and 'ideas man' as much as a skilled composer, and this marked out The Specials as a group able to transcend the ska revivalist limits of its genesis. But he was not alone in writing songs that had substance. Fellow 2-Toners, The Beat, cast a boldly direct vote of no confidence in Thatcher with 'Stand Down Margaret', while another multi-racial band from Birmingham hailed the endemic nature of the unemployment that marked her tenure by naming themselves after the official government name for the forms that were required by those who faced the ignominy of signing on – UB 40. They would go on to become the most successful act in British reggae over the next four decades, where they would incorporate the sound of homegrown lovers rock into a repertoire of originals and classic Jamaican songs, notably 'Red, Red Wine'. Their output in the early 1980s was heavily focused on protest songs that reflected the misery of the Thatcher years, above all on singles such as 'One in Ten', which decried the high rates of joblessness in the Midlands and, more importantly, the way that individuals were being dehumanised and reduced to nothing more than statistics by an indifferent state apparatus.

Woah is me
While UB 40 and The Specials brought politics into the mainstream of popular culture in the early 1980s, the artists who had preceded them in the late 1970s and whose work has been covered in previous chapters, were still producing important music. Steel Pulse, Aswad and Misty in Roots made notable albums, particularly the latter's *Wise and Foolish*, but it was Linton Kwesi Johnson who hit a creative peak on his peerless *Bass Culture*, an album that contained a piece of searing social commentary that gave vent to the frustration of the rebel generation in language attuned to prevailing circumstances: 'Inglan Is a Bitch'.[2]

Given the strength of such statements, made all the more resonant in a climate of patriotic fervour whipped up by the Falklands war, during which *The Sun* sank to new depths with its egregious 'Gotcha!' headline,

Johnson made reggae poetry that countered such vessels of infantile nationalism. His political verse had a cargo of truth.

Meanwhile, soul, the other genre embraced and developed by young artists of African Caribbean heritage and which had a multi-cultural audience, had become increasingly associated with the glitzy escapism if not the hedonism of a club scene centred on 'all-dayers' up and down the country, or raucous 'weekenders' at the holiday camp in Caister, where the entertainment could involve 'tribes' donning theatrical costumes or sloshing around at a foam party, sitting on the floor to perform a rowing dance, as well as dancing hard to extended mixes of hot US imports. The clearest sign of the kitsch extremes to which this behaviour could go was the phenomenon of 'moonin', namely dropping trousers and baring buttocks. As much as the motivation may have been harmless fun, these antics ran decidedly counter to African Caribbean social mores. It was a point of divergence between Black and white working class norms, and was met with contempt by the reggae boys.

Although London, with its iconic clubs such as Crackers, was a mothership for this scene, there were important satellites in the suburbia of Greater London and Kent and Essex, home to The Lacy Lady, Goldmine, Flicks and Zero Six, where the more moneyed patrons would arrive in Ford Capris or Escorts with fluffy dice and windshield stickers that read 'If it moves funk it', while other venues in the Midlands and the North also had their place in this history, such as the Powerhouse in Birmingham, Rock City in Nottingham, Tiffany's in Leeds, Seventh Heaven in Doncaster and Rafters in Manchester. These clubs defined the social life of an entire generation.

Another phenomenon of the US disco scene of the mid-1970s, roller skating to the soundtrack of the latest funk jams, also made its way to the UK, and venues such as Alexandra Palace, Pickett's Lock and The Electric Ballroom in London, Mecca Roller World in Birmingham, Silver Blades in Leeds and Roller World in Colchester became meeting points for whoever wanted to spin and slide on four small wheels, another athletic discipline in Black dance culture.

Such activities reinforced the impression that soul was above all recreational, materialist and escapist for hardworking young people of colour, those lucky enough to have jobs and sufficient purchasing power to acquire the paraphernalia of choice, from tapered trousers and canvas belts to cheesecloth shirts and box jackets, and enjoy a wild night out.

There was now a substantial conceptual and lyrical divide between the two flagship genres of Black music in Britain. Soul was as light as reggae was heavy. Soul was as frivolous as reggae was serious. Soul was as apolitical as reggae was political. Soul was largely not made a part of Rock Against Racism. Reggae was. Soul had love songs. Reggae had rebel tunes.

But if bland declarations of passion, laments over rejection or boasts of sexual conquest were prevalent in soul, it was nonetheless the format for occasional message songs. Light of the World's 'Who Are You (Who Do You Think You Are?) mused on identity. Central Line's 'Man at the Top denounced the hollow nature of showy glamour and material success. Junior Giscombe's 'Too Late' was a poignant meditation on the violence meted out to a woman by her man when he comes home 'intoxicated from the club', providing a sobering contrast to the youthful exuberance of his big breakout hit 'Mama Used to Say'.[3] He gave us dark and light, calling out misogyny while making us dance. Soul was saying something to whoever was prepared to listen.

The prime example came from one of the biggest floor fillers of the early 1980s: '(Somebody) Help Me Out' by Beggar & Co, a band that was an offshoot of Light of the World, who, as noted in the previous chapter, knew all too well the oppressive ways of the British state This new composition was inspired by firsthand observation of what life was becoming under a Tory government waging war on trade unions and ushering in the privatisation of social utilities. Peaking at number 15 in the national singles chart in 1981, the song was a response to an alarming phenomenon of the Thatcher era: homelessness. The decision by Kenny Wellington and his bandmates to don the kind of raggedy coats and torn hats that would have made them plausible extras for an all-Black cast of *Oliver Twist* when they appeared on *Top of the Pops* to perform the hit was sparked by an encounter with one of the growing number of often young people for whom a cardboard box was refuge and shelter.

> We were in Whitechapel; we actually came across a homeless person, a nice guy, the usual *Can you give us a quid*? Which we duly did. But it was like a no brainer to then have a name like Beggar & Co. Was it a response to the austerity under Thatcher? Absolutely! It was that encounter with a homeless person who says *You got a cigarette?* That made us think. With (guitarist) Breeze McKreith we were just thinking, isn't it interesting how people are walking past this man, a human being, and they've made this judgment? They don't know how he came to be in that situation, they don't see a person... That's why we sang 'please give me a chance!' That was our way of talking about what was going on, about the homeless people in Britain at the time.[4]

'(Somebody) Help Me Out' was set to a funky backbeat, crisp rhythm guitar, heavy brass in a moody minor key that set up some dramatic breakdowns – all the elements that made people take to the floor, without necessarily listening to what the band was saying, because the assumption was that soul boys were politically apathetic. Also notable was the subtle linguistic code in the music. The catchy vocal chant 'woah woah woah', one of the prime hooks of the song, concealed an intentionally oblique literary reference: 'Woah as in... woe,' explained Wellington. 'We couldn't say woe is me, and we weren't trying to be overly clever, but the song...it is a tale of woe. We knew what we were on about, but not everybody got it.'[5] It resonated with some of the other notable lyrics of the time, such as the line from 'Ghost Town' – 'government leaving de yoot on the shelf', and 'Inglan is a Bitch', where Linton Kwesi Johnson vividly lays bare the exploitation of workers who struggle on a lickle wage packit because of the bossman's big tax rackit, and worse still, as unions crumbled, fall under the swinging axe of redundancy. 'The last fifteen years them get mih labour/Now after fifteen years mih fall out of favour.'

So, the opposition between reggae and soul in their respective treatment of political subjects was not as absolute as it looked. If Beggar & Co, The Specials and Linton Kwesi Johnson attracted different audiences in the early 1980s, they were all bound by the desire to speak out. Maybe the collective consciousness could be summarised thus: Somebody help me out of this ghost town because Inglan is a bitch.

Most Important Meal of the Day
Thought provoking messages aside, Linton Kwesi Johnson, The Specials and Beggar & Co had another notable thing in common: they were part of a generation of artists that valued musicianship. Reggae, dub poetry and jazz-funk, although perceived and marketed as separate entities, all involved outstanding musicians, regardless of the differing approaches to rhythm and arrangement that had defined each genre. With the words came expert sounds. People had to be able to play. The musicians who worked with Johnson, none more so than bassist-bandleader Dennis Bovell and guitarist John Kpiaye, were invaluable components of the process of bringing to life an entire world of meaning and emotion, so that the ricochet of a rimshot, the hiss of a 'flying V' cymbal, the crack of a guitar or the slur of an organ enhanced the sensory experience initiated by a well written lyric. What was played synergised with what was said. As artists wedded to Rastafarian philosophy said: Word, sound and power.

The balance between those elements can shift, though. Power can come when sound replaces word, when drums evoke speech and bass becomes culture. A song that brilliantly extends the LKJ-Specials-Beggar & Co axis is one that is profoundly lyrical yet it has no lyrics at all. It is one of the seminal Black British instrumentals. 'Warrior Charge'[6] by Aswad, the highlight of the soundtrack of the movie *Babylon*, the 1980 masterpiece by Franco Rosso,[7] which lionises sound system culture in Britain and lays bare the racist brutality of police harassment. The sturdy drive of the rhythm section and the mighty roar of the brass, both elements deployed with superbly judged economy, make the arrangement an irrepressible anthem of resistance. The horns are like heavy blows against Empire. And at a climactic moment in the piece there is a short, glowering harmonica solo. The effect is devastating. One of the oldest instruments in the African-American musical canon, the humble little mouth organ, has to be clamped against a microphone to be heard above the other instruments, but it has sonic and emotional cut-through. It reconnects with the blues and R&B in the midst of reggae and reminds the world of the long relationship between these different forms. In the provoking push and pull between acoustic and electric devices, an historic instrument has never sounded so thoroughly modern.

While the harmonica lends an ancestral character to 'Warrior Charge', a highpoint in roots reggae, another 'old' instrument used in music that crossed the lines between calypso and jazz-funk was the steel pan from Trinidad Carnival. It was played by Annise Hadeed in The Breakfast Band, a multi-racial seven-piece that also featured drummer Richard Bailey, bassist Kuma Harada, guitarist Winston Delandro, keyboardist James Lascelles, saxophonist Ken Eley and percussionist Tony Maronie. Between them, the individual members had played with a host of iconic artists in the 1970s, including blues rock superstar guitarist Jeff Beck, best-selling pop-reggae singer Johnny Nash and boundary breaking South African jazz saxophonist, Dudu Pukwana. Foregoing the economically steady world of session work, they came together to jam at a rehearsal studio in Camden, north London and a farm in Suffolk, made cassette tapes of their spontaneous trading of riffs and then started to shape them into songs after listening back. What they produced was highly eclectic and the group enjoyed a major underground hit with a lively tune called 'L.A. 14', driven by heavy slap bass, a soaring melodic line and intricate rhythmic breakdowns that found favour with the 'Brit funk' and jazz-funk audience that had taken artists such as Incognito, Morrissey Mullen and Central Line to their hearts.

However, as Richard Bailey, a former member of the early 1970s Black rock combo Batti Mamzelle explains, The Breakfast Band stood out:

> I think we were definitely part of the jazz-funk scene as we were playing the same venues in London as several of those bands like the Half Moon in Putney. The only difference was that we had the steel pan, which identified us more with the Caribbean. Also the other bands had vocalists at some point, whereas we were all instrumental, so there was only so far we could go with that. Because they had singers, they were more in line with the funk and soul thing, and we were told a few times to bring in vocalists. Although we played funk we also played music that didn't fit in because of the Caribbean thing. We did reggae and funk and soca, and sometimes it was all in the same song, so to sell it became a lot more difficult.[8]

The comment points to areas of convergence and divergence among several genres and sub-genres in Black music in Britain in the early 1980s, and how the question of whether a song had words or not did matter to some promoters and listeners. But as steel pan player Annise Hadeed points out, The Breakfast band shared an audience with several combos who were playing salsa and Latin-jazz, which also found favour with UK audiences. He noted:

> I don't think we consciously set out to be a part of any scene to be honest. But around that time you heard people like Cayenne, Gonzalez and Roberto Pla and they had this Afro-Cuban thing that was also very popular and it kind of went with what we did too.[9]

In other words, there was an interest in non-western rhythms that was anything but new when one considers that there had been a vogue for Latin music since the 1950s, as exemplified by the popular bandleader Edmundo Ros. The Breakfast Band maintained the rhythmic heritage of the Caribbean but placed it in a contemporary context with the use of electric instruments, synthesizers and bass guitar. It is worth noting that as the group came to prominence, a steel band movement was growing around the country with bands such as Ebony, with whom Hadeed and Bailey worked, becoming community organisations that provided basic musical training for youngsters, as well as sustaining Carnival culture.

If never as influential as reggae, Trinidadian music was still present in Britain in a variety of settings. Millions of viewers heard the ringing cowbell of 'Soul Limbo', the tribute to calypso by American soul legends Booker T & The MGs which was used as the theme for the BBC's Test Match cricket programmes, and Caribbean rhythms permeated mainstream pop more than one might have imagined. Sometimes it was in the shape of a massive one-off hit like Arrow's 'Hot Hot Hot!', the song that introduced many UK listeners to the sound of soca, whilst Howard Jones used steel pans and a fey, light pop-reggae beat on the chart smash 'Like to Get to Know You Well.' But the band that enjoyed commercial success and really showed the limitations of genre definitions was Kid Creole & The Coconuts. They were from New York, and they took the UK by storm with the spirit of Port of Spain. Although marketed as a soul-funk-Latin combo, they were obviously steeped in the sound of Trinidad, with all its jostling rhythms and piquant word play, as can be heard on any number one of the fabulous hit singles they made in the early 1980s, above all 'Annie, I'm Not Your Daddy', a bitingly funny calypso that Lord Kitchener or Sparrow would have been proud of. When the band's leader, August Darnell, produced a UK funk act, Funkapolitan, Annise Hadeed brought his steel drums to the fete. He and other members of The Breakfast Band also deployed their rhythmic ingenuity on the songs of other

British soul artists, such as Billy Ocean, the Trinidadian vocalist who had been making quality pop-R&B since the late 1960s. And there was more scintillating pan on Central Line's 'Lovely Day', an enchanting song built on a misty soca groove, wavering synthesizer chords and chugging guitar.

Most interesting of all was Linx's 'Intuition'. Although there was no steel pan on this track, the instrument was clearly implied by the bright, buoyant quality of the counter-melodic keyboards which gave the arrangement the upbeat breezy character of steelband and calypso. In other words, here is more evidence of the cultural pluralism in Black British music that goes against the prevailing narrative that bands were always applying an American template. Earth, Wind & Fire remained an essential building block of Linx's development, but the 'Caribbean retentions', both in rhythm and timbre, suggested not just what Black British bands were listening to, but the life they were leading, that they were attending carnival each year and enjoying and absorbing the sounds of steel bands, without questioning whether or not they might fit into their own creative thinking. They were still hearing the West Indian accents of their parents and engaging in different ways with the 'mother country'. Even as Jamaica, Trinidad and Barbados were becoming remoter political abstractions to them, a diversity of Caribbean idioms reached musicians' ears. The band Central Line was named after the key artery in the London tube network, a signifier that could not have been more metropolitan. But what is the subject of Central Line's 'Lovely Day'? The West Indian island of Dominica. And what language did the singers use in the interlude in the latter stages of that superb composition? Creole. They didn't learn that on an O-Level French course.

Eye to I
The song is a moment of magic, a spark of genius. Just when you think you understand what the Caribbean is, 'Lovely Day' doesn't so much pull the rug from under your feet as shift the centre of your geo-cultural assumptions, sending you on a trip to an island that is neither Jamaica nor Trinidad nor Barbados. Listeners may have fallen under the spell of the song's melodic chants but very few people would have understood the spoken word passage because it was in Dominican Creole, so the Caribbean was simultaneously within and beyond our cognitive grasp. In fact, 'Lovely Day', with its irresistibly seductive rhythm and joyous motifs, could not be a greater symbol of the protean alchemy of the region and what its essence meant to young Black Britons. We knew it but we did not know it. We recognised certain but not *all* manifestations of our heartlands. Central Line came to school us.

And there was such an intriguing contrast between the low grainy character of Camelle Hinds' soliloquy and the falsetto style dominant at the time in UK soul, as exemplified by the likes of Junior Giscombe, Leee

John and David Joseph, all singing in deference to U.S. legends such as Curtis Mayfield, Marvin Gaye and Eddie Kendricks. Central Line had offered a piece of Black popular music stamped 'made in Britain' that was impossible to pigeonhole. It had elements of soca, R&B, funk, salsa and jazz but was bounded by none of them.

From a marketing point of view the mutability of Central Line challenged a music business that preferred predictability, though the band's other notable tracks, such as 'Walking into Sunshine' could be more clearly aligned to a New York sub-genre of soul called 'boogie'. The upside of the band's shape-shifting and risk-taking has been a legacy that has not devalued over time, setting an example to any new artists who have the courage to pursue their own artistic paths away from standardised templates or reductive definitions.

Another interesting band that came along at roughly the same time and had an even more unorthodox stance was I-Level. Its lead singer, Sam Jones, advocated originality and individuality above all else. As much as he admired American soul voices, he would not emulate them:

> I realised at some point that there are a million artists that can do that. So I figured that maybe the lack of vibrato I have in my voice, maybe from the early years in the choir, makes me sing differently. But that might be what made our music different from other soul artists who were around at the time, I suppose.[10]

Consisting of Jones, bassist-producer Joe Dworniak and keyboardist Duncan Bridgeman, I-Level released their debut single 'Give Me' in 1982, and it made an immediate impression because of the beautiful oddity of its musical patchwork, which knitted together futuristic electronic textures, tightly marshalled funk bass and Jones' svelte tone, hard to place but suffused with a glowing sensuality and shorn of the swirling melisma that was integral to the American gospel tradition. He stood out in the UK soul scene when the band produced further releases, including 'Minefield', a more uptempo number bolstered by mighty brass, and 'Teacher', which strangely hybridised synth-pop and hard groove, confirming that the group straddled a number of styles. Jones counted David Grant of Linx among his friends, but always felt like something of a musical outsider. 'I never saw us as part of the UK soul scene or whatever,' he explained. 'I was just interested in making music and doing what I do.'[11]

Jones's backstory is fascinating. His parents were from Sierra Leone and he grew up in Scotland. His father had studied at Edinburgh University but moved the family to Rutherglen to the south east of Glasgow in the early 1960s, where, as Jones recalls, 'the horrendous racism toughened me up a bit', though he did join a local choir, his first foray into music. Things changed when the family moved to London, around 1969, for Jones to attend secondary school. They initially settled in Harlesden before moving to Wembley, then Ladbroke Grove, in the west of the city, a hub of the West Indian community. This brought about a major cultural shift in Jones life. He recalled:

> I was about eleven. I met all these kids from the Caribbean. It was fascinating for me because previous to that I hadn't known much about the various genres of music. I remember Paul Simon's 'Mother and Child Reunion'. I didn't know that was called reggae. I loved that song and when I came to London I discovered a whole world of reggae and I had lots of friends from the Caribbean and it became a real fascination for me. And that steered me towards becoming a musician. It was kind of weird that I'd end up in a reggae band after not really growing up in that music.[12]

Jones was one of the few Black British artists of African heritage to gravitate towards Jamaican music rather than, as had been the case for many of his generation, Afro-rock or other styles derived from Ghanaian or Nigerian rhythms. The first group he joined, The Chaldeans, was signed to Island by Chris Blackwell, though they never released any recorded material. But the connection with one of the foremost labels in Black music in Britain put Jones at the heart of the reggae community in London, and this brought him literally to the legend's door. 'I was accustomed to going to visit Bob Marley through a friend of mine who was in a band called Sons of Jah. Bob would call me "African", as he wasn't keen on Sam, he'd just call me African!' chuckled Jones, who had joined a reggae group called Brimstone. Jones recalled:

> When we did our first gig at Metro club, Bob was in the audience standing there right in front of us. I got accustomed to meeting lots of Jamaican musicians and started going to Jamaica at an early age before I started going to Africa. I was living there for about a year. I met so many people, like the producer Niney the Observer, he was the first person to take me to Jamaica and in this country... the first person to put me in the studio was [rocksteady legend] Alton Ellis. I sang on an album of his in the mid 70s.[13]

A few years later, Brimstone recorded singles such as 'Release Me' for Karnak, an independent label that grew from the Karnak House Caribbean Arts Centre in Ladbroke Grove, and also toured Europe, finding receptive audiences for their blend of roots and lover's rock. Change came with a chance encounter, though. When Brimstone went to record at Music Works studio in Finsbury Park in north London, Jones met Joe Dworniak who was employed there as an engineer, and after an informal chat at the session, he played the singer a demo. Jones said:

> I thought I like the sound of that, and at that time I was getting more and

more interested in genres other than reggae, so when Joe played it to me I thought ok, I can write something to this, so I went away and I did and played it to the guys, Joe and a keyboard player he knew called Duncan Bridgeman and they both liked it.[14]

That was the beginning of I-Level. They embraced soul, funk, rock and synth-pop, while not totally abandoning Jones's origins in reggae. One of the band's best tunes, 'Historical Nights', is an entrancing roots number that could, to all intents and purposes, have been a Brimstone outtake. But whether the band was creating something that leaned to the Caribbean or to Black America, their sound was shaped by the fact that Dworniak was a skilled engineer as well as bassist, and along with Bridgeman he took a keen interest in technology and studio techniques. Jones noted that:

We were very into experimental sounds. There was an overlap between the traditional methods of recording on two-inch tape, with instruments being played directly, and MIDI (Musical Instrument Digital Interface, which advanced the use of electronics and software in pop). MIDI was just coming in when we were doing our first album. And then you had Linn Drum, Oberheim DMX and all those drum machines… they were new things. There was also the Fairlight synthesizer; we had to hire one of those in to the studio; it cost an arm and a leg back then. We tried a lot of things. I played a lot of keys but Duncan was the main keyboard player. I-Level was definitely a kind of electronica group as well as a soul group. Some tracks have a mixture of drum machines and live drums. And Joe had a style of using quarter-inch tape to do what we called 'spinning in'. You'd record on quarter-inch and then spin in to two-inch tape which would be the equivalent of sampling today.[15]

On tracks such as 'Give Me', 'Number 4' and 'In the Sand' the band created a beautifully bizarre vocabulary that stood in an undefined space between live performance, with the bounce of bass and ripple of percussion prominent in many arrangements, and post-production, in which crafted electronic timbres had a kind of glisten and glow, suggesting that chords were as much sculpted into being as they were played on a keyboard. There was a subtle sheen in much of I-Level's music that looked forward to what was actively marketed as synth-pop in the early 1980s, on the back of the success of groups such as Depeche Mode and Soft Cell, but regardless of their eclecticism, Jones and co were still largely perceived as soul.

I-Level also unveiled an artfully sombre quality on their later material. Songs like 'In the River' had a dramatic weight in the drum sounds and a barrage of hard-edged keys that again showed that Jones, Dworniak and Bridgeman had created a unique vocabulary that did not lend itself to any neat categorisation. Stylistically, the band was a tantalising oddity.

Joy Spring
The strain of experimentalism I-Level embodied could be found elsewhere in Black music in Britain at the time, particularly among artists who wanted to explore the sonic possibilities of new synthesisers, electronics and studio technology. The question was whether there was space for them in the mainstream music industry.

In Scotland, an endearingly off-the-wall combo called Set the Tone released several singles and one album, *Shiftin' Air Affair*, which revealed them as marauding mavericks who took funk in an confrontationally raucous direction and combined that with austere, metallic-like keyboard effects to produce a signature that was in the tradition of dance music but also resonated with the burgeoning sub-genre known as electro, an important precursor of what would become hip-hop. Cold and hard ruled.

Set the Tone exemplified the potential for musicians who had been part of rock and soul combos, such as Simple Minds and Love and Money, to morph into something that had a youthful irreverence as well as interesting musical ideas. Moreover, the sight of the group's Black female vocalist Evelyn Asiedu singing alongside white singer, Chris Morgan, put them in the long lineage of British multi-racial groups.

From Bristol came Float Up CP, which arose phoenix-like out of the ashes of Rip, Rig & Panic to make music that blended an upbeat happy-go-lucky ambiance with spiky dissonances, as on its debut single, 'Joy's Address', while another band called Brilliant mixed punk and funk in a gutsy but very melodic style that deployed June Montana's vocals and Youth's production to good effect on strong singles such as 'Love is War'. Then there was Floy Joy, a Sheffield act that was equally interesting in sound and personnel. Shaun and Michael Ward were the players, while Don Was of US pop-funk upstarts Was Not Was was the producer. Carroll Thompson, one of the revered 'queens of lover's rock', was the singer. On tracks such as the stupendous 'Burn 'Down a Rhythm', with its sledgehammer beat and thick sludge of baritone saxophone, the band ingeniously re-channelled classic R&B and soul in a way that was similar to some of these groups, yet sounded unique in terms of textures, and above all in the mix, which had a strong dub flavour.

Taken together, these groups could be seen as forming a pattern that any halfway decent commentator could have spotted. A group led by white male musicians was fronted by a Black female vocalist. The women in question were for the most part not actively involved in the writing process, a fact which might have given them less of a stake in the material they performed, yet Carroll Thompson made an absolutely essential contribution to Floy Joy, so that if you removed her voice from the recordings they would not be the same at all. Similarly, 'Temptation' by Heaven 17, another soul-pop-electronica act from Sheffield, was a great song made greater still by the soaring choruses of Carol Kenyon, one of the most versatile session vocalists of the 1980s who worked with jazz-funkers Morrissey Mullen, pop-rocker Chris Rea and global electro-pop stars Jon & Vangelis.

Other Black British women in this period who did significant work included Ruth Rogers-Wright. Under the name of Moontwist she cut a couple of superb singles, the best being 'Sight and Sound', a track which had the relaxed grace of a classic jazz ballad but also a shadowy, skulking, brooding character that made it a perfect backdrop for very unsettling times, especially as the melody was given a dramatic edge by the dark-toned, quite masculine voice of the singer, who defied prevailing gender norms in how she dressed as well as how she performed. Then Rogers-Wright emigrated to Australia and disappeared from British view, though she established a career in Australia that continues to the present, with an album called *The Book of Ruth* in 2011, and she performs many concerts featuring the songs of Nina Simone.

But in general, transience was the experience of too many talented Black artists. Some issued music on independent labels, while others, though signed by well-established, successful imprints, did not release more than a handful of singles and a few albums at the most. It seems that A & R departments rarely adopted a long term view of their artists' development but signed them with an eye on short term profit, to be dropped if that target was not reached. Carol Kenyon released singles, but never an album, on Columbia.

Even so, enough material survives from the early 1980s to make it clear that it was a vital period in the history of Black music in Britain precisely because of the arrival of musicians who fell tantalisingly between rather than squarely into genres. Whether they were inter-genre, extra-genre, or an 'inbetweenie' Britishisation of pop, groups such as I-Level, Set the Tone, and Floy Joy took African American and Caribbean elements and inventively shaped them into something that was new.

Notes

1. Blair Peach was a New Zealand-born teacher who died after being struck on the head by a member of the SPG (Special Patrol Group) during an Anti-Nazi league demonstration in Southall, west London in 1979. No officer was ever charged. Linton Kwesi Johnson paid tribute to Peach on his composition 'Reggae Fi Peach'.
2. Linton Kwesi Johnson, *Bass Culture* (Island, 1980).
3. Junior Giscombe's 'Mama Used To Say' was a big hit in America.
4. Interview with the author, June 2022.
5. Ibid.

6. 'Warrior Charge' featured Jamaican veterans trombonist Vin Gordon and saxophonist Michael 'Bami' Rose, formerly of soul pioneers Cymande.
7. Franco Rosso was an Italian-born British filmmaker whose body of work also included the 1973 documentary *The Mangrove 9*, which was scripted by John La Rose and the 1979 documentary *Dread Beat an' Blood*, a profile of Linton Kwesi Johnson.
8. Interview with the author, September 2022.
9. Ibid.
10. Interview with the author, July 2022.
11. Ibid.
12. Ibid.
13. Ibid.
14. Ibid.
15. Ibid.

17 GREEN IS THE COLOUR

'Our freedom didn't just come like that. We worked very hard. The campaign to release Mandela and all political prisoners was the most effective work.'
— Sebothane Julian Bahula

Kulture clash
Nothing prepared me for Monsoon. When the band appeared on *Top of the Pops* in 1981 to perform 'Ever So Lonely', they treated schoolchildren of the Thatcher generation to a series of firsts. Never before had I seen musicians seated. Never before had I seen the long neck and bulbous base of a sitar, or been engulfed in the sound of its glistening strings. Never before had I seen a singer such as Sheila Chandra move confidently to a beat caught between raga and Western pop. She counteracted the prevailing image of the music of the Indian subcontinent as a soundtrack to tandoori dining or, worse still, the appalling racism peddled by movies such as *Carry On Up the Khyber* or the television show *It Ain't Half Hot Mum*, both of which presented Asians as comically superstitious and subservient underlings who had to know their place in the brutal hierarchy of the glorious British Raj.

'Ever So Lonely' was a bright, catchy song that built a coherent synthesis from a variety of cultural and musical elements. With its whiplash backbeat, rhythmic energy, intriguing blend of high-pitched Indian percussion, acoustic piano chords and an evanescent melody, it was an appealing composition, especially to ears that were unfamiliar with those elements. Yet not everybody heard the same thing.

'I hated that record,' says Pervez Bilgrami. 'To me it was very much a kind of manufactured Asian music for the mainstream and the lyrics weren't saying anything to me.'[1] That damning verdict is a reminder that what is fresh to a consumer outside a particular culture can be stale to those inside it, especially if they have taken a radical artistic path. Bilgrami was the lead singer of an Asian punk band, Alien Kulture. It was formed in 1979 by Bilgrami, bassist Ausaf Abbas, and drummer Azhar Rana, who were all part of the South Asian, mainly Pakistani community in Balham, south London, with the addition of white guitarist, Huw Jones. They played unapologetically noisy, shouty, highly provocative songs that were largely inspired by the Sex Pistols, deviating comprehensively from the rhythmic sophistication of the music of their parents. The whole ethos of the band was to reflect their lived experience at the heart of a culture clash between themselves and their parents' generation, as well as the hostility and violence they faced on the streets in the era of National Front campaigns and feral skinhead gangs. With the police as the main issue for young African Caribbeans, the experiences of the two communities were largely perceived as unrelated. The question of selfhood was highly complex, as were frames of reference. There were embryonic black Britons but there were as yet no British Asians. That was because the latter were more invisible, and in a literal and figurative sense less comprehensible to the mainstream. People mocked my parents for their strong Trinidadian accents, but they poured much greater scorn on Asians because they spoke not just one but in many cases several languages that most Brits could *not* understand, which made the mockery all the more caustic as racists were reduced, quite pathetically, to producing what they thought were the speech rhythms and timbres of Hindi or Urdu, not that they knew the difference between the two, or the many peoples of South Asia. Bilgrami explained, 'We came from all over the world but we were grouped together by one word, and that was Paki. I don't think we really had an identity. Black kids were cool, they had reggae they brought their culture over from Jamaica… White people liked to dance to it.'[2]

The spectacle of 'Paki bashing', so widespread in the era of Thatcher, happy as she was to stoke the fire of casual street violence against ethnic minorities by making statements about Britain being 'swamped' by alien cultures, provided the backdrop as well as the name of the band of Abbas, Bilgrami, Rana and Jones. But not only did they have to go through the ordeal of having groups of skinheads turn up at their gigs to run amok, they also incurred the wrath of their own elders who took great exception to songs such as 'Arranged Marriage'. The band's febrile music was moulded in the pop aesthetic of short bursts of energy rather than any more advanced structural ambition, but they had a specific goal. 'We had to kind of force our way into the closed shop of black and white musicians,' Bilgrami said. 'We had to gatecrash the party by playing music people identified with, which was punk but we sang about these things that had just not been sung about before.'[3]

Alien Kulture brought to light subjects that needed to be aired such as what they saw as 'a two-way problem between children and parents'. In a 1981 interview, the band's drummer, Azhar Rana, explained:

> We feel one of the main problems facing Asian youth arises from the fact that they are under the influence of two cultures, eastern cultural influence coming mainly from the parents and the western from the media… schools… And often this results in real problems… identity crisis. They don't know what culture they should adopt.[4]

As far as Alien Kulture were concerned, the dilemma was not reducible to a binary choice. There was no need to adopt one culture at the expense of the other and every reason to embrace Eastern and Western ways on terms the individual found palatable, such as wearing traditional Indian garments with Dr Martens boots, the apparel of choice for kids who were punks, ska revivalists and skinheads alike. Bilgrami was of a mind that these elements were not incompatible: 'I don't know why you can't be happy with both cultures.'[5]

Finding a harmonious space between the mores of their parents and those of their adopted homeland was a challenge. There was an inordinate amount of baggage placed on the shoulders of Black and Asian youth in Britain by dint of the legacy of colonial history, with its entrenched notions of white superiority, and its legacy of white paranoia over the threat posed by the settlement of former subjects of Empire and their offspring in Britain. Bilgrami's words implied a wish that could only be achieved through action, so the band became part of the Rock Against Racism movement (see Chapter 12), and at concerts under that banner saw animosity and misconceptions up close and personal. Bassist Ausaf Abbas recalled:

> When we were in Birmingham, we were playing a RAR gig there and when we'd finished a skinhead came up to one of us and said that I didn't use to like Pakis before but there's obviously no difference and I think you're alright... And it's that sort of image, because what's been happening is that a lot of people think that Asians don't mix, and that they want to stand outside but that's not true. I think the feeling of the band and quite a lot of our friends, and I'm sure the vast number of other Asian youth, is that we are here to stay in Britain, and we are here to fight and that we've got to stand up for what we believe in and what we want.[6]

There were both positive and negative role models for this stand. Jaz Coleman, charismatic front man of the influential post-punk band, Killing Joke, and Norman Watt-Roy, excellent bassist of Ian Dury & The Blockheads, both had Asian heritage, as did one of the biggest pop stars of the period, Freddie Mercury, though he felt compelled to suppress his original identity as Farrokh Bulsara and claim that he was Persian rather than Indian, to avoid the inevitable public stigma. At the time it was not cool to be brown.

Both the Indo-pop of Monsoon and the Asian punk of Alien Kulture were new creative paths that diverged from those followed by previous generations, those who had arrived in the UK from the Indian subcontinent in the late 1950s and early 1960s. Then, Indian composers and virtuoso players such as John Mayer and Diwan Motihar briefly became part of the British jazz scene, notably working with Jamaican saxophonist, Joe

Harriott and St Vincent trumpeter, Shake Keane. Also important were George Khan, born in London to a Punjabi father and English mother, and Olaf Vas, a Kenyan Asian; both were highly respected saxophonists, the former enjoying a long stint in the band of Mike Westbrook.

Living Off the Dohl
Beyond jazz, punk and Indo-pop, the genre of music that became most readily identified with Asian communities in Britain in the 1980s was a new thing called bhangra. It was an example of how strong local traditions can be reshaped by a change of environment or the kind of organic shift in social outlook we think of as modernity. Derived from Punjabi folk music, the name bhangra designated dance as well as song and was centred around the sharp crack of the dohl drum, a conic-shaped percussion instrument slung around the waist and hit with a stick, often in short, punchy phrases that laid the foundation for vocal chants which would be given supersized volume by guests at weddings and parties. Pervez Bigrami of Alien Kulture says that, aware of the roots of bhangra, they almost got in on the act:

> We had this song 'Liberation Dance', which was about Zimbabwe's independence. We thought that if we ever recorded this we'd put bhangra on it to give it that heavy percussive feel but we broke up, so we were the bhangra group that never was. We were too early.[7]

Although the roots of the music in the UK reached back to the 1960s and 1970s, it was really in the 1980s that bhangra hit a peak of popularity when its sonic palette was altered by the arrival of both new ideas and instruments. In the vanguard of the movement was a band called Alaap from Southall, west London. They joined forces with a Kashmiri-born arranger, Deepak Khazanchi, who introduced elements of disco and electronic production into their traditional percussive base on an album called *Teri Chunni De Sitare*. It caused a sensation, providing a model for groups that sprang up in the Punjabi diaspora in Britain, notably in Midlands' cities such as Birmingham, Coventry and Wolverhampton. The large audiences for Alaap and bhangra's other prime movers such as Holle Holle, who drew up to 3,000 fans to gigs, attracted substantial media attention, as Sabita Banerji and Gerd Baumann explain:

> Images of girls in glittering dresses and energetic boys flocking to the largest discos in central London captivated the mainstream press that had assumed Asian youth to be shy and introverted, oppressed by authoritarian, ultra conservative parents.[8]

Indeed, the bhangra of Alaap, the Indi-pop of Monsoon and the punk of Alien Kulture, significantly broadened the scope of Asian cultural identity between the early to mid-1980s, and while the emergence of these artists did not mean that the great British public stopped making snide remarks at the sight of a turban or sari, creative individuals with brown skins were breaking new ground. *My Beautiful Launderette* (1985), with its daring massala of the generation gap in an Asian household, the fine line between peer pressure-led racism and homosexual romance, and perhaps, most provocatively of all, the desire of a minority group to buy *into* rather than out of the Thatcherite dream was undoubtedly the British Asian cultural artefact that reached the biggest UK audience. If the film, directed by Stephen Frears and scripted by Hanif Kureishi, was one of the key productions of Channel 4 on the big screen, then the same station also took significant steps forward in its representation of both Asian and Black communities in shows such as *Eastern Eye, Black On Black* and *The Bandung File*. Farrukh Dhondy, Darcus Howe and Tariq Ali all played major parts, either off or on camera, in documenting the experience of ethnic minorities in Britain and making international news programmes from a Black perspective.

Another World
Chapter 8 documented the success of Osibisa as the founding fathers of what was called Afro-rock in the 1970s. Though, commercially, the band was on the wane in the 1980s, there was a plethora of exciting new music being made in Africa and also a shift in the perception of how well it compared to pop from either America or the United Kingdom. As a schoolboy with very little knowledge of African artists beyond Osibisa (who had dazzled me and my parents when we saw them on TV playing 'Sunshine Day'), I still mostly heard the view that the music from Ghana and Nigeria was either 'strange' or 'repetitive'. But when the journalist and photographer Sue Steward (who covered Latin and non-western music) was asked why there was a growing attraction to African music, she gave this answer: 'We were just so bored of rock at that time. It sounded so dead.'

Steward was amongst those who realised that there was much to be gained from looking outwards, adopting an international rather than national or purely European perspective and embracing artists from around the world. To that end Peter Gabriel, of the successful progressive rock band Genesis, launched an important new festival, World of Music and Dance (WOMAD) in 1982 at Shepton Mallet in Somerset, far from traditional rock festival heartlands of Reading or Knebworth.

At the inaugural event, the line-up was cross-genre as well as trans-geographical and inter-generational: legendary American expatriate trumpeter, Don Cherry, who had long had a global musical outlook; British ska-pop heroes, The Beat; The Drummers of Burundi, (aka The Royal Burundi Drummers); Liverpudlian new-wavers, Echo & The Bunnymen; Cameroonian-Nigerian high life sensation Prince Nico Mbarga & Rocafill Jazz; Scottish rockers, Simple Minds; Indian sitarist Imrat Khan; and the Irish folk band, The Chieftains.

To promote the festival, WEA records issued a 'benefit double album', *Music and Rhythm*,[9] which featured calypso legend, Mighty Sparrow, respected Jamaican trombonist, Rico Rodriguez, experimental American jazz trumpeter, Jon Hassell and Pakistani vocalist, Nusrat Fateh Ali Khan. As stated in the sleeve notes, Gabriel's vision was for greater inclusion in the pop music canon. He wrote:

> The W.O.M.A.D festival intends to focus wider UK public attention upon the traditional and contemporary arts of non-western cultures, as practiced in this country and throughout the world. We hope that this record may provide an open and varied introduction to a few of the countless musical traditions which thrive everywhere over the populated world.

Black Britain was also showcased. One of the most significant appearances at WOMAD was the Ekome National Dance Company, an ensemble from Bristol that revealed a complex and stimulating relationship between Africa and its Diaspora. The group's repertoire was largely rooted in the rhythms and choreography of Ghana, yet the bulk of its members were of Caribbean heritage, a focus that resonated with the Afro-centricity professed in UK by some groups that had Jamaican roots.

WOMAD was also staged at Morecambe Bay in Lancashire and throughout the 1980s it grew as a national phenomenon. Perhaps Peter Gabriel's primary achievement as a curator was to bring together disparate listeners or at least usher western rock fans towards non-western music. British audiences familiar with XTC and The Beat discovered the unfamiliar sound of Malawian xylophonist Lonesi Chewane or Nigerian Hi-Life singer Prince Nico Mbarga. And the sight of Echo & The Bunnymen meeting The Royal Burundi Drummers or Gabriel playing with Indian violin virtuoso L. Shankar recalled similar unions of the past, such as the Rolling Stones and Ginger Johnson's African drummers, though knowledge of such stimulating encounters of the late 1960s may well have been confined to a minority of popular music listeners. In any case, WOMAD became a key fixture on the UK festival circuit that still attracts audiences of up to 140,000 to its annual festivals and also has international editions. Gabriel also founded a recording studio in Box, Wiltshire as well as label, both operating under the name of Real World, creating a diverse roster based on the same ethos as WOMAD. Among his many signings was the former Monsoon singer, Sheila Chandra, who made a number of interesting solo albums.

This period saw a significant shift in the market segmentation of music, as the idea of packaging non-western artists under new terms gained more traction. The advent of WOMAD coincided with the inception of a genre, a loose translation of what the French called 'La sono mondiale' or 'Les Musiques Du Monde', prompted by a groundswell of quite extraordinary artists from Francophone West Africa, such as Youssou N'Dour, Oumou Sangare, Salif Keita and Angelique Kidjo, who revealed that cities such as Dakar, Bamoko and Cotonou were creative powerhouses that Paris, London and New York should not underrate.

But exactly what the term 'World Music' meant was by no means clear, and its lack of precise definition could be seen as akin to any promotional tool that seeks to hedge its bets, in order to push product to new markets. A number of progressive African idioms, such as Hi-life, Afro-rock and Afrobeat had existed prior to the advent of World Music, but there was no logical sense of how all these strands fitted together.

Over the years I have met artists who have raised no objection to the concept of World Music because they are grateful for the practical opportunities provided, namely festival bookings and media interest. On the other hand, many others have been contemptuous of the label because of what they feel are its patronising, post-colonial connotations, namely that self-appointed Western powerbrokers have deigned to create a general umbrella term that, regardless of any positive intent to place non-western artists on a par with western ones, ironically frames them in a reductive way. Nobody put it better than South African vocal legend Miriam Makeba: 'They might as well call it Third World music. That's what they really mean, the west looking at us as exotic. We could also call English pop a kind of World Music because that's what is sounds like to us.'[10]

How questions of definition and self-definition play out is inevitably shaped by an international recording and touring industry in which financial power and the means of production are mostly centred in Europe and America. The fact that many African artists had to travel to Europe and Britain to further their careers underlines the realities of this hierarchy.

Whether or not WOMAD brought new commercial impetus to non-western artists, the dynamic personalities involved in African music in Britain still continued to present important events. Promoter Wala Danga programmed acts from all over the continent at the Limpopo club at the Africa Centre, Covent Garden in Central London. This was also the base for African Dawn, an interesting collective of African, Caribbean and Central American artists (including the Grenadian writer, Merle Collins) whose highly political songs and poems broached anything from the oppression of black people in South Africa to the imperialist American interventions in Grenada and El Salvador.

Also important in the growth of audiences for African music in Britain was the record label and shop, Sterns, which distributed the groundbreaking music of Francophone African artists, and also signed bands based in Britain. One such was Hi Life International. As the name suggests they stood firmly in the lineage of West African dance music, though they were also adept at other styles such as soukous, reflecting the lively multi-cultural scene in London in which Caribbean, white English and African players mixed freely. A six-piece featuring vocalist-guitarist Kwabena Oduro Kwarteng, tenor saxophonist Frank Williams and trumpeter Stu Hamer, among others, the group fulfilled its mission statement to make 'music to wake the dead' on the highly enjoyable, club-friendly albums *Travel & See* and *Na Wa Fo*.

Anansi tales
Regardless of whether or not World Music did open up a new audience for African artists, there had long been and continued to be an appreciation of music from around the world in Britain, though this has not always been recognised. The 'soul boy' youth cult has tended to be equated with either US or UK funk and jazz-funk, but a wide range of Afro-Latin music was an integral part of that scene because of the irresistibility of its rhythmic content, which underpinned the huge quantity of 'floor fillers' that found favour with dancers in clubs up and down the country. There may be an element of social snobbery at play here, too, as the working-class nature of that 'soul boy' constituency didn't chime with the idea of 'World Music' as the preserve of a more middle-class audience with sophisticated tastes. As it was, soul boys were sufficiently advanced listeners to tune into music from Brazil that had a strong grounding in African rhythms. Artists such as Azymuth, Gilberto Gil and Tania Maria were hugely popular because they straddled jazz, funk, soul and Latin-American genres, all energized by percussion and polyrhythms.

There were also DJs with open minds who tuned into classic and contemporary African artists, that a World Music audience would have lapped up, and programmed in soul and jazz sets. Received narratives state that Andy Kershaw, Charlie Gillett, Gerry Lyseight, Ian & Ray, Max Reinhardt and Rita Ray all furthered the cause of African and Latin American artists both on the radio and in clubs, and this is true, but there was also the seminal British jazz-funk DJ, Robbie Vincent[11] who got behind outstanding 'motherland' artists such as Cameroonian saxophonist Manu Dibango, the man with the 'big blow', and Ghanaian vocalist-guitarist George Darko, whose enchanting 'Hi-Life Time' was a tune that Vincent 'hammered' in 1983, making it clear that this music was totally compatible with the songs of Light of the World, The Crusaders and Brass Construction. Vincent endorsed other artists from Ghana. Kabbala were led by two

London-based brothers, Michael and Isaac Ospanin, both percussionists, with the latter also playing trombone. They released a superb 12" single, 'Ashewo Ara', that, loosely picking up from where Osibisa had left off, caused an absolute frenzy in soul clubs. The constant ricochets of cowbells, bongos and congas against a steady, funky, slapped bass, wiry guitar riffs, splashy electric piano, roaring horns and stirring vocal chants proved an irresistible combination whose elements clearly overlapped with the standard vocabulary of jazz-funk.

Last but not least there was George Lee, a saxophonist who had been making music in Britain in a variety of different fields, from reggae and jazz to spoken word poetry, since the late 1960s. He unveiled a new group called Anansi that featured musicians such as percussionist Nana Tsiboe, a master drummer whose credits ranged from pop icons such as Paul McCartney to jazz artists like Trevor Watts. Also on board were the excellent South African bassist Ernest Mothle, and the highly respected Trinidadian guitarist, Winston Delandro, a member of the Caribbean-fusion ensemble, The Breakfast Band, who had also played sessions with Lee for American soul-reggae star, Johnny Nash.

Lee's brilliance lay in both composition and improvisation. The album *Anansi* saw him use a wide range of African and Latin rhythms on material which moved stealthily from joyous upbeat dance to deeply poignant ballads on which Lee sometimes added wordless vocals, lending a vaguely folk-like character to music that had a high degree of harmonic finesse. The single, 'Sea Shells', issued prior to the release of the LP, proved a winner on Robbie Vincent's radio show. It created a perfect bridge between African American and African musical cultures insofar as the main beat was taut, minimal funk, which was bolstered by a steady rumble of congas. But it was the ascending horns that really drew the listener in. Lee played a unison saxophone and flute line that was full of dashing, darting phrases that became more intricate after several breaks, creating the kind of whirling momentum that recalled the note-laden performances of classic bebop era combos. There was a real effervescence in the arrangement and an attention to detail in each part of the score that caught the ear, while the snap of the beat underneath ensured that the song was also a surefire floor filler.

At this time, a notable new player arrived in the international music business. In 1981, South African entrepreneur Clive Calder founded a record label, Jive, which enjoyed substantial success in pop and R&B, though the imprint's name referred to 'township jive' or 'Soweto beat', and that reference became more explicit when a subsidiary, Jive Afrika, was launched. Several DJs picked up on some of its key releases, particularly the eponymous album by Sakhile, a very gifted South African jazz combo whose music was characterised by rhythmic imagination, haunting vocals, rich melodic motifs and strident solos, particularly from saxophonist, Barney Rachabane.

One of Sakhile's compatriots, the veteran trumpeter Hugh Masekela, also became their label mate and released a single 'Don't Go Lose It Baby' in 1984 that made waves. The song's dominant marimba riff, hotly aggressive in rhythmic attack, bewitching in timbre, was a perfectly programmed pneumatic drill in the midst of sensual female vocals and swift flugelhorn motifs. Much tension was created by the flurries of brass around the hard solid drive of the central percussive loop. The track was important because there was a growing strand of American dance music that employed Atari drum machines and Fairlight synthesizers, which was being marketed as 'electro', and Masekela's song stood as an African counterpart to this vocabulary, a prototype Afro-Techno or Bush Techno. In fact, the album from which it came was called *Techno Bush*, a playful evocation of an encounter between state-of-the-art electronics and traditional rhythmic traditions. There was an additional coded message. The music was recorded at a mobile studio at The Woodpecker Inn, Gaborone in Botswana, as there was no other facility available at the time, though much of the post-production was done at Battery in Willesden, north London. The transcontinental character of the album marked Masekela's status as an exile from apartheid who had an ongoing relationship with Britain, where he had recorded back in the early 1970s.

Freedom Sounds
Masekela was one of the most vocal critics of white minority rule in South Africa and the single that followed 'Don't Go Lose It Baby' was a cover of Fela Anikulapo Kuti's 'Lady', whose B-side contained 'Stimela', a deeply affecting ballad about the exploitation of migrant labourers, mostly from Namibia, Lesotho and Zimbabwe, who toiled for next to nothing in the diamond mines of South Africa. The piece was a memorable denunciation of capitalism in concert with racism.

In any case, during the 1980s, powerful financial institutions in Britain, such as Barclays Bank (which had major interests in South Africa) actively supported the apartheid regime and promoters with deep pockets offered pay packets large enough to entice major international artists, including The Beach Boys, Status Quo, Shirley Bassey, Rod Stewart and Elton John, to break a United Nations boycott and appear at the luxury resort and casino Sun City. All the while, Margaret Thatcher denounced the African National Congress as a terrorist organisation and Young Conservatives wanted to see Mandela hung.

Yet there was also a gradual shift in public opinion in the UK, which saw people who were not especially 'conscious' grow more aware of the dehumanising conditions to which the indigenous population was subjected in townships, and it became increasingly clear that however brutal the repression, the resistance against it would not be silenced. Culture was a major weapon. Plays such as *Woza Albert*,[12] an ingenious satire on the second coming of Jesus Christ under apartheid, which toured Britain and other European countries, had a powerful impact on those who saw it. Other events also acted as a wake-up call. My parents were ashamed when the West Indies 'rebel tours' of the early 1980s saw several black cricketers they had once admired defy an international ban on playing in South Africa. They explained the signficance of their outrage to me.

But it was the imprisonment of Nelson Mandela that remained the focal point for campaigning against the apartheid regime. Political action, in the form of benefit gigs, often with South African guest speakers, had taken place in Britain since the 1950s. Thirty years later, the tide of activity was rising. On Sunday 17 July 1983, a gala concert called *African Sounds! For Mandela* took place at Alexandra Palace in London, to mark Mandela's 65th birthday, drawing an audience of close to 3,000. Julian Bahula of the band Jabula, an important member of the exiled South African artist community in Britain, as noted in Chapter 5, was the driving force behind the event, which was hugely important because much of the rightwing mainstream media had fallen in line with the Conservative government's desire to undermine the legitimacy of Mandela's political position.

Bahula knew that it was the power of Mandela's growing celebrity that had to be harnessed. As he said, 'It will help bring awareness of people to know what's happening in South Africa. Nelson Mandela is internationally known as the leader of the people.' And it is clear from the archive footage of the event that those who attended came not just for the music but because they were aware of the imprisonment of the ANC figurehead. There had been campaigning in schools and universities up and down the country before the event. Years later Bahula reflected:

> The Alexandra palace Mandela concert was an eye-opener for many, many people, those who supported our struggle and those who didn't support our struggle as well. Our freedom didn't just come like that. We worked very hard. The campaign to release Mandela and all political prisoners was the most effective work.[13]

The appearance of Hugh Masekela as well as multi-cultural London bands such as the very danceable Orchestra Jazira, made the concert a release of joyous energy as well as a space for urgent political statements. A significant chain of events was also set off. One of the audience members was Jerry Dammers, of The Specials, who just a few years prior had shown his desire to reflect the prevailingly downcast mood of Thatcher's Britain with his seminal composition 'Ghost Town'. Hearing Bahula and others marked an important epiphany for him.

> The first time I came into contact with live African music was at the 65th birthday concert (at Alexandra Palace). Years earlier, when I was 15, when the Springboks toured Britain, I stuck stickers around my school, urging people to go and demonstrate against the Springboks as part of the sanctions campaign. I managed to rally about two people to demonstrate but maybe this old school friend remembered that when he saw me in the street just by chance and told me about this concert. So I thought I'd go and check it out. Like most people in my generation, I'd never heard of Nelson Mandela.[14]

After attending the gig, Dammers decided to make the campaign to free Mandela the focal point of a song on which he had been working. In 1984, 'Free Nelson Mandela', with its infectious organ shuffle, skipping horns and churchy female backing vocals, made a splash internationally, becoming a top ten hit in the UK, Dutch and Belgian singles charts, and climbing to number one in New Zealand. Dali Tambo, son of the then ANC president, Oliver Tambo, asked Dammers to launch a British version of Artists United Against Apartheid, the collective headed by Little Steven in America, which featured a rainbow coalition of stars such as Bob Dylan, Herbie Hancock, Lou Reed, Gil Scott-Heron and Linton Kwesi Johnson and had released 'Sun City', a fervent exhortation to boycott South Africa's entertainment mecca.

Under the Free Mandela banner, Dammers started to assemble bands to play benefit gigs, gradually building a momentum that took him from small venues such as the Fridge in Brixton to an open-air event in Clapham Common that drew 200,000. 'It was the culmination of an anti-apartheid demonstration,' he recalled. 'We organised it with the anti-apartheid movement. We had really big names there, Peter Gabriel, Gil Scott-Heron, Hugh Masekela, Boy George... Sade.'[15]

This movement reached its apex at the 70th birthday, Free Nelson Mandela concert at Wembley stadium in 1988. On the bill were some of the biggest names in British and American pop at the time, including Simple Minds, Whitney Houston, Sting, Stevie Wonder, George Michael, Al Green, Joe Cocker, Aswad and Sly & Robbie, while among the South Africans were Amabutho Male Chorus, Jonathan Butler, Hugh Masekela, Miriam Makeba, Mahlathini and the Mahotella Queens.

The global impact of the concert was substantial, especially with the fillip of a BBC broadcast, despite fierce criticism from 24 Tory MPs who were still convinced that support for the ANC was support for terrorism. The efforts of Dammers and producer Tony Hollingsworth in putting on the concert were undeniable. Yet the event couldn't evade the play of power dynamics, of who appeared on the final bill, how much stage time was allocated to each act, and where they came in the running order. Political principles met the clashing agendas of promoters, managers and agents.

Similar issues were also faced by the Rock Against Racism movement years before. Ensuring that artists who were most politically relevant to 'the cause' were not sidelined for those with more famous names, the obvious case in point being Julian Bahula, who sadly did not play Wembley, became a cause for concern for Dammers, who later conceded that the programming could have been done differently:

> My priority was getting the message across to as many people as possible. But at the same time I think the actual exiled musicians did get a raw deal because they were the most committed and they probably deserved more of a profile than they got.[15]

But to their credit, both the single 'Free Nelson Mandela' and the Wembley gig were notably more racially diverse than the Band Aid and Live Aid projects initiated by Bob Geldof and Midge Ure, a few years prior to raise money for the Ethiopian famine. The conspicuous absence of Black British artists from the recording of the single 'Do They Know It's Christmas?', an omission made all the more salient by the appearance of a few members of the African American soul combos Kool & The Gang and Shalamar, gave the impression that UK musicians of African Caribbean heritage were invisible, or at best still deemed to be 'specialist' rather than mainstream, for all the appearances on *Top of the Pops* or Radio One. It was clear that the organisers thought they could not credibly front a fundraising appeal on a national scale. And this was at a time when Eddy Grant was at his commercial peak, enjoying the run of hits kickstarted by 'Electric Avenue'. He had been singing notable songs about Africa for many years, but then again, maybe he wouldn't have agreed to lend his voice to the astonishingly, insultingly Eurocentric if not utterly meaningless lyric penned by the Band Aid's writers: 'There won't be snow in Africa this Christmas.' Is that so?

Green is the colour
Band Aid was not the sole initiative of its kind. In 1985, Leon Leiffer, a singer known for his work with The Mighty Soul Rebels and The Blackstones founded British Reggae Artists Famine Appeal (BRAFA) and brought together a multitude of prominent names in the reggae community to record a charity single, 'Let's Make Africa Green Again'. Gene Rondo helped co-ordinate the project, Tony Douglas wrote lyrics for the song and Eddy Grant provided his studio free of charge. Winston Reedy, Byron Otis, Dennis Brown, The Pioneers, The Blackstones, Janet Kay, Christine McNab, Keith Drummond, The Undivided Roots, Aswad, Trevor Walters, and Junior English were among the many vocalists who took part. A crack backing band featured drummer Jah Bunny, bassist Ras Elroy Bailey, guitarist Ken Kendrick, trumpeter Eddie 'Tan Tan' Thornton

and saxophonist Michael 'Bami' Rose. Leiffer was clear about the central motivation and challenge of BRAFA:

> We reggae artists, even though we sing I love you and those kind of songs, we're singing about roots and culture. I think we should really do something to help these people. I took the initiative to *The Voice* newspaper, which was based in Hackney and they gave me the facilities to use, like the fax machine and the telephone, before any Bob Geldof or any Joe Public was known, but I had to abandon that after the stress it was giving me. After three weeks I knocked it on the head but if wasn't for my wife Faye Addison I wouldn't have picked myself up.[16]

Several of the BRAFA members were forthright about what the project meant in terms of race relations. Pauline Reid, of lovers rock pioneers, Brown Sugar, noted that there was a distinct resentment at their exclusion from the Band Aid initiative:

> The images that we saw of the Ethiopian famine in 1984 – I think the press reported it as biblical – and it stung us as a community. It was great of Bob Geldof but there was a lack of representation of black people and black artists that were here, particularly black British artists. It was for me amazing that Leon Leiffer decided to pull this effort together and when you think of how much they raised.

Trevor Walters added:

> It was always being done by a load of white people. We as black people never got the opportunity or were invited, let's put it that way, to do anything or to make a contribution.[17]

Perhaps more importantly there was a real sense of community action at a grass-roots level. Leiffer invited 200 musicians, singers and local schoolchildren to take part in the recording session, rather than considering who had the greatest commercial draw or cultural kudos, which was essentially how Band Aid had been framed, right down to the photo shoot with its clear focus on A-listers. For inclusion in Leiffer's project you didn't have to be somebody of recognised stature:

> Even though the professional musicians and singers were there, we never turned our nose up at anybody. Anybody... the non-singer, the little singer... it was a happy feeling and people were glad to be there.[18]

Inevitably the next stage of the operation was putting on a gig. There was precious little coverage in the national press of BRAFA, which, one can surmise, reflected negative attitudes towards Hackney given its prevailing association with crime, and the stigma that clung to Black people in the wake of the national riots of 1981. West Indians largely passed as thugs not charity workers. Only *The Hackney Echo* put the project on the front page of its edition of Thursday May 15 1986, right next to a piece on television astrologer Russell Grant. The opening lines read 'Black Music Festival in the Park to be held in Shoreditch Park to raise funds for famine-starved Africa'. With no intended irony, the piece spoke of 'Hackney's answer to Live Aid', when it might have been more appropriate to talk of Hackney doing what it saw fit to do *regardless* of the high profile of Live Aid. In any case BRAFA drew an audience of over 10,000 to its event.

BRAFA reflected a spirit of independence in the Black British musical community and its desire to have its voice heard on an important subject should be seen in the wider context of militant activity by expatriate African artists, such as Julian Bahula's 'Freedom Sounds For Mandela' concert, as well as a general reverence for Africa as a spiritual homeland.

The evidence that fundraising for a disaster on the scale of the Ethiopian famine could have been more effective if it included Black British and international Black artists can be seen in an initiative that was roughly contemporary to 'Make Africa Green Again'. This was a double A-sided charity record by the collective Starvation/Tam Tam Pour L'Ethiopie, which pooled the resources of the British reggae and West African music scenes. The first song on the single, 'Starvation', was written by George Agard, Jackie Robinson and Sydney Crooks of Jamaican rocksteady legends, The Pioneers, who performed alongside several of the UK bands they had inspired, such as The Specials, General Public (born of The Beat), Madness and UB 40, along with percussionist Gaspar Lawal, session royalty since the 1970s. The horn section comprised a young English trombonist, Annie Whitehead and trumpeter Dick Cuthell, who was an engineer and producer at Island Records. The second song, 'Tam Tam Pour L'Ethiopie' featured veteran Cameroonian saxophonist Manu Dibango, Nigerian guitarist King Sunny Ade, Malian vocalist Salif Keita and Guinean kora player Mory Kante, who had gone mainstream with a huge global hit 'Yeke Yeke'. The bouncy pop-edged reggae of 'Starvation' is pleasant enough, but 'Tam Tam Pour L'Ethiopie' (Drums for Ethiopia) was especially interesting, with an intriguing patchwork of sounds knitted together over a smart rhythm that uses both traditional percussion and electronic Linn drums played by the peerless Tony Allen, one of the key architects of Afrobeat. As was the case with BRAFA, there is an integrity to the music that matches the nobility of the sentiment behind it, not least by including in the same space artists divided in location by the legacy of the slave trade and divided by language as a result of European colonialism: Jamaicans, Nigerians, Black Britons, Cameroonians, Guineans and Malians. The immense cultural breadth of 'Tam Tam Pour L'Ethiopie' is symbolised by the use of five languages – Douala, Wolof, Lingala, Malinke and Swahili – which gave a pan-African dimension to the whole project. The third track on the 12" single, 'Haunted', placed a British vocal group under the spotlight. The piece was written by Dick Cuthell and had a lead vocal by Satch Dixon, but the sumptuous choruses were sung by an ensemble called Afrodiziak, which comprised Claudia Fontaine, Naomi Thomson and Caron Wheeler (who, a decade before, had been part of lover's rock pioneers, Brown Sugar). They had lent their heavenly harmonies to important political statements such as 'Black Pride' and now they were doing something to make Black people proud, and this gave the 'Starvation/Tam Tam Pour L'Ethiopie' initiative an emotional and conceptual weight that has stood the test of time.

Maybe the ultimate purpose of these songs is to make us rethink what Africa means, or rather embrace the change required in Europe to recognise and redress the role it has played in its underdevelopment. More than occasional act of charity, a major recalibration of the relationship needs to take place.

Notes

1. Interview with the author, September 2022.
2. Ibid.
3. Ibid.
4. *Something Else*, BBC TV, 1980.
5. Ibid.
6. Ibid.
7. Ibid.
8. Sabita Banerji and Gerd Baumann, 'Bhangra 1984-8: Fusion and Professionalisation in a Genre of South Asian Dance Music', in *Black Music in Britain*, ed. Paul Oliver (OUP, 1990).
9. Various artists *Music and Rhythm* (WEA, 1982).
10. Interview with the author, 2005.
11. Robbie Vincent presented a highly influential soul and jazz-funk show on BBC Radio London from the mid 1970s to the mid 1980s.
12. *Woza Albert* by Percy Mtwa, Mbongeni Ngema and Barney Simon opened at the Market Theater in Johannesburg in 1981 and subsequently toured Europe and America.
13. *African Sounds for Mandela*, BBC documentary, 1983.
14. Ibid.
15. Ibid.
16. Hackney Museum On-line, 07 October, 2021.
17. Ibid.
18. Ibid.

18. YOUNG AMERICANS... WHO ARE BLACK AND FROM BRITAIN.

Factory lost a shedload of fans because they went 'Ian Curtis would be turning in his grave if he knew that you'd sell out, doing this disco funky dance stuff!'
— Tony Henry of 52nd Street on cultural politics in Manchester.

Paradise Found
'You Don't haffi dread to be Rasta'. This adage conveys the primacy of religion over fashion, of credo over hairdo, the recognition that locks do not make a true follower of the articles of faith put forward by Bob Marley, Burning Spear, Aswad and other influential reggae artists from Jamaica and Britain. They consolidated an African Caribbean identity around the non-Western cosmology of Rastafarianism. All praises be to Jah, not Jesus. But Christianity still held sway over many in the Black community in post-war Britain, as it had done in Black America where, by the last decades of slavery, most though not all enslaved people were members of the established denominational churches or of unofficial Black-led congregations which were often persecuted. In the Anglophone Caribbean, slave-owners remained hostile to Christian missionaries, particularly Baptists, but after emancipation, church-going massively increased. There was frequently tension between the denominational churches that remained almost wholly led by whites, and independent Black-led churches that Africanised versions of Christianity. Membership of churches with British origins or of the independent 'sects' as they tended to be described, was very much a matter of class, colour and colonial notions of respectability. By the time of postwar West Indian migration to Britain, worshippers came from many denominations, though a growing minority attended the Pentecostal churches that had sprung up rapidly in the 20th century Caribbean, an American import that frequently became Africanised. By the early 1980s, West Indian settlers and their children, often made to feel unwelcome in mainstream churches, found in their own houses of praise the benefits of community leadership, social cohesion and artistic training. With Black churches came gospel music.

This was by no means new. In the 1870s, the Fisk Jubilee Singers, the

African American vocal group discussed in Volume 1, had toured the UK, astounding the great and the good, including Queen Victoria, with their performances of sacred songs, and they had even created a legacy of sorts when one of their members, Thomas Rutland, opted to settle in Harrogate, Yorkshire. He would go on to become a legendary music teacher in the area.

Almost a century later, several choirs rose to prominence during the Thatcher years when Black churches became an ever more important place of emotional solace and material safety from the vioence of the streets and the police brutality that represented a very real danger to Black youth. For parents, keeping their children attached to the church was a form of both sanctuary and opportunity. Quite apart from giving believers the opportunity to lift their voices and sing, churches with bands sometimes made instruments available to those who were minded to learn. In any action shot of a Gospel choir, you'll see a band, usually comprising drums, guitar, bass and organ, the latter providing the emblematic sound associated with Black sacred music.

The exact nature of the relationship between sacred and secular songs has always been fluid and intriguing, with the likes of Al Green, Aretha Franklin, Philip Bailey (of Earth, Wind & Fire) and Rance Allen moving back and forth between the two genres for large parts of their respective careers. And the idea that those who listened to tales of heartbreak or desire would have no truck with compositions dedicated to godly values was challenged by the crossover success of fine 1980s gospel ensembles such as The Winans, an African American group from Detroit, whose 'Let My People Go' was a superb composition that drew its title from the Bible and joined it to a highly political lyric that denounced the evils of apartheid in South Africa.

As important as the song's lyrics were, its arrangement also caught the ear with a combination of jazz, funk and subtle passages of electronic sequencing and drum programming that created a sound palette that was decidedly up-to-date, making it clear that gospel, one of the central pillars of the Western Black music tradition, could evolve with a contemporary approach to writing, performing and production.

In Britain in the 1980s, a new group of young musicians, trained in the church, were developing a gospel-soul hybrid that captured the imagination of mainstream Black music listeners. Paradise was centred on two musical families, the Edwards (bassist, Junior and organist, Phil) and the Crosses (pianist, Victor and drummer, Billy, brothers of the talented lovers rock singer, Sandra Cross). Their place of worship was the Calvary Temple Church in south London. The group later picked up multi-instrumentalist Lincoln Anderson, and became The Reapers,[1] before the arrival of singers Doug Williams and Paul Johnson.

Weaned on the standard gospel repertoire of Black churches up and down the country, players such as Anderson had taken a keen interest in the cutting edge of African American secular music in its many transformations in sound and structure. The new approaches to rhythm and the embrace of electric instruments of the 'fusion' era greatly inspired The Reapers just as it had the roughly contemporaneous Brit-funk and jazz-funk bands like Light of the World, discussed in previous chapters. These two ensembles shared similar references, namely The Crusaders, Herbie Hancock and Chick Corea, though there was a divide between them in terms of lyrical content and the venues in which they appeared.

LOTW evoked the unabashed glamour and hedonism of 'dancin' and swingin' whilst The Reapers penned lyrics that upheld wholesome Christian principles. Yet Light of the World – a nod to funk combo Kool & The Gang's 1974 album *Light of Worlds* – was actually how Jesus defined himself in debate with the Jews in John 8:12. This uncannily mirrored the final name change of The Reapers when they became Paradise, the place of perfect fulfilment that Jesus promised the thieves crucified alongside him. Originally, the band was called Return to Paradise, which was a nod to Corea's seminal jazz-rock ensemble Return to Forever.

The young Londoners also lent an ear to reggae and this chain of secular-religious references underlined the way the line between sacred and profane had long been crossed in African-Diasporan music, though some in the churches were dogmatic about what constituted an *acceptable* gospel song. Thus, when Paradise decided to break with standard templates, there was no small amount of fire and brimstone hurled at them, as manager Mike Martin recalls:

> We have had several distasteful comments about presenting the Gospel through our particular style of music. I believe every person is entitled to their opinion, but as Christians we must be careful not to let our opinions or tastes hinder the growth of other Christians. God is not restricted to one particular way. God can work through any form of music; we do not have to conform to one particular style.[2]

Vocalist Doug Williams noted more specific reasons for the flak:

> Because we were not afraid to use contemporary sounds, we were labelled as being 'worldly', especially compared to the conservative and very traditional Pentecostal stuff. We did the outrageous thing of playing reggae on our albums and that was the devil's music.[3]

That troublesome eclecticism defined the three excellent albums Paradise recorded between 1980 and 1983 – their eponymous debut, *Paradise*, *World's Midnight* and *Love Is the Answer*. Their merits rested on the impressive writing and arranging of the band that enriched melodic skills with a finesse that largely drew on their love for jazz-fusion.

The best track Paradise ever made, a brilliant single called 'One Mind Two Hearts', became a hit in soul circles, and although the gospel identity of the band was never denied, the lyric could be read as both a romantic ode and a devotional piece. Above all, the arrangement offered a series of effective contrasts, from understated piano chords and guitar picking, to clipped, incisive percussion and emphatic synth stabs that were all carefully placed around a lead vocal that glides over the pulse with understated authority. It was delivered in a falsetto pitch that fitted into the lineage of soul legends reared in the church, such as Curtis Mayfield.

This was sophisticated soul music that was deeply rooted in gospel, trading the familiar vocabulary of hot Hammond organ riffs and rousing harmonies for a sound palette that had considerable nuance and attention to detail, comparing favourably to the music of African-American pace-setters such as Anita Baker and Luther Vandross. Paradise did not record more than the aforesaid albums, though its vocalist Paul Johnson later embarked on a solo career of some note.

Another group that emerged at roughly the same time and ploughed a more traditional furrow in bringing together many voices as a kind of congregation on stage was the London Community Gospel Choir (L.C.G.C). Under the direction of the Reverend Bazil Meade, this powerful vocal ensemble had a political premise insofar as it drew members from the many denominations of the Black churches in the capital rather than defining itself as strictly Pentecostal or Adventist, and this united front resonated with the group's desire to foster a rehabilitation of the West Indian community in the wake of the early 1980s riots.

Buoyed by a show-stopping appearance on the television show *Black on Black*, L.C.G.C. gathered considerable momentum, particularly when they recorded a single 'Fill My Cup' that crossed over onto soul radio, with Invicta as an early champion. The track had a tightly regulated funk groove and a bumping boogie-style bassline that worked effectively with the sweeping crescendos of the 27-strong choir. Again, the use of the glowing polyphonic keyboards – one of the dominant sounds of soul at the time – made the song strike a chord with clubgoers. Smartly turned out, with female choir members in modestly cut dresses and men in dark suits – barring Reverend Meade who wore a natty grey number – L.C.G.C. had a freshness about them that broke the image of the ultra starchy Caribbean choirs which encased women in neat two-piece skirt suits, gloves and pillbox hats as necessary manifestations of sanctity.

While 'Fill My Cup' had fine singing and playing it was also enhanced by the input of the highly talented sound engineer, Godwin Logie, whose work behind the scenes at the mixing desk really deserved to be recognised. A key member of the production staff at Island Records, Logie had worked with leading reggae artists such as Black Uhuru and Inner Circle, and had brought a fantastically crisp, clear sound to David Joseph, a former member of Hi-Tension, who in 1983 was enjoying a sizeable club hit with 'You Can't Hide Your Love.'[4]

With its imaginatively flute-like, charmingly funky keyboards, the vibrato pronounced so as to lend a whistling feel to the notes, and bubbling bassline, the song had a progressive sound that compared favourably to any dance music being made by Americans. In fact, there was also a mix by the legendary New York DJ Larry Levan. But though it was a massive floor filler, 'You Can't Hide Your Love' did not achieve commensurate mainstream success. This was at a time when the so-called 'Brit funk' wave had already started to decline as the early pacesetters Hi-Tension, LOTW, Linx, Second Image, Freeez, and Central Line were either disbanding for good or entering a long period of recording inactivity. By the mid-1980s, Imagination, after enjoying a run of hits, were falling from their commercial peak, while Level 42, who'd had scant success with a jazz-inclined sound, made a mainstream breakthrough with songs that were significantly more pop-slanted. By contrast, a number of white acts, who were heavily influenced by soul and disco, notably Spandau Ballet, achieved big commercial success, and even though they flagged up their influences clearly enough, name-checking Marvin Gaye on their number one single 'True', they were marketed as mainstream pop.

Beginning of the Ends

New names, new energy, new ideas were needed in Black British music. Another generation of artists had to be nurtured, which was the scenario played out by the London combo, Loose Ends. They were given a big break when trumpeter-pianist-composer, Steve Nichol, handed over a song on his Walkman to A&R man, Mick Clark, who had brokered a deal for the highly original I-Level with Virgin a few years before and now did the same for Loose Ends. It had up to nine players involved, but the core was Nichol, vocalist Jayne Eugene and bassist-guitarist-vocalist Carl McIntosh, who were all of Jamaican heritage. Their debut single, 'We've Arrived', was a competent piece of mid-tempo soul; the follow up, 'In the Sky', marked a step forward in its arrangement and richness of instrumentation. The song was produced by Chris and Eddie Amoo of The Real Thing, whose manager, Tony Hall (who issued music by Jamaican jazz legend Dizzy Reece in the 1950s) had also added Loose Ends to his roster. Chris Amoo recalled:

> The band was on Virgin, and they got on to Tony and asked him if we would produce them. They had a song called 'In the Sky', so me and Eddie took them into the studio, but we realised straightaway that the

line-up wasn't good enough to do what we wanted. So, we took Steve Nichol, Carl McIntosh and Jayne Eugene aside and said we're gonna bring in a few guys to work alongside you. Carl said fine. So we brought in drummer Nigel Martinez, guitarist Victor Linton and a keyboard player and put them, Carl, Jayne and Steve together. We also sang on 'In the Sky ', too. It was a very good track.[5]

Despite the artistic success of the collaboration and the support lent to the band by the specialist Black music press and radio, the direction of Loose Ends was still not entirely set, and there was a change of producer for the next single, 'Don't Hold Back Your Love'. This was Peter Walsh, known for his work with the Sex Pistols, a choice that embodied the incongruity of Virgin's foray into soul. Carl McIntosh soon realised that Loose Ends were signed to a label that was broaching uncharted territory. As he said, 'These guys were rockers, basically. There are no black music personnel that know black music or dance music in that division of A&R. We were totally lost.'[6]

Yet if that mismatch was worrying, the clinching of a US deal with the MCA label was major progress. Just as David Bowie had done in the 1970s, Loose Ends headed to the legendary Sigma studio in Philadelphia to become new 'Young Americans' who happened to be Black and from Britain. While in the city of brotherly love, Loose Ends would meet many of their heroes, including saxophonist Grover Washington jnr, vocalist Phyllis Hyman, keyboardist-arranger Dexter Wansel – all of whom were monumental figures in the canon of jazz-fusion and soul, typified by the lushly produced song, 'The Sound of Philadelphia' (T.S.O.P), which heralded a series of unforgettable anthems on love and politics that became to the 1970s what Motown had been to the 1960s.

The man who shaped the destiny of Loose Ends was a young producer called Nick Martinelli, an Italian American who was building his profile through work with popular soul artists such as Change, Tavares and Evelyn 'Champagne' King. Nichol referred to Martinelli as 'the fourth member' of the band, because he created the sonic soundscape for the original material, enhancing the songs through his interest in new technology and the aesthetic of the 'remix' where the sequencing and programming of rhythms vied with the input of 'real instruments'. When he heard a new Nichol-McIntosh composition, 'Hanging on a String', Martinelli decided that it should be adapted to capture the flavour of two cutting-edge American producers, Jam & Lewis, who were enjoying huge success through their work with acts such as the SOS band. The result was sensational. On its release in 1985, 'Hanging on a String' became a Transatlantic hit, climbing to number 13 in the UK Singles chart and topping the Billboard R&B chart, a feat that had never before been achieved by a British band.

Similarities between the beat used by Loose Ends and Jam & Lewis may have fed a longstanding narrative that where the Americans led, the British followed, but it would be equally valid to contend that 'Hanging on a String' was essentially a US-UK collaboration, under the aegis of a Philadelphia producer. More to the point, the distinctively sharp flicker and metallic texture of the percussive rhythm heralded what was to be a sea change in Black popular music.

The arrival of the 'numbers gear' – Roland 808, MPC 60, MPC 3000 Linn 9000 – was forcing a reassessment of both writing and producing. If you could find the sounds you wanted to hear on a single machine it saved the expense of bringing in a bunch of session players. Yet if the patented groove of Jam & Lewis, who would later snub a collaboration with Loose Ends in favour of one with British synth-pop stars, The Human League, was at the core of the sound of 'Hanging on a String', there is no denying the breadth of creativity in the arrangement. While Carl McIntosh and Jayne Eugene's voices belonged to an established duet tradition, here they were used on a tight funk track rather than the more common romantic ballad. The combination of thick slabs of synth bass and the grinding pentatonic guitar lines lent solidity to a medium tempo arrangement, making it heavy without being busy. What created real communion on the dancefloor was the way the chorus glided upwards before hitting the rhyming rejoinder of 'You never told me you were waiting, contemplating'. That heavenly line made it clear that Loose Ends had the ability to add myriad melodic layers to a basic song structure; this amounted to much more than being Jam & Lewis lite. Indeed, the repertoire they created over four albums – *A Little Spice, So Where Are You?, Zagora* and *The Real Chuckeeboo* – displayed a musical ambition much greater than any naysayers claimed. Stylistically, they had range. The hints of Jamaican riddim that underpinned 'Johnny Broadhead', the breezy Latin beats flowing through the title track of 'A Little Spice' and above all the wonderfully subtle harmonic landscape of 'Gonna Make You Mine' point to Nichol's classical training and McIntosh's ingenuity as a multi-instrumentalist. Asking to what extent this was British or American soul seems less important than recognising the coherence with which Loose Ends straddled genres as well as geographical spaces. Taken as a whole, their songbook built a bridge between funk, electronica, dub and jazz, which made them much more than an average R&B act. They created soul music with a sophistication that was not alien to improvising musicians.

In sartorial flair and promotional design they were glamour incarnate. But there was an edge. Carl McIntosh had dreadlocks at a time when this was mostly unheard of for soul boys. He wasn't a Rastafarian but he sported a key symbol of reggae culture. There were few if any American R&B artists who did that. Loose Ends also performed energetic dance moves, of which McIntosh's simultaneous over-the-head handclap and knee-raise to waist height was the stuff of legend. And these Londoners enjoyed success beyond their wildest dreams. Making it big in the States for artists in their twenties led to surreal experiences. As McIntosh recalled years later with a beaming smile:

> The whole thing in America was an eye opener. I'm not sure where to start with it. It's so big, I mean you go from not being able to get any airplay in your own country to Number One in America. It's incredible. We were getting into limos and the phone was ringing with chart predictions of number one next week. There's motorbikes each side of the limo. It's madness, just ordinary people in the limo. We'd go to restaurants like that if we can. I wanna go to the West Indian shop… bring the motorbikes![7]

Inevitably, the success created pressure. Long tours, notably with Freddie Jackson, one of the biggest new names in soul in the 1980s, started to take their toll on Loose Ends, and disagreements over the creative direction of the group led to Steve Nichol, Jane Eugene and Carl McIntosh going their separate ways, though the latter did resume work under the original name of the band in 1990. Their body of work has more than stood the test of time and they joined the many other notable acts in the history of Black music in Britain who would find themselves lionised by a new generation of hip-hop and R&B producers in the millennium.

Another Northern Soul
In their heyday, Loose Ends made many dynamic appearances on *Top of the Pops* and were introduced to the audience by DJs such as Janice Long, one of the few females to break into the all-male cabal of Radio One presenters of the show. She called them 'the best soul band in the country.' That may well have been true but a Liverpudlian such as Long would have been interested to know that in Manchester there was a group that could also lay claim to that superlative, even though their profile was considerably lower. 52nd Street was one of the best British groups of the 1980s in any genre. Their blend of elements was formidable. Tony Henry, John Dennison and Tony Bowry were excellent players and writers; Diane Charlemagne was one of the outstanding singers of her generation, and Ten Records, a subsidiary of the Virgin label, made the right call in sending them to Philadelphia in 1985 to make *Children of the Night*, an impressive debut album that consolidated their reputation.

Songs such as 'Tell Me (How It Feels)', 'Look I've Heard', 'I Can't Let You Go', and the title track had the right quotient of melodic beauty, rhythmic ingenuity and textural creativity, created by a skilled use of synthesizers and electronica, to compare favourably with the work of any contemporary soul, rock and pop acts.

Although the involvement of producer Nick Martinelli may have lent 52nd Street kudos, as it did their British peers, Loose Ends, it was really the compositional quality of their material, particularly the way they switched from winsome melancholy to a darker, moodier energy, that excelled. 'You're My Last Chance' has a finely crafted verse that builds to a powerful release of tension in the chorus, accentuating the force and fragility of Charlemagne's voice against a backdrop of wobbly keyboard bass and whirring, vapour trails of noise. The synth timbres were enticing but also ghostly. A dissonant nails-on-the-blackboard scratch, very similar to that used thrillingly on in a new machine-based funk called electro, underscored a lyric that described the troubled state of mind of an individual on the verge of a breakdown, a lost soul crying out for help. A purring Brazilian cuica in the latter stage of the song consolidated the punchy, piercing clavé beats that were at the rhythmic centre of the arrangement, giving it an understated but perceptible Latin American character. This was a very modern piece of soul music that had a producer's sheen yet still enough heart to keep it from being swallowed whole by a machine aesthetic. Or maybe the relationship between producer and band at this point yielded a fruitful creative synergy.

The clout Martinelli had in the industry because of his big chart hits, several with Loose Ends, made him an obvious choice of collaborator but there were limitations in terms of the palette he sought to craft for the band. There was too great a focus on programming and not enough on live playing to really suit 52nd Street. In fact, Tony Henry, a talented guitarist who was the centrifugal force of the band, was less keen on working with Martinelli, more in recording at the legendary Sigma studio in Philadelphia, where other Brits – Loose Ends and David Bowie – had also worked.

But 52nd Street had already won over fans in America through their second single, 'Cool as Ice', which had made the Billboard chart, and the buzz was enhanced by further releases, 'Can't Afford' and 'You're My Last Chance', so there was a healthy interest in the young Mancunians when they flew out to record in Philadelphia in the summer of 1984. As Tony Henry recalled:

> Sigma was booked for the summer. We got to meet all these legends... Teddy Pendergrass, even though he was wheelchair bound at the time. Terri Wells, the crème de la crème of Philadelphia came in to see us because they were all dead fascinated with Diane (Charlemagne)'s voice. The moment news got out that there was this British girl and her voice is just phenomenal they all came over.[8]

But the visitor the band was most star-struck by was Phyllis Hyman, one of the great soul and jazz singers of the 1970s and 80s. 'She was 6ft 1 in heels and smelled of heaven', recalled Henry. Such was the impact the Brits were making, they were even actively considered as writers for Hyman's next album. Hence 'Children of the Night' and 'I Can't Let You Go' were initially earmarked for her, but Martinelli was so impressed with the melodies that he vetoed the idea, knowing that they were integral to the artistic statement of the album. 'He listens to the songs and says you *can't* give that to Phyllis Hyman,' said Henry wryly.

Martinelli was not, though, retained as producer on 52nd Street's second album *Something's Going On*. That responsibility went to a musician highly respected for his work with Miles Davis and Chick Corea, as well as his own solo projects at the height of the fusion years. This was American drummer and composer, Lenny White. Perhaps unsurprisingly, given his jazz background, White struck much more of a chord with Tony Henry who was astounded by the phenomenal cast of supporting musicians who were recruited for the recording, including saxophonist Michael Brecker, one of the great exponents of his instrument in the 1980s.

Recorded in 1986, *Something's Going On* marked a considerable shift in the evolution of 52nd Street because there was a greater balance between studio production, the use of technological means, and live instrumentation. On the one hand, there were songs such 'Are You Receiving Me?', a startling mosaic of strange shards and slivers of noise that was created from a session in which Henry and White focused their attention on the sonic possibilities of Roland, Juno and Jupiter synthesizers. On the other hand, there was 'What Did I Do Wrong?', an affecting ballad about the travails of a single parent. Finally, there was the magnificent title track, a harmonically sophisticated piece with smart shifts of tempo and rhythm that was the nearest 52nd Street came to the jazz anthems that had been a major source of inspiration during their formative years.

As Henry recalls, the experience of making *Something's Going On* was greatly enhanced by the genial atmosphere in the studio, partly because of the slew of accomplished players who stopped by to see what the Brits were up to, following the success of their first album. White's stature in jazz and soul was reflected by the company he kept. 'Bernard Wright, Weldon Irvine, Stanley Clarke, Marcus Miller (all solo artists who, between them, had played with Tom Browne, Nina Simone, Pharoah Sanders, Miles Davis, Luther Vandross and Aretha Franklin) were all hanging around the studio,' Henry explained with a chuckle. 'I mean all the people we grew up listening to because of the connection with Lenny White.'

For their part, the African Americans were intrigued by the presence of the African Caribbeans from the north of England. They learned things. As Henry reported:

> We've got a couple of characters in our band. The Americans loved Tony Bowry who would just keep you up all night with stories. They'd all come to the studio hang around with us but they'd all want Tony to

tell them stories about Withenshaw and Moss Side in Manchester. The Americans just loved it and they loved his voice. So they all just came to the studio, some of them played and some just hung around and had a chat with us. They were people that we'd hero-worshipped.[9]

Sadly, *Something's Going On*, with its higher degree of experimentation and risk taking, did not fare well commercially, and it marked the beginning of the strained final phase of 52nd Street that would end with an album being recorded and aborted in the late 1980s. That ill-fated project took them to Los Angeles for a year, where life in the Hollywood Hills, with neighbours including Madonna, provided little succour to Tony Henry, who saw his material being discarded when a power struggle took place as a new producer, John Barnes, sought to impose his own vision on the group.

It was all a long way from Manchester. Or rather Bolton, where Tony Henry was born and raised. His Jamaican parents had previously lived in Birmingham but were drawn to the north by the prospect of work on the railways and in civil engineering in the 1950s, though Henry's father was actually a shoemaker who found gainful employment in the Timpson's chain. At the age of eight, Henry played a sidedrum in the local Boys Brigade, the London branch of which had incidentally supplied brass instruments to 'Brit funk' heroes Light of the World. Later, he took up guitar, playing in a small band in church, soaking up gospel to complement the reggae, country, soul and jazz on the family Dansette. By the age of fifteen, Henry was in a rock band doing Beatles covers before he formed Solid Heat, a jazz-funk ensemble whose bassist, Wayne Ellis, went on to front a Thin Lizzy tribute act called Limehouse Lizzy. Henry gigged in Leeds, Scotland and Wales in the late 1970s and his band was offered the chance to support The Elgins, a lesser known Motown act from the 1960s who now had no original members but were using Black British singers to keep their franchise alive. It was a turning point because Henry saw that working on the nostalgia circuit clashed with his ambition to be an original artist, and he had to make a choice. There was also an interesting crossing of paths with a soon to be famous UK group . As Henry noted:

> We went to Stoke Newington in London. The Elgins were these singers and musicians called Ashley Ingram, Leee John and Errol Kennedy. Really, they were training us up to take over; they'd had enough and wanted to pass it on to another set of musicians. We were excited for about a day, then we looked at each other when we went back to the hotel and said, I don't think this is us. So the next day I said to Ashley and Leee, You know what, I've enjoyed being with you but we wanna make it on our own. We don't wanna be a back up band. So we went back home and carried on gigging. Next thing we saw *Top of the Pops*…Leee and Ashley were there as Imagination![10]

Solid Heat plied their trade in Bolton, but Henry, for practical reasons, was spending more time in Manchester. He went to the city's instrument shops such as A1 to buy guitar strings and it was there that he met local players such as bassist Derrick Johnson, drummer Tony Thompson, and keyboard player John Dennison, who were looking for a guitarist to join a band that performed soul and jazz-funk. They already had a guitarist, but they thought he was 'a bit biblical', which was ironic because, as noted at the start of this chapter, it was in the churches that young African Caribbeans had access to good musical training, and two of the best known players in Manchester, Barry and Lawrence Stewart, were weaned on sacred music. There was also a band called The Faithful Youth Challengers, (later The Challengers), whose profile was raised when it branched out into the secular world, appearing at the Manchester jazz venue, The Band on the Wall, and also in a Granada television documentary.

The Black Factory
Tony Henry started jamming with the musicians he met at A1 and finding that they had a much higher standards than the Bolton crew, he signed up and moved to Manchester permanently in 1979, settling in the historic West Indian area, Moss Side. The band became 52nd Street. In the late 1970s and early 1980s, the Manchester soul scene did not have a high national profile. The biggest act, Sweet Sensation, who had enjoyed a hit with 'Sad Sweet Dreamer', had disbanded, though its golden-voiced singer, Marcel King, was still performing. Most of the active bands were not known outside the city and in some cases personnel overlapped. For example, Adventure was founded by saxophonist Eric Gooden, who would later join 52nd Street, while Spooky was born of the ashes of Sweet Sensation and featured their drummer Mike Hallyday. Also launching a solo career was vocalist, Rikki Patrick, who had formerly replaced Marcel King in Sweet Sensation. By consensus, the hottest local funk act was The Reality Band who Henry remembers as 'a cross between Hi-Tension and LOTW' and he lamented the fact that they never managed to get signed. Even so, there was a healthy club scene. Since the early 1970s, The Twisted Wheel, had been a temple of Northern Soul, and others followed, playing soul, funk, jazz and Latin music, such as Placemate 7, Rafters, Rufus, Legends and Club Berlin. Among the local DJs, Colin Curtis and Mike Shaft, both of whom, especially the former, were highly rated by other selectors in London and the South, were the most renowned.

Despite this local Black musical talent pool, Manchester was known first and foremost for the post-punk of Joy Division and the record label that championed it, Factory, founded by Tony Wilson, a broadcaster on Granada television, and Alan Erasmus. Joy Division had made a breakthrough with their albums *Unknown Pleasures* and *Closer*, winning plaudits from NME and BBC Radio One's John Peel, but following the suicide of lead singer, Ian Curtis, there was a huge void to be filled.

Although Factory has been perceived as a purveyor of white British rock, it had a Black music input from its early days, through the band A Certain Ratio, whose drummer, Donald Johnson, anchored the sparks of abrasive noise around him and infused it with an infectious very danceable funk. He was also the brother of 52nd Street's original bassist, Derrick Johnson. At the instigation of A&R man Rob Gretton, a major Black music fan, Factory signed 52nd Street, much to the dismay of talent scouts busy touting the band to majors like RCA and Warner, who could not see the logic in a soul band throwing in its lot with 'that punk label'. But it made sense because the love of soul music was soaked into the walls of Mancunian clubs. Rob Gretton had a vision for Factory to be reborn with a funkier, dancefloor friendly character, so the signing of 52nd Street, whose debut single, 'Cool as Ice/Twice as Nice', created a buzzing clubland vibe, made sense. As if to consolidate the shift, guitarist Bernard Sumner, an original member of Joy Division, signed up to the new recruits. Tony Henry explained:

> Within a month of us being with Factory, Bernard joined the band. Rob said to him you need to go with these guys and learn from them. So all of a sudden Bernard was at rehearsals, gigging with us. He had a little moog synthesizer making all sorts of squawky noises at the back. People used to come to us and say who's the white guy? Oh that's Barney! He used to come to all-dayers with us. There's a great interview of Bernard talking about his times with 52nd Street. The thing with the white press is… Bernard always says to me 'Tony, countless times I tell them about 52nd Street and the importance of that band on Factory and they don't want to print it.'[11]

Given the lingering contempt for disco of many rock writers, with soul being tainted by association, it is little surprise that the history of 'Black Factory' has been hidden. Bristol bands such as The Pop Group and Rip, Rig & Panic showed that punk, avant-garde jazz and funk could make for interesting bedfellows, but the grip of tribalism has been hard to loosen. Or was the fact that 52nd Street were not American – the 'real thing' – part of the problem?

In any case, after the band started to attract interest in America, Gretton tracked down Marcel King from Sweet Sensation and signed him to make a quite brilliant song in 1984, 'Reach for Love', that showcased the beauty of King's voice as well as Bernard Sumner and Donald Johnson's ability to produce soulful electronic grooves that would fill any floor, such as at a new club called The Hacienda. This had opened just a few years before.

It was part of Rob Gretton's masterplan to pivot Factory away from punk and towards dance music, and when Sumner founded New Order and the band had a huge hit with a beat-heavy track, 'Blue Monday', the vision was on the way to being fulfilled. But Tony Henry, having had first-hand experience of the sequence of events, makes an interesting point about the tiresome culture wars that ensued, revealing in the process the blatant bias that has had an impact on prevailing historical narratives:

> Factory lost a shedload of fans because they went, 'Ian Curtis would be turning in his grave if he knew that you'd sell out, doing this disco funky dance stuff!' But Bernard Sumner was doing music that he'd always wanted to do. On car journeys when we talked about Clash and Elvis Costello, Bernard talked about Janet and Michael Jackson, Shep Pettibone (the great New York producer-remixer) and Kashif (a big name in 1980s soul). We were looking at each other going 'Bernard, you are a soul boy!' And he just laughed! We were like, how have you gotten away with it all these years, being really into black music but being forced to do punk? And he just said, well you know, that's life, really.
>
> A lot of people come to my website today and they say Oh, I didn't know how influential 52nd Street were to Factory. But it's not the done thing to say it, because people don't want to associate signing 52nd Street with getting their main people from the label to learn the rhythms we were producing and taking that back to their bands.[12]

Tony Henry was well aware that the dominant image of soul music in some quarters was as a genre that lacked the 'cool' of punk or reggae. Yet it wasn't as if cultural-racial lines weren't being crossed on the Manchester scene. Magazine, arguably one of the most interesting of post-punk groups, had an excellent black bassist, Barry Adamson, who nailed the popping groove of their cover of Sly & The Family Stone's timeless 'Thank You (Falettinme Be Mice Elf Agin)'. The funk was too good to forego. Having said that, acting funky could be problematic. When 52nd Street played the Hacienda, they did the unthinkable. They *talked* to the audience, they engaged with people. It broke with the orthodoxy of aloofness if not haughty aggression that defined the bulk of punk bands and reinforced the perception of soul as something soft if not self-indulgent, a sin compounded by the band's commitment to stretches of improvisation. Guitar solos drew the ire of Factory bosses.

If differences of opinion existed on musical aesthetics, there was also a wider backdrop of negative attitudes towards people of colour in a city like Manchester, which, like Birmingham, Bolton, Bristol, Liverpool, London and Nottingham, had been rocked by major civil disturbances in the years that immediately preceded the rise of the Hacienda. Many city centre venues did not welcome a largely black clientele and enforced the most superficial rules to deny access – above all, the 'No hats' line. In fact, socialising in the north came with certain caveats that had to be observed, as those who came of age at the time attest. Aniff Akinola, a Mancunian of Jamaican heritage, who along with pianist-producer Colin Thorpe formed the soul-jazz act, Chapter & The Verse in the late 1980s, reports an undercurrent of racism:

> As a black kid when you'd go out in town on Saturday, you weren't getting drunk. Black kids didn't get drunk, you couldn't *risk* being drunk Your only safe space would be in your shebeens and after things clubs. Those places would have a higher number of black people. I think in the other places I'd say that the black kids went in groups and they stuck together and were very kind of protective of one another.

They would travel outside of the city but that also entailed dangers.

> I remember going to Scotland. I've got a scar on the side of my head where it kicked off, where Glaswegians didn't take nicely to black guys being in Glasgow. It was the mid 80s, I remember. But you know I went to a club in Wigan not far from Wigan Casino; it's called Cassanelli's, it's a restaurant but they used to do a night there once a month. Somebody gave me a lift there and they said I can't give you a lift back. So I thought shit, I'm stuck. It's about 20 miles away. I started to walk home. I'm walking in bleached jeans, Cuban heels, suede tasselled jacket. The culture of thumbing a lift and hitch hiking was still prevalent then. I thought let me try. So I get down the road and I actually passed the Wigan Casino. First car drives past... aaaah no luck... Second car... 'Fuck off you black bastard!' The thumb went back in its pocket and it's never been out since. My point being that who you were and *where* you were created a vulnerability for us in them days. And that had an effect on nights you'd attend, where you'd go and who you'd go with and how you'd behave in them places.[13]

This is one of the reasons why the Hacienda, regardless of it being part of Factory, a commercial operation that had roots in the punk scene, was important for the growth of integration in the Manchester club scene, at least in terms of the visibility of people of colour within the upper echelons of the management structure. Akinlola recalled that:

> The licensee of The Hacienda was a black guy, Leroy Richardson. His name was over the Factory door! If you're running a business and you punt on a black guy in Manchester under Chief Inspector James Anderton (who notoriously advocated going in 'fast and hard' during the Moss Side riots in the 1980s) it tells me that you don't give a shit!
> You were putting black people in positions of power without con-

demnation. Those were important things because I certainly didn't know any other places that have got a black licensee over the door and we saw Leroy behind the bar with black staff. It meant a lot.[13]

Notes

1. There is a later all-female group also called The Reapers.
2. Steve Alexander Smith, *British Black Gospel* (Monarch, 2009), p.161.
3. Ibid, p.163.
4. David Joseph, *You Can't Hide Your Love* (Mango/Island) 1983.
5. Interview with the author, May 2022.
6. Red Bull Music Academy, 3 September 2017.
7. Ibid.
8. Interview with the author, August 2022.
9. Ibid
10. Ibid
11. Ibid.
12. Ibid.
13. Ibid.

19 THE WORLD HEARS THE GHETTO

'Rhythmic in a rub a dub style... in a different style... him skank it in a ragga man style... him skank it in a yard man style. Him born a Chapeltown where de culture is strong.'
— Edward Lynch, Phoenix Dance Company, Leeds

'They just assumed I was American.'
— Juliet Roberts, Working Week, London.

'An A&R man came to one of our gigs and the feedback... what he said to our manager was they're great dancers and great singers, but the guy third from the end is too black. That was me.'
— Mark Swaby, Jazz Defektors, Manchester.

Gained in translation
In November 1982, the *Times Education Supplement* published an article by Ray Honeyford, a Manchester-born teacher who worked in a school in Bradford. The op-ed followed two letters by Honeyford to the same publication, and a controversial article in the right-wing *Salisbury Review*, criticising the idea of multiculturalism. It railed against falling standards in schools with high numbers of pupils of Indian, Bangladeshi and Pakistani heritage, and argued against the idea that 'British-born Asian children [could] begin their mastery of English by being taught in Urdu.' Language was a source of conflict.

The resulting controversy led to Honeyford's suspension, though he was later reinstated. Honeyford took potshots at the 'political correctness' that led to his removal, cementing the idea that he was bold enough to put his head above the parapet and say what the silent majority was thinking. In England, everybody had a duty to speak English because the persistence of other languages was a threat to a coherent 'British/English' cultural identity. Yet though reduced to diametrically opposed positions, a folk hero for the right and hate figure for the Asian community, Honeyford was broaching an important subject, though he expressed it in a crudely offensive way, in denial of historical realities. Honeyford failed to ask why people from the ex-Raj, ghettoised in a single area of one city might be inclined to hold onto their own language, especially when thuggish white youth and mainstream television sitcoms[1] poured scorn on the accent and vocabulary of Asians who *did* speak English, though they had no problem eating their food. It was not easy to stomach that pick 'n' mix attitude when you were being 'othered'. Brown people were here only to serve and be mocked in the process.

Since the beginning of Empire, Britain's language had itself been colonised in reverse, not least in the field of music where both instruments and genres brought new nouns into the mainstream. Words that are now taken for granted – tabla, sitar, ska or reggae – came to enhance the English lexicon because there simply was no English equivalent for them. The reality has always been the coexistence and cross-fertilisation of languages and those who have attempted to keep languages and culture 'pure' have always failed miserably. However, this did not prevent the hypocrisy of those who insisted on only English being spoken in Bradford when few British colonial settlers in the Empire had ceased to speak English or bothered to learn the languages of the countries under their rule.

By contrast, a true visionary, the African American singer-actor-political activist, Paul Robeson, sat down in the library of the School of Oriental and African Studies in London in the 1920s to broaden his mind with the vocabulary of Asante, Ga and Twi because he saw the value of what were then commonly known as the 'barbarous dialects' of the Dark Continent. He did not think that these tongues were in any way backward or beneath the rank of common western languages. Robeson was in keeping with the development of scientific linguistics that recognised the intellectual equality of all mother tongues and lamented the disappearance of any language as a loss of a unique and necessary diversity in the world.

Perhaps with no intended nod to the Honeyford Affair, a new band by the name of Fun Boy Three, whose members Terry Hall, Neville Staple and Lynval Golding were formerly part of Coventry's 2 Tone heroes, The Specials, released a thought-provoking song 'Our Lips are Sealed', which took aim at power, whether of a faceless corporation or a repressive government. Set to a languorous beat that perfectly suited the understated, plaintive vocal, the track came in two versions. The B-side featured lyrics in Urdu.

Any research on England as a multi-lingual as well as multi-cultural society should lend an ear to this mesmerising work. For many of us, the Urdu side was impossible to understand, but the finesse of the music, the grace of the rhythm and beauty of the sound of the language were undeniable. Striking too was the idea of two vocabularies permeating the same artistic space. Such multilingualism was by no means a novel idea. Popular music had exhibited such tendencies for years, as exemplified by Louis Armstrong's French songs, Nat 'King' Cole's Spanish and David Bowie's German.

As the Honeyford affair lingered, in 1984 a single was released that told a story that further fed into the debate on 'linguistic confusion'. 'Cockney Translation' by Smiley Culture, a South London dee-jay of Jamaican heritage, was a light-hearted but meaningful evocation of the reality of a world where the lexicons of the East End of London and the 'back o' yard' of Kingston coexisted and interacted, creating a cultural duality that through the verve of the artist's performance showed an enrichment rather than an impoverishment of the contemporary British society from which it flowed. The accompanying video took place in a school classroom and the artist was cast in the role of a friendly teacher. All the kids were Black.

The song's sparse drum and bass foundation, flecked by piano syncopations that were ear-catching jolts to the steadiness of the meter, was a perfect foil for the fluidity of Smiley's lyrics. His narrative was smartly constructed insofar as he observed not just the differences between the Jamaican and English vernaculars, but the wider naming traditions into which they fitted. Cockneys were called Terry, Arthur and Del Boy, Jamaicans were Winston, Lloyd and Leroy; Cockneys had mates, Jamaicans had spars; Cockneys called the police the Old Bill, Jamaicans dubbed them dutty Babylon; Cockneys used the homophobic slur of iron (iron hoof = poof), Jamaicans said batty man; Cockneys gave encouragement in the form of 'Be first my son!', Jamaicans hollered: 'We just say g'wan!'

'Cockney Translation' made it clear that 'common people', Black and white, expressed themselves with a richness that, although developed outside of books, would eventually be the subject of them. 18th-century 'scholars' had derided a West Indian poet writing in Latin as no more than an imitative parrot, but here was a 20th-century Dee-Jay flying over a forest of words like a hummingbird. Smiley's informal reportage laid bare what he heard around him without adopting a judgmental stance, except that whilst he celebrated invention, he did not condone insult. He simply told the world what he heard, what he knew about the way people *really* spoke, recognising that Britain was in the grip of linguistic change. Code switching between formal and informal modes of speech had always been a pragmatic and necessary part of a lived reality for Black people; Smiley Culture astutely recognised the existence of new, hybrid codes.

'Police Officer', the follow-up single to 'Cockney Translation' announced Smiley as an important new force in British reggae in the early 1980s. It adopted a similarly witty approach to the much more contentious issue of the relationship between the police and Black youth, with Smiley using his timbral flexibility to move between his natural voice and an imitation of 'the old bill' who is carrying out a stop and search and arrest. The song has a bitterly ironic legacy because the artist later lost his life in a police raid on his home in circumstances that remained unexplained.

Smiley Culture epitomised the art of 'toasting' that was integral to the world of sound systems. As Britain entered the 1980s, this just about portable, self-contained means of entertainment, towers of speakers carefully constructed so as to produce the most gargantuan vibrations, particularly in low registers, focused on the role of the 'selecta' who decided what discs would resonate most with an audience. But the 'mike man', who would improvise, 'chat' or 'toast' lyrics, just as an emcee would at a showbusiness event, was also a key component of the operation. His skill was not to be taken lightly, and the incumbent had to display sufficient intellect and wit, broaching everything from serious social commentary to ribald rub-a-dub humour to have an extended opportunity to perform at a dance. This could involve an apprenticeship that ran to a few years. During that prep time, the would-be toaster had to coin lyrics that were original within the broad scope of Jamaican oral culture rather than rehashing tired tropes that had been in use for years.

Smiley Culture, who was known for his personal catchphrases such as 'slam bam', came up through the ranks of Saxon Studio International, along with one of the other key DJs of the period, Tippa Irie. In Jamaica, the likes of Yellowman, who did many legendary performances in Britain, also came to prominence. There was also the hugely talented Macka B, born in Wolverhampton, to Jamaican parents. He made his debut on the Lord Barley sound system but became increasingly drawn to Rastafarianism and founded his own operation, Exodus, with friends before he started to appear regularly with Jah Wasifa in neighbouring Birmingham. Macka's reputation grew sufficiently for him to bring his wit and wisdom to radio shows, and he then moved his creative output to another level when he collaborated with the talented producer, Mad Professor (Neil Fraser), and recorded songs which showcased the full extent of his powers of observation as well as his penchant for irreverence. 'Baked Bean & Egg' was a wry comment on British cuisine, while 'Wet Look Crazy' was a stupendously funny riff on the latest glossy hairstyle in fashion among African Americans and Caribbeans, which was not so much drip-dry as the drip that kept on dripping. No greater sign of the beguiling nature of entwined cultural references came than in Macka's cute rhyming of a Black woman called Flo with Olympic runner Sebastian Coe, so as to denote the urgency of the new craze. A sprint to the nearest salon was on.

Lyrics such as these made it clear that the art of toasting was about day-to-day reporting. Whoever dared to grip the mike had a responsibility to construct narratives that were distinctively original in delivery and meaningful to their listening community, sometimes referencing current events, sometimes embarking on poetic flights of an altogether more abstract nature

Dee-jays such as Macka B and Smiley Culture had to be, like their Jamaican inspirations such as U-Roy, I-Roy and Big Youth, larger than life characters with sufficient charisma to win over live crowds as well as translate to the small screen. Both of the Brits would appear on the important Black magazine television shows *Ebony* and *Club Mix*.

Out of the Ashes

The power of toasting took it into a very different context: contemporary dance. In 1983, the Leeds-based Phoenix Dance Company presented its inaugural show 'Forming the Phoenix'. While the performances by David Hamilton, Merville Jones, Vilmore James and Donald Edwards were striking, the sight and sound of another member of the company, Edward Lynch on stage with a mic caught the attention by dint of its sheer subversion and originality. The combination of the carefully mapped body movements and the rhythmic delivery of the lyrics proved exciting because these two disciplines were for the most part mutually exclusive in British culture. People would wine 'n' grine to toasting when they went to a sound system dance, but here was a key part of Jamaican oral culture, the art of talking on the beat, brought into a formal setting in which an audience would *watch* and appreciate choreography. As Lynch later explained, there was a considerable spontaneity in the way these two worlds came together:

> One day I was just sat down singing while they were doing the dance and David (Hamilton) just came over to me and said, that's a good idea we've always wanted somebody to toast, how about toasting for the piece? I said you're joking? He said 'Go on... I said alright, I'll try it then.[2]

Forming the Phoenix was the origin story of Phoenix Dance Company. As the performers leapt through the air, Lynch, through his lyrics, presented miniature pithy profiles of his colleagues, emphasising that each one had their own personality and individual way of expressing themselves. It was a celebration not just of who these artists were but where they came from. When Lynch spoke of Donald Edwards, he gave praise to where he and all the others were nurtured. 'Rhythmic in a rub a dub style... in a different style... him skank it in a ragga man style... him skank it in a yard man style. Him born a Chapeltown where de culture is strong.'[3]

The heart of the Caribbean community in Leeds, Chapeltown was noted for its historic carnival, calypso singers and sound systems, which in the early 1980s, when Phoenix was formed, included Genesis and Magnum Force 45. So when Lynch said: 'Me come inna de company just a chat me lyric', he was referencing the wider cultural backdrop of his heartland. As one might expect, reggae was an integral part of the lives of the Phoenix members and the music for *Forming the Phoenix* was *A New Chapter of Dub*, one of the crowning glories of the discography of Aswad. The combination of a London band and a dance company from Leeds, both of Caribbean heritage, was a key moment in Black British culture in the 1980s, bridging regional and metropolitan creative hubs, a brilliant symbiosis of national and local talents.

Phoenix was a Yorkshire phenomenon. Though David Hamilton had moved to London to attend the London School of Contemporary Dance, he *returned* to Leeds and resumed dancing after he had temporarily stopped to focus on martial arts. The idea of forming Phoenix came to him shortly after. The significance of Phoenix was recognised by a full length documentary on The South Bank Show, one of the major television arts programmes in the 1980s. As members of the company gave insights into their backgrounds and motivations, it was clear that all saw the necessity of developing a style of their own, even if being able to train at a national dance school might have made them 'technically better'.

Footage of the dancers walking through Chapeltown, some of them with the then state of the art Walkman clipped to their waistbands, mingling with local residents, added to the sense of grassroots identity at the heart of Phoenix. At one point, Vilmore James, who was once an accomplished amateur boxer, states that he could have made more money bobbing and weaving in the ring rather than leaping and twisting in a studio, reminding the viewer that opportunities and rewards in the world of dance remained limited.

Phoenix made significant progress as a company, winning plaudits in an Arts Council Report, receiving a grant and touring for up to 42 weeks a year. Yet they still encountered scepticism because of a key decision they took at an early stage of their history. The company would work within a public education framework, running workshops to teach kids 'calypso, jazz and contemporary all in one go', rather than a commercial one. Pauline Fitzmorris, Phoenix's manager, saw the maddeningly negative connotations of this engagement:

> People assumed that if you're working in the community and taking dance out to people, dancing in church halls or whatever, that you're only doing that because you can't somehow make it in to the big time, and the big time is the big theatres.

While overcoming perceptions of inferior status, Phoenix also endeavoured to be recognised as dancers rather than Black dancers. The Nicholas brothers (Fayard and Harold), towering figures in the history of African American choreography, were sources of inspiration for their all-action vocabulary, with its swirling, bending, dipping, flying splits, and liquidly gymnastic grace, which had taken New York swing era styles such as the lindy hop and jitterbug to high levels of artistic excellence.

However, Phoenix were also aware that their own tendency towards a high-energy style with 'a lot of jumps and stuff' could easily turn to a stereotype. Hence they explored new territory with choreographers such as Veronica Lewis who took them away from tight and aggressive movements and created intriguing originals works such as *Traffic Variations*, which was danced to a baroque flute sonata. And as much as they saw the need to broaden their repertoire, the Phoenix dancers were, as David Hamilton forcefully put it, intent on constantly learning and developing. If, in their precious spare time, they were still doing the things that Black British youth did, such as spinning under the glittery mirror ball of a local disco, then they were also engaged with other forms of Black music. One of the most striking of Phoenix's early pieces, *Speak Like a Child*, choreographed by Darshan Bhuller, a British-Asian who trained at the London School of Contemporary Dance, saw them perform with an acoustic jazz trio, that showcased an ability to be reflective and serene as well as explosive and dynamic. Phoenix was a major cultural phenomenon in the 1980s, and played a vital role in maintaining the deep historical link betweeen Black dance and Black music, integrating Caribbean and African-American idioms, from reggae to jazz, with verve and imagination.

A Drop of the Hard Stuff
Throughout the North, Midlands and London there were other troupes, most not formally trained, that were also developing a style of choreography set to jazz, which reflected shifts in the outlook and imagination of those who were active in club culture. The phenomenon was called 'jazz dance', and it marked a response to decisions made by DJs to be more adventurous and challenging in the way they put their sets together, which itself fed off the energy of those on the floor.

This specific strand of music and dance grew out of the soul scene where a thirst for records with different rhythms and timbres was never ending. In Manchester, a Black dance crew called Optical Illusion, comprising Mark Swaby, an aspiring medical student, Barry Wilkes, Tony Blades and Sautz, a well-known graffiti artist in Moss Side, home to all of them, had honed their moves to funk for some years. But their eyes and ears had new information to process. As Mark Swaby told me in a North London pub in 2022, the early 1980s saw the local club scene changing:

> When I first got into the scene it was mainly soul, then DJs like Colin Curtis started to play jazz-funk, more instrumentals, George Duke, Azymuth and The Crusaders. And then it turned into 'the hard stuff', jazz, Brazilian jazz, Latin jazz and the dance got more intense. There was a change. During that period, a group of people from Birmingham came down to Club Berlin. They dressed fantastically… long trench coats and hats, and when they went on the floor they just killed it!
>
> They didn't have a name but there was a couple of twins. That changed the whole scene in Manchester because they were very balletic

and influenced a lot of the dancers. We'd go down to Birmingham, we wouldn't even dance, we'd just observe what they were doing, take it back to Manchester and add our own stuff to it.[4]

Soon after, Optical Illusion became the Jazz Defektors and in the fullness of time other crews with a similar vision, such as Brothers in Jazz from Leeds, whose members Irven Lewis and Wayne James *were* trained at the Urdang Academy, rose to prominence while the pioneers with no name from Birmingham kept doing their thing in various cities. Rock City in Nottingham also became a focal point for jazz dance, while in Bristol the Floor Technicians made a name for themselves. As for London, it had the IDJ (I Dance Jazz) whose core members included Marshall Smith, Gary Nurse, Jerry Barry and Milton McAlpine.[5]

All of the above had a wide choreographic range. Fast spins, jumps, and splits were common, with a degree of acrobatics involved, and the traces of 'hoofing' and tap dance traditions were visible, though some crews also leaned towards ballet. The emphasis was on freestyle, with each dancer endeavouring to devise an original set of moves, but Swaby did notice what he thought was an interesting regional stylistic divide. 'London was all below the waist, purely footwork; there were no arm movements. There was a complete contrast between what was happening in the north, really Birmingham upwards and London.'[5] As for the music, it was usually at high tempo with a frantic rhythmic drive that would push dancers to create moves that were more and more outlandish; showmanship was at a premium. Humour also worked. Oscar of the Floor Technicians did a fantastic Charlie Chaplin's waddle and twirled an invisible walking stick.

One of the organising principles of the soul scene was the division of a club space into areas devoted to specific genres, so it became commonplace to have a 'main room' hosting funk and boogie, often with bright lights, and a smaller annex or 'jazz room', usually more dimly lit, where the dancing was significantly more athletic. And there were DJs such as Paul Murphy, who had a residency at the Electric Ballroom in Camden, north London, and realised that what was in some quarters deemed passé – the 1950s and 1960s sound of hard bop, with its gospel and bluesy yearnings or modal jazz with its repeated riffs and expansive solos, or Latin jazz with its barrage of congas, cowbells and bongos – could win the hearts, minds and feet of those who had been weaned on American demigods such as Earth, Wind & Fire and British disciples like Light of the World at kitschy events where soul boys would dress up like New York cops or ancient Romans as they got up to get down. Here is testimony of just how radical some DJs were in the early 1980s when it came to redefining what could pass as dance music. As one soul boy remembered: 'I went out to a soul all-dayer at the Pink Flamingo in Luton, an appalling event… a toga party, in the main room they were playing all the soul hits. And in the jazz room Bob Jones was playing "Impressions" by John Coltrane, I just thought "fuck me!" And people were dancing to it.'[6]

This was indeed a giant step in terms of how one person hears a piece of music and envisions the possible effect it may have on others. 'Impressions' was perceived first and foremost as 'art' rather than dance music, a piece of high concept jazz recorded in 1963 that most would not have considered to have any appeal to soul boys two decades down the line. But therein lies the depth of Jones' imagination, or rather his ability to hear something others could not: the imperiously piercing cry of the saxophone, the unrelenting, agitated push of the rhythm section, the glinting piano, the throbbing double bass and the sizzling ride cymbal combine in a tidal wave of energy; a feverish tension engulfs every chorus. The beat is a whirl, a whizzing gyration. It swings. And the music is acoustic. It really is the 'hard stuff', challenging and inspiring to ears fed on a diet of all things electric.

The 'soul boy' who saw Jones drop the Coltrane bomb was Simon Booth, a south Londoner who had broadened his knowledge of jazz history when he worked at a record shop called Moles in Kings Cross in the centre of town. That moment made it clear that the jazz made decades earlier could still be contemporary in resonance. Booth was also an able guitarist-songwriter who loved Brazilian, Afro-Cuban and African American music. This shaped the tunes he wrote himself, firstly for a group called Weekend, whose 'View from Her Room' had become a much-loved anthem at London's Electric Ballroom, and secondly with the ensemble that succeeded it, Working Week. Its debut single 'Venceremos' was an explosive, ambitious, intricately scored samba that was dedicated to the dancers at that very venue.

Booth had a connection with other groups such as Everything But the Girl and Sade, with the vocalist from the first group, Tracey Thorn, and the saxophonist from the second, Stuart Mathewman, appearing on 'Venceremos'. Other London-based bands with jazz leanings such as Animal Nightlife, Blue Rondo a la Turk and its offshoot, Matt Bianco, drew media attention, and enjoyed variable chart success. Sade would become one of the biggest acts of the decade.

Up in Manchester, Latin jazz group Kalima and Carmel (led by vocalist Carmel McCourt) made their debuts, while The Jazz Defektors started singing as well as dancing and recruited musicians to back them. These artists were Black, white, and multiracial, and for the most part had an image that was proudly retro chic, wearing swing and bebop era clobber, such as double-breasted suits, kipper ties, berets and dark glasses which could be snapped up at emporiums such as Afflex Palace in Manchester and Flip in London. People were going back to the past to find what would make them stand out in the present, as well as listening to old music that was unlike anything that was new.

When Astrud Gilberto's 'The Girl from Ipanema', the Brazilian bossa nova classic of 1962, which had a major influence on all of the above, was reissued and made the British charts, there was talk of a new wave in jazz, complete with opportunistic ad agencies scrambling to cast lifestyle products against a smoke-filled monochrome backdrop. The style press also picked up on this trend, with journalists such as Robert Elms becoming a notable chronicler of events as *The Face* magazine hailed "Rebirth of the Cool: Jazz Age Britain', and camera crews rushed to venues like The Wag in Soho, where DJs such as Paul Murphy, Andy McConnell and Baz Fe Jazz brought more classic music to a new generation. The fact that two legendary African American expatriates – the tap dancer Will Gaines and singer Slim Gaillard, who had been part of the original 'golden age of the 1950s' – attended nights lent extra credibility to the whole scene. Though not credited at the time, Colin Curtis and Hewan Clarke's sessions at Club Berlin in Manchester should also have been placed under the spotlight.

Another significant band was the Tommy Chase quartet, whose leader was a veteran drummer from Manchester who welcomed the interest of a new, younger, non-specialist audience who tended to be less judgmental than the older 'buffs' to whom he had been playing. With his younger sidemen, including saxophonist Alan Barnes, pianist Mark Edwards and double bassist Alec Dankworth (son of English jazz legend John Dankworth and Jamaican-British singer Cleo Laine), Chase gave punters a credible recreation of the 1950s school of hard bop, which was being heard again because Blue Note, the definitive jazz label of that era, had started to reissue albums by the originators of the music. Chase was a player with well-honed technique, full of energetic drive, and he and his band, sharply styled a la Blue Note record sleeves, became a studied, enjoyable homage to such as Art Blakey, Hank Mobley and Lee Morgan. Chase did *not* bring any singers into the fold but welcomed the new wave of jazz dancers. His concerts with IDJ were the stuff of legend, having an authenticity that was not always found among some of these bands who, for the most part, enjoyed far greater commercial success, probably because, as they were sufficiently candid to state, they played what was a kind of jazz-inflected pop. Mark Swaby of The Jazz Defektors recalled:

> We thought we'd have that punk attitude to jazz and because we were going against the idea that as a jazz musician you had to pay your dues and learn an instrument… Because we had vocals, we said we're defectors, we're defecting *away* from the original route into jazz. We didn't play instruments; all we had was our voices and dance moves; that's where the name came from. We tried to make jazz more accessible to people, the vocal Latin and Brazilian side, we did songs, we had that in mind.[7]

Although Working Week had an impressively high standard of musicianship, the band nonetheless put a greater accent on composition than improvisation, in keeping with Simon Booth's love of verse and chorus as well as passages in which players would 'blow'. As Booth said:

> We were, for want of a better word, a pop group because we were song-based. I just wanted to get a bunch of musicians together and make music for this burgeoning underground club scene and have it song-based. I'm interested in lyrics. I wanted to write songs, not take long guitar solos. Through the lyric you can affect people. Sure we did solos, but we didn't want to imitate bebop. We just wanted to make music that was London. When I see the video of 'Venceremos', the zeitgeist is very London, not New York or Rio De Janeiro. In terms of its musical geography, it was based in that 80s London soul scene (and the 'jazz room' stuff that was related to it).[8]

Indeed 'Venceremos' provided a snapshot of a British scene that was vigorously eclectic, with the sight of the IDJ dancers kicking up a storm over turbulent batucada Brazilian rhythms, a powerful encapsulation of a new energy. The input of English pianist Kim Burton, Colombian bassist Chucho Merchan and Brazilian percussionist Bosco D'Oliveira was also crucial. The piece was overtly political, denouncing the Pinochet regime in Chile for murdering Victor Jara, the poet-singer-dissident, who was a hero to Booth, an activist since his youth. Working Week was an avowedly left-leaning band that played Italy's Communist festival at Reggio Emilia and pursued social commentary throughout its magnificent debut album *Working Nights*. The writing by Booth and saxophonist Larry Stabbins, an excellent player from Bristol with a background in avant-garde jazz, was consistently good. It captured the stark austerity of the Thatcher years, particularly on pieces such as 'Sweet Nothing', and 'Autumn Boy', an affectingly sombre melody around which an unsettling string arrangement was wrapped, telling the tale of a blighted soul, very possibly an unemployed teenager or young miner, who wants to 'kick it all down and build it up again', a common sentiment at the time among the millions who were assigned to society's scrapheap and forced to 'watch their town die'. The lyrics were uncompromisingly painful and truthful.

The sole cover on the album, a version of Marvin Gaye's 'Inner City Blues', although written some fifteen years prior to Booth and Stabbins's own songs, could not have been more relevant. What was going on then, in terms of social injustice, corporate greed and failure of government in 1960s America was what was going in 1980s Britain, as Juliet Roberts was all too aware: 'Those words of Marvin, "This ain't living!", resonated then with what was happening under Thatcher, as it still does now. You can put it on now and it's still saying something that was the power of the music.'[9]

Too Black, Too Jazz

Juliet Roberts was a very interesting singer (with Working Week between 1984-88) with a strikingly low voice that did not venture into upper register acrobatics or flyaway scat solos that can tip jazz vocals into cliché if not executed precisely. She could be as commanding as she was subtle. Her performance on 'Autumn Boy' was perhaps the best example of her ability to shift her tone and texture in line with the changes of key and emotional ambiance of the piece, whose melody reflected the influence of the legendary Brazilian composer, Milton Nascimento. There was also little or no layering of her voice, which stood alone, apart from the occasional harmonies of Leroy Osborne, known for his work with Sade. Several Working Week songs have a rich orchestral backdrop, but Roberts's voice always stands out with its dark-hued gravitas.

As much as Working Week had a multi-cultural dimension, Booth was well aware that the combination of a Black female singer and two white male musicians could still ruffle some feathers in a British music industry with little understanding of the origins of the band or the realities of the soul and jazz dance scene they represented. Roberts was not slow to pick up on the race-related projections:

> People assumed I was American because of the professionalism (which they didn't associate with black Britons). And at that time, Sade, Everything but the Girl (and, later, Swing Out Sister) were all happening and they had mixed race or white singers, so they defined the British pop-jazz thing and they just assumed I was American. They just didn't think that I could be a Black British woman in that context.[10]

While that comment pointed to subtle prejudice on the UK music scene, there were also far more alarming episodes to note. Mark Swaby, of the Jazz Defektors, heard racism expressed much more directly. He recalled: 'An A&R man came to one of our gigs and the feedback… what he said to our manager was they're great dancers and great singers but the guy third from the end is too black. That was me.'[11]

Despite the international success of Black British soul artists such as Junior Giscombe and Loose Ends, the lack of Black representation at corporate level in the music industry was still stark. When there were Black people in A&R, management and promotion they could challenge such attitudes. Chief among these was the late Erskine Thompson, a Brummie of Caribbean origin, who was instrumental in the careers of Loose Ends and other soul acts such as Total Contrast, and of lovers' rock stars Maxi Priest and Carroll Thompson. He had the means to put together multi-artist tours of Black British artists which helped launch the career of a young Juliet Roberts, who explained: 'It was Total Contrast, me, Loose Ends, Sid Haywoode and P.P Arnold. Erskine just put us in a van and we'd be out on the road.'[12]

Roberts was a Londoner whose parents came from the Grenadian Carriacou community, which was largely centred on the Harrow Road in West London. She had debuted as a teenager in a reggae band called Black Jade and maintained a friendship with several prominent artists working in the genre, such as Drummie Zeb from Aswad and Carroll Thompson. She recalled:

> In the early 80s, we all came together, having some success – let's go over there, let's do that – jam sessions at places like Browns and Xenon in the West End of London. There were so many opportunities to create something… I mean you could go out and do jam sessions five nights a week. At the time we were all just trying to jam and find our own way. I'd meet Carroll [Thompson] in Harrow, who had many other musicians at her house. It was time when everyone knew each other and we 'fused' different ideas and sounds and Erskine [Thompson] was a kind of link.[13]

Another musician who Roberts knew well because, like her, he was also from the Harrow Road area, was a young saxophonist by the name of Courtney Pine. He had cut his teeth on sessions for reggae artists, with one of his first notable solos on Clint Eastwood & General Saint's 'Stop That Train', a club hit in 1983, which was a cover of an achingly beautiful melody that had been sung by the rocksteady duo, Keith & Tex, and produced by Derrick Harriott back in 1967.

Reggae offered a space for aspiring players to develop, and although his work on 'Stop That Train' showed that Pine had a firm grip on its specific rhythmic character, he was becoming more and more interested in the history of jazz, as epitomised by great saxophone soloists such as John Coltrane, Charlie Parker and Sidney Bechet. In the three years that followed his debut as a sideman, Pine, whose parents hailed from Jamaica, started to make considerable progress as an improviser and attended workshops run by the drummer and bandleader (most notably of the Spontaneous Music Ensemble) John Stevens, and also became a member of the big band led by Rolling Stones drummer, Charlie Watts,[14] who never disengaged from his enduring love of jazz.

Pine came to the attention of Island records and signed to the label as an artist in his own right. He had formed a band with a number of other young Black Britons who had reggae roots, such as double bassist Gary Crosby and drummer Mark Mondesir, while pianist Julian Joseph had a dual classical and jazz background. Pine started to record his debut album at two London studios, Angel and Power Plant, the latter run by Robin Millar who had produced Sade and Working Week.

Released in 1986, *Journey to the Urge Within* was one of the most significant releases of the decade. It was an outright commercial success, peaking at number 39 in the UK album charts and earning a silver disc for over 250,000 copies sold, wholly impressive stats for a debut jazz album by a saxophonist still only twenty-two years old. As a result, Pine was the subject of significant media interest, from the mainstream press, such as *The Guardian*, who hailed him as an artist of 'enormous potential', and specialist publications such as *The Wire*, whose cover he graced, complete with beret – and a well-cut suit, a form of attire that was the norm for a new generation of young African American musicians investigating the heritage of acoustic jazz, spearheaded by such performers as the gifted New Orleans trumpeter Wynton Marsalis.

Children, Get Your Culture
Most importantly, the album saw Pine largely deliver on the pre-release hype. He had a strength of tone and smart turn of phrase that acknowledged the core vocabulary of the twin pillars of post-bop saxophone modernism, John Coltrane and Sonny Rollins, and displayed a maturity beyond his years, daring to edge towards the kind of lengthy, dense solos that had characterised the harmonically and rhythmically challenging verve of his role models. This was another case of the beauty of acoustic music coming into its own. The sound was 'unplugged' and powerful.

Pine unveiled several appealing original compositions such as 'Miss-Interpret', 'I Believe' and 'As We Would Say' but there were also reprises of classic songs by two African American jazz legends who had also inspired him – Horace Silver's 'Peace' and Wayne Shorter's 'Dolores'. These tracks were very much a recognition of those who had blazed a trail for him, and Pine acquitted himself well, particularly on the second piece, which saw him play soprano saxophone, also showing that his band could convincingly negotiate an energetic high tempo swing rhythm. The other cover on the album came entirely out of left field. This was an anthem of Black British soul of the 1970s, The Real Thing's 'Children of the Ghetto.' A new interpretation of a hard bop Blue Note classic this was not. Against expectation Pine reprised an electric ballad.

As noted in Chapter 13, this song was one of the definitive documents of the experience of a new generation of people of colour whose lives were being blighted by racism and unemployment, a song that foresaw the riots that rocked the country just a few years before the release of Pine's album. Pine explained in his sleeve notes for the album that one of his originals, C.G.C., expressed 'the joys and sorrows' of his parents following their 'exodus' to this country, whilst his choice of 'Children of the Ghetto,' was intended to create a continuum between the bittersweet experience of the two Caribbean generations, those who came to Britain and those who were born here.

Reflecting on the idea behind the song, Chris Amoo of The Real Thing said: 'It was supposed to be like a classic jazz ballad.' Pine's take on the song took it even further in that direction. The use of an acoustic palette and a low tempo evoked the timeless tales of heartache and love, sung by Billie Holiday or played by her soulmate, tenor saxist Lester Young, or any of his followers, from Dexter Gordon to John Coltrane.

There was great attention to detail in the re-imagining of 'Children of the Ghetto'. Gary Crosby's double bass provided a solid anchor in the low register, Mark Mondesir's light, crisp rimshots and breathy ride cymbal made the atmosphere intimate, while Ian Mussington's congas provided a sensual understated stream of beats under the song's central pulse. Everything was serene. Julian Joseph's piano and Martin Taylor's guitar brought a tranquil embroidery to the arrangement, their chords slender rather than heavy, embellishing the harmonic palette of the music without splashing too much obtrusive colour upon it. In the midst of these acoustic instruments was a piece of kit that took the band away from the jazz tradition: the synthesizer played by Roy Carter, a longstanding presence in British soul, who had worked with Heatwave, Central Line and, most pertinently, The Real Thing. Carter drew creamy legato notes or 'pads' from his keyboard that brought another layer of violin-like softness and warmth to the ensemble, just as had been the case on countless 1970s R&B tunes made by groups who could not afford to hire 'real' string sections. The trail of synth-strings, a whisper under the main chords, is not inconsequential because, as an electric sound slipped into an otherwise acoustic palette, it pushes the 'pure' jazz ensemble into an idiomatic space that is connected to popular music. All these elements strike a balance between strength and sensitivity, making us feel that this melody in a minor key has a noble grace as well as a deep poignancy, suggesting, even before the words are factored in, that we are listening to a ballad that presents a notworthy comment on a subject of importance.

'Children of the Ghetto' was also, of course, defined by two sounds: Courtney Pine's tenor saxophone and Susaye Greene's voice, and their synergy was vital to the overarching narrative of the performance. They combine to create a quite majestic opening fanfare, with the two trading fleeting but dramatic phrases, the former trilling powerfully, almost like the ringing bell of a town cryer and the latter bursting into life with a declamation of the title and the song's theme of 'Running wild and free', which is stretched out into impassioned adlibs. And as the song unfolds, Greene unveils a quite beautiful range of colours and textures. Her falsetto has the quality of flickering light that contrasts with her low tones that have an almost sulky intimacy. The second time she sings the line 'to the sky', a vital three-word redemption song for Black British youth, Greene whirls upwards with an operatic flourish. This release of energy is followed by a Pine solo that provides a bold contrast because the notes are long and sustained, the phrasing nonchalant rather than urgent, the harmonic variations reined in so as to create a distinct feeling of reflection if not introspection. Pine's subtleties enhance the lyrical depth of the song, implying through concise phrasing and careful tonal understatement that the ghetto children are having a moment to ponder, gathering their thoughts rather than rushing into action. It is time to think, it is time to heal, it is time to rise.

In the coda, Pine and Greene trade lines that bring the arrangement full circle, as the two figures move back to centre stage, just as they were in the prelude. The sound of the saxophone here acquires a touch more density and Pine picks up on and repeats the quicksilver scatted vocal lines before the two elements blend into unison on the three-note phrase that had such emotional meaning earlier in the performance: 'to the sky'. The children are looking up.

From A-level to next level
Susaye Greene exemplified the complex history of Black music in Britain. She was an African-American expatriate, who had once been a member of The Supremes and also proved herself to be a talented writer. She settled in London following a 1984 tour with Stevie Wonder, extending a line of Black women from the USA who enriched the musical history of the UK that included P.P. Arnold, Madeline Bell, and Gloria and Salena Jones.

'Children of the Ghetto' itself had already made an Atlantic crossing. Two years prior to Pine's 1986 version, it was reprised by Philip Bailey, percussionist-vocalist with Earth, Wind & Fire, who featured it on his album *Chinese Wall*, produced by the English drummer-vocalist Phil Collins. Bailey's falsetto floated across a new arrangement which cleverly juxtaposed a blues-rock electric guitar with pert rolls of timbales, which gave the music quite a different sound to the Real Thing's original, though it retained the song's blend of deep pathos and nascent hope. The melody sounded as noble as ever.

The song had travelled from Black Liverpool to Black London via Black Chicago, moving between electric and acoustic settings, a trajectory that summed up continuing cultural exchange within the Black Diaspora. We have thought of the Great American songbook as an invaluable resource in popular music and jazz for the best part of a century, but now I'd argue that two other repertoires of excellence should be considered: The Great African American and The Great Black British songbooks.

By accident or design, Courtney Pine's *Journey to the Urge Within* made that point. Horace Silver, Wayne Shorter *and* The Real Thing, in addition to the saxophonist's own original music, all make the track listing. The span of sources draws a coherent line between apparently unrelated points in time and space of significant cultural achievements by people of colour. A broader focus on the UK could have brought the likes of Eddy Grant,

Cymande, Matumbi, Joan Armatrading,[15] Labi Siffre, Steel Pulse, Linton Kwesi Johnson, Janet Kay, Light of the World, I-Level, Loose Ends, 52nd Street, Rip, Rig & Panic, Floy Joy and Ruth Rogers-Wright into the frame.

These are artists who have excelled against a socio-economic and political backdrop that has been challenging if not debilitating. Racial discrimination in daily life – from violent assault by thugs to substandard accommodation; from discrimination in employment to systematic persecution by the police – have been its most shockingly visible manifestations. But it is in the area of education, specifically the low expectation of the capabilities of Black children that has been one of the greatest stumbling blocks to progress, as Courtney Pine testified:

> I myself was doing A-level music and I was told that there wouldn't be any point in me doing it because I wouldn't get into college eventually, so I may as well leave school. So there was me. I had to leave school because my music teacher didn't have faith that I could do the A-Level. And that's what happens to a lot of guys. So there isn't that pressure to get proficient on your instrument to play jazz. That's why I think that there haven't been many young black jazz musicians.[16]

Given this situation, Pine took an initiative that paralleled those of countless minority groups who felt that their only option was self-sufficiency and organising with like-minded souls, as exemplified by the various 'co-ops and collectives' launched by African American improvising musicians from as early as the 1910s. Pine founded TAJA – The Abibi Jazz Arts – with a communal perspective. He explained:

> It's an organisation to make more black musicians aware of jazz, make more people aware of Afro-classical music, which is jazz. We just sent out letters to people, got on television, told people what this thing's about. We just held workshops, and I got a lot of my musicians out of that. I'm trying to get more young black musicians involved in playing jazz.[17]

The big band that grew from the project was The Jazz Warriors, an ensemble that included major talents from Pine's generation and the preceding ones: Gail Thompson, Steve Williamson, Gary Crosby, Orphy Robinson, Cleveland Watkiss, Ray Carless, Kevin Robinson, Philip Bent, Alan Weekes, Adrian Reid and Andy Grappy to name but some. They went on to win international acclaim. For the most part *they* were the children of the ghetto. Now they would be heard far beyond its borders.

Notes

1. I'm thinking of *It Ain't Half Hot Mum*, *Mind Your Language* and *Curry and Chips*.
2. *Forming The Phoenix*, South Bank Show, LWT, 1984 (Dir. Kim Evans).
3. Interview with the author, September, 2022.
4. Ibid.
5. Ibid.
6. Ibid.
7. Ibid.
8. Ibid.
9. Ibid.
10. Ibid.
11. Ibid.
12. Ibid.
13. Ibid.
14. Charlie Watts big band also featured soloists such as Evan Parker, British titan of the avant-garde.
15. Courtney Pine covered Joan Armatrading's 'Love and Affection' on his album *Back in the Day* (Blue Thumb), 2000.
16. *South of Watford*, 1986. Presenter, Hugh Laurie. LWT.
17. Ibid.
18. Ibid.

OUTRODUCTION

HEAD TO THE SKY

The geographical journey undertaken by the song 'Children of the Ghetto' is a significant one. It was originally written in Liverpool, a major British slave port, and covered by artists in London, the central hub of African Caribbean migration in the UK, and Chicago, an iconic city in the history of Black music in America. A story of second-class citizenship, of marginalisation, of resilience, a new weary blues for the austerity of the 1980s, was thus told in several different parts of the African Diaspora. The song came to cross the waters.

The stylistic journey of 'Children of the Ghetto' is no less interesting. It was conceived by soul vocal group The Real Thing as a jazz ballad and became just that when covered by saxophonist Courtney Pine, whose expansive, expressive solos were signiifcantly enhanced by the input of US singer, Susaye Greene. Another version of the song by her compatriot, Philip Bailey, really brought the music full circle, as he was the lead singer of the legendary soul-funk band Earth, Wind & Fire, a major influence on all the aforementioned.

While the endorsement of one of the defining acts in the history of Black music in America proved that Black music in Britain had come of age, the accolades have taken other forms in more recent times. If the cover version was a staple strategy of both popular music and jazz throughout the first half of the 20th century, then the second saw a dramatic shift occasioned by the advent of new electronic technologies.

Instead of learning to play the themes of others, a new generation of DJs, producers and beatmakers began to take selected breaks directly from old recordings, choice cuts from a once dead musical carcass, and use them as a basis for 'joints' of their own, cooked back to life by a master chef of sound. The sample became the song. Or at least it acted as the programmed-sequenced backing, and the virtual band over which new storytellers or rappers could drop their rhymes in the genre that would be known as hip-hop.

Given that the immortal 'Funky Drummer' had the funkiest drumming, it made sense for this visionary piece by James Brown, ably assisted by Clyde Stubblefield, to be the most ubiquitous loop in the 'old school' of the new music. But there were brothers from another island rather than another planet who captured ears, hearts and minds. The proliferation of beats mined in the UK by US rappers is one of the most empowering stories of Black music in Britain. Hearing the deft poetry of Common set to the gorgeous melodic soul-folk of Linda Lewis, or the offbeat musings of Eminem bolted on to Labi Siffre's fraught blues-funk was a revelation, because it brought these largely forgotten artists back to millions of new listeners around the world, even if they were initially unaware of who they were. The emcees and producers took centre stage while the sonic sources they used remained under wraps.

Of all the British inductees in the 'sampled' hall of fame, none is more revered than Cymande. In 2024, *Gettin' It Back*, a superb documentary directed by Tim McKenzie-Smith, told the story of the group in illuminating and engaging detail. A major strand in the narrative was the enormous impact made by the south London based combo, which did the bulk of its recording between the early and mid 1970s, on the world of electronic dance music and hip-hop in the 1980s and 1990s. The likes of Raze, De La Soul, The Fugees and EPMD all used Cymande's irresistibly bouncy basslines and dynamic drumbeats to good effect, but it was the Parisian rapper MC Solaar who made the most significant cultural statement by way of 'Bouge De La'. This unforgettable song, which exuded such boyish charm and kittenish humour, was built on the central see-saw bass line of Cymande's debut single 'The Message', and it marked a hugely significant moment in recent popular music. It presented hip-hop as a truly global phenomenon. An African American genre was given a new linguistic and cultural dimension by verses rapped not in English but in French by an 'Afropean', Claude M'Barali, who was born in Senegal and raised in Paris. In other words, this was a long creative chain linking several parts of the Black Diaspora.

And in the middle of it was a band of brothers from Jamaica, Guyana and St. Vincent who had made London their home. The fact that they had chosen to name themselves with the Creole term Cymande, which sounds uncannily close to a Caribbean phrase such as 'see man deh', further underlines the enormous cultural complexity that is being played out here. The march of new technology, the timelessness of old beats and the dance of French rhymes that one might call *le flow*, synergise in a song made in Black Britain but raised between America and Europe. If the inspirational Jamaican poet Louise Bennett spoke of 'colonisation in reverse' to hail the enduring linguistic impact of the West Indies on Empire, then this was a case of colonisation as three-point turn. Rhythm and speech formed an irresistible life-affirming force.

As much as Cymande are now perceived as the soul band loved by hip-hop, they were always much more than artists who could be pinned down in a single category. Of course, they had a command of African American idioms, above all the energetic polyrhythms that made funk so appealing, as well as the improvisatory skills and compositional ambition that are integral to jazz. And the other main elements of their work were emphatically Caribbean – Jamaican and Guyanese folk melodies as well as the drums and vernacular of Rastafarianism, the non-western belief system whose followers, lest we forget, were once objects of great scorn. These disparate elements coalesced seamlessly to create something that resisted definition, while the musicians, who were fully aware of their Blackness in the harsh landscape of the UK music industry, steadfastly refused political compromise. What they created is one of the great legacies of post-Windrush culture. Their music is unique.

It might be appropriate to say it was conceived in the Caribbean and birthed in Britain, a triumph of imagination that accompanied the challenge of immigration. In any case, the key figures in *Children of the Ghetto* have shown a similar quality. They also reflected the dynamic, evolutionary nature of a Black British vernacular that has a wide range of Caribbean and English colloquialisms flowing from lived experience up and down the country, be it a Leeds Chapeltown upbringing, or a London childhood that is marked by cockney translations.

While there is no greater sign of the creative heights scaled by artists in this country than the expansion of genres and styles that took place in the period covered by this book, the strength of character of individual composers, lyric writers, singers and players has been remarkable. Eddy Grant, Dennis Bovell, Doris Troy, Joan Armatrading, Linda Lewis, Ruth Rogers-Wright and Labi Siffre all made music that has stood the test of time and achieved the enviable feat of bringing a wholly personal slant to what is a recognised idiom, or, perhaps more excitingly, showing that the border between styles is fluid rather than rigid. While a band such as Osibisa stand as one of the best known exponents of music that built a bridge between several eras and cultures, namely the sensual acoustic timbres of west African hi-life and the explosive electric vibrations of western rock and funk, there are many other practitioners who, although not blessed with comparable commercial success, deserve a place in the pantheon. Indeed the unheralded wave of 1970s black British rock acts such as Gass, Batti Mamzelle and Demon Fuzz made beguiling music.

In the 1980s, Rip, Rig & Panic, with their torrid, turbulent, politically charged songs, which were as much avant-garde as they were pop, are an exemplar of the richness of the Bristol scene while Floy Joy could be described as a regional-metropolitan marvel. The band comprised, the Ward brothers, horn player Michael and keyboardist-bassist-guitarist Shaun, both weaned on soul, funk and jazz in Sheffield, and one of London's feted queens of lovers' rock, Carroll Thompson. The music they made together was fantastically bizarre, knitting off-kilter themes and pounding, menacingly muscular grooves into songs that were both seductive and cryptic.

If Thompson, a highly accomplished composer in her own right, embodied a kind of free artistic spirit who was wont to appear in a number of different contexts, then she had a loose parallel in Sam Jones, a fine singer raised in Scotland to Sierra Leonean parents, who made his name with roots reggae combo, Brimstone, before going on to found I-Level with bassist Jo Dworniak and keyboardist Duncan Bridgeman. What they created together was marketed as soul, but it made such inventive use of synthesizers, sequencing and early sampling ideas that the end result was often a kind of offbeat electronica with more soulfulness than is usually associated with the genre. I-Level stood between many genres.

This idiomatic experimentation and hybridisation that mark significant moments in Black music in Britain from the late 1960s to the early 1980s has provided an overarching theme for *Children of the Ghetto*, but the other recurrent element is the high standard of performance among successive generations. The arrival of a new wave of jazz musicians is an appropriate conclusion to the book, as it powerfully underlines this continuum. The likes of Courtney Pine, Steve Williamson, Gail Thompson, Orphy Robinson, Gary Crosby, Cleveland Watkiss, Kevin Robinson, Mark Mondesir, Alan Weekes and Philip Bent, among many others, was a major *story* because they signalled the ability young Black improvisers to pursue unexpected career paths. Many of them had cut their teeth on reggae, lovers' rock and soul bands and no eyebrows would have been raised if they had continued down those roads. But their decision to explore the acoustic tradition of Coltrane, Rollins and Monk marked a fresh development that cannot be taken for granted.

The big band that brought them together, The Jazz Warriors, was an exciting vehicle for this cohort of players who had grown up under the dark cloud of Thatcherism, but they had the means to make a direct connection to the far-reaching history of Black music in Britain by including in their ranks the marvellous trumpeter, Harry Beckett, who had arrived on these shores in the 1950s and been an indefatigable presence on many scenes in the decades that followed. If ever there was an artistic role model, then he was surely it. Pine, the most lionised figure among the young hopefuls, had a keen interest in what he called in song his 'forefathers' fathers' dreams.' It was clear that this new generation was well aware of the trials and tribulations of those who had come before them and laid down roots. Leaving the Caribbean and settling in England in the postwar period was a leap of faith that entailed sacrifice and resilience. Pine was in the full glare of media attention as the archetypal 'young man with a horn', but he came from *somewhere*. His elders and their aspirations were thus acknowledged and perhaps vicariously fulfilled. For words of encouragement in their endeavour, the saxophonist and his peers needed to look no further than the chorus of 'Children of the Ghetto', the song he covered. Find peace, stay strong, walk tall. *Keep your head to the sky.*

SELECTED DISCOGRAPHY

Gloria Jones, 'Tainted Love' (Champion, 1965)
Diane & Nicky, 'Me and You' (Columbia, 1966)
Jimmy James & The Vagabonds, 'Come to Me Softly' (Piccadilly, 1966)
The Foundations, 'Baby Now That I've Found You' (Pye, 1967)
The Pyramids, 'Train Tour to Rainbow City' (President, 1967)
P.P Arnold, 'Dreamin'' (Immediate, 1968)
The Cats, 'Swan Lake' (BAF, 1968)
The Equals, Police on My Back (President, 1968)
Root & Jenny Jackson, 'Lean on Me' (Beacon, 1968)
Max Romeo, 'Wet Dream' (Pama, 1968)
Joe E. Young & The Toniks, 'Got That Feeling' (Toast, 1968)
The Upsetters, 'Return of Django' (Upsetter, 1969)
Joyce Bond, 'You Don't Stand a Chance' (Upfront, 1970)
C.C.S, 'Whole Lotta Love' (CBS/Rak, 1970)
The Clangers, 'Dance of the Clangers' (Beacon, 1970)
Gass, 'Juju' (Polydor, 1970)
Doris Troy, 'Give Me Back My Dynamite' (Apple, 1970)
The Equals, 'Black Skin Blue Eyed Boys' (President, 1970)
Hot Chocolate Band, 'Give Peace a Chance' (Apple, 1970)
Assagai, 'Beka' (Vertigo, 1971)
Brotherhood of Breath, 'MRA' (RCA/Neon, 1971)
Osibisa, 'Music for Gong Gong' (MCA, 1971)
Labi Siffre, 'Bless the Telephone' (Pye, 1971)
Labi Siffre, 'It Must Be Love' (Pye, 1971)
Akido, 'Awade (We Have Come)' (Mercury, 1972)
Mustapha Tettey Addy, 'Ewe Atsimivu' (Tangent, 1972)
Joan Armatrading, 'City Girl' (Cube, 1972)
Joe Cocker, 'Woman to Woman' (A&M, 1972)
Cymande, 'Bra' (Janus, 1972)
Cymande, 'The Message' (Janus, 1972)
Linda Lewis, 'Waterbaby' (Reprise, 1972)
Hugh Masekela, 'Inner Crisis' (Blue Thumb, 1972)
Blue Mink, 'Whole Lotta Love' (Regal Zonophone, 1972)
Reebop Kwaku, 'Bah Zagapam' (Island, 1972)
The Peddlers, 'I Have Seen' (Philips, 1972)
Thin Lizzy, 'Black Boys on the Corner' (Decca, 1972)
Brian Auger's Oblivion Express, 'Happiness is Just Around the Bend' (CBS, 1973)
Hot Chocolate, 'Brother Louie' (RAK, 1973)
Marsha Hunt, 'Man to Woman' (Fontana, 1973)
Matumbi, Brother Louie (GG's, 1973)

Matumbi, 'Wipe Them Out' (Duke, 1973)
Third World, Shango (Island, 1973)
Batti Mamzelle, 'I See the Light' (Cube, 1974)
Gonzalez, 'Funky Frith Street' (EMI, 1974)
Average White Band, 'Schoolboy Crush' (Atlantic, 1975)
Clancy, 'Move On' (Warner, 1975)
Louisa Mark, 'Caught You in a Lie' (Safari, 1975)
Love Childs Afro-Cuban Blues Band, 'Black Skin Blue Eyed Boys' (Roulette, 1975)
Labi Siffre, 'I Got The' (EMI, 1975)
Sweet Sensation, 'Mr. Cool' (Pye, 1975)
Thin Lizzy, 'Half-Caste' (Vertigo, 1975)
Joan Armatrading, 'Love and Affection' (A&M, 1976)
Joan Armatrading, 'Tall in the Saddle' (A&M, 1976)
Demon Fuzz, 'Remember Biafra' (Paco, 1976)
F.B.I., 'Talking Bout Love' (Good Earth, 1976)
Jabula, 'Thunder into Our Hearts' (Caroline, 1976)
The Real Thing, 'Hallelujah Man' (Pye, 1976)
Brown Sugar, 'I'm in Love with a Dreadlocks' (Lover's Rock, 1977)
Cimarons, 'Living on the Dole' (Ronco, 1977)
Eddy Grant, 'Race Hate' (ICE, 1977)
Heatwave, 'The Groove Line' (GTO, 1977)
Hummingbird, 'You Can't Hide Love' (A&M, 1977)
Moon, All Night (Epic, 1977)
Remi Kabaka, 'Future of a 1000 Years' (Island, 1977)
Hi-Tension, 'Hi-Tension' (Island, 1978)
Joshua Moses, 'Pretty Girl' (Shoc Wave, 1978)
X-Ray Spex, 'Germ Free Adolescents' (EMI, 1978)
Steel Pulse, 'Soldiers' (Island, 1978)
Joan Armatrading, 'How Cruel' (A&M, 1979)
Capital Letters, 'Headline News' (Greensleeves, 1979)
Ian Dury & The Blockheads, 'Inbetweenies' (Stiff, 1979)
HI-Tension, 'There's a Reason' (Island, 1979)
Light of the World, 'Liv Togevver' (The Greater London Funkathon) (Ensign, 1979)
Linton Kwesi Johnson, 'Sonny's Lettah (Anti-Sus Poem)' (Island, 1979)
Janet Kay, 'Silly Games' (Scope, 1979)
Misty in Roots, 'Judas Iscariote' (People Unite, 1979)
Maric Pierre 'Choose Me' (Trojan, 1979)
The Real Thing, 'Children of the Ghetto' (Pye, 1979)
Jean Adebambo, 'Paradise' (Santic, 1980)
Aswad, 'Warrior Charge' (Island, 1980)
Linton Kwesi Johnson, 'Inglan Is a Bitch' (Island, 1980)

Beggar & Co, '(Somebody) Help Me Out' (Ensign, 1981)
Blue Rondo a la Turk, 'Sarava' (Virgin, 1981)
Breakfast Band, 'L.A 14' (Disc Empire, 1981)
Eddy Grant, 'Timewarp' (ICE, 1981)
Eddy Grant, 'Walking on Sunshine' (ICE, 1981)
The Specials, 'Ghost Town' (Two Tone, 1981)
Talisman, 'Run Come Girl' (Recreational, 1981)
Billy Ocean, 'Calypso Funkin'' (Epic, 1982)
Alaap, Teri Chunni De Sitare (Alaap, 1982)
Roy Alton, 'If You Want Me' (Island, 1982)
Funkapolitan, 'War' (London, 1982)
I-Level, 'Give Me' (Virgin, 1982)
Jabula, 'Botlokwa' (Plane, 1982)
Junior Giscombe, 'Too Late' (Mercury, 1982)
Kabbala, 'Ashewo Ara' (Red Flame, 1982)
Lonesi Chewane & Joni Hetara, 'Mkazi Wa Mulomo' (WEA, 1982)
Rip, Rig & Panic, 'You're My Kind of Climate' (Virgin, 1982)
Set the Tone, 'Dance Sucker' (Island, 1982)
Weekend, 'The View from Her Room' (Rough Trade, 1982)
Candy McKenzie, 'Remind Me' (Intense, 1983)
Central Line, 'Lovely Day' (Mercury, 1983)
Clint Eastwood & General Saint, 'Stop That Train' (Greensleeves, 1983)
Fun Boy Three, 'Our Lips Are Sealed' (Chrysalis, 1983)
I-Level, 'Historical Nights' (Virgin, 1983)
David Joseph, 'You Can't Hide Your Love' (Island, 1983)
Paradise, 'One Mind Two Hearts' (Priority, 1983)
Black Roots, 'Signs & Wonders' (Kick, 1984)
Floy Joy, 'Burn Down a Rhythm' (Virgin, 1984)
Kalima, 'The Smiling Hour' (Factory, 1984)
L.C.G.C, 'Fill My Cup' (Island, 1984)
George Lee's Anansi, 'Seashells' (Ebusia, 1984)
Working Week, 'Venceremos (We Will Win)' (Paladin, 1984)
52nd Street, 'You're My Last Chance' (10 Records, 1985)
Brafa Team, 'Let's Make Africa Green Again' (Island, 1985)
Loose Ends, 'Hangin' on a String' (Virgin, 1985)
Moontwist, 'Sight and Sound' (Certain, 1985)
Smiley Culture, 'Cockney Translation' (Polydor, 1985)
Starvation/Tam Tam Pour L'Ethiopie, 'Starvation' (Zarjazz, 1985)
Tommy Chase Quartet, 'Sunset Eyes' (Paladin, 1985)
Macka B, 'Wet Look Crazy' (Ariwa, 1986)
Courtney Pine, 'Children of the Ghetto' (Island, 1986)
Pam Hall, 'Perfidia' (World Enterprise, 1987)
The Jazz Defektors, 'Bounce Back' (CBS, 1987)

INDEX

52nd Street, 279-282: *Children of the Night*, 279-280; 'Your My Last Chance', 'Cool as Ice', 280; recording in Philadelphia, 280-281; *Something's Going On*, 281; use of synthesizers, 281
70 Proof (Black British soul band), 230
Abbas, Ausaf (Alien Kulture), 255, 257
Abbensetts, Michael (writer), *Empire Road*, 178
Acquaye, Neemoi 'Speedy' (drummer), 123
Addy, Mustapha Tettey, *Master Drummer from Ghana*, 115; *Kpanlogo Party*, 115-116
Adebambo, Jean (singer), 212, 214
Adjaye, Peter, aka AJ Kwame, 121
Africa Centre, 116, 261
Africa embraced as the core of Black identity, 116
African and the Caribbean music, influenced by funk, 100, 101
African Dawn (performance group), 261-262
African drumming in British rock, 123-124
Afrocult Foundation (composer), *Black Goddess*, 123
Afrodiziak, on 'Tam Tam Pour Ethiopie', 270
Afro-Latin rhythms, embrace of, 195, 197, 262-263, 278, 297
Afro-Rock, and Afro-Funk, 10, 117, 118, 120 (See also Osibisa)
Akido (Afro-Rock band), 'Psychedelic Baby', 117
Akinlola, Aniff (Chapter & the Verse), 286
Alaap (bhangra band), *Teri Chunni De Sitare*, 258
Alan Bown Set, The, 24
Ali, Tariq, 259
Alien Kulture (Asian British punk band), 255, 259; 'Arranged Marriage', 256; punk and addressing Asian British generational divide, 256-257; as part of RAR, 257, 'Liberation Dance', 258

Allen, Tony (drummer), 101, 269
Allendale, Eric (The Foundations), 18
Alphonso, Roland (Jamaican saxophonist), 25, 57
Alton, Roy, 221-222, *Mas in the Grove, Carnival in Ladbroke Grove*, 222
Amoo, Chris (The Real Thing), 147, 188, 195; producing Loose Ends, 276; 302
Amoo, Eddy (The Real Thing), 147, 148, 195-199; producing Loose Ends, 276
Animals, The, 16
Anti-Apartheid Campaign and musicians, 264-267
Anti-Nazi League, 183
Antonioni, Michelangelo, *Blow Up*, 15, 91
Archer, Elizabeth, 'Feel Like Making Love', 216
Armatrading, Joan, 10, 11, 154-161, 166, 172, 308: biography, 154-156; problems of marketing a Black singer who didn't sing 'Black' music and crosses genres, 157, 158, 160-161; 'City Girl', 157; *Whatever's for Us*, 157-158; 'Love and Affection' 158; use of top-class musicians, 159; locating her in a Black tradition, 160; feminism and sexual identity, 166; politics in 'How Cruel', 200
Armstrong, Louis, 34, 47, 52, 186, 203
Arnold, P.P., 86, 89-91, *Catch My Soul*, 89, 'Piccaninny', 90, 'Dreamin', 91; on the mistreatment of a Black woman in the music industry, 91, 94
Artists United Against Apartheid, 266
Assagai (see also Feza, Pukwana, Moholo-Moholo, Afro-Rock), 'Telephone Girl', 117
Aswad, 10, 174-176: influence of Rastafarianism, 175-176; *Aswad, Hulet*, 175-176; 'Can't Stand the Pressure', 175; 'Judgment Day', 175-176; 'Warrior Charge', 245-246; as backers of Burning Spear and link up

with Marley's band, 176; 268
Atmosfear (Soul-funk group), 232
Auger, Brian, 144
Average White Band (soul-funk), 'Pick up the Pieces', 110-111
Bah, Reebop Kwaku, 123, *Reebop and Anthony Reebop Kwaku Bah*, 124
Bahula, Sebothane Julian (Jabula), 78, 265, 267
Bailey, Philip (ex Earth Wind & Fire), version of 'Children of the Ghetto', 303
Bailey, Richard (Batti Mamzelle), 246
Baker, Ginger 101, 122, Airforce, 123
Baldry, Long John, 92
Banks, Darrell, 'Open the Doors to Your Heart', 27
Bar-Kays, The (funk band), 'Soul Finger' 26
Basie, Count, 118, 163
Bassey, Shirley, 42, 84, 86, 167, 204, 219 n.2, 264
Batti Mamzelle, *I See the Light*, 124-125; 308
BBC radio, as barrier to Black music, 65, 69, 73
Beacon (label), 21, 57
Beat & Commercial (Gopthal labels), 60
Beat, The, 'Stand Down Margaret', 239, 242
Beatles, 15, 16, 23, 28, 38, 39, 58, 67, 86, 88, 96, 142
Beaton, Norman (actor), 178, 188, 194
Beckett, Harry (jazz trumpeter), 75-76, *Flare Up*, 80; 309
Beggar & Co, '(Somebody) Help Me Out', 244-245
Bell, Eric (Thin Lizzy), 132, 133, 134
Bell, Madeline, with Blue Mink, 86, *Bell's A Poppin'*, 87; solo career, 89; with Hummingbird, 152
Benjamin, Sharon, 'Mr Guy', 225
Bennett, Louise, 307
Bennett, Val, 61
Berry, Chuck, 47
Bhangra, 11, 258-259
Bilgrami, Pervez (Alien Kulture), 255, 256, 258
Birmingham, 10, 31, 43, 66, 71, 74, 75, 156, 177, 178-179, 183, 184, 188, 196, 239, 242, 243, 257, 294; Handsworth, as a Jamaican community, 178
Black American musical influences, 15, 16, 19, stage presence, dance-steps and dress, 17,
Black and born and educated in Britain, emergence of a Black British identity, 32-33
Black British music, as a regional phenomenon, 21; see Bristol, Coventry, Birmingham, Liverpool, Manchester
Black British psychedelia, 24, 48, 125
Black churches in Britain as sanctuaries and sources of gospel music, 273-274
Black Diamonds, The, 20, 21
Black Joy (film), musical soundtrack, 194
Black Music, and its ethnic ownership, 34-35; the 'inimitable' Black voice, 34-35, on authenticity and essentialism, 35-36; for a non-essentialist aesthetics, 36
Black Parents Association, 75
Black political resistance in Britain, 43-44, 64-65; in the George Lindo case, 204-206; at the Notting Hill Carnival, 222-223; the uprisings of 1981 in Brixton, Toxteth, Moss Side & St Paul's, 238-239
Black Roots (Bristol reggae band), 'Bristol Rock', 224
Black Slate (reggae band), 'Amigo', 186
Black Unity and Freedom Party, 64
Black Velvet, 'Peace and Love is the Message', 'Clown', 57
Black/white singing duos, 31, 37, 88, 95
Blacking up, survivals, 33, 34, Olivier as Othello, *The Black and White Minstrel Show*, 33-34, in *Catch My Soul*, 89
Blackwell, Chris, 60, 61
Blake, Eaton (Matumbi, aka Jah Blake), 177
Blue Aces, The, 27
Blue Mink, 86-87, 95, *Live at the Talk of the Town*, 86, 'Good Morning Freedom', 87, 'Melting Pot', 87
Blue-eyed Soul, 35-36, 110-111

Bob Adams and the Echoes, 20
Bodysnatchers (ska revival), 239
Bolan, Marc, 92
Bond, Joyce, *Ska and Soul*, 28; *Soul of Change*, 28-29
Booker T & the MGs, 56, 68, 120
Booth, Simon (Weekend and Working Week), 295, 298
Boothe, Ken, 55, 61
Boundary crossing of genres, 125-127
Bovell, Dennis (Matumbi, aka Blackbeard), 10, 60, 99, 308; interview, 68-69, 144: influences, 68, (Cymande), 107; 'Brother Louie', 143; connections with Bob Marley and Family Man (Barrett), 176; formation and naming of Matumbi, 177; as architect of lovers rock as 'smooch reggae', 211-212; as producer of Janet Kay, 216-217; as engineer producer, 226
Bowie, David, flirtation with fascism, 183
Bowry, Tony (52nd Street), 279
'Boys in Blue' (Light of the World), 9
Bradshaw, Tiny, 'Train Kept A-Rollin'', 16
BRAFA, 267-270
Braithwaite, E.R., *To Sir, With Love*, 32
Breakfast Band, the, 'L.A. 14', 246, 263
Brevett, Lloyd, 25
Bridgeman, Duncan (I-Level), 251
Brilliant, 'Love Is War', 252
Brimstone, 'Come and Take Me', 214, 250
Bristol, 10, 71, 223, 224-226, 227, 228, 252, 260, 284, 295, 298, 308
Britain as a hub for African music, 101
British Black Panther Movement, 64, 87
British funk, 102, 177, 232, 234, 252, 274; decline of, 276
British music industry, its class and race hierarchy, 17, 37, 38; power of DJ's, 17-18; problems with multi-racialism and Black women, 18, 89, 98
British reggae, its birth, 67; the club circuit and backing Jamaican stars, 71, British versions and outselling Jamaican originals, 71

British soul based on American models, 17, 19; invidious comparisons, 20
'Brother Louie' (Hot Chocolate and Matumbi), 9, 141; its success in American cover versions, 143; Matumbi's version, 143
Brotherhood of Breath, 77-78, 'MRA', 77, 'Davashe's Dream', 78
Brothers in Jazz (jazz dance) 295
Brown, Errol (Black Roots), 224
Brown Sugar (vocal trio), 213, 'Black Pride' and 'Dreaming of Zion', 213
Brown, Errol, Hot Chocolate Band, 60, 67, interview, 67-68, 142
Brown, James, 'Soul Power', 25, 41, 100, 101, 120, 152, 227, 306
Buckmaster, Paul (The Real Thing), 199
Bullimore, Tony, The Bamboo Club, Bristol, 224-225
Burke, Pat (The Foundations), 18
Burke, Solomon (soul singer), 20, 25, 96
Burke, Vanley (photographer), 73, 74-75
Burton, Nick (sound system operator), 174
Buster, Prince (Cecil Campbell), 51, 56, 57, 239
Butetown, as the home of Cardiff's Black community, including Shirley Bassey, 204; the myths and harsh realities of its multiracialism, 204
C.C.S., Collective Consciousness Society, 79-82, 86: mixed genres but not fusion, 80; use of top jazz musicians, 80, '(I Can't Get No) Satisfaction, 81; use of rare time signatures, 81; 'Whole Lotta Love', 81-82 as theme for Top of the Pops,
Cadogan, Susan, 212
Calder, Clive, Jive and Jive Afrika labels, 263
California Ballroom, The (Dunstable), as a hotspot soul venue, 27
Callier, Terry, 160
Calypso, as an outdated form in the 1970s, 220; soul-calypso into soca, 220-221
Cameron, Earl (actor), 33, 144, 173, *Fear of Strangers*, 173
Cameron, John, 80, 151
Campbell, Ambrose, 7

Capital Letters (reggae band), *Headline News*, 186
CARD, Campaign Against Racial Discrimination, as a moderate organisation, 43-44, 64
Carriacou, 15, 20, 110, 156, 300
Cary, Joyce (novelist), *Mister Johnson*, 177
Catch My Soul (musical), 89, 91, 94, 98 n. 2, 125
Catlin, Pauline (Brown Sugar) 213
Cats, The, 'Swan Lake', 70
Central Line, 'Man at the Top', 244, 'Lovely Day', 248-249; 'Walking into Sunshine', 249
Challengers, The (Manchester gospel band), 283
Chaman, Clive, 152
Chandler, Chas, 129
Chandra, Sheila (Monsoon), 255, 261
Charlemagne, Diane (52nd Street), 279
Charles, Ray, 15, 40, 41, 45 n.9, 228
Chen, Colston 'Coley' (The Vagabonds), 23
Cherry, Neneh (Rip, Rig & Panic), 226
Chewane, Lonesi (WOMAD), 260
Chic (funk band), 149
Children of the Ghetto, the author's goals and rationale, 12-14
'Children of the Ghetto', song, versions of, see The Real Thing, Courtney Pine, Philip Bailey
Cimarons, The, 70-71, 'Living on the Dole', 193-194; 214
Clancy (soul band), 151, *Seriously Speaking* and *Every Day*, 151-152
Clangers, The (rocksteady), 'Dance of the Clangers', 57
Clapton, Eric, racism of, 34, 183
Clark, Vivian (Brimstone), interview, 214-215
Clash, The, reggae covers, 183; 184, 189, 190, 285
Clayton, Merry, 'Turner's Murder', 97
Cliff, Jimmy, 61, 63, 65, 71, 224
Clinton, George, 49
Coard, Bernard, 'How the West Indian Child Is Made Educationally Subnormal', 75
Cocker, Joe, 110
Cole, Nat 'King', 25

Coleman, Jaz (Killing Joke), 257
Coleman, Ornette, 78
Collins, Bootsy, 49
Collins, Merle, 262
Coloured Raisins (aka Black Velvet), 'One Way Love', 57
Commission for Racial Equality, 172
Compilation albums as a solution to distribution problems, 61
Conteh, John, film roles, 148
Cook, Roger (Blue Mink), 86, 88
Cooke, Sam, 26, 36, 225
Corea, Chick, 274
Cortez, Jayne, 210
Coulam, Roger (Blue Mink), 86
Covay, Don (R&B), 'See-Saw', 50
Coventry, 10, 54, 239, 241, 258, 289
Cover versions, 24, 27, 28, 67, 86, 92
Cregan, Jim, 168
Cropper, Steve, 34
Crosby, Gary (Courtney Pine band), 300, 302
Cross, Sandra, 218
Cross-genre influences, from jazz, 79, Soft Machine, CCS, 79-80
Crusaders, The, 232, 234, 274
Cultural exchange, the Caribbean and Britain, linguistic, 58; musical, 71-72
Curtis, Clem (The Foundations), 18
Cymande, 10, 99, 102-106: influence of Rastafarianism, 102, 107; jazz, soul and calypso, 102, as a pan-Caribbean ensemble, 103, 'The Message', 104; creativity not matched by sales, 104; the band's instrumentation, 105; 'Bra', and calypso flavour, and its sampling in 'Jack the Groove', 105-106; 'The Dove', 106-107; influence on other Black British musicians, 107-108; the problems of band size and economics, 109; sampled by Raze, De La Soul, The Fugees, EPMD and MC Solaar, 307
Dammers, Jerry, Black musical influences including ska, 239; formation of The Specials, 239; involvement in Free Nelson Mandela concerts, 265-266; issue of celebrity and ignored exiled South African musicians, 267
Danga, Wala (African music promoter), 261

Darko, George, 'Hi-Life Time', 263
Darnell, August (Kid Creole and the Coconuts), 247
Davis, Miles, as an influence, 47, 103, 199
Day, Jennifer, 'Together', 215
Dee, Joey, 103, 107
Dekker, Desmond, 'Israelites', 56, 62, 63
Delandro, Winston, 263
Demon Fuzz, 10, *Afreaka*, 125-126; 308
Denning, Chris (DJ), 17, 18
Dennison, John (52nd Street), 279
Dhondy, Farrukh (writer), 64, 65, 87, 259
Diane (Ferraz) and Nicky (Scott), as a mixed duo, 37, 'Me and You', 37
Dibango Manu, 100, 101, 262, 269
Disco, 149; roller-skating disco, 243
Discrimination, in housing, 55; in education, 75
Dixon, Errol, *Blues in the Big City*, 22
Dodd, Sir Coxone, 25
'Dole Age' (Talisman), 9
Dole, as the iconic term of 1970s precarity, 193-194; The Cimarons, 'Living on the Dole', 193-194; song used in *Black Joy* (film), 194
Domino, Fats, 163
Donaldson, Bunny (Matumbi, aka Jah Bunny), 177
Dub or reggae poetry, 9, 209
Dub, 211, 219, 225, 226, 240, 252
Dupree, Champion Jack, 20
Dury, Ian and the Blackheads, as a multiracial band, 228; engagement with Black American music, 228-229, 'Hit Me with Your Rhythm Stick', 228
Dworniak, Joe (I-Level), 250, 251
Dyani, Johnny (South African jazz), 76
Dzidzornu, Rocky, 123
Earth, Wind & Fire, 152, 153, 230, 248, 273, 295, 303, 306
Eclecticism and musical mavericks, 10, 11, 88, 99
Edwards, Donald (Phoenix Dance Co.), 292
Egbuna, Obi (activist), 64, 65
Ekome National Dance Company, 260
Electro-funk, 280
Ellington, Duke, 77, 118, 188, 203

Elliot, Mike (The Foundations), 18
Ellis, Alton, 56, 216, 218, 250
Empire Road, 177, 178, 179, 188, 190
English, Junior, 'In Loving You', 176
Equals, The, 10, 46, 47; Equals Explosion, 48, Equals at the Top, 48, as a precursor of 'glamrock', 49; 'I'm a Poor Man', 50-51, 'Black Skin Blue Eyed Boys', 51, 87, 145; Born Ya!, 'Funky Like a Train', 221
Eugene, Jayne (Loose Ends), 276, 278
F.B.I. (see also Root Jackson), 109, 'The Time is Right to Leave the City', 110
Factory (label and organisation, Manchester), 284-287: Black band, A Certain Ratio, 284; first signers of 52nd Street, 284
Fame, Georgie, 35
Famine Relief, Band Aid and its Eurocentric whiteness, 267
Farlowe, Chris, 35-36, Stormy Monday, 36-37, 'Out of Time', 37
Feeny, Margaret, 116
Feminism in Black British music, 93, 97
Feza, Mongezi, 76
Fisk Jubilee Singers, 272
Fitzmorris, Pauline (Phoenix Dance Co. manager), 293
Float Up CP, ex- Rip, Rig & Panic, 'Joy's Address', 252
Floor Technicians (jazz dance) 295
Floy Joy, 'Burn Down a Rhythm', 252; 308
Floyd, Eddie, 25
Ford, Barry (Clancy), 151
Forde, Brinsley (Aswad, aka Chaka B), 11, acting career, 174, formation of Aswad, 174;
Foster, Keith (aka Tito Simon), 28-29, 'You Don't Stand a Chance', 29
Foundations, The, 17, 18, 19, 20 *From the Foundations*, 'Baby, Now that I've Found You', 18, 19; 'Build Me Up Buttercup, 19, 'My Little Chickadee', 20
Four Aces (club), 66
Francis, Cordell (Black Roots), 224
Franklin, Aretha, 15, 21, 25, 29, 36, 152, 194, 212, 273, 281

Freeaz (Soul-funk group), 232, 234
Fun Boy Three, 'Our Lips Are Sealed', Urdu B-side, 289
Funk, 10, 100-101, 102-105, 106, , 108, 109, 134, 144, 164, 197, 226, 275, 308; the role of drummers, 100
Funkees, The, 101
Gabbidon, Basil (Steel Pulse), 178
Gabbidon, Colin (Steel Pulse), 178
Gabriel, Peter, 259, 260, 266
Gad, Tony (Aswad), 216
Gage, Peter (Geno Washington), 26
Garrick, Michael, 84
Gaye, Angus, (Aswad, aka Drummie Zeb) 174, in *Step Forward Youth*, 175; 300
Gaylads, The, 55
Genesis (sound system), 292
'Ghost Town' (The Specials), 9
Gibb, Barry, 90
Gillett, Charlie, 262
Giovanni, Nikki, 210
Giscombe, Junior, 'Too Late', 'Mama Used to Say', 244; 299
Glaxo Babies (Bristol band), *Nine Months to the Disco*, 227
Goins, Herbie, 27, 150, 167
Golding, Lynval (Fun Boy Three), 289
Gomez, Tony (The Foundations), 18
Gonsales, Pablo, 106, 107
Gonzalez, 101-102, 108, 111, 142, 144, 247, 'Funky Frith Street', 102
Goode, Coleridge, 84
Gopthal, Lee, 60
Gordon, Lincoln and Derv (The Equals), 47
Gospel music in Britain, 273-276; cross-over with soul, 273
Grant, Eddy, 10, 308; memories of Guyana, 46-47; musical ambitions and influences, 47, 49; on The Equals as a multiracial band, 48; psychedelic fashions and theatrical performances, 48-49; Caribbean retentions in the music, calypso in 'Baby Come Back' and 'I'm a Poor Man', 50, 51; political edge in 'Black Skin Blue Eyed Boys', 51; 'Police on My Back', 52, 'Train Tour to Rainbow City' 56; Black politics in *Message Man*, 200; as originator of a proto-soca, in 'Walking on Sunshine', 'Time Warp', 221

Greenaway, Roger (Blue Mink), 88
Greene, Susaye, 303, 304, 306
Grenades, The, 27
Greyhound, 'Black and White', 69
Griffiths, Donald, (Aswad) 174
Griffiths, Marcia, 212
Grimes, Carol (singer/songwriter), 110
Gurnah, Abdulrazak (novelist), 32
Hacienda (Manchester club), gradual integration of Black music and players, 285-286
Hadeed, Annise, 246, 247
Hair, 91-92
Hall, Audrey, 'Heart of Stone', 215
Hall, John, 47
Hall, Pam, 'Perfidia', 215
Hall, Terry (The Specials, Fun Boy Three), 241, 289
Hall, Tony, 147, 276
Hamilton, David (Phoenix Dance Co.), 292, 293
Hancock, Herbie, 15, 274
Harriott, Derek, 55
Harriott, Joe, 7, 11, 83-85, *Freeform* and *Abstract*, 83; 258
Harris, Dennis, Lovers Rock record label, 212
Harrison, Nick (The Real Thing), 199
Harry J & The All Stars, 'Liquidator', 69
Hassan, Leila, 64
Havens, Richie, 160
Hawkins, Screamin' J, 49
Heart and Souls, 27
Heatwave, 11, *Too Hot to Handle*, 150-151
Heaven 17, 'Temptation', 252
Hemmings, Courtney, (Aswad, aka Khaki) 174
Hendrix, Jimi, 11, 15, 33, 126, 129
Henry, Tony (52nd Street), 272, 279, 280, 281, 282; origins in Manchester, 282-283, as part of 52nd Street, 284, 285
Henry, Tony (Misty in Roots), 185
Hi Life International, *Travel & See*, *Na Wa Fo*, 262
Hi-life, 118
Hinds, David (Steel Pulse), 10, 178, as reader of Black revolutionary texts

INDEX

and writer of 'Soldiers', 181-182; interview, 181-182, 183
Hi-Tension, 230-231; 'The British Hustle', 229, 'High Tension', 230; dwindling success, 231
Holder, Ram John, 22, 57
Holiday, Billie, 163
Holland-Dozier-Holland, 16
Holle Holle (bhangra band), 258
Honeyford, Ray, critic of multiculturalism, 288-289
Hot Chocolate Band, 10, 60, 141, 142, 'Give Peace a Chance', 67-68, 'Brother Louie', 142-142; 'The Street', 144; commercial success, 144
Hot Waxx (Black British soul band), 230
Howe, Darcus, 53, 64, 222-223, 259
Huddersfield, 20
Hudson People (Black British soul band), 230
Hummingbird, *We Can't Go on Meeting Like This* and *Diamond Nights*, 152
Hunt, Marsha, 86, 91-94: Hair, 91-92; White Trash, 'I Walk on Gilded Splinters', 92, *Woman Child*, 92-93; Marsha Hunt's 22 and gender relations in *Attention! Marsha Hunt!*, 'Man to Woman', 93
Hunt, Vernon (Misty in Roots), 185
Huntley, Jessica and Eric, Bogle L'Ouverture Press, 207
IDJ (I Dance Jazz), 295
I-Level, 'Give Me', 249, 276; 'Historical Nights', 251; experimental use of synthesisers and electronica, 251; 'In the River', 251
Imagination (funk band), 276
Impressions, The, 21
Institute for Race Relations, 64
Interracial sexual & marital unions, 51, 87, 89, 93-94; in films, 142
Jabula (exiled South African band), 78, *Thunder into Our Hearts*, 79; 265
Jackson, Jenny (Monica), 21
Jackson, Root, 15, 20-22; Root and Jenny Jackson and the Hightimers, 21, 57, 'So Far Away', 21-22,
Jamaican music, emergence of new styles, 55-56, 62; imported to Britain, 56

Jamaican music, influence of soul, 25, 99-100
James, C.L.R., 43, 64
James, Etta, 15,
James, Jimmy, and the Vagabonds, 22-23; *Ska-Time*, 22-23; *The New Religion*, 24; 'Come to Me Softly', 24-25
James, Vilmore (Phoenix Dance Co.), 292, 293
Jazz dance, 294-296
Jazz Defektors, 294, 297
Jazz Warriors, 304, 309
Jazz, 10, continuing space for Black musicians in UK, 75-76
Jimi Hendrix Experience, 48
Johns, Glyn, 158
Johnson, Ginger, 7, 103, 122
Johnson, Linton Kwesi, 9, 60, 65, 203, 206; political growth in British Black Panthers, Race Today collective and Caribbean Artists Movement, 206; mentoring by John La Rose and Andrew Salkey, 206; publication of *Dread, Beat an Blood*, 207; on the influence of reggae dee-jays, 207; working with Rasta Love, 207; Bovell and recording of *Dread, Beat an Blood* as Poet and the Roots, 207-208; 'It Dread Inna Inglan', 208; LKJ's network of allied groups, 208; evolution of dub or reggae poetry, 209; *Forces of Victory*, 210; LKJ's 'verité style and recognition of the need for pleasure, 210; Sus law and 'Sonny's Lettah', 223; Bass Culture, 'Inglan Is a Bitch', 242-243, 245
Jones, Gloria, 94-96, *Share My Love*, 94, partnership with Marc Bolan, 94-95, 'Tainted Love', 95
Jones, Huw (Alien Kulture), 255
Jones, Merville (Phoenix Dance Co.), 292
Jones, Sam (I-Level), 249-250, joins The Chaldeans and then Brimstone, 250; interview 251; 309
Jones, Tom, 38, 86
Jones-Lecointe, Althea, 64
Joseph, David (Hi-Tension), 'You Can't Hide Your Love', 276
Joseph, Julian (Courtney Pine band, 300

Joseph, Winston Raphael, 125
Kabaka, Remi, 123
Kabbala, 'Ashewo Ara', 263
Kandidate (Black British soul band), 230
Kay, Janet, 10, 216-217, 'Lovin' You' 216, biography, 216; 'Silly Games', 216-217; 268
Keane, Shake, 85, 258
Kelly, Pat, 55
Kelly, Sam, 104, 111
Kenyon, Carol (Heaven 17), 'Temptation', 253
Kershaw, Andy, 262
Khan, George, 258
Khazanchi, Deepak, 258
Kid Creole and the Coconuts, 247-248
King (label), 16
King, Ben E., 25, 86, 111
King, Marcel (Sweet Sensation), 283, 'Reach for Love', 284-285
Kirk, Rahsaan Roland, 103, 226
Kitchener, Lord, 7, 23, 63, 220, 247
Kokomo, 110
Kong, Leslie, 61
Kool and the Gang, 109, 177, 230, 231, 267
Korner, Alexis, 80
Kpiaye, John (The Cats), interview, 69-70; on Louisa Mark, 212-213, on lovers rock, 231-214; as composer, synthesizer player on lovers rock recordings, 217
Kureishi, Hanif, 259
Kuti, Fela, 79, 100-101, 122, *London Scene*, 101
La Rose, John, poet, publisher and activist, 75, 206
Lake, Ray (The Real Thing), 197-199
Language and descriptions of race and ethnicity, 88, 135, 143
Last Poets, The, 210
Latin and Afro-Cuban styles, 247
Lawal, Gaspar, 123, 151, 159, 269
Leadbelly, 160
League of Empire Loyalists, 141
Led Zeppelin, 81, 82, 86
Lee, George (Anansi), *Anansi*, 263, 'Sea Shells', 263
Leeds, Chapeltown, 10, 292-293
Leiffer, Leon (The Mighty Soul Rebels), 267; founds British Reggae Artists Famine Appeal (BRAFA), 267-270; 'Let's Make Africa Green Again', 267; BRAFA as community action, 268-269;
Letts, Don, as influential DJ, 189
Level 42 (Soul-funk group), 232, 276
Levine, Stewart, 76
Lewis, Linda, 152, 166-170, 308: 'Red Light Ladies', 166-167; biography, 167; *Say No More...*, 168; vocal qualities, 167; *Lark*, 168-169; 'Waterbaby', 169, 'Little Indians' and London identity, 169-170; battles with music industry over forced diva identity, 170; sampled by Common, 307
LGBTQI identities, 166
Light of the World (Black British soul-funk-jazz band), 10, 220, 'Liv Togevver', Black artists with Cockney voices, 229, 235, 'Swingin'', 231; involvement with jazz at Goldsmiths College, 233; hostility in clubs devoted to reggae and soca, 233-234; 'London Town' and 'Time', 'Boys in Blue' on *Round Trip*, 234-235; 'Who Are You (Who Do You Think You Are', 244; 274
Lindo, George, framing by the police and jailing as a miscarriage of justice, 205; protests in Bradford,
Linton, Vic (The Real Thing), 199
Live and Let Die, 113-114
Liverpool, 38-39, 43, 146; and slavery, 8
Lloyd, Patrick, 47
Logie, Godwin (sound engineer), 275-276
London Community Gospel Choir, 'Fill My Cup', 275
Loose Ends, 276-279, 299: 'Don't Hold Back Your Love', 277; work in Philadelphia, 277-278; compared to Jam & Lewis, 277, 278; 'Hanging on a String', 278; use of electronica, 278; 'Gonna Make You Mine', 278; split, 279
Lord Kitchener, 7, 23
Love Thy Neighbour, 113
Lovers Rock, 10, 211-219: Dennis

Bovell as architect of 'smooch reggae', 211-212; as producer and promoter of women vocalists, 212; youthfulness of singers, 213-214; versions of Black American soul, 216
Lulu, 16
Lynch, Edward (Phoenix Dance Co.), 11, 288, 292
Lynott, Phil, 11, 128-140: beginnings of Thin Lizzy, 128-129; as a complex personality, 129, as bass guitar player, 129-130; the funk component, 130; *Vagabonds of the Western World* at the crossroads of rock and funk with a blues flavour, 130; biography as a mixed-race child brought up in Ireland, 131-132; Lynott's reflections on race and identity, 'Black Boys on the Corner', 'Half-caste', 133-136; reggae elements, 136; *Solo in Soho*, 'Ode to the Black Man', 136-137; Phil Lynott & the Soul Band, 137; Lynott on Dublin and Black identity, 138-139, in 'Dublin', 139; admiration for Hendrix, 139; on the stresses that led to Lynott's early death, 140
Lynott, Philomena, 131
Lynx, 'Intuition', 248
Macbeth, Peter (The Foundations), 18
Macka B, 'Baked Bean & Egg' and 'Wet Look Crazy', 291
Mackay, Delbert, (Misty in Roots), 185
Mad Professor (Neil Fraser), 291
Madness, 239
Mafia & Fluxy, 218
Magnum Force 45 (sound system), 292
Mailer, Norman, on the 'white Negro', 33
Makeba, Miriam, 261
Malombo, 78
Mama Dragon (film, Menelik Shabazz), 218
Manchester, 10, 146, 279, 283-287; racism in 286-287
Mandela, Nelson, campaign for the release of, 265-266; Africa Sounds!, 265
Mangrove 9, 64, 173
Mark, Louisa, 'Caught You in a Lie', 212, 213; 215

Marley, Bob, in Britain, 73; influence on British reggae musicians, 176; love, pleasure as well as militancy in *Kaya*, 210; influence on lovers rock with songs like 'Could You Be Loved' and 'Is This Love?' 211
Marley, Rita, 212
Martin, Mike (Paradise), 274
Martinelli, Nick, 277, 280
Martinez, Nigel (The Real Thing), 199
Masekela, Hugh, *Home Is Where the Music Is*, 76; 'Don't Go Lose It Baby', *Techno Bush*, 264; 265
Matata, 101, 102
Mathis, Johnny, 25
Matthewson, Ron, 159
Matumbi (see Dennis Bovell), 10, 68, 'Wipe Them Out', 'Go Back Home', 72; Rastafarian vision, 177; *Seven Seals*, 177; elements of funk, R&B and soul, 177; 'Empire Road' and TV sitcom, 177-178
Maverick Sound, 66
Maximum Joy (Bristol band), 227
Mayer, John, 11, 258
Mayfield, Curtis, 24, 104, 108, 195, 196, 228, 249, 275
Mbarga, Prince Nico, 260
McClean, Godfrey, 101, 125
McDonald, Ian, 53, 64
McGrath, Paul, 139-140
McGregor, Chris, 76, 77-78
McGriff, Jimmie, 56
McIntosh, Carl (Loose Ends), 276, 278
McKenzie, Candy, as a precursor of lovers rock, 'Thinking of You' 217-218
McNair, Harold, 80, 81, 82-83
McQueen, Ronald (Steel Pulse), 178
Meade, Reverend Bazil, 275
Melodians, The, 55
Mercury, Freddie (Farrokh Busara), 257
Miller, Count 'Prince', 23
Miller, Harry, 76
Misty in Roots, 10, 184-186: launched own label, People Unite, 185; championed by John Peel, 185; *Wise and Foolish*, 185, 242; *Live at the Counter-Eurovision*, 185-186; 'Judas Iscariote', 185-186

Mittoo, Jackie, 57, 185
Moholo-Moholo, Louis, 76
Mondesir, Mark (Courtney Pine band, 300, 302
Monk, Thelonious, 78
Monsoon, 'Ever So Lonely', 255, 257
Moon, *Too Close for Comfort* and *Turning Tides*, 152
Moore, Johnny, 25
Morais, Trevor, 38-39, 43 (The Peddlers), and the Beatles, 39; interview, 42-43
Morgan, Derrick, 61
Morris, Olive, 64
Moses, Joshua, Full Force and Power band, 'House of Dread', 'The Suffering', 'Africa Is Our Land', 225-26
Mothle, Ernest, 263
Motihar, Diwan, 258
Motown, 16, 19, 24, 25, 38, 50, 61, 67, 94, 100, 152, 160, 277
Mowatt, Judy, 212
Muhammad, Idris, 100
Multiracialism in Black British music, 11, 18, 47, 48, 88
My Beautiful Laundrette, 259
Napier-Bell, Simon, 31, 37, 38
Nash, Johnny, 73, 99
National Front, 8, street violence, 141; infiltration of football crowds and racism against Black players, 141-142
Nelson, Pete (The Real Thing), 199
Nelson, Sammy, 44
Nestor, Pam, 156-157
New Beacon Books, 206
New Cross massacre, 237
Ngozi, Kondwani (Black Roots), 224
Nichol, Steve (Loose Ends), 276, 278
Northern Soul, 95-96, 98 n.10, 167, 283
Notting Hill Carnival, 222-223
O'Gilvie, Delroy (Black Roots), 224
Oban, George, (Aswad, aka Ras Oban) 174
Oblivion Express, 145
Odetta, 160
Ogun (label), 76, 77
Okoro, Michael, 69
Oluwale, David, killing by Leeds police, 54-55

Olympic Runners, 111
Optical Illusion (jazz dance), 294; becomes Jazz Defektors, 295
Orchestra Jazira, 265
Osbourne, Mike, 77, 80
Osei, Teddy, 113, biography, 118-119, interview, 119-120
Osibisa, 10, 113, 118-122, 259, 308: cross-over success, 118, origins as Cat's Paw, 119; the Osibisa sound, 'Music for Gong Gong', tradition and modernity,120; 'Spirits Up Above' and 'Woyaya' as examples of range and adventurous use of meters, 121
Ové, Horace, 62; *Pressure*, 172-173, BFI and delay in its release, 173; portrayal of police racism and intergenerational differences within Black community, 173
Pablo, Augustus, 'Lovers Rock', 211
Padget, Betty, 'My Eyes Adored You', 215
'Paki', as the generic racist insult, 256
Palmer Brothers, Harry, Jeff & Carl, Pama label, 62
Paradise (gospel group), 273-275; influence of reggae, 274; Paradise, World's Midnight, Love Is the Answer, 275; 'One Mind Two Hearts', 275
Paragons, The, 55
Parker, Victor, funeral procession for a Black jazz guitarist in Cardiff, 203; traditional jazz and the jam session, 204; a Tiger Bay Rasta as a sign of the complexity and dispersal of the Black British community and persistence of older musical forms, 205
Patterson, Tyrone, 69
Patwa, use of in songs, 63
Peach, Blair, SPG killing of, 238
Peddlers, The, 38-42, as Merseysiders, 38-39; Live at the Pickwick, 39;
Peel, John, champion of reggae bands, 185, 224
Perry, Lee Scratch, 56
Peters, Julian (Misty in Roots), 185
Phillips, Roy (The Peddlers), 40, 'The Lost Continent', 40; 'Girlie, P.S. I Love You', 40; 'Nobody Likes Me', 40-41; 'On a Clear Day', 41; as a

source of sampling, 41-42; Suite London, with the LPO, 42
Phoenix Dance Company, 292-294; *Forming the Phoenix*, toasting and dance 292; *Speak Like a Child*, 294
Pickett, Wilson, 21, 25
Pierre, Marie, 212
Pine, Courtney, 300-304, 306: session player on reggae recordings, 300; huge success of *Journey to the Urge Within*, 300-303; Pine's influences, 301; choice of tracks, 301; choice of 'Children of the Ghetto', 302; Susaye Greene's vocals, 302-303; formation of the Abibi Jazz Arts (TAJA), 304; formation of a big band, The Jazz Warriors, 304
Pioneers, The, 62, 268, 269
Poitier, Sidney, 114
'Police on My Back' (The Equals), 9
Police, as persecutors of Black people, 46, 52-54, 64; as subject of songs, 52; in the George Lindo case, 205-206; at Carnival, 222-223; Special Control Group (SPG) and Operation Swamp, 237
Poly Styrene (X-Ray Spex, born Marianne Joan Elliott-Said), 190-193: biography, 191; 'Germ Free Adolescents', 191; sharp lyrics on consumerism, celebrity and capitalism, 191-192; 'Plastic Bag', 191-192; exploration of bi-racial identity, 192; experience of misogyny, 192-193
Powell, Enoch, 'Rivers of Blood', 31-32
Powell, June, 'Please Mr. Please', 215
Priest, Maxi, 299
Pukwana, Dudu, 76, 78, *Blue Notes for Mongezi*, 79
Punk and reggae, attractions and divisions, 189-190; Mikey Massive on incompatibility, 189; Mykaell Riley on the confusion of playing with The Stranglers and The Clash, 190; racist skinheads and reggae, 190
Purdie, Bernard 'Pretty', 152
Pyramids, The, 'Train Tour to Rainbow City' 56
R&B, 10, 15, 16, 19, 20, 22, 24, 25, 35, 36, 40, 47, 50, 88, 94, 96, 125, 130, 131, 150, 164, 177, 227

Ra, Sun, 77
Race Relations Acts, 54, 172
Race Today (journal), 64
Racial hostility, 7, 31-34, 52; racism experienced by Black musicians, 44, 84, 89-90; racism in British media culture, 33, 34, 89, 113-114
Racist images of Asian in popular films and TV, 255
Radicals (Bristol reggae band), 224
Rana, Azhar (Alien Kulture), 255, 256
Ranglin, Ernie, 55
Ranking, Glen, (Stone Mafia Sound) interview, 66
Rastafarianism, growth in Britain, 72, 74; influence on music, 107-108; adoptions by bands like Matumbi and Aswad, 175-177, 189
Reality Band, The (Manchester funk band), 283
Real World (label), 261
Reapers, The, 273-274; become Paradise, 274
Redding, Otis, 15, 21, 36; *Otis Blue/Otis Redding Sings Soul*, 25
Reece, Dizzy, 7
Reedy, Winston (Cimarons), 70
Reeves, Martha and the Vandellas, 16
Reggae and gender, the secondary position of women in Jamaican reggae, 212; the increasing prominence of women in British reggae through lovers rock, 212-214; absence of women at the recording controls, 214
Reggae, its emergence and importation to Britain, 62; its worldwide influence, 99-100; reggae and covers of soul, 144; its emergence into the mainstream with Marley, 183; the division between politics and pleasure, the 'Frontline' and lovers rock, 210-211;
Reid, Duke, 60, 61
Reid, Pauline (Brown Sugar), on BRAFA, 268
Restriction (Bristol reggae band), 224
Richard, Little, 49, 163
Richardson, Wendell, 124
Riley, Howard, 233
Riley, Mykaell, 178, on varieties of

Rastafarianism in Birmingham and rejecting oversimplifications of Black identity, 179; involvement with Rock Against Racism and criticism of Clapton, 184

Rip, Rig & Panic, 10, 308; explosive energy and subversive critiques of Thatcherism, 226-227; God; I Am Cold; Attitude, 227; 'Your My Kind of Climate' and 'Storm the Reality Asylum', 227

Roberts, Juliet (Working Week), 288; 'Autumn Boy', 299; 300

Roberts, Sonny (owner of first Black recording studio), Planetone and Orbitone labels, 221-222

Robeson, Paul, 289

Robinson, Smokey, and the Miracles, 16, 24

Rock Against Racism, 11, 183; the conflict between status, personalities and politics, 201-202; fighting racism at the heart of rock, 202

Rock musicians with Asian heritage, 257

Rocksteady, 10, 55-56, 57, 58, 61, 62, 63, 68, 69, 70, 178, 183, 211, 230, 269, 300

Rodriguez, Rico, 241

Rogers-Wright, Ruth (Moontwist), 'Sight and Sound', 253, 308

Rolling Stones, 16

Rollins, Sonny, 84, 220, 301, 309

Romeo, Max, 'Wet Dream', 58, 'Melting Pot', 88

Ross, Annie, 39, 163

Ross, Diana, and the Supremes, 16, 17

Rosso, Franco (filmmaker), *Babylon*, 219, 245

Royal Burundi Drummers, 260

Rutland, Thomas, 273

Ruts, The, 'Babylon's Burning' and 'Jah War', 184-185

Sager, Gareth (Rip, Rig & Panic), 226

Sakhile (jazz combo), 264

Salkey, Andrew, 206, 207

Sam and Dave, 25

Sampling, 306-307

Sampson, Chesley (Misty in Roots), 185

Saunders, Red (Rock Against Racism), 183-184; on RAR's musical choices, 201

Savanna (Soul-funk group), 232

Saxon Studio International, 291

Scarman report, 238

Schloss, Cynthia, 'Sad Movies', 215

Schroeder, John, 103, 104

Scipio, Steve 99, 106-107

Scott-Heron, Gil, 210

Scotty, 63

Second Image (Soul-funk group), 232

Selector, The, 239, 'Three-Minute Hero', 239

Selvon, Samuel, The Lonely Londoners, The Housing Lark, 55

Semenya, Caius, 76

Set the Tone, *Shiftin' Air Affair*, 252

Sexism in album covers, 61

Shabbazz, Menelik (filmmaker), *Step Forward Youth*, 173-174, on reggae as Black British cultural identity, 174; *Mama Dragon*, 218

Shankar, L., 260

Shelly, Count, 66

Sherwood, Adrian, 227

Siffre, Labi, 10, 161-166, 308: defying expectations and genre crossing, 161-162; 'It Must Be Love', 162-163; influences and admirations, 163; Remember My Song, 163-164; 'Sadie and the Devil' 164; 'I Got The', 164; Siffre on the craft of song, 165-166; criticism of racial boundaries, 166; sexuality, 166; sampled by Eminem, 307

Simms, Carol (Brown Sugar), 213

Ska revival, and 2-Tone, 239-242; disapproval of reggae purists, 240

Ska, 55

Skidmore, Alan, 77, 80

Slade, 128

Slickers, The, 63

Small, Millie, 'My Boy Lollypop', 55, 62

Smiley Culture, 'Cockney Translation', 290; 'Police Officer', 290

Smythe, Tony (NCCL), 53

Snow, Phoebe, 160

Soca, 220

Soft Machine, 79

Solid Heat (see Tony Henry), 282-283

Sonny's Lettah' (LKJ), 9

Soul in Britain, 10, 17, 25-26; unfairly seen as nonpolitical compared to reggae, 201, 202; re-emergence with Black British bands, 230; escapism of club scene, the assumed soul/reggae divide, 243-244
Soul Vendors, 25
Sound systems, 66-67, 174; 291, role of selecta and mike man, 291; in Leeds, 292
South African musicians in Britain, 76-77
Sparrow, Mighty, 23, 50, 220, 247, 260
Specials, The, 10, 239, 'Gangsters', 239; 'Stereotypes', 240; 'Ghost Town', 240-241; 269
Springfield, Dusty, 16
St Pierre, Roger, 35, 36, 108, 109
Stabbins, Larry (Working Week), 298
Staple, Neville (The Specials, Fun Boy Three), 239, 289
Starvation/ Tam Tam Pour Ethiopie Collective, 269-270
Stax, 16, 25
Steel pan, use in Black British music (see Batti Mamzelle, The Breakfast Band), 246; revival of steel band culture in Britain, 247
Steel Pulse, 10, 178-182; touring with Marley but mixed responses to Rastafarianism, 178; *Handsworth Revolution*, as an exploration of a new Black British and located identity, 179-180; Pan-Africanist and aphoristic lyrics, 189; space for joy in 'Macka Splaff', 181; banning of 'Ku Klux Klan' by Radio One, 181; David Hinds as reader of Black revolutionary texts and writer of 'Soldiers', 181-182; 'Equality', 182; fighting the stigma of not being (Jamaican) authentic, 183; support from some punks bands and Rock Against Racism, 183
Steward, Sue, 259
Stobart, Kathy, 233
Stone, Sly, 49
Straighten Up (compilation series), 62
Stubblefield, Clyde, 100
Suckle, Count, 66
Summers, Andy, 159

Sun City and musicians who breached the boycott, 264
Sundae Times, 90, *Us Coloured Kids*, 124
Supplementary schooling, 75
Supremes, The, 16, 17
Surman. John, 77, 80
Sus laws, 8, 205, 223-224, 235
Swaby, Mark (Jazz Defektors), 288, 294, 299; on regional variations in jazz dance, 295
Sweet Sensation (Manchester soul band), 145-146, 'Sad Sweet Dreamer', 146; 283
Symarip, 'Skinhead Moonstomp', 69, as 'Zubaba' in *A Warm December*, 114
Tabane, Philip, 78
Tait, Lynn, 55
Talisman, 10, 'Dole Age', 223-224, 'Run Come Girl', 226
Tambo, Oliver, 266
Taylor, Richard, *Equal Before the Law*, 52-53
Tella, Sylvia, 218
Temperton, Rod, 11, 150
Tench, Bobby, 101, 125, 152
Tharpe, Sister Rosetta, 36
Thatcher, Margaret, racist of images of migrant 'swamping', 208, 256
The Enchanter, Neville, 66
The Front Line (TV series), 224
The Gass, *Juju*, 125, 308
The Harder They Come (film), 63
'The Message', 9
The Pop Group, *Y* (produced by Dennis Bovell, 226
The Real Thing (see also the Amoo brothers), 8, 10, 14, 146, 306; smooth soul in 'You to Me Are Everything, 146-147; the political turn of self-written songs and listening to politicised African American music, 195-196; Stanhope Street, Toxteth as roots and the real ghetto, 195, 196; the importance of Stanley House as a venue, 196-197; *4 from 8*, 195-200: 'Plastic Man' 197; Children of the Ghetto' and jazz feel, 8, 14, 197-200, 238; lack of commercial success because of previous reputation, 199
The Rick 'n' Beckers, 27

Thin Lizzy, 11 (see Phil Lynott)
Third World, *Aiye Keta*, 123
This is Soul, 25
Thomas, Carla, 25
Thomas, Nicky, 62, 65, 'B.B.C.', 66, 71
Thompson, Carroll, 'What Colour', Hopelessly in Love', 218; with Floy Joy, 'Burn Down the Rhythm', 252; 299, 300; 308-309
Thompson, Derek, 44
Thompson, Erskine (promoter), 299-300
Thornton, Eddie 'Tan Tan', 241, 268
Thorup, Peter, 80
Tighten Up, compilation album series, 61
Tippa Irie, 291
Toasting, see Smiley Culture, 290
Tommy Chase Quartet, and connection with jazz dance, 297-298
Toots and the Maytals, 63, 'Pressure Drop', 65
Tormé, Mel, 163
Tosh, Peter, 176
Toxteth (Liverpool), 14, 195
Traffic (group), 123
Trojan Records (label), 60, 61, 62, 65, 71, 144, 174, 215
Troy, Doris, 96-97: The Sweet Inspirations, 96; *Doris Troy*, 'Dynamite', 96-97; 308
Tsiboe, Nana, 263
Two Gentlemen Sharing (film), 22, 93
Tyson, Delvin (Misty in Roots), 185
Tyson, Walford 'Poco' (Misty in Roots), 185
UB 40, 'One in Ten', 242, 269
Ugandan Asians, arrival, 141
UK Players (Soul-funk group), 232
Upsetters, The, 'Return of Django', 56
Upstairs at Ronnie's, 102
Vas, Olaf, 258
Vin, Duke, 66
Vincent, Robbie, 262-263
Virgin Records, the Frontline Series, 210-211
Walters, Trevor, on BRAFA, 268
Washington, Geno, 17, and the Ramjam Band, 23-24, 26
Watt-Roy, Norman (Ian Dury & the Blockheads), 257

Weedon, Bert, 70
Weekend, 'View from Her Room', 296
Wellington, Kenny (Light of the World), 229; interview on local London soul-funk groups, 231-232, 236; on Beggar & Co.'s '(Somebody) Help Me Out', 244-245
West Indian influences on Black British music, 22
West Indian Standing Conference, 53
Wheeler, Caron (Brown Sugar), 213, 270
White adoption of Black styles, 12, 33
White singers and the blues, 36
White youth talking 'Black', 241
White, Lennie, 281
'Whole Lotta Love', (Led Zeppelin, CCS, Blue Mink), 81, 82, 86
Wilder brothers, Keith and Johnie, 11, 150
Williams, Doug (Paradise), 274
Williams, Joe, 163
Willis, Larry, 76
Winans, The, 'Let My People Go', 273
Windrush (generation), 7, 9, 63
Winwood, Stevie, 123
'Wipe Them Out', 9
WOMAD, 259, 260, 261; *Music and Rhythm album*, 260
Wonder, Stevie, 16
Working Week, 'Venceremos', 296, 298; Working Nights, 298
World Music, 259-262; WOMAD, 259; the debate over its marketing, 261-262
Woyaya (Heaven Knows), 9
Woza Albert (play), 265
X-O-Dus (reggae band), 186
X-Ray Spex, 190-193
Yardbirds, The, 15
Young, Colin, 26
Young, Joe E., and the Toniks, *Soul Buster*, 26

ABOUT THE AUTHOR

Kevin Le Gendre is a journalist and broadcaster with a special interest in black music, literature and culture. Since the late 1990s he has written about soul, funk, jazz and hip-hop, as well as about the work of African and Caribbean authors for many publications, including *Echoes, Jazzwise, The Guardian, The Independent,* Qwest TV (France) and Times Literary Supplement Online. He contributes to BBC Radio arts programmes and has presented several documentaries. His other books include *Soul Unsung (Reflections on the Band in Black Popular Music)* and *Hear My Train A Comin': The Songs of Jimi Hendrix*.

ALSO BY KEVIN LE GENDRE

Don't Stop the Carnival: Black Music in Britain
ISBN: 9781845233617; pp. 374; pub. 2018; £19.99

'Expansive, meticulous and revelatory', *The Wire*. 'The definitive text on this subject'; *Songlines*. 'A meticulous, sweeping and vivid history of black British music', Diana Evans, *Financial Times*.

Don't Stop the Carnival is the story of Black music in Britain from Tudor times to the mid 1960s. It is a story framed by slavery, empire, colonialism and the flow of music around the Black Atlantic of Africa, the Caribbean, the USA and Great Britain. It is about the passage of temporary but influential visitors such as the Fisk Jubilee Singers, the Southern Syncopated Orchestra and Paul Robeson; about the post-1945 migration of people from the colonial empire to Britain; about the new energies released by independence in the ex-colonies that created new musical forms such as ska, rocksteady and West African high life.

It is the story of a struggle against racism, but also of institutions like the military that provided spaces for black musicians from the middle ages to the mid-20th century. It is the story of individuals such as the trumpeter John Blanke in the court of Henry VIII, Ignatius Sancho writing minuets in the 18th century, Billy Waters scraping the catgut on the streets, the violinist George Bridgewater and his falling-out with Beethoven, the composer Samuel Coleridge-Taylor whose music is still played today, and popular 1930's entertainers such as "Hutch" and Ken "Snakehips" Johnson. Above all, it is the story of those who changed the face of British music in the post-war period in ways that continue to evolve in the present.

It is the story of actual Windrush arrivals such as the calypsonian, Lord Kitchener, and singer, Mona Baptiste; of Edric Connor, Cy Grant and Winifred Atwell who made inroads into the BBC and British hearts; of those who brought calypso and steel band to Britain's streets; of Caribbean jazz musicians such as Leslie Thompson, Joe Harriott, Dizzy Reece and Andy Hamilton; of great West African high lifers such as Ambrose Campbell and Ginger Johnson; of escapees from apartheid South Africa, such as Louis Moholo-Moholo who brought the sounds of Soweto to British jazz; and of that great worker across steelband, jazz and African music, Russell Henderson. Based on extensive research and many first-hand interviews, Kevin Le Gendre's book recognises that much important development took place in cities such as Manchester, Leeds, Liverpool, Cardiff and Bristol, as well as London. He brings together a keen sense of history and the ability to describe music in both vivid and meaningful ways.

In 2019, *Don't Stop the Carnival* won Best History in the category of Best Historical Research in Recorded Roots or World Music in the Association for Recorded Sound Collections (ARSC) Awards for Excellence.

ABOUT PEEPAL TREE

Peepal Tree Press has been decolonising bookshelves since 1985, with our focus on Caribbean and Black British writing. We are an independent, specialist publisher supported by the Arts Council of England since 2011 and part of the national portfolio since 2015. In 2024, we established a partnership with HopeRoad Publishing.

Peepal Tree's list is balanced between fiction, poetry and non-fiction, including both academic texts and creative memoirs. We insist our academic titles are accessible to the general reader. By the end of 2024, we will have published 490 books by 320 different authors, including those published in our anthologies. Most of our titles remain in print. Our books have won the Costa Prize, T.S. Eliot, Forward, OCM Bocas, Guyana and Casa de las Americas prizes.

From the beginning, women and LGBTQ+ authors have been fully represented in our lists. We have focused on the new by publishing many first-time authors and have restored to print important Caribbean books in all genres in our Caribbean Classics Series. We have also published overlooked material from the past as a way of challenging received ideas about the Caribbean canon.

As an ACE funded organisation, Peepal Tree supports writer development projects both nationally (Inscribe) and locally (the Readers and Writers Group in Leeds).

We see decolonisation as about overthrowing and repairing an oppressive, economically exploitative and racist power relationship. Many of our books explore the halting, difficult process of overcoming four hundred years of colonialism in the Caribbean in the post-independence period. We see decolonisation as also needing to happen in Britain. We are committed to ending British amnesia over the destructiveness of empire and colonialism, and promoting an understanding of how Britain's long relationship with the Caribbean has contributed to the making of British society in both positive and negative ways. As a publisher, we have taken a stand on supporting Palestinian rights for freedom from a brutal colonial occupation and denial of statehood.

We hope that you enjoyed reading your book as much as we did publishing it. Your purchase directly supports writers to flourish, so thank you. Keep in touch with our newsletter at https://www.peepaltreepress.com/subscribe, discover all our books, and a wealth of other information at www.peepaltrcepress.com, and join us on social media @peepaltreepress